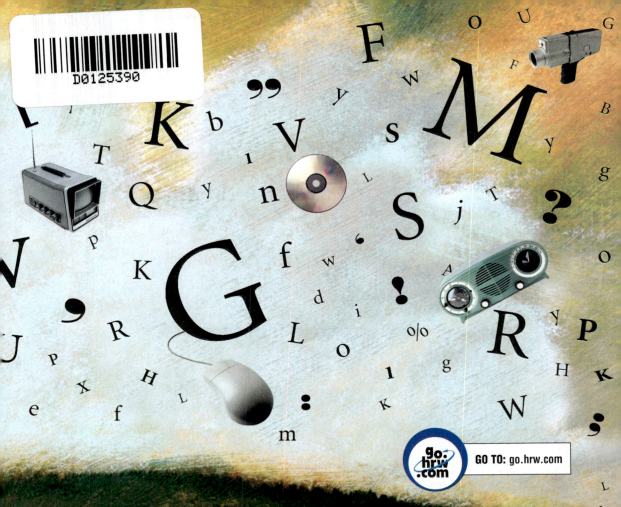

Parts of Speech Overview

Identification and Function

Diagnostic Preview

Identifying Parts of Speech

For each sentence in the following paragraph, write each italicized word or word group and tell how it is used—as a *noun, pronoun, adjective, verb, adverb, preposition, conjunction,* or *interjection.*

EXAMPLES   In parts of **[1]** *India,* for a **[2]** *few* weeks every year, it rains continually.

    1. India—noun

    2. few—adjective

After months **[1]** *of* drought, the **[2]** *storm* clouds build up in the **[3]** *sky* and the torrential deluge **[4]** *begins.* **[5]** *Well,* it is April in India, **[6]** *monsoon* season. In India **[7]** *and* neighboring Bangladesh, the monsoon **[8]** *usually* continues from **[9]** *late* spring to early fall. **[10]** *During* that time **[11]** *it* brings heavy rains **[12]** *that* are beneficial to crops, but **[13]** *some* monsoons **[14]** *can be* deadly if their **[15]** *rains* are abnormally heavy.

Monsoons are created **[16]** *when* there is a great difference **[17]** *between* the temperatures of hot air over the sea and cold air over the land. **[18]** *Southwesterly* winds carry warm, moist air up from the Indian Ocean and **[19]** *collide* with cooler air over the landmass. **[20]** *The* result is a downpour that can last for weeks.

The Noun

1a. A *noun* names a person, a place, a thing, or an idea.

Persons	architect	travelers	family	Kira Alvarez
Places	restaurant	islands	wilderness	Salt Lake City
Things	computer	sailboats	insects	Brooklyn Bridge
Ideas	education	beliefs	ambition	utopianism

Common and Proper Nouns

A *common noun* names any one of a group of persons, places, things, or ideas. A *proper noun* names a particular person, place, thing, or idea. Generally, common nouns are not capitalized unless they begin a sentence or are part of a title; proper nouns are capitalized.

Reference Note

For more information about **capitalization of nouns,** see page 271.

Common Nouns	Proper Nouns
woman	Sylvia Bryan, Eda Seasongood, Queen Hatshepsut
nation	South Korea, Canada, Mexico, United States
event	World Series, Mardi Gras, World War II
holiday	Memorial Day, Thanksgiving Day, Fourth of July
language	English, Japanese, American Sign Language
painter	Pablo Picasso, Mary Cassatt, Jackson Pollock
athlete	Michelle Kwan, Michael Jordan, Vijay Singh

Concrete and Abstract Nouns

A *concrete noun* names a person, place, or thing that can be perceived by one or more of the senses (sight, hearing, taste, touch, and smell). An *abstract noun* names an idea, a feeling, a quality, or a characteristic.

Concrete Nouns	fire, garlic, cotton, horses, Liberty Bell
Abstract Nouns	self-confidence, strength, charm, ability, Zen

Reference Note

For information on using **verbs and pronouns that agree with collective nouns,** see pages 102 and 115.

Reference Note

For information on words or word groups that may serve as nouns, see **verbals and verbal phrases** (page 58) and **subordinate clauses** (page 77).

Oral Practice **Classifying Nouns**

Read each of the following nouns aloud, and classify it as either *concrete* or *abstract*.

EXAMPLE **1.** satisfaction

          1. *satisfaction—abstract*

1. tradition	6. honor	11. palm trees	16. sand dune
2. flower	7. security	12. Mr. Nakamura	17. pencil
3. courage	8. lake	13. tears	18. commitment
4. cafeteria	9. happiness	14. suspicion	19. hope
5. dancers	10. bench	15. self-esteem	20. Mackinac Bridge

Collective Nouns

The singular form of a *collective noun* names a group.

Collective Nouns				
audience	bunch	fleet	jury	pride
batch	cluster	flock	litter	set
bouquet	crew	group	pack	staff
brood	family	herd	pod	swarm

Compound Nouns

A *compound noun* consists of two or more words that together name a person, a place, a thing, or an idea. A compound noun may be written as one word, as separate words, or as a hyphenated word.

One Word	sidewalk, tablecloth, Greenland
Separate Words	attorney general, telephone pole, Empire State Building
Hyphenated Word	daughter-in-law, jack-o'-lantern, great-grandfather

NOTE When you are not sure how to write a compound noun, look it up in a dictionary.

Review A **Classifying Nouns**

Classify the italicized noun in each of the following sentences as *common, proper, collective,* or *compound.*

EXAMPLE   **1.** Didn't you want a *treehouse* when you were a child?

1. *common, compound*

1. *Republicans,* sometimes known as members of the Grand Old Party, use an elephant as their symbol.
2. After his term as the prime minister of Japan, Eisaku Sato was awarded the *Nobel Peace Prize* in recognition of his efforts toward nuclear disarmament.
3. Lamar and Yancy rowed to the middle of the lake to escape the *swarm* of mosquitoes on the shore.
4. Off the coast of Guam lies the deepest place in the ocean—the *Mariana Trench.*
5. Well, yes, I do enjoy the *Modern Jazz Quartet.*
6. *Reality* almost always falls short of ideals.
7. Standing regally in the shallow pool was a huge *flock* of flamingos.
8. Give me a *bunch* of those shasta daisies, please.
9. *Lucky* will never sit on command unless you train him.
10. Although the heritage and name of *boogie-woogie* may be African, that jazz sound is purely American.

┌HELP─
Some nouns in Review A have more than one classification.

The Pronoun

1b. **A *pronoun* is a word used in place of one or more nouns or pronouns.**

EXAMPLES   Angelo borrowed a hammer and some nails. **He** will return **them** tomorrow. [The pronoun *He* takes the place of the noun *Angelo.* The pronoun *them* takes the place of the nouns *hammer* and *nails.*]

Several of the students have entered the essay contest because **they** are extremely interested in the topic. [The pronoun *they* takes the place of the pronoun *Several.*]

The word that a pronoun stands for is called the ***antecedent*** of the pronoun. In the preceding examples, *Angelo* is the antecedent of *He; hammer* and *nails* are the antecedents of *them;* and *Several* is the antecedent of *they.*

Reference Note
For more information about **antecedents,** see page 111.

Personal Pronouns

A *personal pronoun* refers to the one speaking (*first person*), the one spoken to (*second person*), or the one spoken about (*third person*).

First Person	I, me, my, mine, we, us, our, ours
Second Person	you, your, yours
Third Person	he, him, his, she, her, hers, it, its, they, them, their, theirs

EXAMPLES   I hope that **you** can help **me** with **my** homework.

He said that **they** would meet **us** outside the theater.

NOTE   This textbook refers to the words *my, your, his, her, its, our,* and *their* as possessive pronouns. However, because these words can come before nouns and tell *which one* or *whose,* some authorities prefer to call them adjectives. Follow your teacher's instructions regarding these words.

TIPS & TRICKS

To determine whether a pronoun is reflexive or intensive, read the sentence aloud and omit the pronoun. If the meaning of the sentence changes, the pronoun is reflexive. If the meaning of the sentence stays the same, the pronoun is intensive.

EXAMPLES
I need a little time for myself. [*I need a little time for* doesn't make sense. The pronoun *myself* is reflexive.]

Did Paul prepare dinner himself? [Without *himself,* the meaning of the sentence stays the same. The pronoun *himself* is intensive.]

HELP
Do not use the nonstandard forms *hisself, theirself,* and *theirselves.* Use *himself* and *themselves* instead.

Reflexive and Intensive Pronouns

A *reflexive pronoun* refers to the subject of a sentence and functions as a complement or as an object of a preposition. An *intensive pronoun* emphasizes its antecedent.

First Person	myself, ourselves
Second Person	yourself, yourselves
Third Person	himself, herself, itself, themselves

REFLEXIVE   Kimiko wrote a note to **herself.**
INTENSIVE   Leonora **herself** organized the school's recycling program.

Demonstrative Pronouns

A *demonstrative pronoun* points out a specific person, place, thing, or idea.

this	that	these	those

EXAMPLES **This** is our favorite song by Ella Fitzgerald.

The apples I picked today taste better than **these.**

> **NOTE** The same words that are used as demonstrative pronouns can also function as **demonstrative adjectives.**
>
> PRONOUN   Her best painting is **this.**
> ADJECTIVE   Her best painting is **this** one.

Reference Note

For more information on **demonstrative adjectives,** see page 11.

Interrogative Pronouns

An *interrogative pronoun* introduces a question.

what	which	who	whom	whose

EXAMPLES   **What** is the answer to the last algebra problem?

Whose is this?

Relative Pronouns

A *relative pronoun* introduces an adjective clause.

that	which	who	whom	whose

EXAMPLES   The house **that** you saw is a historical landmark.

She is the woman **who** is running for mayor.

Reference Note

For more information on **relative pronouns** and **adjective clauses,** see page 78. For information on when to use **who or whom,** see page 137.

Indefinite Pronouns

An *indefinite pronoun* refers to a person, a place, a thing, or an idea that may or may not be specifically named.

all	each other	most	one another
another	either	much	other
any	everybody	neither	several
anybody	everyone	nobody	some
anyone	everything	none	somebody
anything	few	no one	someone
both	many	nothing	something
each	more	one	such

Reference Note

For information on the **agreement of indefinite pronouns with verbs,** see page 99. For information on **indefinite pronouns used with other pronouns,** see page 111.

EXAMPLES   I have packed **everything** we will need for the trip.

Has **anyone** seen my binoculars?

NOTE Many of the pronouns you have studied so far may also be used as adjectives.

whose basketball   **this** girl   **more** paper   **each** apple

Exercise 1 Identifying Pronouns

Identify the pronouns in the following sentences. Then, classify each pronoun as *personal, reflexive, intensive, demonstrative, interrogative, relative,* or *indefinite*.

EXAMPLE   1. Someone told me they had moved to Iowa.

1. *Someone—indefinite; me—personal; they—personal*

1. Devon himself knew everyone who had a ticket or could get one for him at a low price.
2. Nobody has bought any of the CDs on sale at the discount store.
3. You won several of the events at the 4-H competition, I hear.
4. Those are photographs of some of the many contemporary politicians who are women.
5. What is the name of the large body of water that borders Ethiopia?
6. Althea Gibson stunned spectators but not herself when she took the singles and doubles titles at Wimbledon in 1957.
7. According to Buddhist belief, a soul detached from all of its desires enters nirvana, which is a state of consciousness, not a place.
8. Most of the participants purchased small souvenirs and such.
9. Either of their formats will work, but we prefer another.
10. According to this article, Sherlock Holmes never actually said "Elementary, my dear Watson."

Review B Identifying Nouns and Pronouns

Tell whether each italicized word or word group in the following paragraph is a *noun* or a *pronoun*.

EXAMPLES   Tessellation is the filling of a plane with shapes so that **[1]** *each* of the **[2]** *shapes* touches the others without any space between them.

1. *pronoun*
2. *noun*

For centuries, cultures all over the world have used tessellated [1] *designs* to decorate fabrics, walls, floors, pottery, and many other everyday things. The [2] *Moors,* for example, were masters at creating intricate tiled walls and floors. Because their [3] *religion* did not allow [4] *them* to make images of any animals or [5] *people,* they worked with geometric shapes. Notice also that [6] *both* of the Moorish designs shown below (left and center) are symmetrical. One twentieth-century Dutch artist [7] *who* was inspired by designs like [8] *these* from Moorish buildings was [9] *M. C. Escher.* [10] *Many* of Escher's designs, however, feature birds, lizards, and other natural [11] *forms.* In addition, he often used asymmetrical [12] *shapes* in [13] *his* interlocking designs. The [14] *one* below on the [15] *right* consists of asymmetrical shapes. In this [16] *pattern* one [17] *kind* of creature interlocks with [18] *another.* In the design on the left—an amazing [19] *achievement*— a single, complicated shape interlocks in two ways with [20] *itself.*

#7 by M.C. Escher, from the Alhambra in Granada, 5" x 5". © M.C. Escher/Cordon Art-Baarn-Holland. All rights reserved.

#8 by M.C. Escher, from the Alhambra in Granada, 5" x 5". © M.C. Escher/Cordon Art-Baarn-Holland. All rights reserved.

Symmetry Drawing E 22 by M.C. Escher. © 1999 Cordon Art-Baarn-Holland. All rights reserved.

The Adjective

1c. An ***adjective*** modifies a noun or a pronoun.

To ***modify*** means "to describe or to make more definite" the meaning of a word. Adjectives modify nouns or pronouns by telling *what kind, which one, how many,* or *how much.*

What Kind?	Which One?	How Many?	How Much?
brown shoes	**those** cars	**ten** boxes	**some** water
English tea	**first** step	**several** books	**less** time
up-to-date look	**last** one	**many** students	**enough** money

Reference Note

For more information on **using modifiers,** see Chapter 9.

Adjectives usually precede the words they modify.

EXAMPLE   The **wild** and **graceful** deer ran through the forest.

For emphasis, however, adjectives sometimes follow the words they modify.

EXAMPLE   The deer, **wild** and **graceful,** ran through the forest.

Adjectives may be separated from the words they modify.

EXAMPLE   The casserole was **delicious.**

NOTE   The adjective in the example above is a predicate adjective. A **predicate adjective** is an adjective that completes the meaning of a linking verb and modifies the subject of the verb.

Reference Note

For more information on **predicate adjectives,** see page 43.

Articles

The most frequently used adjectives are *a, an,* and *the.* These words are called **articles.** *A* and *an* are called **indefinite articles** because they refer to any member of a general group. *A* is used before a word beginning with a consonant sound. *An* is used before a word beginning with a vowel sound. *The* is called the **definite article** because it refers to someone or something in particular.

EXAMPLES   Jorge drew pictures of **a** pelican and **an** albatross.

For **an** hour I rode through **the** park in **a** horse-drawn carriage. [*An* is used before *hour* because *hour* begins with a vowel sound.]

Maple Avenue is **a** one-way street. [*A* is used before *one-way* because *one-way* begins with a consonant sound.]

The lion is often called "**the** king of **the** beasts."

Adjective or Pronoun?

A word may be used as one part of speech in one context and as a different part of speech in another context. For example, the following words may be used as adjectives or as pronouns.

all	each	more	one	such	those
another	either	most	other	that	what
any	few	much	several	these	which
both	many	neither	some	this	whose

Remember that an adjective modifies a noun or a pronoun and that a pronoun takes the place of a noun or pronoun.

ADJECTIVE   **Which** museum did you visit? [*Which* modifies the noun *museum.*]

PRONOUN   **Which** did you visit? [*Which* takes the place of the noun *museum.*]

ADJECTIVE   Leslie Marmon Silko wrote **these** stories. [*These* modifies the noun *stories.*]

PRONOUN   Leslie Marmon Silko wrote **these.** [*These* takes the place of the noun *stories.*]

NOTE The words *this, that, these,* and *those* are called **demonstrative adjectives** when they modify nouns or pronouns, and they are called **demonstrative pronouns** when they take the place of nouns or pronouns.

Reference Note

For more information about **demonstrative pronouns,** see page 6.

Adjective or Noun?

Some words can be used as nouns or adjectives.

Nouns	Adjectives
business	**business** letter
saxophone	**saxophone** player
tuna	**tuna** salad
United States	**United States** government

Notice in the last example above that the proper noun *United States* is capitalized whether it is used as an adjective or as a noun.

NOTE Some word groups make up compound nouns.

EXAMPLES   road map, blood bank, soap opera, country club, United States of America, Spanish moss, merry-go-round

By checking an up-to-date dictionary, you can avoid confusing an adjective with a word that is considered part of a compound noun.

Reference Note

For more about **compound nouns,** see page 4.

Proper Adjectives

An adjective that is formed from a proper noun is called a *proper adjective.*

Proper Nouns	Proper Adjectives
New Mexico	**New Mexican** food
Islam	**Islamic** teachings
Faust	**Faustian** bargain
Rubens	**Rubenesque** model
Christmas	**Christmas** tree

Exercise 2 Identifying Adjectives and the Words They Modify

Identify the adjectives and the words they modify in each of the following sentences. Do not include the articles *a*, *an*, and *the*.

EXAMPLE   1. Put those aluminum cans in that empty box in the hall closet.

          1. *those, aluminum—cans; that, empty—box; hall—closet*

1. John lives on this street.
2. You need four cups of flour for this recipe.
3. Your new apartment, so spacious and sunny, certainly seems ideal.
4. The image of the eagle is quite powerful in many American Indian cultures today.
5. To which bookstore did you go?
6. All of the books on these shelves were written by eighteenth-century French writers.
7. Neither film was enjoyable.
8. The local stores open at 9:00 A.M.
9. Speaking of the space program, which astronaut do you admire more—Lt. Col. Eileen Collins or Dr. Mae C. Jemison?
10. Tomás bought a new tie for the dance.

Review C Identifying Nouns, Pronouns, and Adjectives

Tell whether each italicized word in the following sentences is used as a *noun*, a *pronoun*, or an *adjective*. If the word is used as an adjective, give the word it modifies.

EXAMPLE   1. *Most* people do not realize the *tremendous* number of books the library has available for *them*.

          1. *Most—adjective—people; tremendous—adjective—number; them—pronoun*

1. Many *shop* owners decided to close *their* shops early.
2. *What* are the *other* choices on the menu?
3. The manuscript for Andrew García's fascinating autobiography was found packed in dynamite *boxes* under his bed five years after *he* had died.
4. We had a *family* reunion at my grandparents' house *last* summer.
5. As people encounter different *ways* of life, *they* gradually alter their speech patterns.
6. Thanks to the development of *digital* recording, symphony *performances* can now be recorded with higher fidelity.
7. *Oboe* players carry extra reeds with *them* because of the possibility that a reed might split during a performance.
8. *Alonzo* had never bought *that* brand before.
9. *Some* of the players felt nervous about the *athletic* contests.
10. *They* were penalized *ten* yards for holding.

The Verb

1d. **A *verb* expresses action or a state of being.**

In this textbook, verbs are classified as (1) action or linking verbs, (2) helping or main verbs, and (3) transitive or intransitive verbs.

Action Verbs and Linking Verbs

An ***action verb*** expresses either physical or mental activity.

Physical	travel	sit	arise	draw	build
Mental	remember	think	believe	consider	know

EXAMPLES   The ancient Egyptians **constructed** elaborate tombs for their rulers. [The verb *constructed* expresses physical activity.]

Do you **recall** the family we met on our vacation last summer? [The verb phrase *Do recall* expresses mental activity.]

A ***linking verb*** connects the subject to a word or word group in the predicate that identifies or describes the subject. Such a word or word group is called a ***subject complement***.

Reference Note

For more on **subject complements,** see page 42.

EXAMPLES Patience **is** the best remedy for many troubles. [The subject complement *remedy* identifies the subject *Patience*.]

He **became** a highly respected sculptor. [The subject complement *sculptor* identifies the subject *He*.]

The dessert **looks** delicious. [The subject complement *delicious* describes the subject *dessert*.]

Commonly Used Linking Verbs			
Forms of *Be*			
am	be	will be	had been
is	can be	could be	shall have been
are	may be	should be	will have been
was	might be	would be	could have been
were	must be	has been	should have been
being	shall be	have been	would have been

Other Common Linking Verbs			
appear	grow	seem	stay
become	look	smell	taste
feel	remain	sound	turn

TIPS & TRICKS

To determine whether a verb in a sentence is a linking verb, substitute a form of the verb *be*. If the sentence makes sense, the verb is probably a linking verb.

LINKING
The milk **smelled** sour.
[The verb *was* can sensibly replace *smelled*: The milk was sour.]

ACTION
I **smelled** the milk to see whether it was fresh. [The verb *was* cannot sensibly replace *smelled*.]

Some verbs may be used as linking verbs or as action verbs.

LINKING The soup **tasted** spicy.
ACTION We **tasted** the soup.

LINKING She **felt** good about her presentation.
ACTION The explorers **felt** rain on their faces.

LINKING The corn **grows** taller every day.
ACTION Mr. Tahir **grows** pomegranates in his garden.

The forms of the verb *be* are not always used as linking verbs. They may be followed by words that tell *where* or *when*. Used in this way, *be* is referred to as a *state-of-being verb*.

EXAMPLE My relatives from Ohio **will be** here tomorrow. [The verb *will be* is followed by *here*, which tells *where*, and *tomorrow*, which tells *when*.]

Main Verbs and Helping Verbs

A *verb phrase* consists of at least one *main verb* and one or more *helping verbs* (also called *auxiliary verbs*).

EXAMPLES   John **will be arriving** at 3:00 P.M. [*Will* and *be* are the helping verbs; *arriving* is the main verb.]

She **should** not **have been told** about her surprise party. [*Should, have,* and *been* are the helping verbs. *Told* is the main verb.]

Commonly Used Helping Verbs				
Forms of *Be*	am	is	are	was
	were	be	being	been
Forms of *Have*	has	have	having	had
Forms of *Do*	do	does	doing	did
Modals	may	can	could	
	might	shall	should	
	must	will	would	

NOTE   Like a one-word verb, a verb phrase may be classified as action or linking.

EXAMPLES   I **have read** every book by Zora Neale Hurston. [action]

Is the koala **sleeping**? [action]

Sandra Day O'Connor **has been** a Supreme Court justice since 1981. [linking]

A *modal* is a helping verb that is joined with a main verb to express an attitude such as necessity or possibility.

EXAMPLES   We **must** be on time if we want to catch the plane. [necessity]

Uncle René said that the entire front of the house **may** need to be replaced. [possibility]

Reference Note

For more on using **modals,** see page 201.

FRANK & ERNEST reprinted by permission of Newspaper Enterprise Association, Inc.

Helping verbs may be separated from the main verb by other words.

EXAMPLES   **Should** we **leave** immediately?

I **have** not **read** Nadine Gordimer's latest novel.

Reference Note

For more about **adverbs,** see page 17.

NOTE   The word *not* and its contraction, *–n't,* are never part of a verb phrase. Instead, they are adverbs telling *to what extent.*

Transitive Verbs and Intransitive Verbs

A *transitive verb* has an *object*—a word that tells *who* or *what* receives the action.

Reference Note

For more about **objects of verbs,** see page 39.

EXAMPLES   Everyone in the school **cheered** the football team during the championship game. [The object *team* receives the action of *cheered.*]

Nikki Giovanni **writes** poetry. [The object *poetry* receives the action of *writes.*]

An *intransitive verb* does not have an object.

EXAMPLES   The gorilla **smiled** at its baby.

Suddenly, the child next to the door **screamed** loudly.

HELP

Most dictionaries group the definitions of verbs according to whether the verbs are used transitively (v.t.) or intransitively (v.i.).

NOTE   Some verbs can be transitive in one sentence and intransitive in another.

TRANSITIVE   We **ate** our lunch quickly.
INTRANSITIVE   We **ate** quickly.

TRANSITIVE   Ms. Marino **measured** the boards carefully.
INTRANSITIVE   Ms. Marino **measured** carefully.

Exercise 3 **Identifying and Classifying Verbs**

Identify the verbs and verb phrases in the following sentences. Then, classify each verb or verb phrase as *transitive action, intransitive action,* or *intransitive linking.* Give the object(s) of each transitive action verb and the subject complement(s) of each linking verb.

EXAMPLE   1.   The word *igloo* derives from the Inuit word *iglu,* which means "house."

          1.   *derives—intransitive action*

               means—transitive action—"house" (object)

┌**HELP**┐

In Exercise 3, look for verbs in subordinate clauses as well as in independent clauses.

1. Throughout its history English has borrowed many words from other languages.
2. Because a newly borrowed word often sounds unfamiliar, people sometimes do not hear it correctly.
3. They will pronounce the word and will spell it as if it had come from other, more familiar English words.
4. The wrong spelling hides the true origin of the word and gives the false impression that its source is contemporary English, when its real source is something else entirely.
5. The word *woodchuck,* for example, might have come from two English words, *wood* and *chuck.*
6. Actually, *woodchuck* came from the Cree *otchek.*
7. Another interesting word of American Indian origin is the Algonquian word *musquash.*
8. When English-speaking settlers adopted the word, it became the animal name *muskrat.*
9. In a similar way, the Dutch word for cabbage salad, *koolsla,* became the English word *coleslaw,* and the French word for a kind of cart, *carriole,* led to the English word *carryall.*
10. Linguists generally know popular but inaccurate word histories as "folk etymology."

The Adverb

1e. An *adverb* modifies a verb, an adjective, or another adverb.

An adverb tells *how, when, where,* or *to what extent* (*how much* or *how long*).

GRAMMAR

┌─ **H E L P** ─

Although many adverbs end in *–ly,* the *–ly* ending does not always signal that a word is an adverb. Some adjectives also end in *–ly:* the *daily* newspaper, an *early* train, an *only* child, a *friendly* person. Further, some words that do not end in *–ly,* such as *now, then, far, already, somewhat, not,* and *right,* are often used as adverbs. To tell whether a word is an adverb, ask yourself these questions:

• Does the word modify a verb, an adjective, or an adverb?

• Does it tell *how, when, where,* or *to what extent?*

If you answer yes to both questions, the word is an adverb.

Reference Note

For information about **adverbs that are used to join words or word groups,** see relative adverbs (page 79) and conjunctive adverbs (page 88).

NOTE Some adverbs can begin questions.

EXAMPLES   **Where** are you going?

When will they return?

Adverbs Modifying Verbs

EXAMPLES   Marian Anderson performed **magnificently.** [*how*]

Marian Anderson performed **earlier.** [*when*]

Marian Anderson performed **there.** [*where*]

Marian Anderson performed **widely.** [*to what extent*]

Adverbs Modifying Adjectives

EXAMPLES   The players are **exceptionally** skillful. [The adverb *exceptionally* modifies the adjective *skillful,* telling *to what extent.*]

The documentary about global warming was thorough **enough.** [The adverb *enough* modifies the adjective *thorough,* telling *to what extent.*]

Adverbs Modifying Other Adverbs

EXAMPLES   Cheetahs can run **extremely** fast. [The adverb *extremely* modifies the adverb *fast,* telling *to what extent.*]

André reacted to the news **rather** calmly. [The adverb *rather* modifies the adverb *calmly,* telling *to what extent.*]

Nouns or Adverbs?

Some words may be used as nouns or as adverbs.

NOUN   They returned to their **home.**

ADVERB   They returned **home** before noon.

NOUN   **Yesterday** was a good day.

ADVERB   The teacher reviewed what had been covered **yesterday.**

When identifying parts of speech, identify as adverbs words that modify verbs, adjectives, and adverbs.

Exercise 4 Identifying Adverbs and the Words They Modify

Identify the adverbs and the words they modify in the following sentences. State whether each adverb tells *how, when, where,* or *to what extent.*

EXAMPLE   1. We went to the museum today, but it was not open.

1. *today—went—when; not—open—to what extent*

1. Her calm, friendly manner always inspired confidence.
2. I understand now what he was saying.
3. The index lists all the book's topics alphabetically.
4. The guests have already left.
5. They thought that the decorations would be too expensive.
6. Maurice Hines and Gregory Hines tap-danced professionally when they were very young children.
7. The messenger said that she felt rather uncertain about which was the quickest route.
8. "Are you quite sure that this is the person you saw?" the detective asked the witness.
9. The teacher told the students, "Take your essays home for revision and return them to me tomorrow."
10. Visitors to China often bring back small figures that have been delicately carved from solid blocks of jade.

Review D Identifying Parts of Speech

Tell whether each italicized word in the following sentences is used as a *noun, pronoun, adjective, verb,* or *adverb.* If the word is used as an adjective or an adverb, give the word or words it modifies.

EXAMPLE   1. *Is* the platypus *indigenous* to *Australia*?

1. *Is—verb; indigenous—adjective—platypus; Australia—noun*

1. He *announced* the names of *all* who had contributed *time* or money.
2. Jesse Owens *won* four gold medals in the 1936 *Olympics.*
3. In *ancient* Rome the new year began on March 1, and September *was* the *seventh* month of the year.
4. In 6000 B.C. the usual transportation for traveling long distances was the *camel* caravan, *which* averaged *eight* miles per hour.
5. The play received *generally* excellent reviews, but several critics were disappointed with the *rather* dull costumes.

S T Y L E   T I P

To keep your writing fresh, try to avoid overusing adverbs such as *very, really,* and *so.* When you can, replace these words with more exact and descriptive words.

EXAMPLES
The lions were **ravenous** [not *very hungry*] after their unsuccessful hunt.

In the land of the Lilliputians, Gulliver appears **gigantic** [not *really tall*].

Hundreds of [not *So many*] people were waiting in line for tickets.

The Adverb   **19**

6. As *we* approached Santoríni, I saw sparkling white houses along the *steep* hillsides.

7. The teacher *posted* a list of students *who* would give *reports* about Sacagawea.

8. *Many* readers complained *angrily* about the editorial that appeared in yesterday's newspaper, but *others* found it amusing.

9. *Silently,* the drifting snow *blanketed* the narrow road.

10. I recall *vividly* that small town in the southern *part* of Texas.

Review E   **Identifying Parts of Speech**

Tell whether each italicized word in the following paragraph is used as a *noun, pronoun, adjective, verb,* or *adverb.* If the word is used as an adjective or an adverb, give the word or words it modifies.

EXAMPLES   I consider my aunt Laurette **[1]** *one* of my **[2]** *best* friends.

    1. one—pronoun

    2. best—adjective—friends

       My aunt Laurette is just about the nicest **[1]** *grown-up* **[2]** *that* I know. I do **[3]** *not* get to see her **[4]** *very* often because she **[5]** *works* in Chicago, but when she comes **[6]** *here* to visit, I'm in heaven. **[7]** *What* do I like about her? For one thing, we share **[8]** *many* interests—both of us play the piano, **[9]** *sew* our own clothes, and love to make **[10]** *puns.* She is also a sympathetic listener and lets me tell about **[11]** *myself* without interrupting or criticizing me. Aunt Laurette shares **[12]** *her* own **[13]** *career* stories with me, and sometimes she even asks me for **[14]** *some* advice. A day with Aunt Laurette **[15]** *is* sometimes silly and sometimes **[16]** *serious,* but it's always a delight. I **[17]** *always* feel relaxed with my aunt Laurette. She's living proof that a person **[18]** *can* go through adolescence and **[19]** *still* emerge as a happy, **[20]** *highly* competent adult!

The Preposition

1f. A *preposition* shows the relationship of a noun or pronoun, called the *object of the preposition,* to another word.

Notice how the prepositions in the examples on the next page show different relationships between the words *ran* (the verb) and *me* (the object of each preposition).

EXAMPLES The playful puppy ran **beside** me.

The playful puppy ran **toward** me.

The playful puppy ran **around** me.

The playful puppy ran **past** me.

The playful puppy ran **after** me.

The playful puppy ran **behind** me.

The playful puppy ran **in front of** me.

A preposition, its object, and any modifiers of the object form a *prepositional phrase.*

"We the people, of the people, for the people, by the people, above the people, under the people, beside the people, behind the people..."

Overly thorough, lesser known Founding Father Clive Fishburne delivers his Preposition Proclamation.

THE QUIGMANS, by Buddy Hickerson, copyright 1993 Los Angeles Times Syndicate. Reprinted with permission.

Commonly Used Prepositions			
about	beneath	in	through
above	beside	inside	throughout
across	besides	into	to
after	between	like	toward
against	beyond	near	under
along	but (meaning	of	underneath
among	"except")	off	until
around	by	on	unto
as	down	out	up
at	during	outside	upon
before	except	over	with
behind	for	past	within
below	from	since	without

Reference Note

For more about **prepositional phrases,** see page 54.

Preposition or Adverb?

Some words in the preceding list may also be used as adverbs. Remember that an adverb is a modifier and does not take an object.

Reference Note

For more about **adverbs,** see page 17.

PREPOSITION We drove **around** the parking lot. [The compound noun *parking lot* is the object of *around*.]

ADVERB We drove **around** for a while. [*Around* modifies the verb *drove*.]

PREPOSITION Vince went **inside** the house. [The noun *house* is the object of *inside*.]

ADVERB Vince went **inside** when the rain started. [*Inside* modifies the verb *went*.]

Reference Note

For more information on **infinitives,** see page 192.

NOTE As a preposition, the word *to* has a noun or a pronoun as an object. Do not confuse a prepositional phrase with an *infinitive*—a verb form often preceded by *to*.

PREPOSITIONAL PHRASES	to the beach	to him and her
INFINITIVES	to remember	to read

A preposition that consists of two or more words is a ***compound preposition.***

Commonly Used Compound Prepositions

according to	because of	in spite of
along with	by means of	instead of
apart from	in addition to	next to
aside from	in front of	on account of
as of	in place of	out of

STYLE TIP

In formal writing and speaking, you should avoid ending a sentence with a preposition. However, prepositions are integral parts of many common English expressions, such as *come up with.*

INFORMAL
This is the solution that the committee has come up with.

Revising such a sentence to avoid ending it with a preposition may result in an awkward or pretentious construction.

AWKWARD
This is the solution up with which the committee has come.

In formal situations, therefore, it may be best to avoid such an expression altogether.

FORMAL
This is the solution that the committee has **proposed.**

EXAMPLES The young sculptor made a scale model of Mount Rushmore **out of** clay.

She placed a photograph of Mount Rushmore **next to** her clay model.

Exercise 5 Writing Prepositions

Supply an appropriate preposition for each blank in the following sentences. Do not use the same preposition twice.

EXAMPLE **1.** _____ the dark blue waters, whales played.

1. *Beneath*

1. Why does your cat always sleep _____ my bed?
2. During the summer, the Dog Star, Sirius, shines _____ the sky.
3. Everyone _____ Julie, our guest of honor, knew about the party.
4. _____ a long struggle, Lithuania won its independence from Russia.
5. Various pieces of electronic equipment were sitting _____ the table.
6. The picnic was postponed _____ rain.
7. _____ the three-hour drive, my little brother took a nap.
8. Have you read _____ the new videophones?
9. Little Turtle was true _____ his word; he kept the treaty.
10. _____ those days, mapmaking has become a much more exact science with multiple levels of precision.

The Conjunction

1g. A *conjunction* joins words or word groups.

Coordinating Conjunctions

A *coordinating conjunction* joins words or word groups that are used in the same way.

Coordinating Conjunctions			
and	for	or	yet
but	nor	so	

EXAMPLES

We found a bat **and** a glove. [The conjunction *and* connects two words.]

They may be hiding in the attic **or** in the basement. [The conjunction *or* connects two phrases.]

Will Rogers once claimed, "My forefathers didn't come over on the Mayflower, **but** they met the boat." [The conjunction *but* connects two clauses.]

Correlative Conjunctions

Correlative conjunctions are pairs of conjunctions that join words or word groups that are used in the same way.

Correlative Conjunctions	
both . . . and	not only . . . but (also)
either . . . or	whether . . . or
neither . . . nor	

EXAMPLES

Both athletes **and** singers must train for long hours. [connects two words]

We searched **not only** behind the garage **but also** under the pecan tree. [connects two phrases]

Either your fuel line is clogged, **or** your carburetor needs adjusting. [connects two clauses]

TIPS & TRICKS

You can remember the coordinating conjunctions as FANBOYS.

For
And
Nor
But
Or
Yet
So

GRAMMAR

Reference Note

For more information about **subordinate clauses,** see page 77.

Subordinating Conjunctions

A *subordinating conjunction* begins a subordinate clause and connects it to an independent clause.

Commonly Used Subordinating Conjunctions			
after	because	since	when
although	before	so that	whenever
as	even though	than	where
as if	how	that	wherever
as much as	if	though	whether
as though	in order that	unless	while
as well as	provided	until	why

EXAMPLES   We arrived late **because** our train was delayed.

Dr. Watson listened quietly **while** Sherlock Holmes explained his theory.

A subordinating conjunction does not always come between the groups of words it joins. It may come at the beginning of a sentence.

EXAMPLE   **While** Sherlock Holmes explained his theory, Dr. Watson listened quietly.

NOTE   Some words can be either prepositions or subordinating conjunctions.

PREPOSITION   **After** the basketball game, we celebrated.

SUBORDINATING
CONJUNCTION   **After** we won the basketball game, we celebrated.

Review F   Identifying Prepositions and Conjunctions; Classifying Conjunctions

For each of the following sentences, identify every word or word group that is the part of speech indicated in parentheses. Then, classify each conjunction as *coordinating, correlative,* or *subordinating.*

EXAMPLE   1. Seeds were removed from short-staple cotton bolls by hand until Eli Whitney invented the cotton gin. (conjunction)

   1. *until—subordinating*

1. Eli Whitney not only invented a new type of cotton gin but also manufactured muskets and other weapons. (*conjunction*)
2. Nowadays we take the idea of interchangeable parts for granted, but it was a revolutionary concept at that time. (*conjunction*)
3. For example, when a rifle is constructed with interchangeable parts, a defective part can be replaced quickly and easily with an identically made piece. (*preposition*)
4. Critical to any system using interchangeable parts is the standardization of parts, and Whitney himself took care of this task when he invented the first milling machine. (*conjunction*)
5. Like most great ideas, the idea of interchangeable parts was not solely one person's; others, Simeon North among them, also played pioneering roles in the Industrial Revolution. (*preposition*)
6. Even though this idea of interchangeable parts originated in Europe, it was Americans who made mass production the practical technique dubbed "the American System." (*conjunction*)
7. Before Eli Whitney introduced the idea of interchangeable parts, manufacturers had to employ many skilled workers. (*preposition*)
8. Although the new technology benefited manufacturers, it cost many workers their jobs. (*conjunction*)
9. Because of the simplicity of Whitney's system, unskilled workers could be used, for only repetitive actions are required by mass production. (*preposition*)
10. Could either Whitney or North have imagined the massive growth of industrialization and its consequences? (*conjunction*)

The Interjection

1h. An *interjection* expresses emotion and has no grammatical relation to the rest of the sentence.

EXAMPLES	ah	hey	oops	uh-oh	whew
	aha	oh	ouch	well	wow

An interjection is often set off from the rest of the sentence by an exclamation point or a comma. An exclamation point indicates strong emotion. A comma indicates mild emotion.

EXAMPLES   **Ouch!** That hurts!

Well, I think you should apologize to her.

Look at the word *report*: Is it a noun? Does it refer to a sudden, loud noise or an account of happenings? If it's a verb, does it mean to transmit information or to show up for duty? Only a sentence's context can tell you. Choose three words, and use a dictionary to find out all their meanings and functions. Write sample sentences for each meaning and function. Then, combine your words with your classmates' to make a mini-dictionary. How many uses on average do your chosen words have? Can you find a word that can be used at least four different ways? How about five ways?

Determining Parts of Speech

1i. The way a word is used in a sentence determines what part of speech the word is.

EXAMPLES   The coach decided that the team needed more **practice.** [noun]

The girls **practice** every Saturday afternoon. [verb]

They will have a **practice** session after school on Wednesday. [adjective]

Dublin, Ireland, was the **home** of the writer James Joyce. [noun]

The last **home** game will be played tomorrow night. [adjective]

We decided to stay **home.** [adverb]

Celine has won the citizenship award **before.** [adverb]

The two candidates debated each other **before** the election. [preposition]

Read the directions **before** you begin answering the questions. [conjunction]

Review G   Identifying the Parts of Speech

Identify the part of speech of each italicized word or word group in the following paragraphs.

EXAMPLE   Playing on the radio was a **[1]** *piano* sonata by Beethoven.

1. piano—adjective

Suddenly the radio announcer interrupted the [**1**] *musical* selection. "A [**2**] *funnel* cloud [**3**] *has been sighted.* [**4**] *All* people should take immediate [**5**] *precautions!*" [**6**] *Those* were the [**7**] *last* words Denise Moore heard [**8**] *before* the electricity went off and the [**9**] *terrible* roar came closer. [**10**] *She* and her two children [**11**] *ran* to the basement [**12**] *quickly.*

When they [**13**] *emerged* forty-five minutes later, [**14**] *they* weren't sure what they might see. [**15**] *Oh,* the terrible wind had [**16**] *truly* performed freakish tricks! It had driven a fork [**17**] *into* a brick up to the handle. It had sucked the [**18**] *wallpaper* from a living room wall [**19**] *but* had left the picture hanging [**20**] *there* intact. It [**21**] *had driven* a blade of grass into a neighbor's [**22**] *back.* Nevertheless, the citizens of the [**23**] *town* considered [**24**] *themselves* lucky because [**25**] *no one* had been seriously injured.

Chapter Review

A. Classifying Nouns

Classify the italicized noun in each of the following sentences as *common, proper, collective,* or *compound*. Some nouns have more than one classification.

1. Our new neighbors recently moved here from *Japan*.

2. Preston looked across the bay and saw the *fleet* of tall ships.

3. My father's favorite kind of music is *rock-and-roll*.

4. Please put the book on the *table*.

5. Isn't that the book that won the *National Book Award* last year?

B. Identifying Pronouns

Identify the pronouns in the following sentences. There may be more than one pronoun in each sentence.

6. Have you ever eaten paella, which is a typical dish of Spain?

7. Each of the sisters has her own computer.

8. We don't understand why Marta didn't do the work herself.

9. Akira Kurosawa was a Japanese filmmaker who made epic films.

10. What can Yung and he order that won't be too expensive?

11. This will be her first time to travel to the capital of Pakistan.

12. Everybody wants to answer the questions that are easy.

13. He insisted on preparing the meal himself.

14. Those tap shoes are mine, but whose are these?

15. That is the money they want to exchange for yen before leaving for Japan.

C. Identifying Adjectives and Adverbs

Identify each italicized word in the following sentences as an *adjective* or an *adverb*.

16. Edgar Degas, the *French* artist, was born in Paris in 1834 into a *well-to-do* family.

17. His art is *usually* classified with the *Impressionist* movement.

18. However, because he did not like to paint *directly* from nature, his style was unlike the styles of the other Impressionists.

19. Degas had an *extraordinary* ability to draw.

20. *This* ability was an *outstanding* characteristic of his art.

21. One of his *favorite* subjects was the theater, where he *frequently* went to observe people.

22. He also studied *Japanese* prints, which influenced his experimentation with *visual* styles.

23. When Degas was *older,* his eyesight began to fail, and he worked *increasingly* in sculpture and pastel.

24. In his sculpture, he was *quite successful* in capturing action.

25. When Degas died in Paris in 1917, he was *relatively unknown.*

D. Identifying and Classifying Verbs and Verb Phrases

Identify the verbs and verb phrases in the following sentences. Then, classify each verb or verb phrase as a *transitive action verb, intransitive action verb,* or *linking verb.*

26. After the first of the year, the weather will turn colder.

27. In art class last semester, Belinda painted a portrait of her parents.

28. Kenzo had thought hard about the question.

29. The baking bread smelled good.

30. I smell burning onions.

E. Identifying the Parts of Speech

Identify each italicized word in the following paragraph as a *noun,* a *pronoun,* an *adjective,* a *verb,* an *adverb,* a *preposition,* a *conjunction,* or an *interjection.*

Our English teacher gave us an [31] *unusual* writing assignment. He asked [32] *each* of us to rewrite a well-known [33] *saying.* [34] *Although* the sentences we wrote were quite [35] *unfamiliar,* we all knew the proverbs. [36] *These* are some examples of our work:

a. The feathered, egg-laying animal that is [37] *among* the first to rise invariably [38] *captures* the small, [39] *elongated,* and legless creature.

b. A person will not be able to retain possession of his or her sweet, baked **[40]** *batter* and devour **[41]** *it* also.

c. **[42]** *Never* place your total **[43]** *number* of small, oval objects that are laid by female birds **[44]** *into* a single receptacle made of woven material.

[45] *If* these sentences **[46]** *sound* strange, read the original versions.

a. The early bird catches the worm.

b. You can't have your cake **[47]** *and* eat it, too.

c. Don't put **[48]** *all* of your eggs in one basket.

[49] *Well,* the originals sound **[50]** *much* better!

Writing Application
Using Adjectives in a Paragraph

Specific, Vivid Adjectives   Your class is having Share the Music Week. Each person will bring in a tape of a favorite piece of music and a paragraph describing it. Write a paragraph describing any piece of music that you like. In your paragraph use at least ten adjectives. Make each adjective as specific as you can.

Prewriting   Write down the names of five pieces of music that you enjoy. Then, decide which piece will make the most interesting topic for your paragraph. Listen to your selection several times. Sit quietly with your eyes closed, and think about how the piece sounds and makes you feel. While you are thinking, jot down any adjectives that occur to you.

Writing   As you write your first draft, include the adjectives that you jotted down. Try to give a clear description of the music. At the same time, imagine what specific details might persuade your class-mates to listen to this piece of music.

Revising   Re-read your paragraph, replacing vague, inexact adjectives with words that are more descriptive. Be sure you have included at least ten adjectives.

Publishing   Proofread your paragraph for any errors in grammar, usage, and mechanics. You might wish to gather the class's music descriptions and arrange them on a bulletin board titled *Share the Music!*

—HELP—
Be sure to get your teacher's approval of your music selection.

CHAPTER

2

The Parts of a Sentence

Subjects, Predicates, Complements

Diagnostic Preview

A. Identifying Subjects, Verbs, and Complements in a Paragraph

Identify the italicized word or word group in each sentence in the following paragraph as a *subject,* a *verb,* or a *complement.* If it is a complement, identify it as a *direct object,* an *indirect object,* a *predicate nominative,* a *predicate adjective,* or an *objective complement.*

EXAMPLE   **[1]** The National Science Foundation (NSF) is undergoing a great *surge* of growth.

1. *complement—direct object*

[1] The NSF is relatively *small* compared with other government agencies, such as the National Institutes of Health and the National Aeronautics and Space Administration. [2] However, it *has* always *accepted* new challenges. [3] In 1991, with funding of only $2.3 billion, the *foundation* began participating in several government programs. [4] *One* of these important programs investigates global climate change. [5] There is another *program* for which the NSF is developing sophisticated computer technology. [6] In a third project, the foundation supports *education* and *literacy* in science and mathematics. [7] How important the project *must have been* to the physicist Walter E. Massey, the foundation's director at that time. [8] Throughout his career,

Dr. Massey has shown *hundreds* of students the excitement of physics, chemistry, biology, and the other sciences. **[9]** In fact, in 1995 Dr. Massey returned to his alma mater, Moreland College, and its students, who historically have been *African Americans.* **[10]** As the school's president, Dr. Massey encourages these students to prove themselves *candidates* for either the NSF programs or some other career in science.

B. Classifying Sentences

Classify each of the following sentences as *declarative, imperative, interrogative,* or *exclamatory.* Then, supply an appropriate end mark after the last word in the sentence.

EXAMPLE **1.** The school is five blocks from here

  1. declarative—here.

11. The umpire called a strike
12. Where did you park the car
13. His hard work earned him a promotion
14. Anita ran errands during most of the day
15. Why did Earl leave the party so early
16. Debbie Allen is a choreographer
17. What a wonderful day we had yesterday
18. Please hold my umbrella for a minute
19. The pear tree grew well in our backyard
20. Leave your classrooms quickly

Sentence or Fragment?

2a. A *sentence* is a word group that contains a subject and a verb and that expresses a complete thought.

A thought is complete when it makes sense by itself.

EXAMPLES   The weary executive had left her briefcase on the train.

For how many years was Winston Churchill the prime minister of Great Britain?

What extraordinary courage the early settlers in North America must have had!

Wait! [The subject of the sentence is understood to be *you.*]

Reference Note
For information on the **understood subject,** see page 36.

STYLE **TIP**

Sentence fragments are commonly used in casual conversation, in written dialogue, and in advertisements. In these situations, the context usually clarifies any confusion caused by the sentence fragment. In formal speaking and writing, however, it is best to use complete sentences for greater clarity.

COMPUTER TIP

Many style-checking software programs can help you identify sentence fragments. If you have access to such a program, use it to help you evaluate your writing.

Reference Note

For information on **revising sentence fragments,** see page 446.

As you can see, a sentence begins with a capital letter and ends with a period, a question mark, or an exclamation point. Do not confuse a sentence with a ***sentence fragment***—a word or word group that may be capitalized and punctuated as a sentence but does not contain both a subject and a verb or does not express a complete thought.

SENTENCE FRAGMENT	Athletes representing 160 nations.
SENTENCE	Athletes representing 160 nations competed in the Olympics.
SENTENCE FRAGMENT	The offices designed for high efficiency.
SENTENCE	The offices have been designed for high efficiency.
SENTENCE FRAGMENT	Plans every month for future growth.
SENTENCE	The board of directors plans every month for future growth.

Oral Practice **Identifying and Correcting Sentence Fragments**

Read aloud the following word groups, some of which are sentence fragments. If a word group is a sentence fragment, revise it aloud to make a complete sentence. If the word group is already a complete sentence, say *"Correct."*

EXAMPLE
1. If a computer disk comes in contact with a strong magnet.

1. *If a computer disk comes in contact with a strong magnet, information on the disk likely will be lost.*

1. To have seen the Parthenon in its glory.
2. Between the towering mountain ridge and the wide ocean only a few miles away.
3. Engaging in endless discussions of pending legislation, especially the new tax bill.
4. One of the few who truly understood and took advantage of the opportunity for profit in personal computing.
5. Although it seemed unlikely, her prediction was soon fulfilled.
6. Not one but two deer appeared.
7. Than we had thought it would be.
8. I, to my surprise, enjoyed the ballet recital.
9. Beside the pool, children splashing each other and laughing at the antics of Uncle Tony.
10. Follow me!

The Subject and the Predicate

2b. Sentences consist of two basic parts: *subjects* and *predicates.* The *subject* tells *whom* or *what* the sentence is about. The *predicate* tells something about the subject.

Note in the following examples that the subject or the predicate may consist of one word or more than one word. Notice also that the subject may appear before or after the predicate or between parts of the predicate.

SUBJECT	PREDICATE
Lightning	struck.

SUBJECT	PREDICATE
Everyone	enjoyed reading *The Piano Lesson.*

SUBJECT	PREDICATE
All of the seeds	sprouted.

PREDICATE	SUBJECT
Into the sky soared	the young eagle.

PREDICATE	SUBJECT	PREDICATE
Where did	your family	go on vacation?

The Simple Subject and the Complete Subject

2c. The *simple subject* is the main word or word group that tells *whom* or *what* the sentence is about. The *complete subject* consists of the simple subject and any words or word groups used to modify the simple subject.

SIMPLE SUBJECT	The **coach** of our hockey team used to play professional hockey.
COMPLETE SUBJECT	**The coach of our hockey team** used to play professional hockey.

SIMPLE SUBJECT	Supported by grants, **scientists** constantly search for a cure for cancer.
COMPLETE SUBJECT	**Supported by grants, scientists** constantly search for a cure for cancer.

The Subject and the Predicate **33**

SIMPLE SUBJECT	The **scenes** that you see in these tapestries show the beauty of Pennsylvania in the 1700s.
COMPLETE SUBJECT	**The scenes that you see in these tapestries** show the beauty of Pennsylvania in the 1700s.
SIMPLE SUBJECT	The **Corn Palace** in Mitchell, South Dakota, is a popular tourist attraction.
COMPLETE SUBJECT	**The Corn Palace in Mitchell, South Dakota,** is a popular tourist attraction.

Reference Note

For more about **compound nouns,** see page 4.

Notice in the last example above that a compound noun, such as *Corn Palace*, may serve as a simple subject because together the two words name one thing.

NOTE In this textbook, the term *subject* usually refers to the simple subject unless otherwise indicated.

The Simple Predicate and the Complete Predicate

2d. The ***simple predicate,*** or ***verb,*** is the main word or word group that tells something about the subject. The ***complete predicate*** consists of the verb and all the words used to modify the verb and complete its meaning.

SIMPLE PREDICATE (VERB)	The puppy **chased** its tail frantically.
COMPLETE PREDICATE	The puppy **chased its tail frantically.**
SIMPLE PREDICATE (VERB)	Catalina **ran** swiftly across the field.
COMPLETE PREDICATE	Catalina **ran swiftly across the field.**
SIMPLE PREDICATE (VERB)	Today another space probe **was** successfully **launched**.
COMPLETE PREDICATE	**Today** another space probe **was successfully launched.**
SIMPLE PREDICATE (VERB)	**Did** Ethan ever **find** his history book?
COMPLETE PREDICATE	**Did** Ethan **ever find his history book**?

Reference Note

For more about **verbs** and **verb phrases,** see pages 13 and 15.

NOTE In this textbook, the term *verb* usually refers to the simple predicate (a one-word verb or a verb phrase) unless otherwise indicated.

The Compound Subject and the Compound Verb

2e. A *compound subject* consists of two or more subjects that are joined by a conjunction and that have the same verb.

The parts of a compound subject are usually joined by the conjunction *and*, *or*, or *nor*.

EXAMPLES   The **ship** and its **cargo** had been lost.

Will **Marva** or **Antonio** drive us to the track meet?

Neither the **sheets** nor the **blanket** should be washed with bleach.

Athens, Delphi, and **Nauplia** are on the mainland of Greece.

2f. A *compound verb* consists of two or more verbs that are joined by a conjunction and that have the same subject.

The parts of a compound verb are usually joined by the conjunction *and*, *but*, *or*, or *nor*.

EXAMPLES   We **chose** a seat near the door and quietly **sat** down.

Sandra **had gone** to the football game but **had left** at halftime.

For exercise I **swim** or **play** racquetball nearly every day.

Unfortunately, Eddie neither **relaxed** nor **did** anything productive this weekend.

Truth **enlightens** the mind, **frees** the spirit, and also **strengthens** the soul.

> **NOTE** Do not mistake a simple sentence containing a compound subject or a compound verb, or both, for a compound sentence. A simple sentence has only one independent clause. A compound sentence has two or more independent clauses.

SIMPLE SENTENCE   **Kendra** and **I have taken** the Scholastic Aptitude Test but **have** not **received** our scores. [compound subject and compound verb]

COMPOUND SENTENCE   **Kendra** and **I have taken** the Scholastic Aptitude Test, but **we have** not **received** our scores.

┌ T I P S & T R I C K S ┐

When you are identifying compound verbs, be sure to include all parts of any verb phrases.

EXAMPLE
Should we **wait** for Ellen or **leave** a note for her?

Reference Note

For information on **independent clauses,** see page 76. For more about **simple and compound sentences,** see page 87.

How to Find the Subject of a Sentence

A simple way to find the subject of a sentence is to ask *Who?* or *What?* before the verb.

EXAMPLES   The **crew** of the racing yacht had worked hard. [Who had worked? *Crew* had worked.]

In their eyes shone **happiness.** [What shone? *Happiness* shone.]

Waiting at the harbor was a huge, cheering **crowd.** [Who was waiting? *Crowd* was waiting.]

Remembering the following guidelines will also help you find the subject of a sentence.

- The subject of a sentence expressing a command or a request is always understood to be *you*, although *you* may not appear in the sentence.

COMMAND   Turn left at the next intersection. [Who is being told to turn? *You* is understood.]

REQUEST   Please tell me the story again. [Who is being asked to tell? *You* is understood.]

The subject of a command or a request is *you* even when the sentence contains a word naming the one or ones spoken to—a **noun of direct address**.

EXAMPLE   Chelsea, [you] close the door, please.

- The subject of a sentence is never in a prepositional phrase.

EXAMPLES   A **group** of students gathered near the main library. [Who gathered? *Group* gathered. *Students* is the object of the preposition *of.*]

One of the paintings by Vincent van Gogh sold for $82.5 million. [What sold? *One* sold. *Paintings* is the object of the preposition *of. Vincent van Gogh* is the object of the preposition *by.*]

Out of the stillness came the loud **sound** of laughter. [What came? *Sound* came. *Stillness* is the object of the preposition *Out of. Laughter* is the object of the preposition *of.*]

- The subject of a sentence expressing a question generally follows the verb or a part of the verb phrase.

TIPS & TRICKS

To help you find the subject and verb of a sentence, try crossing out any prepositional phrases.

EXAMPLE
The charcoal ~~in the grill~~ caught ~~on fire~~.
Subject: charcoal
Verb: caught

Reference Note

For information about **prepositional phrases,** see page 54.

EXAMPLES   Is the **dog** in the house? [What is? *Dog* is.]

When was **Madeleine Albright** appointed secretary of state of the United States? [Who was appointed? *Madeleine Albright* was appointed.]

- The word *there* or *here* is almost never the subject of a sentence.

EXAMPLES   There is the famous ***Mona Lisa.*** [What is there? *Mona Lisa is there.*]

Here are your **gloves.** [What are here? *Gloves* are here.]

In the two examples above, the words *there* and *here* are used as adverbs telling *where*.

NOTE   The word *there* also may be used as an ***expletive***—a word that fills out the structure of a sentence but does not add to the meaning. In the following example, *there* does not tell *where* but serves only to make the structure of the sentence complete.

EXAMPLE   There is a soccer **game** after school this Friday. [What is? *Game* is.]

FRANK & ERNEST reprinted by permission of Newspaper Enterprise Association, Inc.

Exercise 1   Identifying Subjects and Verbs

For each of the following sentences, identify the subject and the verb. Be sure to include all parts of a compound subject or a compound verb and all parts of verb phrases.

EXAMPLE   1. In ancient Japan, fierce samurai like the one shown on the next page ruled society with an iron hand.

1. *subject—samurai; verb—ruled*

1. The men, women, and children of the peasant class lived in terror of these landlord-warriors.

HELP

In Exercise 1, if the subject is understood to be *you*, write *(you)*.

2. A samurai's powerful position gave him the right to kill any disobedient or disrespectful peasant.
3. Did anyone in Japan refuse a samurai's requests?
4. There was one dedicated group of rebels, called ninja, meaning "stealers in."
5. Off to the barren mountain regions of Iga and Koga fled the ninja people with their families.
6. There they could train their children in the martial arts of ninjutsu.
7. Lessons in camouflage, escape, and evasion were taught to children as young as one or two years of age.
8. The ninja sneaked down into the settled areas and struck at the samurai in any way possible.
9. In time, the ninja warriors gained a reputation all over Japan and were feared by the mighty samurai.
10. Hand me the book about Japan and the ninja warriors.

Complements

2g. **A** *complement* **is a word or word group that completes the meaning of a verb.**

Some sentences contain only a subject and a verb. The subject may be expressed or may be understood.

EXAMPLES
      S   **V**
    Everyone participated.

   V
   Stop! [The subject *you* is understood.]

Often, however, the predicate of a sentence also includes at least one complement. Without the complement or complements in the predicate, the subject and the verb may not express a complete thought.

              S   **V**
INCOMPLETE   Jose Canseco caught

             S   **V**   **C**
COMPLETE   Jose Canseco caught the **ball.**

             S **V**
INCOMPLETE   They sent

             S **V** **C**   **C**
COMPLETE   They sent **us** an **invitation.**

	S	**V**	
INCOMPLETE	The judges named		

	S	**V**	**C**	**C**
COMPLETE	The judges named **Consuelo** the **winner.**			

	S	**V**
INCOMPLETE	Denzel Washington is	

	S	**V**	**C**
COMPLETE	Denzel Washington is an **actor.**		

	S	**V**
INCOMPLETE	The players seem	

	S	**V**	**C**
COMPLETE	The players seem **weary.**		

	V S	
INCOMPLETE	Is this	

	V S	**C**	
COMPLETE	Is this **what you want**?		

As you can see in the preceding examples, a complement may be a noun, a pronoun, or an adjective and may consist of one word or a group of words.

NOTE Do not mistake an adverb or an object of a preposition for a complement.

ADVERB	Janna writes **well.** [The adverb *well* tells how Janna writes.]
OBJECT OF A PREPOSITION	Janna writes for the school **newspaper.** [The noun *newspaper* is the object of the preposition *for.*]
COMPLEMENT	Janna writes adventure **stories.** [The noun *stories* completes the meaning of *writes.*]

The Direct Object

2h. A *direct object* is a noun, pronoun, or word group that tells who or what receives the action of the verb or that shows the result of the action.

A direct object answers the question "Whom?" or "What?" after a transitive verb.

TIPS & TRICKS

Both independent and subordinate clauses contain subjects, verbs, and, sometimes, complements. In the last example to the left, the parts of the subordinate clause are as follows:

　C　S　V
　what you want

Reference Note

For information on **adverbs,** see page 17. For information on **objects of prepositions,** see page 20.

Reference Note

For information about **transitive verbs,** see page 16.

EXAMPLES   Drought destroyed **whatever we planted.** [Destroyed what? Whatever we planted.]

The journalist interviewed the **astronauts** before and after their flight. [Interviewed whom? Astronauts.]

Felicia invited **me** to the party. [Invited whom? Me.]

Do toads cause **warts**? [Do cause what? Warts.]

A direct object may be compound.

EXAMPLES   The dog chased **Eli** and **me** through the park.

Did Beethoven compose **sonatas** and **symphonies**?

NOTE For emphasis, the direct object may precede the subject and verb.

EXAMPLE   What a compelling **speech** he gave! [Gave what? Speech.]

The Indirect Object

2i. An ***indirect object*** **is a noun, pronoun, or word group that precedes a direct object and tells *to whom* or *to what* (or *for whom* or *for what*) the action of the verb is done.**

EXAMPLES   Ms. Cruz showed our **class** a great video about Moorish architecture. [Showed to whom? Class.]

The animal trainer fed the **bears** fish. [Fed to what? Bears.]

Their artistic skill won **them** honors. [Won for whom? Them.]

Will Julia buy her pet **terrier** a new rhinestone collar? [Buy for what? Terrier.]

NOTE Do not confuse an indirect object with an object of the preposition *to* or *for*.

INDIRECT OBJECT   The principal gave **her** the award.

OBJECT OF A PREPOSITION   The principal gave the award to **her**. [*Her* is the object of the preposition *to*.]

Reference Note

For information on **prepositional phrases,** see page 54.

An indirect object may be compound.

EXAMPLES   The architect showed **Mom** and **Dad** the plans for the new family room.

Are the judges giving **whoever finishes first** or **whoever does the best job** the prize?

The Objective Complement

2j. An **_objective complement_** is a word or word group that helps complete the meaning of a transitive verb by identifying or modifying the direct object.

An objective complement may be a noun, a pronoun, or an adjective.

EXAMPLES   The members elected Carlotta **secretary.** [The noun _secretary_ identifies the direct object _Carlotta._]

They considered all the prize money **theirs.** [The pronoun _theirs_ identifies the direct object _money._]

Years of hard work had made her **successful.** [The adjective _successful_ modifies the direct object _her._]

Only a few verbs take an objective complement: _consider, make,_ and verbs that can be replaced by _consider_ or _make,_ such as _appoint, call, choose, elect, keep, name, cut, paint,_ and _sweep._

EXAMPLES   Many literary historians call [_or_ consider] Shakespeare the greatest **dramatist** of all time.

The flood had swept [_or_ had made] the valley **clean.**

Will the committee appoint [_or_ make] her the new interim **leader?**

Children, keep [_or_ make] it **quiet** in there.

An objective complement may be compound.

EXAMPLES   The Gibsons named their two cats **Bruno** and **Waldo.**

Charlena painted her old bicycle **black** and **silver.**

Cut my bangs **short** and **straight,** please.

NOTE   For emphasis, the objective complement may precede the subject, verb, and direct object.

EXAMPLE   What an exciting **adventure** our science teacher made the field trip!

Exercise 2 Identifying Direct Objects, Indirect Objects, and Objective Complements

Identify each complement in the following sentences as a *direct object*, an *indirect object*, or an *objective complement*.

EXAMPLE 1. Tutankhamen's tomb contained a candleholder.

   1. *candleholder—direct object*

1. Candles have tremendous appeal as decorative, religious, and utilitarian objects.
2. Every year candle makers use many tons of paraffin.
3. Before the invention of electricity, many people lit their homes with candles.
4. Candles on the dinner table can make even an average meal special.
5. Many of the early colonists in America made their own candles.
6. Nowadays, candle making offers hobbyists a relaxing and rewarding pastime.
7. These pictures show you the steps in candle making.
8. Incense mixed into the melted wax will give your candles a pleasant scent.
9. You can also dye candle wax various colors.
10. I like to make mine blue and white.

The Subject Complement

A *subject complement* is a word or word group in the predicate that identifies or describes the subject. A subject complement completes the meaning of a linking verb. There are two kinds of subject complements: *predicate nominatives* and *predicate adjectives*.

2k. A *predicate nominative* is a word or word group that is in the predicate and that identifies the subject or refers to it.

A predicate nominative may be a noun, a pronoun, or a word group that functions as a noun. A predicate nominative completes the meaning of a linking verb.

EXAMPLES   Adela Rogers St. Johns became a famous **journalist.** [The noun *journalist* refers to the subject *Adela Rogers St. Johns.*]

        Of all the dancers, Marcelo was the most experienced **one.** [The pronoun *one* refers to the subject *Marcelo.*]

        A reliable, fuel-efficient car is **what we need.** [The noun clause *what we need* refers to the subject *car.*]

A predicate nominative may be compound.

EXAMPLES   The two candidates for class treasurer are **Marco** and **I.**

        Was that **oatmeal** or cold **cereal** Marilla had for breakfast?

        South Dakota's chief crops are **corn, wheat,** and **oats.**

2l. A *predicate adjective* is an adjective that is in the predicate and that modifies the subject.

A predicate adjective completes the meaning of a linking verb.

EXAMPLES   The ocean is **calm.** [The adjective *calm* modifies the subject *ocean.*]

        Does that orange taste **bitter**? [The adjective *bitter* modifies the subject *orange.*]

        All of the astronauts look **confident.** [The adjective *confident* modifies the subject *All.*]

A predicate adjective may be compound.

EXAMPLES   Does this blouse look **pink** or **mauve** to you?

        Most parrots are **noisy, colorful,** and **sociable.**

NOTE For emphasis, a subject complement may precede the subject and verb.

| PREDICATE NOMINATIVE | What an outstanding basketball **player** Michael Jordan was! [The noun *player* refers to the subject *Michael Jordan.*] |
| PREDICATE ADJECTIVE | How **talented** she is! [The adjective *talented* modifies the subject *she.*] |

Reference Note

For more about **noun clauses,** see page 80.

┌HELP─

Do not assume that every adjective in the predicate is a predicate adjective. Ask yourself what the adjective modifies.

EXAMPLES

These Korean folk tales are **ancient.** [The adjective *ancient* is a predicate adjective because it modifies the subject *folk tales.*]

These Korean folk tales are **ancient** stories. [The adjective *ancient* is not a predicate adjective because it modifies the predicate nominative *stories.*]

Remember that a predicate adjective modifies only the subject.

TIPS & TRICKS

When you are identifying types of complements, check first to see whether the verbs in the sentences are action or linking. Remember that only action verbs have direct objects, indirect objects, and objective complements and that only linking verbs have predicate nominatives and predicate adjectives.

Exercise 3 Identifying Linking Verbs and Subject Complements

Identify the linking verb and the subject complement in each of the following sentences. Indicate whether the complement is a *predicate nominative* or a *predicate adjective*.

EXAMPLE   1. Pluto is the smallest planet in our solar system.

   1. *linking verb—is; subject complement—planet—predicate nominative*

1. The most common deer in India is a species of axis deer.
2. Many people feel concerned about the depletion of the world's natural resources.
3. Wilhelm Roentgen was the discoverer of the X-ray.
4. Is Jane Austen the author of *Pride and Prejudice*?
5. The violin solo sounded beautiful.
6. The animals grew restless at the sound of the crackling flames.
7. Harriet Tubman was active in the Underground Railroad.
8. Icy is the stare of the glacier.
9. Why does the spaghetti sauce taste too spicy?
10. What a massive work of carved stone the Great Sphinx is!

Review A Identifying the Parts of Sentences

For each of the following sentences, identify the sentence part indicated in parentheses. Be sure to include all parts of a compound subject, a compound verb, or a verb phrase.

EXAMPLE   1. (*simple subject*) The people of New Orleans are famous for their creativity with food as well as with music.

   1. *people*

1. (*complete subject*) Both Creole cooking and Cajun cooking flourish in the kitchens of the city's French Quarter.
2. (*complete predicate*) Some visitors to New Orleans have trouble telling the difference between these two similar styles of food preparation.
3. (*indirect object*) My aunt, a restaurant critic, showed me the differences between Creole cooking and Cajun cooking.
4. (*verb*) The French founders of New Orleans developed the Creole style of cooking.
5. (*predicate nominative*) The *beignet*, a square doughnut, and *boudin*, a spicy sausage, are tasty local favorites from French cuisine.

6. (*simple subject*) In Creole dishes, there are also tangy traces of Spanish, African, and Caribbean cooking.

7. (*verb*) Cajun cooking is Creole's peppery country cousin and was born in the rural bayou areas surrounding New Orleans.

8. (*predicate adjective*) My aunt's favorite Cajun treat, alligator gumbo, is wonderfully thick and spicy.

9. (*direct object*) Don't those little red shellfish resemble tiny lobsters?

10. (*objective complement*) They're New Orleans crawfish, and I declare them the tastiest morsels that I've ever eaten!

Classification of Sentences

2m. Sentences may be classified according to purpose.

(1) A *declarative sentence* makes a statement and ends with a period.

EXAMPLES   The lock on the front door is broken.

David Glasgow Farragut led Union naval forces against the Confederacy in 1864 in the Battle of Mobile Bay.

(2) An *interrogative sentence* asks a question and ends with a question mark.

EXAMPLES   Have you seen a sculpture by Augusta Savage?

What is the capital of New Mexico?

(3) An *imperative sentence* makes a request or gives a command. Most imperative sentences end with a period. A strong command ends with an exclamation point.

EXAMPLES   Please pass the salad. [request]

Call this number in case of an emergency. [mild command]

Watch out! [strong command]

Reference Note

For information on **classifying sentences according to structure,** see page 87.

MEETING THE CHALLENGE

Take a tour of your school, inside and out, copying down all the imperative sentences you can find. You'll probably find instructions for many activities, from getting off the bus in the right place, to signing in at the office if you're late, and even to joining school organizations. Some commands may be very short: "Recycle!" Rewrite these imperative sentences as declarative and interrogative sentences. How would the school atmosphere change if your revised sentences replaced the commands?

Reference Note

For information about the **understood subject**, see page 36.

STYLE **TIP**

Sometimes a writer will use more than one end mark to express intense emotion or a combination of emotions.

EXAMPLES
Bill yelled, "Pass me the ball‼" [intense emotion]

"They did what⁉" gasped Irene. [combination of curiosity and surprise]

Using such double punctuation is acceptable in most informal writing and in writing fiction, especially in dialogue. However, in formal writing, such as essays and business letters, use only one end mark at a time.

NOTE The subject of an imperative sentence is always understood to be *you*, although *you* may not appear in the sentence.

(4) An ***exclamatory sentence*** shows excitement or expresses strong feeling and ends with an exclamation point.

EXAMPLES   What a great singer she is!

Ah, you have discovered the secret!

Ouch! That really hurt!

Exercise 4 **Identifying the Four Kinds of Sentences**

Identify each of the following sentences as *declarative, imperative, interrogative,* or *exclamatory.* Also, supply an appropriate end mark after the last word in each sentence.

EXAMPLE   1. In 1829, Louis Braille developed a system of writing for people with visual impairments

    1. *declarative—impairments.*

1. Anyone with a little free time and a generous heart can help make the world of books available to people with visual impairments
2. Have you ever wondered how Braille schoolbooks are created for students with visual impairments
3. Imagine dozens and dozens of volunteers, all with their fingers flying across the keys of machines that look much like miniature typewriters
4. Different combinations of six keys on the machines make the raised-dot patterns that represent letters and numbers in Braille
5. First, Braille typists take a course to learn how to use the machines
6. Once you learn how, typing in Braille isn't difficult at all
7. If I participate, can I work at home in my spare time
8. What rewarding volunteer work this is
9. When I considered how much time I waste every week, I decided to use that time constructively by volunteering to help create Braille textbooks
10. If you know someone who might be interested in participating, help him or her find out how to get in touch with a Braille association in your community

Identifying Subjects, Verbs, and Complements

Identify the italicized word or word group in each of the following sentences as a *subject*, a *verb*, or a *complement*. If it is a complement, identify it as a *direct object*, an *indirect object*, an *objective complement*, a *predicate nominative*, or a *predicate adjective*.

EXAMPLES
1. *Sally* visited San Antonio last summer.
1. *subject*

2. The bull *cantered* across the field.
2. *verb*

3. Haven't you told *her* the news yet?
3. *complement—indirect object*

1. Rondos are five-part *arrangements* of instrumental music in the form a b a c a b a, in which c is frequently replaced by a developmental passage.
2. Many modern movies are *incomprehensible* to me; I prefer musicals from the 1950s.
3. The prolonged drought last year *destroyed* a great number of crops throughout the Southwest.
4. In September 1998, the German people elected Gerhard Schroeder *chancellor of Germany.*
5. Ms. Villanueva, our art history teacher, showed the freshman *class* a video about the Mexican artist Diego Rivera.
6. The architect proudly displayed the *blueprints* for the new house to his prospective buyers.
7. After the trial, Justice Robinson declared herself *satisfied* with the jury's verdict.
8. On our trans-Sahara trek, we had a very experienced and capable *guide* whose talent was finding water.
9. Handing Mr. Stoddard his term paper, *Cameron* remembered that he had forgotten to include a bibliography.
10. What a remarkable *woman* Mother Teresa of Calcutta was!

Writing Sentences

Write your own sentences according to the guidelines on the following page. In your sentences, underline the sentence parts that are indicated by the italicized words. Also, use a variety of subjects, verbs, and complements in your sentences.

EXAMPLE   **1.** Write an imperative sentence with an *understood subject.*

    1. <u>*(You)* Stop right there</u>!

1. Write a declarative sentence with a *compound subject.*

2. Write an interrogative sentence with a *compound verb.*

3. Write an exclamatory sentence with a *direct object.*

4. Write an imperative sentence with a *compound direct object.*

5. Write a declarative sentence with an *indirect object.*

6. Write a declarative sentence with a *predicate nominative.*

7. Write an interrogative sentence with a *compound predicate adjective.*

8. Write a declarative sentence with an *objective complement.*

9. Write an imperative sentence with an *indirect object.*

10. Write a declarative sentence with a *predicate adjective.*

SHOE © Tribune Media Services, Inc. All rights reserved.
Reprinted with permission.

Chapter Review

A. Identifying Sentences and Sentence Fragments

Identify each of the following word groups as a *sentence* or a *sentence fragment.*

1. What the fastest-growing spectator sport in the United States is.
2. It is stock car racing, according to the National Association for Stock Car Auto Racing (NASCAR).
3. The sport in the 1930s on dirt tracks in the Southeast.
4. Did you know that today it's a two-billion-dollar-a-year industry?
5. That's a lot of money!

B. Identifying Subjects and Verbs

For each of the following sentences, identify the simple subject and the verb. Be sure to include all parts of a compound subject or a compound verb and all words in a verb phrase. If the subject is understood to be *you,* write *(you).*

6. The students, teachers, and staff of the school gathered in the auditorium.
7. The mechanic's knowledge of automobile repair is incredibly comprehensive.
8. Does someone in your family know French?
9. There were several loaves of bread on the windowsill.
10. The Ecology Club met in the park on Saturday and collected trash all morning.
11. Over the outfield fence flew the home-run ball.
12. Here at chess camp even casual players can learn useful chess strategies.
13. Professional athletes from baseball, hockey, and football joined forces for the charity fundraiser.
14. Both the director and the screenwriter offered opinions about the location manager's choices.
15. Please shut the door behind you.

C. Identifying Complements

In each of the following sentences, identify the italicized complement as a *direct object*, an *indirect object*, an *objective complement*, a *predicate nominative*, or a *predicate adjective*.

16. Please don't send any *samples* unless someone requests them.
17. Shirley Chisholm was the first *woman* to run for president of the United States.
18. The photographer gave *us* a picture she had taken of the school.
19. The director and the cast discussed the first *act* but decided not to change it.
20. The woman who called is an insurance *agent*.
21. At this point my plans for the future are quite *indefinite*.
22. Would you consider Maya *reliable*?
23. In her will, Ms. Vos left her *nurse* a share of the fortune.
24. Had Bob lost all *sense* of direction while wandering in the woods?
25. The table that we found in the basement was a valuable *antique*.
26. The people elected Jimmy Carter *president* in 1976.
27. Those dishes seem *worthless* to everyone except Ms. Lammers.
28. Kelly and I want to paint the room *blue*.
29. The original Trans-Siberian Railroad line is the world's largest *railway*.
30. The reporter asked the exhausted *survivors* too many questions.

D. Identifying the Four Kinds of Sentences

Identify each of the following sentences as *declarative, interrogative, imperative,* or *exclamatory.* Also, write the last word in the sentence, and supply an appropriate end mark.

31. What a spectacular sunset that is
32. I bought this Hawaiian shirt at a thrift store
33. Does it fit me well
34. Look out for the car
35. If Anna wants to apply to college, she should pick up some application information from the guidance counselor's office
36. Which '60s singing group is your favorite, the Beatles or the Beach Boys
37. How silly that all seems now

38. Judy asked Steve whether she should get her new cat declawed

39. Pick up your pack, and follow the guide

40. Was Cole Porter the composer of the song "Night and Day," or was it someone else

Writing Application
Combining Sentences in a Letter

Using Compound Subjects and Compound Verbs

You have just won the new car of your choice! All you need to do now is to decide what model and options you want. The car will be shipped to your local dealership. Write a letter to the sponsors of the contest thanking them for the prize and telling them what kind of car you want. Name six or more options that you've chosen for your car. Money is no object! In your letter, use at least three sentences with compound subjects and two sentences with compound verbs.

Prewriting   First, you will need to decide what kind of car you'd like to have. Then, list the options that you would like to have on the car. You can have as many options as you like. Choose wisely, though—don't pick options that you really wouldn't use.

Writing   Address your letter to an imaginary contest sponsor. Begin by thanking the sponsor for your prize. Then, describe your dream car as clearly and specifically as possible.

Revising   As you evaluate and revise your letter, you may think of more options you'd like to include. Check to see that your letter includes at least three sentences with compound subjects and two sentences with compound verbs. If it doesn't, you will need to combine or rewrite some sentences in the letter.

Publishing   Check the grammar, spelling, and punctuation of your letter. Be sure that your letter follows one of the standard business-letter forms. You and your classmates may wish to post your letters along with pictures of your "dream cars" on a bulletin board.

The Phrase

Kinds of Phrases and Their Functions

Diagnostic Preview

A. Identifying Phrases

Identify the italicized phrase in each of the following sentences as a *prepositional phrase*, a *participial phrase*, a *gerund phrase*, an *infinitive phrase*, or an *appositive phrase*.

EXAMPLE   1. *Talking after the bell rings* is strictly forbidden.
            1. *gerund phrase*

1. *Working on the school newspaper* has taught me responsibility.
2. *Delayed by the snowstorm,* the flight from Chicago to Seattle was finally cleared for takeoff.
3. Today's crossword puzzle is difficult *to complete correctly.*
4. At the beginning of class today, we sang "La Marseillaise," *the French national anthem.*
5. If you want *to go to the concert tonight,* give me a call after school.
6. Preserving rare and valuable books and documents is one of the challenges *facing the Library of Congress.*
7. The emu, *a flightless bird from Australia,* is similar to the ostrich.
8. Franklin's history report was about Booker T. Washington, the founder *of the Tuskegee Institute.*
9. Refreshed by the cool breeze, I didn't object to *going back to work.*
10. The United States has been greatly enriched *by many diverse cultures.*

B. Identifying Phrases

Identify each italicized phrase in the following paragraph as a *prepositional phrase*, a *participial phrase*, a *gerund phrase*, an *infinitive phrase*, or an *appositive phrase*.

EXAMPLE   Here is an informative article **[1]** *about Charles Albert Bender.*

1. prepositional phrase

By **[11]** *being elected to the Baseball Hall of Fame in 1953,* Charles Albert Bender became a symbol of pride for American Indians. Bender, **[12]** *born in 1883 on White Earth Reservation, Minnesota,* was half Chippewa. He was better known to fans as "Chief," **[13]** *the nickname given to him by his teammates.* **[14]** *Pitching for the Philadelphia Athletics* was his first job in baseball. Although he played only briefly **[15]** *for a semipro team,* he pitched a four-hit victory in his first major-league game. He won twenty-three games and lost only five during the 1910 season, **[16]** *the best season of his career.* **[17]** *During that same year,* he had an earned run average of 1.58. If it was crucial **[18]** *to win a game,* Connie Mack, the Athletics' manager, would always send Bender to the mound. **[19]** *Finishing with a lifetime total of 212 wins and only 128 losses,* Bender led the American League three times in winning percentage. His last full active year as a pitcher was 1917, but he returned to the mound **[20]** *to pitch one inning for the White Sox in 1925.*

┌─HELP─
In the Diagnostic Preview, do not separately identify a prepositional phrase that is part of another kind of phrase.

What Is a Phrase?

3a. A *phrase* is a group of related words that is used as a single part of speech and that does not contain both a verb and its subject.

VERB PHRASE	has been canceled [no subject]
PREPOSITIONAL PHRASE	before the party [no subject or verb]
INFINITIVE PHRASE	to buy bread [no subject or verb]

NOTE   A group of words that has both a subject and a verb is called a *clause.*

EXAMPLES   the field trip has been canceled [independent clause]

before the party started [subordinate clause]

Reference Note

For more about **clauses,** see Chapter 4.

Prepositional Phrases

Reference Note

For a list of **commonly used prepositions,** see page 21.

3b. A *prepositional phrase* includes a preposition, the object of the preposition, and any modifiers of that object.

EXAMPLES   The tall building **with the red roof** is our new library. [The noun *roof* is the object of the preposition *with.* The adjectives *the* and *red* modify *roof.*]

Next to it is the old library. [The pronoun *it* is the object of the compound preposition *Next to.*]

An object of a preposition may be compound.

EXAMPLE   The female cardinal is brownish red and has red markings **on its wings and tail.** [Both *wings* and *tail* are objects of the preposition *on.*]

S T Y L E   T I P

Prepositional phrases are handy for adding descriptive information to writing. Used excessively, however, these phrases can make writing wordy and stilted.

WORDY
With great care, Julia put on her blouse made of silk, fastened her necklace of pearls, and, with leisure, surveyed the results in the mirror.

REVISED
Carefully, Julia put on her silk blouse, fastened her pearl necklace, and leisurely surveyed the results in the mirror.

The Adjective Phrase

3c. A prepositional phrase that modifies a noun or a pronoun is called an *adjective phrase.*

An adjective phrase tells *what kind(s)* or *which one(s).*

EXAMPLE   Many **of these books** include short stories **for young readers.** [*Of these books* modifies the pronoun *Many,* telling *which ones. For young readers* modifies the noun *short stories,* telling *what kind.*]

An adjective phrase generally follows the word it modifies. That word may be the object of another preposition.

EXAMPLE   Diego Rivera's experiments **with fresco painting on large walls** resulted in beautiful murals. [*With fresco painting* modifies the noun *experiments. On large walls* modifies the noun *painting,* the object of the preposition *with.*]

More than one adjective phrase may modify the same word.

EXAMPLE   Rivera developed a style **of his own with simplified figures and bold colors.** [The two phrases *of his own* and *with simplified figures and bold colors* modify the noun *style.*]

Reference Note

For more about **compound nouns,** see page 4.

NOTE   If an adjective phrase is combined with a noun to form a compound noun, the entire group of words is considered a noun.

EXAMPLES   work of art   Habitat for Humanity

hole in one   board of education

Exercise 1 Identifying Adjective Phrases and the Words They Modify

Each of the following sentences contains at least one adjective phrase. Identify each adjective phrase and the word it modifies.

EXAMPLE
    1. The small Scandinavian animal in this photograph is called a lemming.

    1. in this photograph—animal

1. Ordinarily, lemmings eat a diet of moss and roots.
2. Every few years, however, their population exceeds their food supply, and they ford streams and lakes, devouring everything in their path and leaving no trace of vegetation.
3. Legend tells us that when the lemmings reach the cliffs along the sea, they leap off and drown.
4. This pattern of behavior was puzzling because it contradicted the basic instinct for self-preservation.
5. Do these animals follow a pattern of self-destruction?
6. Recently, scientific study of these animals has revealed that this lore about them is untrue and that most lemmings become victims of predators or starvation.
7. Cozy homes underneath the ground protect young lemmings.
8. Bits of grass line their burrows' walls and floors.
9. Even growing numbers of hungry foxes and owls cannot significantly reduce the number of lemmings; second-year population increases by a factor of thirty are not unusual.
10. The cycle from plenty to starvation begins again every four years.

The Adverb Phrase

3d. **A prepositional phrase that modifies a verb, an adjective, or an adverb is called an *adverb phrase*.**

An adverb phrase tells *how, when, where, why,* or *to what extent* (*how long* or *how far*).

    An adverb phrase may modify a verb.

EXAMPLE
    During the Civil War, Louisa May Alcott worked **as a nurse in a hospital for six weeks.** [Each phrase modifies the verb *worked. During the Civil War* tells *when, as a nurse* tells *how, in a hospital* tells *where,* and *for six weeks* tells *how long.*]

┌ **HELP** ─
Be careful not to confuse a prepositional phrase beginning with *to* with an infinitive or infinitive phrase beginning with *to* (*to swim, to know, to see*). Remember, a preposition always has a noun or pronoun as an object.

Reference Note
For more about **infinitives** and **infinitive phrases,** see page 64.

As you can see in the example on the previous page, more than one adverb phrase can modify the same word. That example also shows that an adverb phrase can precede the word it modifies.

An adverb phrase may modify an adjective.

EXAMPLE   Louisa May Alcott wrote *Little Women,* a novel rich **in New England traditions.** [*In New England traditions* modifies the adjective *rich,* telling *how rich.*]

An adverb phrase may modify an adverb.

EXAMPLE   Too late **for Alcott and other early suffragists,** United States voting laws were changed. [*For Alcott and other early suffragists* modifies the adverb *late,* telling *how late.*]

Exercise 2 **Identifying Adverb Phrases and the Words They Modify**

Each of the following sentences contains at least one adverb phrase. Identify each adverb phrase and the word or words it modifies.

EXAMPLE   1. Chinua Achebe's first novel, *Things Fall Apart,* was published in 1958.

   1. *in 1958—was published*

1. The trees were bent nearly double in the wind.
2. I got the twins ready for bed at 7:30 P.M.
3. In the classic Japanese movie *The Seven Samurai,* fierce professional warriors save a village from bandits.
4. They were assembled on benches for the presentation.
5. Especially for the children, the mariachi band played "The Mexican Hat Dance."
6. Fear sometimes springs from ignorance.
7. Is this outfit appropriate for a job interview?
8. The elephant dozed in the shade.

9. The first mass-produced car, the Model T, was built from 1908 until 1927.

10. Duncan is sitting in his chair, eating a bowl of oatmeal.

Review A Identifying Prepositional Phrases

For each sentence in the following paragraph, list all the prepositional phrases. Be sure to include any prepositional phrase that modifies the object of another preposition. Then, tell whether each prepositional phrase is an *adjective phrase* or an *adverb phrase*. Be prepared to give the word that each prepositional phrase modifies and to identify the word as a *noun*, a *pronoun*, a *verb*, an *adjective*, or an *adverb*.

EXAMPLE **[1]** From what part of the world do these strange-looking objects come?

1. *From what part—adverb phrase; of the world—adjective phrase*

HELP

In the example for Review A, *from what part* modifies the verb *do come. Of the world* modifies the noun *part.*

[1] These items come from Africa, and they belong to the family of musical instruments called *mbiras.* [2] Almost the size of a paperback book, these small *mbiras,* called *kalimbas,* are made of smooth, warm-colored wood. [3] The instrument is called a thumb box by some people because players pluck the steel keys with their thumbs to play melodies. [4] There is also a sound hole like the one on a guitar. [5] When players pluck one or more keys, the notes resonate inside the box. [6] The *kalimba* sounds like a cross between a small xylophone and a set of wind chimes. [7] It is easily carried in a pocket or back-pack, and it is easy to play. [8] Nearly everybody enjoys the soft, light sound, even when a player hits a wrong note with both thumbs! [9] Instruments similar to the *kalimba* were noted by Portuguese explorers in the sixteenth century along the East African coast. [10] In 1586, Father Dos Santos, a Portuguese traveler, wrote that native *mbira* players pluck the keys lightly, "as a good player strikes those of a harpsichord," producing "a sweet and gentle harmony of accordant sounds."

Verbals and Verbal Phrases

Verbals are formed from verbs but are used as nouns, adjectives, and adverbs. The three kinds of verbals are the *participle*, the *gerund*, and the *infinitive*. A **verbal phrase** consists of a verbal and its modifiers and complements. The three kinds of verbal phrases are the *participial phrase*, the *gerund phrase*, and the *infinitive phrase*.

The Participle

3e. A *participle* is a verb form that can be used as an adjective.

Present participles end in *–ing.*

EXAMPLES Esperanza sees the **singing** canary near the window. [*Singing,* a form of the verb *sing,* modifies the noun *canary.*]

Waving, the campers boarded the bus. [*Waving,* a form of the verb *wave,* modifies the noun *campers.*]

We could hear it **moving** in the underbrush. [*Moving,* a form of the verb *move,* modifies the pronoun *it.*]

Most past participles end in *–d* or *–ed.* Others are irregularly formed.

EXAMPLES The **baked** chicken with yellow rice tasted delicious. [*Baked,* a form of the verb *bake,* modifies the noun *chicken.*]

Confused and **frightened,** they fled into the jungle. [*Confused,* a form of the verb *confuse,* and *frightened,* a form of the verb *frighten,* modify the pronoun *they.*]

In your own words, define each term **given** below. [*Given,* a form of the verb *give,* modifies the noun *term.*]

The perfect tense of a participle is formed with *having* or with *having been.*

EXAMPLES **Having worked** all day, Abe was ready for a rest.

Having been washed, the car gleamed in the sun.

NOTE Do not confuse a participle used as an adjective with a participle used as part of a verb phrase.

ADJECTIVE The Smithsonian Institution, **located** in Washington, D.C., is the largest museum in the world.

VERB PHRASE The Smithsonian Institution, which **is located** in Washington, D.C., is the largest museum in the world.

Reference Note

For more information on the **forms of participles,** see page 162. For a discussion of **irregular verbs,** see page 164.

The Participial Phrase

3f. A *participial phrase* consists of a participle and any modifiers or complements the participle has. The entire phrase is used as an adjective.

EXAMPLES **Speaking eloquently,** Julian Bond enthralled the audience. [The participial phrase modifies the noun *Julian Bond*. The adverb *eloquently* modifies the present participle *Speaking*.]

Nodding his head, the defendant admitted his guilt. [The participial phrase modifies the noun *defendant*. The noun *head* is the direct object of the present participle *Nodding*.]

Encouraged by his family, he submitted his book of poems for publication. [The participial phrase modifies the pronoun *he*. The adverb phrase *by his family* modifies the past participle *Encouraged*.]

Florence Griffith-Joyner, **sometimes known as Flo Jo,** held the U.S. national record for the women's 100-meter dash. [The participial phrase modifies the noun *Florence Griffith-Joyner*. The adverb *sometimes* modifies the past participle *known*. The adverb phrase *as Flo Jo* modifies *known*.]

The Absolute Phrase

An *absolute phrase* consists of (1) a participle or participial phrase, (2) a noun or pronoun that the participle or participial phrase modifies, and (3) any other modifiers of that noun or pronoun. The entire word group is used as an adverb to modify an independent clause of a sentence.

An absolute phrase has no direct grammatical connection to any word in the independent clause it modifies. Rather, the phrase modifies the entire clause by telling *when*, *why*, or *how*.

EXAMPLES **The costumes having been made,** the actors prepared for their dress rehearsal. [The perfect participle *having been made* modifies the noun *costumes*. The absolute phrase modifies the independent clause by telling *when* the actors prepared for their dress rehearsal.]

Dark clouds threatening a storm, the hikers searched anxiously for shelter. [The participial phrase *threatening a storm* modifies the noun *clouds*. The absolute phrase modifies the independent clause by telling *why* the hikers searched anxiously for shelter.]

STYLE TIP

When writing a sentence with a participial phrase, be sure to place the phrase as close as possible to the word it modifies. Otherwise, the phrase may appear to modify another word, and the sentence may not make sense.

MISPLACED
Singing in the trees, the birdwatchers heard the wild canaries walking along the path.

IMPROVED
Walking along the path, the birdwatchers heard the wild canaries **singing in the trees.**

Reference Note

For more information about **misplaced participial phrases,** see page 230. For more about the **punctuation of participial phrases,** see page 306.

Identifying Participial Phrases and the Words They Modify

Each of the following sentences contains at least one participial phrase. Identify each participial phrase and the word or words it modifies.

EXAMPLE
1. The Kentucky Derby, considered the first jewel in the Triple Crown of thoroughbred racing, is held each year on the first Saturday in May at Churchill Downs in Louisville, Kentucky.

1. *considered the first jewel in the Triple Crown of thoroughbred racing—Kentucky Derby*

1. Known as Johnny Appleseed, John Chapman distributed apple seeds and saplings to families headed west.
2. Needing a steady wind for flight, the albatross rarely crosses the equator.
3. At the reptile exhibit, we saw forty adders coiled together.
4. The salmon, deriving the pink color of its flesh from its diet, feeds on shrimplike crustaceans.
5. Having been aided by good weather and clear skies, the sailors rejoiced as they sailed into port.
6. Smiling broadly, our champion entered the hall.
7. I would love to see the hibiscus bursting into bloom in the spring; it must be quite a sight!
8. Sparta and Athens, putting aside their own rivalry, joined forces to fight the Persians.
9. Trained on an overhead trellis, a rosebush growing in Tombstone, Arizona, covers approximately 8,000 square feet of aerial space.
10. Searching through old clothes in a trunk, John found a map showing the location of a treasure buried on the shore.

Identifying Prepositional and Participial Phrases and the Words They Modify

Identify each italicized phrase in the following sentences as a *prepositional phrase* or a *participial phrase*. Then, give the word or words each phrase modifies. Do not separately identify a prepositional phrase that is part of a participial phrase.

EXAMPLE
1. *Delighted by the play,* the critic applauded *with great enthusiasm.*

1. *Delighted by the play—participial phrase—critic; with great enthusiasm—prepositional phrase—applauded*

1. Mahalia Jackson, perhaps one of the greatest blues-influenced singers *since Bessie Smith*, would sing only religious songs.
2. Her version of "Silent Night" was one *of the all-time best-selling records* in Denmark.
3. *Known for his imaginative style*, architect Minoru Yamasaki designed the Federal Reserve Bank, *located in Richmond, Virginia*.
4. *Having been rejected by six publishers*, the story *of Peter Rabbit* was finally published privately *by Beatrix Potter*.
5. *Setting out in a thirty-one-foot ketch*, Sharon Sites Adams, a woman *from California*, sailed *across the Pacific Ocean* alone.
6. In 1932, Amelia Earhart, *trying for a new record*, began her solo flight *over the Atlantic Ocean*.
7. Maria Tallchief, an Osage Indian, was the prima ballerina *of the New York City Ballet company*.
8. *Dancing to acclaim in both the United States and Europe*, she was known *for her brilliant interpretation* of Stravinsky's <u>The Firebird</u>.
9. *Continuing her research on radium after her husband's death*, Marie Curie received the Nobel Prize *in chemistry*.
10. *First elected to the House of Representatives in 1968*, Shirley Chisholm was the first African American female member *of Congress*.

The Gerund

3g. A *gerund* is a verb form ending in *–ing* that is used as a noun.

SUBJECT	**Swimming** quickly tired us.
PREDICATE NOMINATIVE	Janetta's hobby is **knitting.**
DIRECT OBJECT	She has always loved **dancing.**
INDIRECT OBJECT	He gave **studying** all his attention.
OBJECT OF PREPOSITION	In **cooking,** use salt sparingly.

Do not confuse a gerund with a present participle used as an adjective or as part of a verb phrase.

GERUND	I enjoyed **volunteering** at the Special Olympics. [direct object of the verb *enjoyed*]
PRESENT PARTICIPLE	All students **volunteering** for the decorating committee should arrive one hour early. [adjective modifying the noun *students*]

Reference Note

For information on **subjects,** see page 33. For information on **predicate nominatives,** see page 42. For information on **direct objects** and **indirect objects,** see page 39. For information on **objects of prepositions,** see page 54.

Verbals and Verbal Phrases **61**

PRESENT PARTICIPLE Chamique is **volunteering** at the food bank this weekend. [part of the verb phrase *is volunteering*]

Reference Note

For information about **possessive forms,** see page 131.

NOTE When writing a noun or a pronoun directly before a gerund, use the possessive form of the noun or pronoun.

EXAMPLES **Rodrigo's** winning the contest surprised no one.

Mom was upset about **our** being late.

Everyone's arriving on time pleased us.

Oral Practice **Identifying Gerunds and Their Functions**

Read the following sentences aloud, and identify the gerunds. Then, identify each gerund as a *subject*, a *direct object*, an *indirect object*, a *predicate nominative*, or an *object of a preposition*.

EXAMPLE 1. By reading the newspaper daily, you can become an informed citizen.

1. *reading—object of a preposition*

1. Judging should be an exercise in objectivity.
2. Do you enjoy skiing?
3. I sometimes dream about flying.
4. Have you ever wished for a career in acting?
5. I have given camping a fair try, but I still do not like it.
6. Some of my friends work at stores in the mall, and others earn extra money by baby-sitting.
7. My doctor says that I should be more physically active, so my new exercise schedule includes jogging.
8. My favorite pastime is snorkeling.
9. Typing is a useful skill that could help you get a job next summer after you graduate.
10. My Navajo grandmother thinks that weaving would be a good hobby for me.

The Gerund Phrase

3h. A *gerund phrase* consists of a gerund and any modifiers or complements the gerund has. The entire phrase is used as a noun.

EXAMPLES **Studying regularly** leads to better grades. [The gerund phrase is the subject of the verb *leads*. The adverb *regularly* modifies the gerund *Studying*.]

My brother likes **working at the travel agency.** [The gerund phrase is the direct object of the verb *likes*. The adverb phrase *at the travel agency* modifies the gerund *working*.]

Maya dreams of **becoming a well-known artist.** [The gerund phrase is the object of the preposition *of*. The noun *artist* is a predicate nominative completing the meaning of the gerund *becoming*.]

One important part of a healthy lifestyle is **eating fresh fruit.** [The gerund phrase is a predicate nominative identifying the subject *part*. The noun *fruit* is the direct object of the gerund *eating*.]

Review C Identifying Participial Phrases and Gerund Phrases

Identify the verbal phrase in each of the following sentences as either a *participial phrase* or a *gerund phrase.*

EXAMPLE **1.** At what age did Se Ri Pak begin playing golf?

 1. playing golf—gerund phrase

1. Mary Shelley wrote *Frankenstein* after having a nightmare about a scientist and his strange experiments.
2. Dr. Mae Jemison became an astronaut by placing among the best fifteen candidates out of two thousand applicants.
3. Beginning with *Pippi Longstocking,* Astrid Lindgren has written a whole series of stories for children.
4. Marian Anderson was the first African American employed as a member of the Metropolitan Opera.
5. Fighting for women's suffrage was Carrie Chapman Catt's mission in life.
6. Appointed principal of the Mason City Iowa High School in 1881, Catt became the city's first female superintendent.
7. The Nineteenth Amendment to the Constitution, adopted in 1920, was largely the result of Catt's efforts.
8. Mildred "Babe" Didrikson, entering the 1932 Olympics as a relatively obscure athlete, won gold and silver medals.
9. Working for *Life* throughout her long career, Margaret Bourke-White was the first female war photographer.
10. Phyllis McGinley, a famous writer of light verse, began publishing her work while she was still in college.

The Infinitive

3i. An *infinitive* is a verb form that can be used as a noun, an adjective, or an adverb. Most infinitives begin with *to*.

Infinitives	
Used as	**Examples**
Nouns	**To fly** was an ambition of humans for many centuries. [subject of *was*]
	Some fishes must swim constantly, or they start **to sink.** [direct object of *start*]
	Darius Freeman's dream is **to act.** [predicate nominative identifying the subject *dream*]
Adjectives	His attempt **to fly** was a failure. [adjective modifying the noun *attempt*]
	The one **to ask** is your guidance counselor. [adjective modifying the pronoun *one*]
Adverbs	With his dog Wolf, Rip Van Winkle went into the woods **to hunt.** [adverb modifying the verb *went*]
	Everyone in the neighborhood was willing **to help.** [adverb modifying the adjective *willing*]

Reference Note

For more information about **prepositional phrases,** see page 54.

NOTE Do not confuse an infinitive with a prepositional phrase that begins with *to*. An infinitive is a verb form. A prepositional phrase beginning with *to* ends with a noun or a pronoun.

INFINITIVES	to write	to forgive	to visit
PREPOSITIONAL PHRASES	to the game	to someone	to them

The word *to*, the sign of the infinitive, is sometimes omitted.

EXAMPLES   Let's [to] **sit** down.

We wouldn't dare [to] **disobey.**

Please make him [to] **stop** that noise.

Thank you for helping me [to] **finish** the mural.

Exercise 4 Identifying Infinitives and Their Functions

Identify the infinitive in each of the following sentences. Then, tell whether it is used as a *noun*, an *adjective*, or an *adverb*. If the infinitive is used as a *noun*, indicate whether it is a *subject*, a *direct object*, or a *predicate nominative*. If the infinitive is used as a modifier, give the word it modifies.

EXAMPLE   1. Swans and geese are fascinating to watch.

1. *to watch—adverb—fascinating*

1. To land on the moon became the national goal of the United States during the 1960s.
2. For me, one of the worst chores is to clean my room.
3. Karl "The Mailman" Malone slam-dunked the ball with one second to go!
4. In my spare time I like to read stories by James Thurber and Laurence Yep.
5. Did you find that book difficult to understand?
6. In our judicial system, the state makes the decision to prosecute the defendant in criminal cases.
7. I did not have time to watch the football game on television.
8. Anita's job was to interview all qualified candidates who had applied for the position.
9. I want to finish the dishes before I go to the movies.
10. Glad to help, Jennifer quickly found a paintbrush and a dropcloth and then started painting the shutters.

The Infinitive Phrase

3j. An *infinitive phrase* consists of an infinitive and any modifiers or complements the infinitive has. The entire phrase can be used as a noun, an adjective, or an adverb.

NOUN   **To finish early** is Peggy's plan. [The infinitive phrase is the subject of the verb *is.* The adverb *early* modifies the infinitive *To finish.*]

NOUN   Reginald wants **to go to the beach with us on Saturday.** [The infinitive phrase is the direct object of the verb *wants.* The adverb phrases *to the beach, with us,* and *on Saturday* modify the infinitive *to go.*]

ADJECTIVE	The team's desire **to win the game** was evident. [The infinitive phrase modifies the noun *desire.* The noun *game* is the direct object of the infinitive *to win.*]
ADVERB	Because of his sprained ankle, Chico was unable **to play in the football game.** [The infinitive phrase modifies the adjective *unable.* The adverb phrase *in the football game* modifies the infinitive *to play.*]

Reference Note

For information about other kinds of **clauses,** see Chapter 4.

Unlike other kinds of verbals, an infinitive may have a subject. An *infinitive clause* consists of an infinitive with a subject and any modifiers and complements the infinitive has. The entire clause is used as a noun. Notice in the second example below that the pronoun (*them*) used as the subject of the infinitive clause is in the objective case.

EXAMPLES	The director wants **Rebecca to star in the play.** [*Rebecca* is the subject of the infinitive *to star.* The entire infinitive clause is the direct object of the verb *wants.*]
	The sergeant commanded **them to march faster.** [*Them* is the subject of the infinitive *to march.* The entire infinitive clause is the direct object of the verb *commanded.*]

COMPUTER TIP

Some style-checking software programs can identify and highlight split infinitives. Using such a program will help you eliminate unnecessary split infinitives from your writing.

NOTE Placing words between the sign of the infinitive, *to,* and the base form results in a *split infinitive.* Generally, you should avoid using split infinitives in formal writing and speech.

SPLIT	The mayor wants to, as soon as possible, meet with her advisors.
REVISED	The mayor wants to meet with her advisors as soon as possible.

Sometimes, however, you may need to use a split infinitive so that the meaning of the sentence is clear.

UNCLEAR	The other team tried unfairly to influence the judges. [Does the adverb *unfairly* modify the verb *tried* or the infinitive *to influence*?]
CLEAR	The other team tried to unfairly influence the judges.

Review D Identifying Participial, Gerund, and Infinitive Phrases

Identify the participial, gerund, and infinitive phrases in the sentences in the paragraph on the next page. For each participial phrase, give the word it modifies. For each gerund phrase, tell what part of a sentence it is. For each infinitive phrase, indicate what part of speech it is.

EXAMPLE **[1]** In Chinese communities all over the world, parading a huge paper dragon is a large part of the New Year's celebration.

1. *parading a huge paper dragon—gerund phrase (subject)*

[1] Dragons are a traditionally honored symbol of happiness to many Chinese people. [2] In ancient Chinese mythology, dragons are responsible for watching over people and bringing rainfall for the crops. [3] There are five different types of dragons, but it is the imperial dragon that is chosen to dance through the streets in traditional New Year's celebrations. [4] The dragon's role is to drive away bad luck and to bring good fortune for the new year. [5] Holding a stick with a white ball on the top, one dancer runs ahead of the dragon figure. [6] The ball symbolizes the highly valued pearl of wisdom, which the dragon chases. [7] The dragon's dance is accompanied by the beating of drums and gongs, the clashing of cymbals, and the popping of firecrackers. [8] The largest dragon figure in the world, similar to the one shown here, measured three meters tall and nearly one hundred meters long. [9] Decorated with thousands of mirrors and silk "scales," this dragon was truly impressive. [10] Because of its great weight and size, it took more than one hundred people, working in shifts, to carry it.

Review E **Identifying Prepositional, Participial, Gerund, and Infinitive Phrases**

Identify each italicized phrase in the following sentences as a *prepositional phrase*, a *participial phrase*, a *gerund phrase*, or an *infinitive phrase*. Do not separately identify a prepositional phrase that is part of another kind of phrase.

EXAMPLE
1. *Celebrating the strength of the human spirit,* Christy Brown's book <u>My Left Foot</u> tells the story *of his life.*

1. *Celebrating the strength of the human spirit*—participial phrase; *of his life*—prepositional phrase

1. Christy Brown, *born with cerebral palsy,* was unable *to speak a single word.*
2. Everyone, *including his family,* assumed he had very little intelligence, because he could not express himself *to anyone.*
3. Christy's left foot was the only limb he could control, and one day he succeeded in *grabbing a piece of chalk with it* and began *to write the word MOTHER on the wooden floor.*
4. Christy's family, *amazed at this remarkable achievement,* suddenly realized that *his leading a full, rewarding life* was not an impossible dream.
5. *Locked inside him,* a nimble intelligence and a mighty determination were waiting *to have their say.*
6. Not only was he capable of *understanding conversation,* but he had also learned *to write and spell* all by himself.
7. *Looking into Christy's eyes that day,* his family might have felt that they were meeting him *for the first time.*
8. *With that one word,* his life changed, and the family made *helping him* a primary goal.
9. *Typing the entire manuscript with his left foot,* Christy Brown was eventually able *to tell his story in this inspiring book about his life.*
10. *Reading his book* will teach you much *about love and courage.*

Appositives and Appositive Phrases

3k. An *appositive* is a noun or a pronoun placed beside another noun or pronoun to identify or describe it.

An appositive usually follows the word it identifies or explains.

EXAMPLES   Both the Tewa and the Hopi are part of the American Indian group **Pueblo.** [The noun *Pueblo* identifies the noun *group*.]

The Hopi-Tewa artist **Dan Namingha** often paints abstract images of Hopi pueblos. [The noun *Dan Namingha* identifies the noun *artist.*]

Tony, did you know that she, **Martha,** won the race? [The noun *Martha* identifies the pronoun *she.*]

Aunt Sheila devotes Saturday mornings to her favorite hobby, **shopping.** [The gerund *shopping* identifies the noun *hobby.*]

Both the winners, **he** and **she,** will get mountain bikes. [The pronouns *he* and *she* identify the noun *winners.*]

For emphasis, however, an appositive may come at the beginning of a sentence.

EXAMPLE   **Conifers,** both redwoods and sequoias bear their seeds in cones. [The noun *Conifers* refers to the nouns *redwoods* and *sequoias.*]

3l. An *appositive phrase* consists of an appositive and any modifiers the appositive has.

EXAMPLES   Did Dan Namingha complete *Red Desert,* **one of his colorful acrylic paintings,** in 1980? [The adjective phrase *of his colorful acrylic paintings* modifies the appositive *one.*]

The Alaska moose, **the largest deer in the world,** inhabits the Kenai Peninsula. [The adjectives *the* and *largest* and the adjective phrase *in the world* modify the appositive *deer.*]

Remember the celebrations held on Monday, January 1, 2001, **the first day of the twenty-first century**? [The adjectives *the* and *first* and the adjective phrase *of the twenty-first century* modify the appositive *day.*]

Exercise 5   Identifying Appositives and Appositive Phrases

Identify the appositive or appositive phrase in each of the following sentences.

EXAMPLE   **1.** I enjoy reading about two colorful trickster figures, the Irish leprechaun and the American Indian Coyote.

1. *the Irish leprechaun and the American Indian Coyote*

1. José Saramago, a Portuguese novelist, won the 1998 Nobel Prize in literature.

Reference Note

For more information about **modifiers,** see Chapter 9.

MEETING THE CHALLENGE

If you stand in front of a bookshelf for a few minutes, chances are you'll encounter several phrases. The titles of many books contain phrases, and the titles of numerous other books actually *are* phrases. By yourself or in a small group, head to the school library for fifteen to twenty minutes, and write down as many titles as you can that contain phrases. Find at least one title for each of the following types of phrases: adjective phrase, adverb phrase, participial phrase, gerund phrase, infinitive phrase, and appositive phrase. When you are finished, share your list with your class.

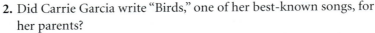

2. Did Carrie Garcia write "Birds," one of her best-known songs, for her parents?
3. There goes the beautiful ship SS *Pericles,* bound for Greece!
4. "Aren't you Paolo Randazzo, the famous center-forward?" they asked excitedly.
5. Our teacher, Mr. Chun, overlooked the whole incident.
6. Sheila's grandmother Sra. Flores loves to listen to Tito Puente.
7. Their dog, a chocolate Labrador, chased a ball along the beach.
8. France is the home of the T.G.V., the fastest train in the world.
9. Ms. Ashoka teaches calculus at King High, a local magnet school.
10. A composer of Armenian ancestry, Aram Khachaturian was known for his exuberant music.

Review F **Identifying Prepositional, Verbal, and Appositive Phrases**

Identify each italicized phrase in the following paragraph as a *prepositional phrase,* a *participial phrase,* a *gerund phrase,* an *infinitive phrase,* or an *appositive phrase.* Do not separately identify a prepositional phrase that is part of another kind of phrase.

EXAMPLE   [1] *Packing effectively for a trip* requires careful thought.
        1. gerund phrase

Each year, thousands of Americans travel to hundreds [1] *of vacation spots in the United States and other countries.* [2] *Anticipating all kinds of weather and activities,* many eager travelers pack far too much clothing and equipment. The most effective way for these travelers to pack is [3] *to set out clothes for the trip* and then to put half of them back. For sightseeing trips, of course, travelers should give particular attention [4] *to walking shoes,* [5] *the most important item of apparel on such trips.* Experienced travelers pack only two or three changes of casual clothing, even if they plan [6] *to be away for some time.* [7] *Taking out the smallest piece of luggage they own,* they study its capacity. It is possible to pack enough clothes for three weeks in a small piece of luggage, [8] *perhaps a duffel bag or shoulder bag.* Passengers can carry such a bag onto an airplane and avoid [9] *waiting at the baggage claim area.* For many people, [10] *doing a bit of hand laundry every few days* is preferable to spending a vacation burdened with heavy suitcases.

Chapter Review

A. Identifying Prepositional Phrases

Write each prepositional phrase in the following sentences, and identify it as an *adjective phrase* or an *adverb phrase*. A sentence may include more than one phrase.

1. My family's cabin in the woods sits near the lakeshore.
2. During the intermission, Mr. Jackson played the pipe organ for the audience.
3. The oregano in the spice rack is fresher than the oregano in the pantry.
4. After the ball, the carriage in the palace courtyard became a pumpkin again.
5. The package arrived too late for Carmina's birthday.
6. Many of the cups on this shelf were made in Mexico.
7. After high school, my mother studied at Calvin College.
8. Add two cans of peeled tomatoes, a tablespoon of mild curry powder, and a cup of brown rice.
9. In *The Hobbit*, the hero of the story finds a magic ring.
10. Does your brother know anything about British history?

B. Identifying Verbal Phrases

Write each verbal phrase in the following sentences, and identify it as a *participial phrase*, a *gerund phrase*, or an *infinitive phrase*.

11. Off the coast of Australia, bottlenose dolphins have been observed with large natural sponges attached to their beaks.
12. Marian's attempt to rescue the cat was covered by a reporter.
13. Shiwonda wants to study law at Vanderbilt.
14. Archaeologists in Bulgaria unearthed a one-room tomb, hollowed out of two boulders, that contained frescoes.
15. Lee prefers swimming in water cooler than 72 degrees Fahrenheit.
16. Jamail spends plenty of time with his new puppy to accustom it to his voice and touch.
17. Mitsuyo's confidence was built up by winning the decathlon.

18. Preparing for the SAT took more time than I thought it would.
19. Shaking her head, Lisa indicated that she wasn't interested in the tour.
20. To learn the basics of French was Lina's main goal.

C. Identifying Appositive Phrases

Write each appositive phrase in the following sentences.

21. Sam, the youngest of Mimi's three cats, likes to climb.
22. Oscar Wilde, the author of *The Importance of Being Earnest,* was known for his sharp wit.
23. The band played "The Stars and Stripes Forever," a march.
24. They have the olive oil I like, the brand with the red label.
25. Winner of the Nobel Prize in literature, Toni Morrison is the author of such novels as *Beloved, Song of Solomon,* and *Paradise.*

D. Identifying Prepositional, Verbal, and Appositive Phrases

Identify each italicized phrase in the following sentences as a *prepositional phrase*, a *participial phrase*, a *gerund phrase*, an *infinitive phrase*, or an *appositive phrase*. Do not separately identify a prepositional phrase that is part of another phrase.

26. *Filling this order* will take at least two weeks.
27. Cuts and bruises, *minor injuries for most children*, are treated by the school nurse.
28. I have an appointment *to meet with the campaign committee*.
29. Ms. Behrman's only comment *on my paper* was that my handwriting was difficult to read.
30. He told me the story of Ta-sunko-witko, *a Sioux chief*.
31. His greatest joy was *seeing the latest science fiction movie*.
32. *Grabbing a sandwich*, René hurried off to join his friends.
33. Mom finally agreed *to buy me a new dress for the dance*.
34. On the top floor are three offices *connected by a hallway*.
35. Her attitude may seem indifferent *to you*.
36. In Israel, farmers use innovative agricultural methods to meet the difficulties of *growing food in a desert country*.
37. Woodrow Wilson, *the U.S. president during World War I*, tried to construct a lasting peace after the war.

38. During our vacation in Hawaii, we saw Mauna Loa, a volcano *rising two and a half miles above sea level.*

39. Withdrawing from the race, the candidate cited personal reasons for her unexpected decision *to return to private life.*

40. To conserve water, many farmers water only the roots of plants, using a series *of underground irrigation pipes.*

Writing Application
Describing a Business

Using Prepositional Phrases   Your school newspaper plans to publish a special careers issue. For a feature page, the editor has invited students to describe businesses they would like to own ten years from now. Think of your business, invent a name for it, and write a paragraph describing it. Use at least five prepositional phrases in your sentences.

Prewriting   Brainstorm ideas for three or four kinds of businesses you would enjoy owning and managing ten years from now. Then, jot down details about your product or service, your location, your equipment, and your customers.

Writing   As you write your first draft, think about your audience. What details about your business would interest your readers? Make sure that you include plenty of specific details.

Revising   Ask a friend to read your paragraph before you revise it. Can your friend clearly imagine your business? If not, add, cut, or rearrange details to make your paragraph clearer and more interesting. If your sentences sound choppy, combine them into longer, smoother sentences. Be sure that you have used at least five prepositional phrases in your paragraph.

Publishing   Check the grammar, spelling, and punctuation of your paragraph. You and your classmates may want to gather your paragraphs into a booklet to include in a class time capsule.

Reference Note

For information on **sentence combining,** see Chapter 18.

The Clause

Independent and Subordinate Clauses

Diagnostic Preview

A. Identifying Independent and Subordinate Clauses

Identify the italicized clause in each of the following sentences as *independent* or *subordinate*. If the italicized clause is subordinate, tell whether it is used as an *adverb*, an *adjective*, or a *noun*.

EXAMPLE 1. Miguel and Bette, *who were visiting us over the Labor Day weekend,* have returned to their home in Rhode Island.

    1. *subordinate; adjective*

1. *Whenever Jorge practices the clarinet,* his neighbor's beagles, Banjo and Randolph, howl.
2. Advertisements encourage people to want products, and *many people cannot distinguish between their passing wants and their essential needs.*
3. In Ms. Weinberg's science class we learned *that chalk is made up mostly of calcium carbonate.*
4. Liliuokalani, *who was the last queen of Hawaii,* wrote "*Aloha Oe*"; she was an accomplished songwriter.
5. Does each of you know *how you can protect yourself* if a tornado strikes our area?

6. *If there is a tornado warning,* go quickly to the lowest level in your house, cover your head with your hands, and lie flat or crouch low until the danger is past.

7. The American Indians *who inhabited the area of Connecticut around the Naugatuck River* were called the Pequots.

8. *American music has been enriched by Ella Fitzgerald, Leslie Uggams, and Lena Horne, three well-known African American vocalists.*

9. *That the girls' volleyball team was well coached* was demonstrated last night when the team won the state championship.

10. *As you enter the school,* the principal's office is the third room on your right.

B. Classifying Sentences According to Structure

Classify each sentence in the following paragraphs as *simple*, *compound*, *complex*, or *compound-complex*.

EXAMPLE **[1]** In January 1991, Phoebe Jeter displayed leadership and courage.

1. *simple*

[11] Just who is this Phoebe Jeter from Sharon, South Carolina? [12] Phoebe Jeter, serving as a lieutenant in the U.S. Army, led a platoon during the Persian Gulf Conflict in 1991. [13] Jeter will always remember the tense January night when she heard the words "Scud alert!" [14] On her orders, thirteen Patriot missiles were fired, and at least two Scud missiles were destroyed. [15] When the Persian Gulf Conflict was over, Jeter had the satisfaction of knowing that she had successfully defended U.S. troops.

[16] That 40 percent of the women who served in the Gulf were African Americans may be an underestimate. [17] Figures have not been released by the Pentagon, but some say the actual number may have been closer to 50 percent. [18] The Persian Gulf Conflict tested the mettle of all female military personnel involved; throughout the conflict, women shared hazardous assignments, primitive living conditions, and various battle responsibilities with men. [19] The professionalism and courage of the women who served in the Gulf earned them considerable respect. [20] Perhaps now, because of soldiers like Phoebe Jeter, people will think differently about the role of women in the United States armed forces.

What Is a Clause?

4a. A *clause* is a word group that contains a verb and its subject and that is used as a sentence or as part of a sentence.

Every clause has a subject and a verb. Not every clause, however, expresses a complete thought. A clause that expresses a complete thought is called an ***independent clause.*** A clause that does not express a complete thought is called a ***subordinate clause.***

SENTENCE	Lichens are plants that are composed of fungi and algae.

                                    S   V

INDEPENDENT   Lichens are plants [complete thought]
CLAUSE

                                    S   V

SUBORDINATE   that are composed of fungi and algae
CLAUSE   [incomplete thought]

The Independent Clause

4b. An *independent* (or *main*) *clause* expresses a complete thought and can stand by itself as a sentence.

                          S   V

EXAMPLES   **Ms. Martin explained the binary number system.**
[one independent clause]

                                  S   V

In the binary system, each number is expressed in

                                S   V

powers of two, and **only the digits 0 and 1 are used.**
[two independent clauses joined by a comma and *and*]

                     S V   **S**

The binary system is a number system; however, **it**

V

is not the only number system. [two independent clauses joined by a semicolon, a conjunctive adverb, and a comma]

                          S V

The binary number system is important to know

          S V

because it is used by computers. [an independent clause combined with a subordinate clause]

┌HELP┐

A subordinate clause that is capitalized and punctuated as a sentence is a ***sentence fragment.***

Reference Note

For information on **correcting sentence fragments,** see page 446.

The Subordinate Clause

4c. A *subordinate* (or *dependent*) *clause* does not express a complete thought and cannot stand by itself as a sentence.

Like a word or a phrase, a subordinate clause can be used as an adjective, a noun, or an adverb in a sentence.

EXAMPLES   that we had collected

what Hui Su named her pet beagle

when Roberto proofread his essay

The thought expressed by a subordinate clause becomes complete when the clause is combined with an independent clause.

EXAMPLES   Mr. Platero took the aluminum cans **that we had collected** to the recycling center. [adjective clause]

Do you know **what Hui Su named her pet beagle**? [noun clause]

When Roberto proofread his essay, he found several typographical errors. [adverb clause]

┌**HELP**──

Subordinate means "lesser in rank or importance."

Exercise 1 **Identifying Independent and Subordinate Clauses**

Identify each italicized word group in the following paragraph as an *independent clause* or a *subordinate clause*.

EXAMPLE   **[1]** The photographs on this page and the next page show *how eggs are processed in a large processing plant.*

    1. subordinate clause

[1] Large plants like the one in the photographs are *where most eggs are processed today.* [2] After an egg is laid, *it gently rolls along the slanted floor of the cage to a narrow conveyor belt.* [3] These narrow conveyor belts converge into one wide belt *that runs directly into the processing plant.* [4] *As soon as the eggs reach the processing*

plant, they are automatically sprayed with detergent and water. [**5**] The eggs then pass through a specially lit inspection area, *where defective eggs can be detected and removed.* [**6**] After the eggs are weighed, *they are separated by weight into groups.* [**7**] Each group of eggs goes onto a separate conveyor belt, *which leads to a forklike lifting device.* [**8**] This device lifts six eggs at a time *while the empty egg cartons wait two feet below it.* [**9**] *The eggs are gently lowered into the cartons,* which are then shipped to grocery stores and supermarkets. [**10**] *What is truly amazing* is that no human hands touch the eggs during the entire process.

STYLE   TIP

Although the use of short, simple sentences is effective at times, overusing them will result in choppy writing. One way to avoid choppy sentences is to change some sentences into subordinate clauses. Furthermore, by using subordinate clauses, you can avoid the unnecessary repetition of words, such as *The Amazon River* in the following example.

CHOPPY
The Amazon River is about 6,276 kilometers in length. The Amazon River is the second-longest river in the world.

SMOOTH
The Amazon River, which is about 6,276 kilometers in length, is the second-longest river in the world.

The Adjective Clause

4d. An *adjective clause* is a subordinate clause that modifies a noun or a pronoun.

An adjective clause follows the word or words that it modifies and tells *what kind* or *which one.*

EXAMPLES   Dr. Charles Richter devised the Richter scale, **which is used to measure the magnitude of earthquakes.** [The adjective clause modifies the noun *scale.*]

Ferdinand Magellan, **who was the commander of the first expedition around the world,** was killed before the end of the journey. [The adjective clause modifies the noun *Ferdinand Magellan.*]

Didn't John Kieran once say, "I am a part of all **that I have read**"? [The adjective clause modifies the pronoun *all.*]

Relative Pronouns

Usually, an adjective clause begins with a ***relative pronoun***—a word that not only relates an adjective clause to the word or words the clause modifies but also serves a function within the clause.

Common Relative Pronouns				
that	which	who	whom	whose

EXAMPLES   Grandma Moses, **who began painting at the age of seventy-six,** became famous for her primitive style. [The relative pronoun *who* relates the adjective clause to the noun *Grandma Moses* and also serves as the subject of the verb *began*.]

The treasure **for which they are searching** belonged to the Aztec emperor Montezuma II. [The relative pronoun *which* relates the adjective clause to the noun *treasure* and serves as the object of the preposition *for*.]

I have read nearly every novel **that Shirley Ann Grau has written.** [The relative pronoun *that* relates the adjective clause to the noun *novel* and serves as the direct object of the verb *has written*.]

To modify a place or time, an adjective clause may begin with *when* or *where*. When used to introduce adjective clauses, these words are called *relative adverbs.*

EXAMPLES   Chim told me about the time **when he backpacked across Luzon.** [The adjective clause modifies the noun *time*.]

Pet birds should be kept in wide cages, **where they have room to fly.** [The adjective clause modifies the noun *cages*.]

Sometimes the relative pronoun or relative adverb is not expressed, but its meaning is understood.

EXAMPLES   The documentary **[that]** I watched yesterday was about Harriet Tubman.

We will never forget the wonderful summer **[when]** we stayed with our grandparents in Mayagüez, Puerto Rico.

Depending on how it is used, an adjective clause is either essential or nonessential. An *essential* (*or restrictive*) *clause* provides information that is necessary to the meaning of a sentence. A *nonessential* (*or nonrestrictive*) *clause* provides additional information that can be omitted without changing the basic meaning of a sentence. Nonessential clauses are set off by commas.

ESSENTIAL   Students **who are going to the track meet** can take the bus at 7:45 A.M. [Omitting the adjective clause would change the basic meaning of the sentence.]

NONESSENTIAL   Nancy Stevens, **whose father is a pediatrician,** plans to study medicine. [The adjective clause gives extra information. Omitting the clause would not affect the basic meaning of the sentence.]

Reference Note

For information on using **who and whom** correctly, see page 137. For information on using **who, that, and which** correctly, see page 258.

Reference Note

For more about **punctuating nonessential clauses,** see page 306.

GRAMMAR

4 d

Exercise 2 **Identifying Adjective Clauses and the Words They Modify**

Identify the adjective clause in each of the following sentences, and give the noun or pronoun that it modifies. Then, tell whether the relative pronoun is used as a *subject, direct object,* or *object of a preposition* in the adjective clause.

EXAMPLE
1. Theo, who is the editor of the school newspaper, wrote an article about the inhumane treatment of laboratory animals.

1. *who is the editor of the school newspaper; Theo; subject*

1. Some of us have read *Native Son,* which Richard Wright published in 1940.
2. The book to which he referred was ordered yesterday.
3. Everyone in the stands at Wimbledon cheered for the player that had the better serve.
4. The fish that I caught yesterday weighed three pounds, but Sally's fish weighed five pounds.
5. The nominee for the prestigious award was a statesman whom everyone admired.
6. It's not easy to understand someone who mumbles.
7. They finally found my briefcase, which had been missing for two weeks.
8. Please indicate the people to whom we should go for help.
9. The guide advised those who enjoy Native American art to visit the new exhibit of Hopi weaving and pottery.
10. In March many countries have festivals that can be traced back to ancient celebrations of spring.

The Noun Clause

4e. A *noun clause* is a subordinate clause that is used as a noun.

A noun clause may be used as a *subject,* a *predicate nominative,* a *direct object,* an *indirect object,* or an *object of a preposition.*

SUBJECT	**That Jim Hynes is a talented writer** is an understatement.
PREDICATE NOMINATIVE	Another course in computers is **what the guidance counselor recommended.**

Reference Note

For more about **subjects, predicate nominatives, direct objects, and indirect objects,** see Chapter 2. For more about **objects of prepositions,** see page 54.

DIRECT OBJECT	The Greek astronomer Ptolemy believed **that the sun orbited the earth.**
INDIRECT OBJECT	The judges will award **whoever has the most original costume** a prize.
OBJECT OF A PREPOSITION	Grandmother Gutiérrez has a kind word for **whomever she meets.**

Common Introductory Words for Noun Clauses				
how	whatever	whether	who	whomever
that	when	which	whoever	whose
what	where	whichever	whom	why

The word that introduces a noun clause may or may not have a grammatical function in the clause.

EXAMPLES   Do you remember **who painted *Washington Crossing the Delaware*?** [The word *who* introduces the noun clause and serves as the subject of the verb *painted*.]

Ms. Eva Picard, an environmentalist, will explain **what the greenhouse effect is.** [The word *what* introduces the noun clause and serves as a predicate nominative completing the meaning of the verb *is*.]

Millicent said **that she would be late.** [The word *that* introduces the noun clause but does not have any grammatical function within the noun clause.]

NOTE   Another type of noun clause is the infinitive clause. An *infinitive clause* consists of an infinitive with a subject, along with any modifiers and complements the infinitive has. The entire infinitive clause can function as the direct object of a verb.

EXAMPLE   I wanted **her to tell the O'Leary twins the story about Mr. Omar.** [The entire infinitive clause is the direct object of the verb *wanted*. *Her* is the subject of the infinitive *to tell*. The infinitive *to tell* has an indirect object, *twins,* and a direct object, *story*.]

Notice that the subject of an infinitive clause is in the objective case and that the infinitive takes the place of a main verb.

Exercise 3 Identifying Noun Clauses

Identify the noun clause in each of the following sentences. Tell whether the noun clause is used as a *subject*, a *predicate nominative*, a *direct object*, an *indirect object*, or an *object of a preposition*.

EXAMPLES 1. Please address your letter to whoever manages the store.

1. *whoever manages the store—object of a preposition*

2. Do you know where the new municipal center is?

2. *where the new municipal center is—direct object*

1. Would you please tell me what the past tense of the verb *swing* is?
2. I will listen carefully to whatever you say.
3. Whatever you decide will be fine with me.
4. Give whoever wants one a free pass.
5. That Jill was worried seemed obvious to us all.
6. Do you know why Eduardo missed the Cinco de Mayo celebration?
7. You can appoint whomever you like.
8. In biology class we learned about how hornets build their nests.
9. A remote desert island was where the pirates buried their treasure.
10. The teacher would like us to prepare the slides.

Review A Distinguishing Between Adjective Clauses and Noun Clauses

Identify the subordinate clause in each of the following sentences. Tell whether the subordinate clause is used as an *adjective* or a *noun*. Then, give the word that each adjective clause modifies, and state whether each noun clause is used as a *subject*, a *predicate nominative*, a *direct object*, or an *object of a preposition*.

EXAMPLE 1. Until recently, scientists believed that the giant sequoias of California were the oldest living trees on earth.

1. *that the giant sequoias of California were the oldest living trees on earth—noun; direct object*

1. Now, however, that honor is given to the bristlecone pine, which is a small, gnarled tree native to the western part of the United States.
2. Botanists estimate that some bristlecone pines are more than six thousand years old.
3. The oldest sequoias are only 2,200 years old, according to those who know.
4. Whoever respects hardiness has to respect the bristlecone.

5. The high altitude of the Rocky Mountains, the bristlecone's natural habitat, is what makes the tree grow so slowly.

6. Do you think that the bristlecone pine will win any beauty contests?

7. Judge by what you can see in the photograph on this page.

8. The bristlecone's needles last on the branches for fifteen to thirty years, a length of time that is extraordinary.

9. Botanists tell us that the bristlecone is a member of the foxtail family.

10. Like all members of this family, the bristlecone has needle clusters that resemble a fox's tail.

The Adverb Clause

4f. An ***adverb clause*** **is a subordinate clause that modifies a verb, an adjective, or an adverb.**

An adverb clause tells *how, when, where, why, to what extent,* or *under what condition.*

EXAMPLES   The pitcher felt **as though all eyes were on him.** [The adverb clause modifies the verb *felt,* telling *how* the pitcher felt.]

Frédéric Chopin made his debut as a concert pianist **when he was eight years old.** [The adverb clause modifies the verb *made,* telling *when* Frédéric Chopin made his debut.]

Ariel takes her new camera **wherever she goes.** [The adverb clause modifies the verb *takes,* telling *where* Ariel takes her new camera.]

Happy **because I had made the team,** I hurried home to tell my parents and older brother the news. [The adverb clause modifies the adjective *Happy,* telling *why* I was happy.]

The water in the lake was much colder **than we had expected.** [The adverb clause modifies the adjective *colder,* telling *to what extent* the water was colder.]

HELP

Some of the words that introduce adverb clauses may also introduce adjective clauses and noun clauses. To determine what type of clause the introductory word begins, look at how the clause is used in the sentence.

ADJECTIVE CLAUSE
The day **when we got our puppy** was a Friday. [The clause modifies the noun *day.*]

NOUN CLAUSE
Does Sam know **when we got our puppy**? [The clause is the direct object of the verb *know.*]

ADVERB CLAUSE
Our older dog sulked a little **when we got our puppy.** [The clause modifies the verb *sulked.*]

The Subordinate Clause   **83**

If we leave now, we will avoid the rush-hour traffic. [The adverb clause modifies the verb *will avoid*, telling *under what condition* we will avoid the traffic.]

NOTE Notice in the example above that an adverb clause that begins a sentence is followed by a comma.

Reference Note

For more about punctuating **introductory adverb clauses,** see page 310.

Subordinating Conjunctions

An adverb clause is introduced by a *subordinating conjunction*—a word or word group that shows the relationship between the adverb clause and the word or words that the clause modifies.

Common Subordinating Conjunctions			
after	as though	provided that	until
although	because	since	when
as	before	so that	whenever
as if	if	than	where
as long as	in order that	though	wherever
as soon as	once	unless	while

Reference Note

The words **after, as, before, since,** and **until** may also be used as **prepositions.** See page 21.

The Elliptical Clause

4g. Part of a clause may be left out when its meaning can be clearly understood from the context of the sentence. Such a clause is called an *elliptical clause.*

Most elliptical clauses are adverb clauses. In each of the adverb clauses in the following examples, the part given in brackets may be omitted because its meaning is clearly understood.

EXAMPLES   Leilana finished her research sooner **than Marta** [did].

While [he was] **painting,** Rembrandt concentrated completely on his work.

NOTE Often the meaning of an elliptical clause depends on the form of the pronoun in the clause.

EXAMPLES   Martine asked her more questions **than I** [asked her].

Martine asked her more questions **than** [she asked] **me.**

Reference Note

For more information about the correct use of **pronouns in elliptical clauses,** see page 134.

Exercise 4 Identifying Adverb Clauses and the Words They Modify

Identify the adverb clause in each of the following sentences, and give the word or words that the clause modifies. Then, state whether the clause tells *how, when, where, why, to what extent,* or *under what condition.* If a clause is elliptical, be prepared to supply the omitted word or words.

HELP

In the example for Exercise 4, the word *is* is omitted from the elliptical clause.

EXAMPLE   1. Thao is quieter than Catherine.

1. *than Catherine—quieter; to what extent*

1. When our school has a fire drill, everyone must go outside.
2. I visited the collection of Aztec artifacts because I wanted to see the religious and solar calendars.
3. She walked until she was too tired to take another step.
4. Because he was late so often, he bought a watch.
5. Gazelles need to be able to run fast so that they can easily escape their predators.
6. Return this revolutionary, new sonic potato peeler for a full refund if you are not completely satisfied.
7. As soon as you're ready, we'll leave.
8. You can set the table while I prepare the salad.
9. Your trip to New York will not be complete unless you see the Alvin Ailey American Dance Theater.
10. You understand the situation much better than I.

Review B Identifying Independent and Subordinate Clauses

Identify each italicized clause in the following paragraph as *independent* or *subordinate.* If the italicized clause is subordinate, tell whether it is used as an *adverb,* an *adjective,* or a *noun.*

EXAMPLE   [1] *When they think of American Indians,* many people immediately picture the Dakota Sioux.

1. *subordinate—adverb*

Do you know [1] *why the Dakota spring to mind*? I think the reason is [2] *that they are known for their impressive eagle-feather headdresses.* Until recently, [3] *if an artist painted or drew Native Americans of any region,* the people were often shown wearing Dakota headdresses, fringed buckskin shirts, and elaborately beaded moccasins. Even paintings of the Pemaquid people meeting the Pilgrims [4] *as they landed on*

COMPUTER TIP

Because an adverb clause does not have a fixed location in a sentence, you must choose where to put the clause. The best place for it is usually a matter of personal taste and style, but often the placement is determined by the context.

If you use a computer, you can easily experiment with the placement of adverb clauses in sentences. Create different versions of the sentence containing the adverb clause, along with the sentences that immediately precede and follow it. Read each version aloud to see how the placement of the clause affects the flow, rhythm, and overall meaning of the passage.

Photo: Charles Milton Bell (1890). From the collection of Kurt Koegler.

Photo: Carl Moon (1905). From the collection of Kurt Koegler.

Cape Cod sometimes show the Pemaquid dressed in the style of the Dakota, [**5**] *who lived far away in the northern plains region.* Artists apparently did not recognize [**6**] *that there are many different American Indian peoples.* Each group has its own traditional clothing, and [**7**] *the variety of Native American dress is truly amazing.* For example, [**8**] *compare the turbans and bearclaw necklaces of the Fox men above with the headband and turquoise jewelry of this Navajo boy.* [**9**] *While these images may not be familiar to you,* they are just as authentic as the image of the Dakota. To see other unique styles of dress, you might want to research the clothing worn by native peoples [**10**] *who live in different regions of the United States.*

Review C Writing Clauses

For each of the following items, supply the type of clause indicated in italics.

EXAMPLE **1.** Do you know _____? (*noun clause*)

1. *Do you know what the phrase "tip of the iceberg" means?*

1. _____, the entire audience stood as one to applaud them. (*adverb clause*)

2. You'd never know it, but the man _____ holds more than one hundred patents. (*adjective clause*)

3. They commanded _____. (*infinitive clause*)

4. I told them _____. (*noun clause*)

5. As we walked by a tall display of potatoes, _____. (*independent clause*)

6. Because the letter was in Chinese, Mrs. Mansfield took it to someone _____. (*adjective clause*)

7. Technology's advance has accelerated _____. (*adverb clause*)

8. In the tackle box were handmade flies _____. (*adjective clause*)

9. _____ should get a medal. (*noun clause*)

10. Africa's wildlife—indeed, animals all over the world—must be protected _____. (*adverb clause*)

┌─ **HELP** ─
Remember that a clause must have both a subject and a verb.

Sentences Classified According to Structure

Reference Note

Sentences may also be **classified according to purpose.** See page 45.

4h. **Depending on its structure, a sentence can be classified as simple, compound, complex, or compound-complex.**

(1) **A *simple sentence* contains one independent clause and no subordinate clauses.**

A simple sentence may contain a compound subject, a compound verb, and any number of phrases.

EXAMPLES Uncle Alan taught me how to play the mandolin.

The spotted owl and the golden-cheeked warbler are endangered species. [compound subject]

Covered with dust and cobwebs, the old bicycle looked terrible but worked just fine. [compound verb]

Reference Note

Independent clauses may be joined by a colon or a dash when the second clause explains or restates the idea of the first clause. For more information, see pages 324 and 328.

Reference Note

For more information on using **semicolons** and **conjunctive adverbs** or **transitional expressions** to join independent clauses, see page 322.

MEETING THE CHALLENGE

Lists of common transitional expressions and conjunctive adverbs are usually arranged alphabetically. Rearrange the lists in your book by *meaning* instead. Which expressions show contrast? a cause-and-effect relationship? other logical relationships? Now, brainstorm other words and phrases to go in these categories. Compare your lists with other students', and compile a master list. After your teacher has checked the list, make a large-print version and, with your teacher's permission, post it in the classroom.

(2) A *compound sentence* contains two or more independent clauses and no subordinate clauses.

The independent clauses in a compound sentence may be joined by a comma and a coordinating conjunction (*and, but, for, nor, or, so,* or *yet*), by a semicolon, or by a semicolon and a conjunctive adverb or a transitional expression.

EXAMPLES Lorenzo's story sounded incredible**, but** it was true. [two independent clauses joined by a comma and the coordinating conjunction *but*]

Althea Gibson was successful at Wimbledon in 1957 and 1958**;** she won the doubles and singles championships both years. [two independent clauses joined by a semicolon]

The defeat of Napoleon at Waterloo was a victory for Britain**; however,** it brought to an end an era of French grandeur. [two independent clauses joined by a semicolon, the conjunctive adverb *however,* and a comma]

Common Conjunctive Adverbs		
also	however	nevertheless
anyway	instead	otherwise
besides	likewise	still
consequently	meanwhile	then
furthermore	moreover	therefore

Common Transitional Expressions		
as a result	for example	in other words
at any rate	in addition	on the contrary
by the way	in fact	on the other hand

NOTE Be careful to distinguish a simple sentence that has either a compound subject or a compound verb from a compound sentence.

SIMPLE SENTENCE The archaeological discovery was made in the fall and was widely acclaimed the following spring. [compound verb]

COMPOUND SENTENCE The archaeological discovery was made in the fall, and it was widely acclaimed the following spring.

(3) A *complex sentence* contains one independent clause and at least one subordinate clause.

EXAMPLES   Thurgood Marshall, who served on the United States Supreme Court for twenty-four years, retired in 1991. [The independent clause is *Thurgood Marshall retired in 1991*. The subordinate clause is *who served on the United States Supreme Court for twenty-four years.*]

While we were on vacation in Washington, D.C., we visited the Folger Shakespeare Library, which is devoted to Shakespeare's legacy. [The independent clause is *we visited the Folger Shakespeare Library*. The subordinate clauses are *While we were on vacation in Washington, D.C.,* and *which is devoted to Shakespeare's legacy.*]

(4) A *compound-complex sentence* contains two or more independent clauses and at least one subordinate clause.

EXAMPLES   My mom just spoke to Mr. Kostas, who runs the neighborhood watch program, and he told her about last night's meeting. [The two independent clauses are *My mom just spoke to Mr. Kostas* and *he told her about last night's meeting*. The subordinate clause is *who runs the neighborhood watch program.*]

Chelsea is only seven years old, but she can already play the violin better than her tutor can. [The two independent clauses are *Chelsea is only seven years old* and *she can already play the violin better*. The subordinate clause is *than her tutor can.*]

Oral Practice   Classifying Sentences According to Structure

Read each of the following sentences aloud, and classify it as *simple, compound, complex,* or *compound-complex.*

EXAMPLE   1. Mr. Faust said that ancient Egyptians used the pith of the papyrus plant to make an early form of paper.

1. *complex*

1. Charles Richard Drew researched blood plasma and helped develop blood banks.

2. Supposedly, if the month of March comes in like a lion, it goes out like a lamb.

3. Many Malaysians believe that sickness will follow the eating of stolen food.

COMPUTER TIP

Computers can help you get a better sense of your own sentence style. If you have style-checking software, run a style check on a paragraph or two (or more) of your writing. The style checker will analyze your writing sample and will provide information such as the number of sentences per paragraph, the kinds of sentences, the average number of words per sentence, and the lengths of the longest and shortest sentences.

If you discover that you tend to use only one or two sentence structures and that your sentences all tend to be of a similar length, you can focus your attention on revising for greater variety.

4. When World War I ended in 1918, many people thought that there would be no more wars; however, twenty-one years later, World War II began in Europe.
5. In his letter to Mrs. Bixby, Abraham Lincoln consoled her for the loss of several sons and hoped that time would ease her sorrow.
6. After the announcement of the final score, all of us fans cheered the team and clapped enthusiastically.
7. In England and Wales, salmon was once king, yet few salmon rivers remain there.
8. The English philosopher Thomas Hobbes once aspired to be a mathematician, but he never fulfilled this ambition.
9. As an older woman, Queen Elizabeth I always wore a dark red wig so that no one knew whether her own hair had grayed or not.
10. The professional tennis star Zina Garrison Jackson devotes time to training and encouraging young inner-city tennis players.

Review D Writing a Variety of Sentence Structures

Write ten sentences according to the following instructions.

EXAMPLE   1. Write a compound sentence containing a semicolon.
1. *You rake the leaves, Janelle; I'll sweep the sidewalk.*

1. Write a simple sentence containing a compound subject.
2. Write a compound sentence containing the conjunction *but.*
3. Write a complex sentence containing an adverb clause modifying a verb.
4. Write a complex sentence containing an adverb clause modifying an adjective.
5. Write a complex sentence containing an adjective clause introduced by the relative pronoun *who.*
6. Write a complex sentence containing an adjective clause introduced by the relative pronoun *that.*
7. Write a complex sentence containing a noun clause used as the subject of the sentence.
8. Write a complex sentence containing a noun clause used as the direct object of the sentence.
9. Write a complex sentence containing an elliptical adverb clause.
10. Write a compound-complex sentence.

Chapter Review

A. Identifying Independent and Subordinate Clauses

Identify the italicized word group in each of the following sentences as an *independent clause* or a *subordinate clause.*

1. My older sister showed us *how she sketches human faces so skillfully.*
2. *Whenever Sue smells ginger,* she remembers her mother's kitchen.
3. *I know a boy* whose grandfather was one of the first astronauts.
4. *Whether the state government should raise the sales tax* was the issue before the legislature that afternoon.
5. *My uncle Leon,* who served in Vietnam, *is now a businessman.*

B. Identifying Adjective Clauses and the Words They Modify

Identify the adjective clause in each of the following sentences, and give the noun or pronoun that it modifies. Then, tell whether the relative pronoun in the adjective clause is used as a *subject,* a *direct object,* or an *object of a preposition.*

6. The lake, which is in Iowa, has swimming facilities.
7. Turn in at the green sign, which shows the way to the boat launch.
8. On the boat ride, wear one of the orange life vests that are available at no extra cost.
9. One lifeguard at the lake, about whom I've told you before, received a medal for saving two children.
10. Everyone whom the lifeguard has assisted is grateful for her training and her bravery.

C. Identifying Noun Clauses

Identify the noun clause in each sentence, and indicate whether it is a *subject,* a *direct object,* an *indirect object,* a *predicate nominative,* or an *object of a preposition.*

11. Did you know that the word *robot* originated from the Czech word *robota?*

12. The year 1921 was when the word was first used; the Czech playwright Karel Capek used it in a play.

13. In many science fiction stories, robots and androids are used for whatever jobs humans are unwilling to do.

14. In *Star Trek: The Next Generation*, the android Data often gives whoever asks him a question a detailed response.

15. How robots will be used in the future remains to be seen.

D. Identifying Adverb Clauses and the Words They Modify

Identify the adverb clause in each of the following sentences, and give the word or words that the clause modifies. Then, state whether the clause tells *how, when, where, why, to what extent,* or *under what condition.*

16. The playwright left the stage after she had made her opening night speech to the audience.

17. Wherever she hiked that spring, Vera enjoyed seeing wildflowers.

18. The meeting ran a little longer than Marcia hoped it would.

19. The team captain played as if winning the championship depended entirely on her.

20. We stopped to eat at the Falafel Hut because we were in a hurry.

21. Whenever you want to rent a bike, ask for information at the bicycle shop.

22. Candida spoke as though she were speaking before a large convention instead of a small class.

23. Mr. Suzuki spread the grass seeds where they would do the most good.

24. The teacher distributed copies of the sheet music so that the class could follow along with the sonata.

25. If you're interested in coming to the movies, please let me know.

E. Classifying Sentences by Structure

Classify each of the following sentences as *simple, compound, complex,* or *compound-complex.*

26. I heard children shouting on the playground as the noise filtered into my room through the closed window.

27. Holding the freshly cut board carefully, Barbara pounded the nail into the wood.

28. Last summer Rita attended band camp, and she met a number of students who were interested in becoming musicians.

29. Last summer, I learned to keep financial records and to place merchandise orders; I also waited on customers.

30. No one will deny that it is the responsibility of a newspaper to report the day's happenings accurately.

Writing Application
Using Sentence Variety in a Guidebook

Sentence Structures   The student council has asked your class to write a guidebook to inform new students and their families about your area. Write an entry for the guidebook, telling about a local attraction that people might enjoy visiting. Use a mix of sentence structures.

Prewriting   Brainstorm points of interest in your city or area. Then, choose one attraction with which you are familiar. Be sure to jot down specific details, such as when the place is open to the public, how much admission is, and why it is worth a visit.

Writing   Begin your guidebook entry by identifying the name, location, and significance of the attraction. Then, capture your readers' interest with a clear, vivid description of the place.

Revising   Ask a friend or family member to read your paragraph. Add, cut, and rearrange details to include all important information. Use sentence-combining techniques to vary the structure of your sentences.

Publishing   Proofread your paragraph for any errors in grammar, usage, and mechanics. Your class may want to compile a guidebook for your area. Double-check all the information included in your paragraphs. Then, type the paragraphs neatly and collect them in a binder. Place your guidebook in the library of your school so that anyone can read it, or make photocopies to give to new students.

Reference Note

For information about **sentence combining,** see Chapter 18.

Agreement

Subject and Verb, Pronoun and Antecedent

Diagnostic Preview

A. Proofreading Sentences for Subject-Verb and Pronoun-Antecedent Agreement

Most of the following sentences contain errors in agreement. If a sentence contains an error in agreement, identify the incorrect verb or pronoun and supply the correct form. If a sentence is already correct, write *C*.

EXAMPLE   **1.** Each of the members of the school board are hoping to be reelected this fall.

　　　　　　1. are hoping—is hoping

1. Half of the members of my history class this year is in the National Honor Society.

2. Over one thousand miles of tunnels travels through El Teniente, the largest copper mine in the world.

3. If she already has needle-nose pliers, she can exchange it for something else at the hardware store.

4. The etchings of Mary Cassatt, an impressionist painter, was definitely influenced by styles used in the prints of the Japanese artists Utamaro and Toyokuni.

5. Under the seat of the car were two dollar bills, seven quarters, and a handful of dimes, pennies, and nickels; they would buy enough gas to get us home.

6. If you see either Veronica or Sabrena in the cafeteria, will you please tell them that I won't be able to go to the mall?

7. Neither Adrianne nor Lillian expect to make the varsity softball team this year; nevertheless, both girls are trying out for it.

8. To learn more about our municipal government, our civics class is planning to invite a number of guest speakers to school.

9. Unfortunately, neither Mayor Ella Hanson nor Mrs. Mary Ann Powell, the assistant mayor, have responded to our invitations to the outdoor concert yet.

10. Try reading *The Borrowers* to your little brother; he'll love it.

B. Proofreading a Paragraph for Subject-Verb and Pronoun-Antecedent Agreement

Most of the sentences in the following paragraph contain errors in agreement. Revise each sentence containing an agreement error to correct the error. If a sentence is already correct, write *C*.

EXAMPLE   [1] My aunt runs Teresa's Treasures, which are next to the access road by the highway.

1. *My aunt runs Teresa's Treasures, which is next to the access road by the highway.*

[11] Clothing, along with jewelry and household goods, are stacked or hung everywhere. [12] Everybody around here knows that they can get great deals there. [13] Ten dollars will buy more there than they will anywhere else in town. [14] I do little chores for Aunt T, and sometimes a few of my friends drops by and helps me. [15] She doesn't like doing the books, but mathematics are easy for me, so I also do the books for her. [16] Aunt T is a member of the Association of Taylor County Businesswomen and lets the group use her empty room for its meetings. [17] Ms. Lincoln, the owner of Acme Appliances, or Mrs. Abbot, the owner of a travel agency, usually brings their tape player. [18] The worst part of the job are the songs the ATCB plays; they're ancient. [19] Don't that old music get to you after a while? [20] Here's something: Yesterday I caught myself humming "A White Sport Coat and a Pink Carnation," and I didn't stop!

Number

Number is the form a word takes to indicate whether the word is singular or plural.

5a. A word that refers to one person, place, thing, or idea is singular in number. A word that refers to more than one is plural in number.

Singular	computer	half-hour	story	this	it
Plural	computers	half-hours	stories	these	they

Agreement of Subject and Verb

5b. A verb should agree in number with its subject.

(1) Singular subjects take singular verbs.

EXAMPLES   My **grandfather trains** dogs.

The **senator is** in favor of the bill.

She owns and **operates** a video store.

That is beautiful!

(2) Plural subjects take plural verbs.

EXAMPLES   My **grandparents train** dogs.

Many **senators are** in favor of the bill.

They own and **operate** a video store.

Those are beautiful!

In a verb phrase, the first helping verb agrees in number with the subject.

EXAMPLES   This **song was performed** by Bonnie Raitt. [singular subject and singular verb phrase]

These **songs were performed** by Bonnie Raitt. [plural subject and plural verb phrase]

Has the **dancer been rehearsing** since noon? [singular subject and singular verb phrase]

Have the **dancers been rehearsing** since noon? [plural subject and plural verb phrase]

Reference Note

For information on **finding the subject,** see page 36.

┌─HELP─

Present-tense verbs, except *be* and *have*, add –s or –es when the subject is third-person singular. Present-tense verbs do not add –s or –es when the subject is a first-person pronoun (*I, we*), a second-person pronoun (*you*), or a third-person plural pronoun (*they*).

Reference Note

For information about **verb phrases,** see page 15.

USAGE

NOTE A gerund phrase or an infinitive phrase used as a complete subject takes a singular verb. Do not be misled by any particular noun in the phrase. The gerund or infinitive serves as a singular simple subject.

EXAMPLES **Writing** verses for greeting cards **sounds** like an interesting job. [The singular verb *sounds* is used because the gerund *Writing*, not the noun *verses* or *cards*, is the subject of the verb.]

To compete in the 2004 Olympics **is** Monica's goal. [The singular verb *is* is used because the infinitive *To compete*, not the noun *Olympics*, is the subject of the verb.]

Reference Note

For information about **gerund phrases and infinitive phrases,** see page 62 and page 65.

Intervening Phrases and Clauses

5c. The number of a subject usually is not determined by a word in a phrase or a clause following the subject.

EXAMPLES This **tape is** by the Boston Pops Orchestra.

This **tape** of songs **is** by the Boston Pops Orchestra. [*Is* agrees with the subject *tape*, not with *songs*, which is part of the prepositional phrase *of songs*.]

The **characters represent** abstract ideas.

The **characters** used in an allegory **represent** abstract ideas. [*Represent* agrees with the subject *characters*, not with *allegory*, which is part of the participial phrase *used in an allegory*.]

The **Great Barrier Reef lies** off northeastern Australia.

The **Great Barrier Reef,** which supports many marine animals, **lies** off northeastern Australia. [*Lies* agrees with the subject *Great Barrier Reef*, not with *animals*, which is part of the adjective clause *which supports many marine animals*.]

HELP

Remember that the subject of a sentence is never in a prepositional phrase.

NOTE Do not be misled by a phrase that begins with a compound preposition such as *along with, as well as, in addition to,* or *together with*. Such a phrase does not affect the number of the subject.

EXAMPLES The **teacher,** as well as her students, **was fascinated** by the exhibit. [singular subject and singular verb]

The **students,** as well as their teacher, **were fascinated** by the exhibit. [plural subject and plural verb]

USAGE

Exercise 1 Identifying Subjects and Verbs That Agree in Number

Identify the subject of the verb in parentheses in each of the following sentences. Then, choose the verb form that agrees in number with the subject.

EXAMPLE

1. The many varieties of American quilts (*reflect, reflects*) the spirit of the people who developed them.

1. *varieties—reflect*

1. During the colonial period, only women of means made quilts; however, by the mid-nineteenth century, women throughout the United States (*was making, were making*) quilts.
2. The abilities that someone needs to make a quilt (*include, includes*) patience, coordination, and a good sense of color and design.
3. A scrapbag full of colorful pieces of cotton and wool fabrics (*was put, were put*) to good use in making a quilt.
4. Usable fabric from worn-out shirts, as well as from other articles of clothing, (*was cut, were cut*) into pieces of various shapes and sizes.
5. The Amish people, known for their beautiful quilting, (*live, lives*) very simply.
6. Amish quilts, which are often brightly colored, (*seem, seems*) to convey the joyous spirits of their makers.
7. Several quilters, gathering at one person's home for a quilting bee, often (*work, works*) on a quilt together.
8. Quilts designed by the Amish usually (*include, includes*) only solid-colored fabrics and not patterned ones.
9. These quilts, which feature colors typical of Amish quilts, (*glow, glows*) with red, purple, blue, pink, and green.
10. In contrast, the clothing worn by Amish women (*is, are*) more subdued in color.

Indefinite Pronouns

5d. Some indefinite pronouns are singular, some are plural, and some can be singular or plural, depending on how they are used.

(1) The following indefinite pronouns are singular: *anybody, anyone, anything, each, either, everybody, everyone, everything, neither, nobody, no one, nothing, one, somebody, someone,* and *something*.

EXAMPLES   **Everyone** in the Pep Club **is wearing** the school colors.

        One of the most beautiful places in North Carolina **is** the Joyce Kilmer Memorial Forest.

        Anything that makes yardwork easier **is** a good gift for Dad.

(2) The following indefinite pronouns are plural: *both, few, many,* and *several*.

EXAMPLES   **Both** of the games **were postponed.**

        Many of our words **derive** from Latin.

        Several of the juniors **have volunteered.**

(3) The indefinite pronouns *all, any, more, most, none,* and *some* may be singular or plural, depending on their meaning in a sentence.

These pronouns are singular when they refer to singular words and are plural when they refer to plural words.

EXAMPLES   **All** of the vegetable garden **has been planted.** [*All* refers to the singular noun *garden.*]

        All of the vegetables **have been planted.** [*All* refers to the plural noun *vegetables.*]

        None of the equipment **was damaged.** [*None* refers to the singular noun *equipment.*]

        None of the machines **were damaged.** [*None* refers to the plural noun *machines.*]

        Most of the food **has already been eaten.** [*Most* refers to the singular noun *food.*]

        Most of the sandwiches **have already been eaten.** [*Most* refers to the plural noun *sandwiches.*]

TIPS & TRICKS

Each, either, neither, and *one* can also be used as adjectives or as parts of correlative conjunctions. Used as these parts of speech, such words cannot function as subjects.

Reference Note

For information on **adjectives,** see page 9. For information on **correlative conjunctions,** see page 23.

COMPUTER TIP

If you use a computer when you write, you may want to create a help file containing lists of indefinite pronouns and their rules for agreement. Fill this file with information that will help you determine whether an indefinite pronoun is used correctly. Then, as you proofread your work, you can access the file whenever you have a question about the agreement between an indefinite pronoun and a verb or another pronoun.

Identifying Subjects and Verbs That Agree in Number

Identify the subject of the verb in parentheses in each of the following sentences. Then, choose the verb form that agrees in number with the subject.

EXAMPLE 1. Not one of the pears (*look, looks*) ripe.

1. one—*looks*

1. Many of the recipes in this cookbook (*is, are*) adaptable to microwave cooking.
2. Neither of my parents (*has, have*) trouble using the metric system.
3. I know that all of the workers (*was, were*) proud to help restore the Statue of Liberty.
4. Most of the English classes in my high school (*stresses, stress*) composition skills.
5. Few of the students (*was, were*) able to spell *bureaucracy* correctly.
6. (*Do, Does*) each of you know what you're supposed to bring?
7. None of the dessert (*remain, remains*), but we can still remember its wonderful taste.
8. Some of the word-processing software (*has, have*) arrived late.
9. Both of the paintings (*shows, show*) the influence of the work of Emilio Sánchez.
10. Everyone visiting Bob and Lynn (*notices, notice*) how well their new puppy behaves.

Compound Subjects

Reference Note

For more about **compound subjects,** see page 35.

A *compound subject* consists of two or more subjects that are joined by a conjunction and that have the same verb.

5e. Subjects joined by *and* usually take a plural verb.

EXAMPLES **Basil** and **thyme are** plants of the mint family.

Following Julius Caesar's death, **Antony, Octavian,** and **Lepidus become** the rulers of Rome.

Subjects joined by *and* may name only one person, place, thing, or idea. Such a compound subject takes a singular verb.

EXAMPLES The **secretary** and **treasurer is** Gretchen. [one person]

Grilled chicken and **rice is** the restaurant's specialty. [one dish]

5f. Singular subjects joined by *or* or *nor* take a singular verb.

EXAMPLES   Neither **Juan** nor **Jeff wants** to see the movie.

Either **Felita** or **Terry sits** in the front row.

Has the **cat** or the **dog been fed** yet?

5g. When a singular subject and a plural subject are joined by *or* or *nor*, the verb agrees with the subject nearer the verb.

EXAMPLES   Neither the **players** nor the **coach was** ready to concede defeat. [The singular subject *coach* is nearer the verb.]

Neither the **coach** nor the **players were** ready to concede defeat. [The plural subject *players* is nearer the verb.]

5
e–g

STYLE   **TIP**

When possible, revise sentences to avoid awkward wordings like those in the examples for **Rule 5g.**

EXAMPLE
The **coach was** not ready to concede defeat, and neither **were** the **players.**

Review A **Correcting Errors in Subject-Verb Agreement**

Most of the following sentences contain verbs that do not agree with their subjects. If the verb does not agree, give the correct form of the verb. If the verb already agrees with its subject, write *C.*

EXAMPLE   **1.** Each of the issues were resolved.

    1. was

1. Emily Dickinson's imagery and verse structure has been analyzed and praised by many critics.
2. One or both of Shakespeare's plays about Henry IV is likely to be performed this summer.
3. The effective date of the new regulations for nuclear power plants have not yet been determined.
4. Each of the region's environmental groups are presenting its recommendations to the governor.
5. Spike Lee, whose movies tackle controversial social issues, has made a great contribution to the film industry.
6. The fact that compact discs do not wear out and do not have to be flipped over make them attractive.
7. The sales representative, with the help of her assistant, plan to expand her territory.
8. Not one of the speakers in the debate on South America appear eager to suggest a solution to the problem.
9. Neither the proposals of the air traffic controllers nor the report of the FAA's committee have been heeded.
10. James Baldwin, along with Richard Wright and Ralph Ellison, rank among the most important writers of the twentieth century.

Special Problems in Subject-Verb Agreement

5h. **When the subject follows the verb, find the subject and make sure that the verb agrees with it.**

TIPS & TRICKS

To find the subject when it follows the verb, invert, or rearrange, the sentence to put the subject first.

EXAMPLES
The **gloves are** here.

A **message was** on her answering machine.

Arsenio is where?

The subject generally follows the verb in sentences beginning with *here* or *there* and in questions.

EXAMPLES   Here **is** the other **glove.**

Here **are** the **gloves.**

There **was** a **message** on her answering machine.

There **were** no **messages** on her answering machine.

Where **is Arsenio?**

Where **are Arsenio** and his **brother?**

NOTE   Contractions such as *here's, there's,* and *where's* contain the verb *is* (*here is, there is,* and *where is*). Use these contractions only with singular subjects.

NONSTANDARD	Here's your keys.
STANDARD	Here **are** your **keys.**
STANDARD	Here**'s** your **set** of keys.

NONSTANDARD	Where's the islands located?
STANDARD	Where **are** the **islands** located?
STANDARD	Where**'s each** of the islands located?

Reference Note

For more information about **collective nouns,** see page 4.

5i. **A collective noun may be either singular or plural, depending on its meaning in a sentence.**

The singular form of a *collective noun* names a group.

Common Collective Nouns			
army	club	family	squadron
assembly	congregation	group	staff
audience	fleet	herd	team
band	flock	number	troop

A collective noun is singular when it refers to the group as a unit and is plural when it refers to the individual members or parts of the group.

SINGULAR	The tour **group is already** on the bus. [The group as a unit is on the bus.]
PLURAL	The tour **group are talking** about what they expect to see. [The members of the group are talking to one another.]

SINGULAR	A **flock** of geese **is flying** over. [The flock is flying as a unit.]
PLURAL	The **flock** of geese **are joining** together in a V-shaped formation. [The members of the flock are joining together.]

N O T E In the expression *number of,* the word *number* is singular when preceded by *the* and is plural when preceded by *a.*

EXAMPLES   **The number** of students taking computer courses **has increased.**

           A number of students taking computer courses **belong** to the Computer Club.

5j. An expression of an amount (a measurement, a percentage, or a fraction, for example) may be singular or plural, depending on how it is used.

An expression of an amount is singular when the amount is thought of as a unit and is plural when the amount is thought of as separate parts.

EXAMPLES   **Five thousand bricks is** a heavy load for this truck. [The bricks are thought of as a unit.]

           Five thousand bricks are scattered on the lot. [The bricks are thought of separately.]

           Two days is the amount of time we will spend visiting each college campus. [one unit]

           Two days of this month **are** school holidays, I believe. [separate days]

A fraction or a percentage is singular when it refers to a singular word and is plural when it refers to a plural word.

EXAMPLES   **One fourth** of our high school's student body **is employed.** [The fraction refers to the singular noun *student body.*]

           One fourth of the students **are employed.** [The fraction refers to the plural noun *students.*]

           Seventy-five percent of the junior class **is** sixteen years old. [The percentage refers to the singular noun *class.*]

           Seventy-five percent of the juniors **are** sixteen years old. [The percentage refers to the plural noun *juniors.*]

Reference Note

For information on **when to spell out numbers** and **when to use numerals,** see page 372.

An expression of measurement (such as length, weight, capacity, or area) is usually singular.

EXAMPLES
Four and seven-tenths inches is the diameter of a CD.

Eight fluid ounces equals one cup.

Two hundred kilometers was the distance we flew in the hot-air balloon.

Exercise 3 Identifying Verbs That Agree with Their Subjects

Identify the subject of each verb in parentheses in each of the following sentences. Then, choose the verb form that agrees in number with the subject.

EXAMPLE
1. The band (*is, are*) tuning their instruments.

1. *band—are*

1. How (*was, were*) the pyramids in Egypt built?
2. The stage crew (*is, are*) working together to make a rapid scene change for Rita Moreno's entrance.
3. Where (*is, are*) the other flight of stairs that go up to the roof?
4. On display in the entrance to the library (*is, are*) several paintings of famous local people.
5. The Hispanic population (*is, are*) one of the two fastest growing ethnic groups in the United States.
6. On our block alone, over two hundred dollars (*was, were*) collected for the American Cancer Society.
7. Of the world's petroleum, approximately one third (*was, were*) produced by the United States at that time.
8. Red beans and rice (*is, are*) sometimes served as a side dish at Cajun meals.
9. Thirty minutes of swimming (*serves, serve*) as a healthful way to get daily exercise.
10. A number of the seeds (*has, have*) failed to sprout.

5k. Some nouns that are plural in form take singular verbs.

The following nouns take singular verbs.

civics	genetics	mathematics	physics
economics	gymnastics	molasses	summons
electronics	linguistics	news	

EXAMPLES   **Physics is** an interesting subject.

The **news was** disappointing.

However, a few nouns take plural verbs even when they refer to single items.

binoculars	pants	shears
eyeglasses	pliers	slacks
Olympics	scissors	trousers

EXAMPLES   The **scissors are** in the sewing basket.

The first modern **Olympics were held** in Athens.

NOTE   Many nouns ending in –*ics*, such as *acoustics, athletics, ethics, politics, statistics,* and *tactics,* may be singular or plural.

EXAMPLES   **Statistics is** a collection of mathematical data.
The **statistics are** misleading.

5l. Even when plural in form, the title of a creative work (such as a book, song, movie, or painting) or the name of a country, a city, or an organization generally takes a singular verb.

EXAMPLES   ***Those Who Ride the Night Winds* was written** by the poet Nikki Giovanni.

"The Birds" is a very scary story.

***Three Musicians* is** a collage painting by Picasso.

In the play *Our Town,* **Grover's Corners represents** the typical American town in the early 1900s.

The Philippines encompasses more than 7,000 islands.

NOTE   The names of some organizations may take singular or plural verbs, depending on how the names are used. When the name refers to the organization as a unit, it takes a singular verb. When the name refers to the members of the organization, it takes a plural verb.

EXAMPLES   The **U.S. Marines is** a separate branch of the Department of the Navy. [The U.S. Marines as a unit is a branch.]
U.S. Marines are stationed all over the world. [Troops are stationed.]

HELP
If you do not know whether a noun that is plural in form is singular or plural in meaning, look in a dictionary.

USAGE

Reference Note

For more information on **predicate nominatives,** see page 42.

5m. **A verb agrees with its subject, but not necessarily with a predicate nominative.**

EXAMPLES   **Han, Phuong Vu,** and **Mary are** Team B.

Team B is Han, Phuong Vu, and Mary.

The featured **attraction is** the exhibits showing how to build a biplane.

The **exhibits** showing how to build a biplane **are** the featured attraction.

5n. **Subjects preceded by** *every* **or** *many a* **take singular verbs.**

EXAMPLES   **Every sophomore** and **junior is** participating.

Many a person supports the cause.

5o. **The contractions** *don't* **and** *doesn't* **should agree with their subjects.**

The word *don't* is the contraction of *do not*. Use *don't* with all plural subjects and with the pronouns *I* and *you*.

EXAMPLES   Some **students don't** have access to a computer.

I don't know how to swim.

Don't you play in the school orchestra?

The word *doesn't* is the contraction of *does not*. Use *doesn't* with all singular subjects except the pronouns *I* and *you*.

EXAMPLES   This **umbrella doesn't** belong to me.

Doesn't he attend Vanderbilt University?

Exercise 4   Choosing the Correct Verb

Choose the correct verb form in parentheses in each of the following sentences.

EXAMPLE   1. He (*doesn't, don't*) have a clue about the surprise party.

       1. *doesn't*

1. The Girl Guides (*is, are*) a scouting organization that was founded in Great Britain.
2. (*Don't, Doesn't*) every boy and girl in the city schools vote in the student council elections?
3. My cousin's favorite comic-book duo (*is, are*) Batman and Robin.

4. In Michigan, I lived in Detroit and then Grand Rapids; Grand Rapids (*were, was*) my favorite place until I moved here.
5. "Seventeen Syllables" (*recounts, recount*) the story of a Japanese American family.
6. This (*doesn't, don't*) make sense to me.
7. Microelectronics, the area of electronics dealing with the design and application of microcircuits, (*have, has*) made possible many of the tremendous advances in computers and robotics in recent years.
8. There (*is, are*) many a slip between the cup and the lip, as my grandpa says.
9. When she is doing needlepoint, Aunt Ching's scissors (*hangs, hang*) around her neck on a red ribbon.
10. Gymnastics (*is, are*) a popular sport at our high school.

Review B   Choosing the Correct Verb

Choose the correct verb form in parentheses in each of the following sentences.

EXAMPLE   1. How many of the foods shown on the next page (*is, are*) native to Central America and North America?

   1. *are*

1. Almost every one of the following sentences (*give, gives*) you a clue to the answer.
2. Popcorn, as well as peanuts, (*was, were*) introduced to European settlers by American Indians.
3. No one in Europe (*was, were*) familiar with the taste of pumpkins, blueberries, or maple syrup until explorers brought these foods back from the Americas.
4. One American food that helped reduce the famine in Europe (*was, were*) potatoes.
5. A field of potatoes (*produce, produces*) almost twice as much food in about half as much growing time as the same field would if it were planted with wheat.
6. News of tomatoes, sweet peppers, beans, and zucchini (*was, were*) received warmly in Europe, and now these foods are the heart and soul of southern Italian cooking.
7. At our school the Original American Chefs (*is, are*) a club that prepares and serves such American Indian foods as baked sweet potatoes and steamed corn pudding.

8. Statistics (*shows, show*) that three fifths of all the crops now in cultivation originated in the Americas.
9. (*Doesn't, Don't*) it seem obvious by now that every one of the foods shown here was first eaten in the Americas?
10. *Indian Givers* (*is, are*) a wonderful book about all kinds of contributions that American Indians have made to the world.

Reference Note

For more about **relative pronouns** and **adjective clauses,** see page 78.

5p. **When the relative pronoun *that, which,* or *who* is the subject of an adjective clause, the verb in the clause agrees with the word to which the relative pronoun refers.**

EXAMPLES Ganymede, **which is** one of Jupiter's satellites, is the largest satellite in our solar system. [*Which* refers to the singular noun *Ganymede.*]

I have neighbors **who raise** tropical fish. [*Who* refers to the plural noun *neighbors.*]

NOTE When preceded by *one of* + a plural word, the relative pronoun generally takes a plural verb. When preceded by *the only one of* + a plural word, the relative pronoun generally takes a singular verb.

EXAMPLES The dodo is **one of the birds that are** extinct.

Pluto is **the only one of the planets that crosses** the orbit of another planet.

Oral Practice 1 **Reviewing Subject-Verb Agreement**

Read each of the following sentences aloud, stressing the italicized words.

1. *Has either* of the essays been graded?

USAGE

2. *Both* of these vegetables, green beans and broccoli, *are* nourishing.

3. Here *are* the *minutes* I took at the meeting.

4. The *salary* that he will earn at his new job *is* the minimum wage.

5. Not *one* of the student drivers *forgets* to fasten the seat belt.

6. Where *are* her *mother and father*?

7. The *coach doesn't* want us to eat sweets.

8. *Several* of the research papers *were* read aloud.

Review C　**Choosing Verbs That Agree with Their Subjects**

Identify the subject of the verb in parentheses in each of the following sentences. Then, choose the verb form that agrees in number with the subject.

EXAMPLES
　　1. Both of the brothers (*play, plays*) in the zydeco band at the Cajun Cafe.
　　1. Both—play

　　2. One of the roads (*run, runs*) past the hospital at the edge of town.
　　2. One—runs

1. Neither the Litchfield exit nor the Torrington exit (*is, are*) the one you should take.

2. The president, after meeting with several advisors, (*has, have*) promised to veto the proposed tax bill.

3. A medical study of World War II veterans (*has, have*) concluded that the veterans have the same health prospects as nonveterans.

4. The list of the greatest baseball players of all time (*is, are*) dominated by outfielders.

5. Babe Ruth, Hank Aaron, Willie Mays, and Joe DiMaggio (*is, are*) all outfielders on the list.

6. The Mariana Trench, located in the Pacific Ocean near the Mariana Islands, (*remains, remain*) the deepest known ocean area in the world.

7. Styles in clothing (*seems, seem*) to change as often as the weather.

8. When (*do, does*) the new telescope at the observatory become operational?

9. Please find out whether the conference room next to the windows (*is, are*) available at 2:00 tomorrow afternoon.

10. These vegetables, which we bought at the market this morning, (*doesn't, don't*) look fresh.

Most of the following sentences contain errors in agreement. If a sentence contains an error in agreement, identify the incorrect verb and supply the correct form. If the sentence is already correct, write *C*.

EXAMPLE   1. Don't the concept of child prodigies fascinate you?

        1. Don't—Doesn't

1. Prodigies, people who have immense talent, is born very infrequently.
2. One of the most interesting child prodigies of this century are young Wang Yani of China.
3. Two and a half years were the age at which Wang began painting.
4. How old do you think she was when this wonderful painting of frolicking monkeys were completed?
5. Neither of us were able to guess correctly that she was only five then.
6. It shouldn't surprise you to learn that *Little Monkeys and Mummy* are the painting's title.
7. The people of China has recognized Wang as a prodigy since she was four years old.
8. By the time she was six, she had painted four thousand pictures.
9. As you can see, wet ink and paint is freely mixed in Wang's pictures, producing interesting puddles and fuzzy edges.
10. Wang Yani is the youngest painter ever whose work have been displayed in a one-person show at the Smithsonian Institution.

USAGE

Agreement of Pronoun and Antecedent

A pronoun usually refers to a noun or another pronoun, which is called the pronoun's *antecedent.*

5q. A pronoun should agree in number, gender, and person with its antecedent.

(1) Singular pronouns refer to singular antecedents. Plural pronouns refer to plural antecedents.

SINGULAR **Sammy Davis, Jr.,** made **his** movie debut in 1931.
PLURAL The **hikers** took **their** canteens with **them.**

(2) Some singular pronouns indicate gender.

The singular pronouns *he, him, his,* and *himself* refer to masculine antecedents. The singular pronouns *she, her, hers,* and *herself* refer to feminine antecedents. The singular pronouns *it, its,* and *itself* refer to antecedents that are neuter (neither masculine nor feminine).

(3) *Person* indicates whether a pronoun refers to the one speaking (*first person*), the one spoken to (*second person*), or the one spoken about (*third person*).

FIRST PERSON **I** need a transcript of **my** grades.
SECOND PERSON Have **you** fastened **your** seat belt?
THIRD PERSON **He** said **they** made **their** own costumes.

Indefinite Pronouns

5r. Some indefinite pronouns are singular, and some are plural. Other indefinite pronouns can be either singular or plural, depending on their meaning.

(1) Use singular pronouns to refer to the indefinite pronouns *anybody, anyone, anything, each, either, everybody, everyone, everything, neither, nobody, no one, nothing, one, somebody, someone,* **and** *something.*

These pronouns do not indicate gender. Often, however, the object in a prepositional phrase that follows such a pronoun indicates the gender of the pronoun.

Reference Note

For more on **antecedents,** see pages 5 and 148.

Reference Note

For information about **personal pronouns,** see page 6.

USAGE

STYLE **TIP**

You can often avoid the awkward *his or her* construction (1) by substituting an article (*a, an,* or *the*) for the construction or (2) by rephrasing the sentence, using the plural forms of both the pronoun and its antecedent.

EXAMPLES
Any interested **person** may send **a** résumé.

All interested **persons** may send **their** résumés.

EXAMPLES   **Each** of the **boys** brought **his** own mitt.

One of the **girls** left **her** sweater on the bus.

If the antecedent may be either masculine or feminine, use both the masculine and feminine pronouns to refer to it.

EXAMPLES   **Anyone** who is going on the field trip needs to bring **his or her** lunch.

Any interested **person** may send **his or her** résumé.

NOTE   In informal situations, plural pronouns are often used to refer to singular antecedents that can be either masculine or feminine.

INFORMAL   **Everybody** stayed late at the dance because **they** were enjoying **themselves.**

Such usage is becoming increasingly popular in writing. In fact, using a singular pronoun to refer to a singular antecedent that is clearly plural in meaning may be misleading in some cases.

MISLEADING   **Everybody** stayed late at the dance because **he or she** was enjoying **himself or herself.** [Since *Everybody* is clearly plural in meaning, the singular constructions *he or she* and *himself or herself,* though grammatically correct, are confusing.]

In formal situations, it is best to revise such sentences to make them both clear and grammatically correct.

EXAMPLE   **All** of the students stayed late at the dance because **they** were enjoying **themselves.**

(2) Use plural pronouns to refer to the indefinite pronouns *both, few, many,* and *several*.

EXAMPLES   **Both** of the debaters persuasively presented **their** arguments.

Several of these coins are worth more than **their** face values.

(3) Use a singular or plural pronoun to refer to the indefinite pronoun *all, any, more, most, none,* or *some,* depending on how it is used in the sentence.

EXAMPLES   **Some** of the computer terminology is difficult to understand; perhaps Ms. Alvarez can clarify **its** meaning. [*Some*
refers to the singular noun terminology.]

Some of the computer terms are difficult to understand;
perhaps Ms. Alvarez can clarify **their** meanings. [*Some* refers
to the plural noun *terms.*]

Oral Practice 2 **Using Correct Pronoun-Antecedent
Agreement**

Read each of the following sentences aloud, stressing the italicized words.

1. *Each* of the girls has prepared *her* presentation.
2. Has *anyone* brought *his or her* compass?
3. *Both* of the teams played *their* best.
4. *Neither* of the kittens has opened *its* eyes yet.
5. *Most* of the tires are on sale; *they* are 25 percent off the regular price.
6. *All* of the casserole is gone; *it* was delicious.
7. Have *many* of the eligible voters cast *their* ballots?
8. *Somebody* should speak up and give *his or her* opinion.

Compound Antecedents

**5s. Use a plural pronoun to refer to two or more antecedents
joined by *and.***

EXAMPLES   If **Joann** and **Benjamin** call, tell **them** that I will not be
home until this evening.

Pilar, Kimberly, and **Laura** have donated **their** time.

Antecedents joined by *and* may name only one person, place,
thing, or idea. Such a compound antecedent takes a singular pronoun.

EXAMPLE   The **corned beef and cabbage** was delicious; I ate two
servings of **it.**

**5t. Use a singular pronoun to refer to two or more singular
antecedents joined by *or* or *nor.***

EXAMPLES   Either **Renaldo** or **Philip** always finishes **his** geometry
homework in class.

Neither **Cindy** nor **Carla** thinks **she** is ready to audition.

USAGE

Using a pronoun to refer to antecedents of different number may create an unclear or awkward sentence.

UNCLEAR	Neither the backup singers nor the lead vocalist was satisfied with her performance. [*Her* agrees with the nearest antecedent, *vocalist*. However, it is unclear whether all the performers were dissatisfied with their own performances or all the performers were dissatisfied only with the lead vocalist's performance.]
UNCLEAR	Neither the lead vocalist nor the backup singers were satisfied with their performance. [*Their* agrees with the nearest antecedent, *singers*. However, it is unclear whether all the performers were dissatisfied with the entire group's performance or all the performers were dissatisfied only with the backup singers' performance.]
AWKWARD	Neither the lead vocalist nor the backup singers were satisfied with her or their performance.

It is best to revise sentences to avoid unclear and awkward constructions like the preceding ones.

REVISED	Neither the lead vocalist nor the backup singers were satisfied with **the** performance.
	All of the singers were dissatisfied with **their** performance.

USAGE

Exercise 5 Supplying Pronouns That Agree with Their Antecedents

Complete each of the following sentences by supplying at least one pronoun that agrees with its antecedent. Use standard formal English.

EXAMPLE   1. Each of the girls took _____ turn at bat.

1. *her*

1. Each student prepares _____ own outline.
2. One of the birds built _____ nest in our chimney.
3. Both Jane and Ruth wrote _____ essays about ecology.
4. If anyone else wants to drive, _____ should tell Mrs. Cruz.
5. Many of the students in our class have turned in _____ reports on the Frida Kahlo exhibit.
6. Not one of the students typed _____ research paper.
7. Neither Angela nor Carrie has given _____ dues to me.
8. Either Mark or David offered to take _____ car.
9. Each of the visitors filled _____ own plate with tacos and fajitas.
10. Everyone in the class has paid _____ lab fees.

Special Problems in Pronoun-Antecedent Agreement

5u. A collective noun can be either singular or plural, depending on how it is used.

A collective noun takes a singular pronoun when the noun refers to the group as a unit. A collective noun takes a plural pronoun when the noun refers to the individual members or parts of the group.

SINGULAR   The **committee** comprised three juniors and two seniors; **its** chairperson was Angelo. [Angelo was chairperson of the committee as a unit.]

PLURAL   The **committee** discussed **their** varied schedules. [The members of the committee had different schedules.]

5v. Some nouns that are plural in form take singular pronouns.

The following nouns take singular pronouns.

civics	gymnastics	news
economics	linguistics	physics
electronics	mathematics	summons
genetics	molasses	

EXAMPLES   We bought several jars of **molasses.** Would you like to have a jar of **it**?

I'm looking forward to studying **physics** next year. **It** is my favorite subject.

However, a few nouns take plural pronouns even when they refer to single items.

binoculars	pants	shears
eyeglasses	pliers	shorts
Olympics	slacks	scissors

EXAMPLES   I have misplaced my **eyeglasses.** Have you seen **them**?

Wherever the **Olympics** are held, **they** attract athletes from all over the world.

Reference Note

For a list of commonly used **collective nouns,** see page 4.

USAGE

NOTE Many nouns ending in –*ics,* such as *acoustics, athletics, ethics, politics,* and *tactics,* may take singular or plural pronouns. Generally, when such a noun names a science, a system, or a skill, the noun takes a singular pronoun. When the noun names qualities, operations, activities, or individual items, the noun takes a plural pronoun.

SINGULAR   She has chosen to pursue a career in **politics**; she has always shown great interest in **it.** [Politics is thought of as a system.]

PLURAL   Some voters support her **politics,** while other voters oppose **them.** [Politics are thought of as activities or ideas.]

5w. Even when plural in form, the title of a creative work (such as a book, song, movie, or painting) or the name of a country or a city generally takes a singular pronoun.

EXAMPLES   I have just finished reading Nina Otero's **"The Bells of Santa Cruz."** Have you read **it**?

Star Wars is my favorite movie. George Lucas wrote and directed **it.**

The **Netherlands,** also called Holland, is situated on the North Sea; **its** capital is Amsterdam.

Located forty-two miles from the Rio Grande is **Las Cruces,** New Mexico. Not far from **it** is University Park, the home of New Mexico State University.

Avid golfers may enjoy dining at **Caddies** because **it** is designed to resemble a golf course and the menu has a golf theme.

NOTE The names of some organizations, though plural in form, may take singular or plural pronouns. When the name refers to the organization as a unit, it takes a singular pronoun. When the name refers to the members of the organization, it takes a plural pronoun.

SINGULAR   The **Evanstown High School Eagles** won all of **its** football games this year. [The team won as a unit.]

PLURAL   Wearing **their** new uniforms, the **Evanstown High School Eagles** posed for pictures for the yearbook. [The members of the team wore separate uniforms.]

5x. The gender and number of a relative pronoun (such as *who,* *which,* or *that*) are determined by its antecedent.

EXAMPLES   **Roseanne, who** knows everyone on **her** block, invited the Guerras to a cookout. [*Who* refers to the singular feminine noun *Roseanne.* Therefore, the singular feminine form *her* is used to agree with *who.*]

The **books that** have stains on **them** will be discarded. [*That* refers to the plural neuter noun *books.* Therefore, the plural neuter form *them* is used to agree with *that.*]

5y. An expression of an amount (a measurement, a percentage, or a fraction, for example) may be singular or plural, depending on how it is used.

EXAMPLES   **Five thousand bricks** is a heavy load; **it** almost ruined the truck's suspension. [The bricks are thought of as a unit.]

Five thousand bricks are scattered on the lot. **They** make walking dangerous. [The bricks are thought of separately.]

We have **ten minutes** to take the quiz; **it** is enough time. [The minutes are thought of as a unit.]

We wasted at least **ten minutes.** We spent **them** sharpening our pencils, asking questions, and putting our books away. [The minutes are thought of separately.]

Two thirds of the casserole is gone; **it** is delicious. [The fraction refers to the singular noun *casserole.*]

Two thirds of the apples are rotten; **they** should be thrown out. [The fraction refers to the plural noun *apples.*]

MEETING THE CHALLENGE

Rules 5j and 5y are two of the more difficult to follow. When is "a dozen eggs" singular, and when is it—or when are they— plural? Review the rules, and then practice them by writing a recipe. Choose a recipe for a favorite food, and write it out in sentences (for instance, "First, beat two eggs until they are blended."). Have a partner check the subject-verb and pronoun-antecedent agreement in your recipe to make sure that you've followed the rules about amounts, fractions, and measurements correctly.

USAGE

Exercise 6   **Proofreading for Pronoun-Antecedent Errors**

Each of the following sentences contains an error in pronoun-antecedent agreement. Identify and correct each error.

EXAMPLE   1. The Drama Club is preparing their annual show.

      1. their—its

1. I read "Ali Baba and the Forty Thieves" and decided to create my own illustrations for them.

2. Bring those pants over here; I'll iron it.

3. We traveled through the Netherlands and across their border into the country of Belgium.

4. Here is where the United Nations meets; their fiftieth anniversary was celebrated in 1995.
5. The sales clerk continued, "Three hundred dollars may seem like a lot, but you'll get a lot of value for them."
6. Thomas is the one who finished their project early.
7. Linguistics has always fascinated me, and I plan to study them in college.
8. If your research requires either a CD-ROM drive or a World Wide Web connection, you will find them in our public library.
9. Around sundown, the herd comes to the river to drink, and they will stay until the lions appear.
10. The band played together for the first time last year, but it had known each other for many years before.

Reference Note

For information on **verb tenses,** see page 182.

Review E **Writing Sentences Demonstrating Agreement**

Write you own original sentences according to the following instructions. Use verbs in present tense only.

EXAMPLE
1. Write a sentence using singular subjects joined by *nor.*

1. *Neither Alessandra nor Kim wants to leave the Mediterranean festival.*

1. Write a sentence using a compound subject joined by *and.*
2. Write a sentence beginning with *Many a.*
3. Write a sentence in which a pronoun refers to the noun *electronics.*
4. Write a sentence using a subject referred to by a relative pronoun.
5. Write a sentence using *Everybody* as the subject.
6. Write a sentence using an indefinite pronoun as the subject.
7. Write a sentence using a singular subject and a plural subject joined by *or.*
8. Write a sentence in which the pronoun *their* is used to refer to the subject.
9. Write a sentence using a gerund phrase as the subject.
10. Write a sentence using a singular subject followed by *as well as.*

Chapter Review

A. Identifying Subjects and Verbs That Agree

Identify the subject of the verb in parentheses for each of the following sentences. Then, choose the form that agrees in number with the subject.

1. Asthma, like other respiratory diseases, (*is, are*) made worse when the air quality is poor.
2. Neither of the ballplayers (*expect, expects*) to be drafted.
3. (*Has, Have*) any of the witnesses been sworn in yet?
4. If you have any questions, remember that either Lili or Roberto (*has, have*) experience with these computers.
5. My family (*is, are*) going to Thailand this summer.
6. In the village of San Ildefonso, two days (*is, are*) not considered a long time to spend polishing one piece of black pottery.
7. In recent years there (*has, have*) been many changes in farming.
8. Exactly one third of the students in my American history class (*is, are*) sophomores.
9. A pair of scissors (*was, were*) lying on the counter.
10. Neither the child nor her parents (*want, wants*) to be interviewed.
11. Cavities (*is, are*) one result of not brushing your teeth often enough.
12. *The Censors* (*is, are*) a book of stories by Luisa Valenzuela.
13. How (*do, does*) the wolf get his bad reputation?
14. The laws of physics (*tell, tells*) us that every action of force (*has, have*) an equal and opposite reaction.
15. John Lennon, Paul McCartney, George Harrison, and Ringo Starr (*was, were*) the Beatles.

B. Supplying Pronouns That Agree with Their Antecedents

Complete each of the following sentences by supplying at least one pronoun that agrees with its antecedent. Then, write the antecedent(s). Be sure to use standard, formal English.

16. Everyone has ____ reason for choosing to drive certain models of cars.

17. The words someone uses in daily conversation tell a great deal about _____ background.
18. If either Theo or Tommy calls, tell _____ I need help.
19. When Suzanne and Anita arrive, would you please help _____ find some good seats?
20. Only one of the girls has finished _____ project.
21. Could either Laura or Suzanne stop _____ before hitting the wall of the skating rink?
22. Anyone who wants to participate can leave _____ name with the secretary.
23. The new marching band made _____ debut at the game last night.
24. Just before the game, the director told the band that _____ new uniforms would arrive next week.
25. My aunt is a professor of economics, and she believes that _____ ought to be part of every student's curriculum.
26. Every turtle on the beach dug _____ own nest.
27. Half of the students had never heard of the book before, but _____ were looking forward to reading it.
28. Alfred Hitchcock's film *The Birds* was on television last night; _____ is one of the scariest movies I've ever seen!
29. Keith lowered the binoculars and handed _____ to me.
30. Neither Sean nor his brothers forgot _____ mother's birthday.

C. Choosing Correct Forms for Subject-Verb and Pronoun-Antecedent Agreement

For each sentence in the following paragraph, choose the word in parentheses that will complete the sentence correctly.

Kenny Walker was the only player in the history of the NFL who [31] (*was, were*) deaf. The Denver Broncos, my favorite team, [32] (*was, were*) smart to choose Walker in the 1990 football draft. Walker certainly [33] (*wasn't, weren't*) going to let his deafness keep him from being a great linebacker. Even today, not everyone [34] (*know, knows*) that spinal meningitis cost Kenny Walker his hearing when he was two years old. Sign language and lip reading [35] (*was, were*) taught to him at a special school, beginning when he was four years old. Because of his hearing impairment, most of the neighborhood boys [36] (*was, were*) unwilling to choose Walker to be on a team. After they saw him play, though, each of them wanted Walker on [37] (*their, his*) team! In all the time that Walker was a professional football player, neither he nor his coaches [38] (*was, were*) much bothered by his deafness. One of the accommodations the Broncos made [39] (*was, were*) to hire an interpreter to sign plays to Walker. Although he couldn't hear a sound on the field, Walker could feel the vibrations in his shoulder pads when the fans in the crowd cheered [40] (*them, him*).

Writing Application
Using Agreement in a Report

Pronoun-Antecedent Agreement   For your term project in history class, you've decided to poll people about what recent events they think will be among the most important events of the decade. Take a poll of at least ten people and write a brief report discussing your findings. Be sure that pronouns you use agree with their antecedents.

Prewriting   First, write down several specific questions that you will ask in your poll. Then, poll your subjects. Be sure to record the answers clearly and accurately and to identify your sources by their full names. After you take your poll, compile lists of the responses.

Writing   As you write your report, identify the answers people gave most frequently to each of your questions. Clearly identify your sources as well as the events you're discussing. You might wrap up your report with a paragraph telling what conclusions you've drawn from the results of the poll.

Revising   Make sure your report follows a clear, logical order. Also be sure you've accurately represented the responses to your poll.

Publishing   Check for pronoun-antecedent agreement, paying special attention to antecedents that are singular indefinite pronouns. Then, proofread your report for any errors in spelling, capitalization, and punctuation. You and your classmates may wish to compile all the responses gathered by your class and present the findings in an article in your school newspaper.

Using Pronouns Correctly
Case Forms of Pronouns

Diagnostic Preview

A. Proofreading Sentences for Correct Pronoun Forms

For each of the following sentences that contains an incorrect pronoun form, identify the error and then give the correct form. If a sentence is already correct, write *C*.

EXAMPLES   **1.** Manuel and him are on the soccer team.

    1. him—he

    2. Did you know that he and she are the new captains of the soccer team?

    2. C

1. Debbie is planning a surprise party for Marita, Jorge, and she.
2. Please send Anna and me a copy of the rough draft that you and she wrote.
3. You and I should probably ask Mr. Beauvais because no one speaks French better than him.
4. Tamisha hopes it will be her and Pete who are appointed to the student council.
5. Us students feel much more confident about repairing cars after taking this course.
6. To who did Justin give that picture of Maria Tallchief?

7. Danielle and myself had our bat mitzvahs in the same month, and she and I both did very well reading from the Torah.
8. Mrs. Kitts says that our knowing facts is less important than our knowing where to find them.
9. I really appreciated you picking me up after school today, and I'm glad you can give me a ride tomorrow.
10. Seriously, whom did you expect would win the blue ribbon?

B. Proofreading a Paragraph for Correct Pronoun Forms

Identify each incorrect pronoun form in the following sentences, and then give the correct form. If a sentence contains no errors, write *C*.

EXAMPLES [1] Meriwether Lewis hired me when him and William Clark set out to explore the Louisiana Territory.

1. *him—he*

[2] The two of them were already famous explorers when my cousin and I joined their expedition.

2. *C*

HELP

In Part B of the Diagnostic Preview, there may be more than one error in a sentence.

USAGE

[11] My cousin John and me were proud to be included in the group that went along with Lewis and Clark. [12] Us cousins were jacks-of-all-trades; both of us did everything from loading pack animals to building campfires. [13] For John and I, one of the best things about the trip was getting to know the other members of the group. [14] Someone who we became good friends with was a strong, friendly man named York. [15] Everyone, including myself, found York to be one of the most fascinating members of the expedition. [16] Many people know that Sacagawea, a Shoshone woman, was an interpreter on the expedition, but York was in many ways as able an interpreter as her. [17] In fact, communicating with the American Indians would have been practically impossible without both Sacagawea and himself. [18] Whenever the expedition met with Native American peoples, Sacagawea would tell her French husband, Charbonneau, what was said between her and them. [19] Charbonneau would then repeat the message in French to York, who would translate the French into English for Lewis, Clark, and the rest of we expedition members. [20] When we needed food and horses, York himself did much of the trading with the Indians because him and them got along very well.

Case

Case is the form that a noun or a pronoun takes to show its relationship to other words in a sentence. In English, there are three cases: *nominative, objective,* and *possessive.*

The form of a noun is the same for both the nominative case and the objective case. For example, a noun used as a subject (nominative case) will have the same form if used as an object (objective case).

NOMINATIVE CASE	The **general** explained the strategy. [subject]
OBJECTIVE CASE	The strategy was explained by the **general.** [object of the preposition *by*]

Reference Note

For more about **forming possessive nouns,** see page 345.

A noun changes its form in the possessive case by adding an apostrophe and an *s* to most singular nouns and only the apostrophe to most plural nouns.

POSSESSIVE CASE	The **general's** explanation was both clear and concise. [singular noun]
	Both **generals'** explanations were clear and concise. [plural noun]

Unlike nouns, most personal pronouns have three forms, one for each case. The form a pronoun takes depends on its function in a sentence.

NOMINATIVE CASE	**We** listened closely to the directions. [subject]
	The winners of the state championship are **they.** [predicate nominative.]
OBJECTIVE CASE	The teacher gave **us** a vocabulary quiz. [indirect object]
	Grandpa Worthington thanked **him** for picking the peaches in the orchard. [direct object]
	Are those flowers for **her**? [object of a preposition]
POSSESSIVE CASE	The teacher collected **our** papers. [possessive pronoun]

Within each case, the forms of the personal pronouns indicate *number, person,* and *gender.*

- *Number* tells you whether the pronoun is singular or plural.
- *Person* tells you whether the pronoun refers to the one(s) speaking (*first person*), the one(s) spoken to (*second person*), or the one(s) spoken about (*third person*).

- **Gender** tells you whether the pronoun is *masculine, feminine,* or *neuter* (neither masculine nor feminine).

Personal Pronouns			
	Nominative Case	Objective Case	Possessive Case
Singular			
First Person	I	me	my, mine
Second Person	you	you	your, yours
Third Person	he, she, it	him, her, it	his, her, hers, its
Plural			
First Person	we	us	our, ours
Second Person	you	you	your, yours
Third Person	they	them	their, theirs

Notice in the chart that *you* and *it* have the same forms for the nominative and the objective cases. All other personal pronouns have different forms for each case. Notice also that only third-person singular pronouns indicate gender.

The Nominative Case

The personal pronouns in the nominative case—*I, you, he, she, it, we,* and *they*—are used as subjects of verbs and as predicate nominatives.

6a. The subject of a verb should be in the nominative case.

EXAMPLES   **We** ordered the concert tickets. [*We* is the subject of the verb *ordered.*]

Why does **she** think that **they** are too expensive? [*She* is the subject of the verb *does think. They* is the subject of the verb *are.*]

He, she, and Shelby have volunteered at the animal shelter. [*He, she,* and *Shelby* are the compound subject of the verb *have volunteered.*]

Ms. Chang said that **he** and **I** should audition. [*He* and *I* are the compound subject of the verb *should audition.*]

STYLE **TIP**

Use the neuter pronoun *it* when referring to an animal unless the gender of the animal is made clear by another word in the sentence.

EXAMPLES
A stablehand led the horse to **its** stall.

That rooster is known for **his** bad temper. [The word *rooster* indicates that the animal is male.]

Eileen's cat, Melanie, kept an eye on the guests from **her** lookout post on top of the refrigerator. [The name *Melanie* indicates that the animal is female.]

USAGE

Reference Note

The **personal pronouns** in the nominative case may also be **used as appositives.** See page 68.

Reference Note

For more about **subjects of verbs,** see page 33.

TIPS & TRICKS

To help you choose the correct pronoun form in a compound subject, try each form separately with the verb.

EXAMPLE
(*She, Her*) and (*I, me*) will make the piñata. [*She will make* or *Her will make? I will make* or *me will make?*]

She and **I** will make the piñata.

Reference Note

For more information about **predicate nominatives,** see page 42.

USAGE

TIPS & TRICKS

Notice that the predicate nominative and the subject of the verb both indicate the same individual(s). To help you identify the correct pronoun form to use as a predicate nominative, try each form as the subject of the verb.

EXAMPLE
The only applicant for the job was (*he, him*). [*He was* or *him was?*]

The only applicant for the job was **he.**

Oral Practice 1   Using Pronouns as Subjects

Read each of the following sentences aloud, stressing the italicized pronoun(s).

1. *You* and *I* will go to the library this afternoon.
2. *We* and *they* have some research to do on Kiowa culture.
3. Either Terrell or *he* will select a topic about the environment.
4. Neither *they* nor *we* should use periodicals older than three months.
5. Both *she* and *I* will write about modern art.
6. Risa, Irena, and *I* might write about Georgia O'Keeffe.
7. Which playwright did Kaye and *she* select?
8. *She* said that *you* and *they* decided to go camping.

6b. A predicate nominative should be in the nominative case.

A ***predicate nominative*** is a word or word group in the predicate that identifies the subject or refers to it.

A pronoun used as a predicate nominative generally follows a form of the verb *be: am, is, are, was, were, be,* or *been.*

EXAMPLES   The chairperson of the prom committee is **she.** [*She* follows *is* and identifies the subject *chairperson.*]

The one who made the comment was **I.** [*I* follows *was* and identifies the subject *one.*]

A predicate nominative may be compound, with a pronoun appearing in combination with a noun or another pronoun.

EXAMPLES   The students who auditioned for the role were **he** and **Carlos.** [*He* and *Carlos* identify the subject *students.*]

The two new debaters are **she** and **I.** [*She* and *I* identify the subject *debaters.*]

Exercise 1   Using Pronouns in the Nominative Case

Complete the following sentences by supplying personal pronouns in the nominative case. For each pronoun you add, tell whether it is used as a *subject* or as a *predicate nominative.* Use a variety of pronouns, but do not use *you* or *it.*

EXAMPLE   1. When Charles L. Blockson was a child, _____ was eager to learn about African American heroes.

1. *he*—subject

1. When he told his teachers of his interest, it was _____ who said that there had been very few black heroes.
2. Certain that _____ must be wrong, Blockson started looking for African Americans in history books.
3. He began to collect books, and _____ showed him plenty of heroic black Americans.
4. Black people had not been inactive in shaping American history, he learned; in fact, _____ had played important roles in most of its key events!
5. When Blockson's great-grandfather was just a teenager, _____ had escaped slavery with the help of the Underground Railroad.
6. It was _____ who inspired Blockson's lifelong interest in the Underground Railroad.
7. It may have been my friends Latisha and _____ who read about Blockson's studies in a magazine article and then gave a report in history class.
8. Using Blockson's map as a source, _____ and _____ made this simplified map of the main Underground Railroad routes to freedom.
9. My ancestors escaped from slavery in Kentucky; therefore, as you can see, _____ must have followed one of the main routes to arrive in Detroit.
10. Latisha's great-great-great-grandmother traveled with her younger brother on the Underground Railroad from Virginia to Toronto, and later both _____ and _____ moved to Detroit to find work.

6
b

STYLE **TIP**

Expressions such as *It's me, This is her,* and *It was them* incorrectly use objective case pronouns as predicate nominatives. Although common in everyday situations, such expressions should be avoided in formal speaking and writing.

USAGE

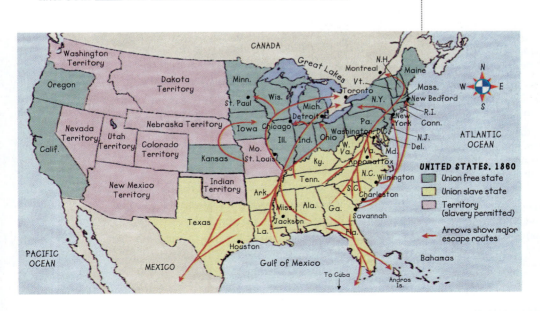

UNITED STATES, 1860
- Union free state
- Union slave state
- Territory (slavery permitted)
- ← Arrows show major escape routes

Reference Note

Personal pronouns in the objective case may also be used as **appositives.** See page 68.

Reference Note

For more about **direct objects,** see page 39. For more about **indirect objects,** see page 40.

The Objective Case

The personal pronouns in the objective case—*me, you, him, her, it, us,* and *them*—are used as direct objects, indirect objects, and objects of prepositions.

6c. A direct object should be in the objective case.

A *direct object* tells *who* or *what* receives the action of the verb.

EXAMPLES   My pen pal from Manila visited **me** last summer.

After the nails scattered all over the garage, we picked **them** up.

Can you drive the girls and **us** home from the game tonight?

6d. An indirect object should be in the objective case.

An *indirect object* often appears in sentences containing direct objects and tells *to whom* or *to what* or *for whom* or *for what* the action of the verb is done. The indirect object usually appears between the verb and a direct object.

EXAMPLES   The coach awarded **her** a varsity letter.

We gathered the chickens and gave **them** some feed.

Has Mr. Sims paid **Jason, Tracy,** and **her** their wages?

NOTE   Do not mistake an object of the preposition *to* or *for* for an indirect object.

INDIRECT OBJECT   Louise wrote **me** a letter.
OBJECT OF PREPOSITION   Louise wrote a letter to **me.** [*Me* is the object of the preposition *to.*]

TIPS & TRICKS

To help you choose the correct pronoun form in a compound direct or indirect object, try each form separately with the verb.

EXAMPLES
The new student asked Kelly and (*I, me*) for directions. [*asked I* or *asked me?*]

The new student asked Kelly and **me** for directions.

The editor in chief gave (*he, him*) and (*she, her*) an interesting assignment. [*gave he* or *gave him? gave she* or *gave her?*]

The editor in chief gave **him** and **her** an interesting assignment.

Oral Practice 2   **Using Pronouns in the Objective Case**

Read the following sentences aloud, stressing the italicized pronouns.

1. The judges chose Carmen and *me.*
2. Do you think that they will provide *us* with what we need?
3. Call either *her* or Rhea about the yearbook deadline.
4. *Him* I like, but don't ask *me* about the others.
5. These instructions confuse my brother and *me.*
6. Give the other girls and *her* the chemistry assignment.
7. Were they accusing *them* or *us?*
8. The success of the car wash surprised Mr. Kahn and *him.*

Exercise 2 Using Pronouns in the Objective Case

Complete the following sentences by supplying personal pronouns in the objective case. For each pronoun you add, tell whether it is used as a *direct object* or an *indirect object*. Use a variety of pronouns, but do not use *you* or *it*.

EXAMPLE   **1.** Marcia drove _____ to the civic center.

     1. us—direct object

1. Have you given Nick and _____ the reading list?
2. Did Bob show _____ his autographed copy of Amy Tan's latest book?
3. Mrs. Martin handed Lena, Chris, and _____ their notebooks.
4. Our teacher has already graded Latoya and _____ on our oral reports to the class.
5. Ms. Guerra has invited both _____ and _____ to the Independence Day Festival.
6. Would you please lend _____ and her the manual for the fax machine?
7. During practice today, the coach taught Patricia and _____ the proper form for the inward dive.
8. The play gave _____ some ideas for a skit.
9. My mother is picking up both you and _____.
10. Please tell _____ about the plans for the junior prom.

6e.   **An object of a preposition should be in the objective case.**

The **object of a preposition** is a noun or pronoun that follows a preposition. The preposition, its object, and any modifiers of the object make a **prepositional phrase.**

EXAMPLES	for **me**	after **her**	next to **them**
	with **us**	beside **him**	between **you** and **me**

Exercise 3 Selecting Pronouns Used as Objects of Prepositions

For each of the following sentences, choose the correct form of the pronoun in parentheses.

EXAMPLE   **1.** The Irish terrier belongs to (*she, her*).

     1. her

1. Would you like to play baseball with Eugenio and (*me, I*)?
2. These photographs were taken by Dwight and (*she, her*).

Reference Note

For more discussion of **prepositional phrases,** see page 54.

TIPS & TRICKS

To help you choose the correct pronoun form in a compound object of a preposition, try each form separately with the preposition.

EXAMPLES

Please return these videotapes to Mr. Mehta and (*she, her*). [*to she* or *to her?*]

Please return these videotapes to Mr. Mehta and **her.**

They want to go camping with (*he, him*) and (*I, me*). [*with he* or *with him? with I* or *with me?*]

They want to go camping with **him** and **me.**

---

3. We can rely on Theresa and (*he, him*) for their help.

4. Would you like to sit next to Elaine and (*me, I*)?

5. There has been much cooperation between the Hispanic Chamber of Commerce and (*we, us*).

6. On the basketball court, teammates like Dave and (*he, him*) seem to read each other's minds.

7. The closing lines of the play will be spoken by you and (*she, her*).

8. We have been studying the early settlers from England and learning about the help that American Indian peoples gave to (*them, they*).

9. Most of the credit belongs to (*we, us*).

10. Steer the ship between the lighthouse and (*them, they*).

Review A Choosing Correct Forms of Personal Pronouns

For each sentence in the following paragraph, choose the correct form of the pronoun in parentheses. Then, tell whether the pronoun is used as a *subject*, a *predicate nominative*, a *direct object*, an *indirect object*, or an *object of a preposition*.

EXAMPLE   During our vacation in Mexico, my grandmother, her brother Luís, and [1] (*I, me*) visited the Oaxaca Valley.

1. *I—subject*

The state of Oaxaca is where [1] (*they, them*) and their two older brothers were born. As we drove through Arrazola, their village, Uncle Luís was amazed to find well-built brick homes where all of [2] (*we, us*) had expected to see bamboo houses. Turning to Grandma, [3] (*he, him*) exclaimed, "Something good has happened here, Nita!" After visiting Arrazola, my relatives and [4] (*I, me*) drove to the city of Oaxaca, which is the state capital, and strolled along its main street. I pointed out some painted woodcarvings to Grandma and showed [5] (*she, her*) and Uncle Luís the ones I liked best. I took this picture of a pair of carved dancing chickens and decided it would be [6] (*they, them*) or a wooden alligator playing a horn that I'd buy for a souvenir. While I was making up my mind, Uncle Luís spoke to the shopkeeper, asking questions of [7] (*he, him*) and his wife. It seems that not long before, a local man named Manuel Jiménez had started making colorful wooden figures and had been selling [8] (*they, them*) to tourists. Seeing his success, others in the Oaxaca Valley began carving, too, and within a few years [9] (*they, them*) and their fanciful woodcarvings had become famous. The imagination, skill, and hard work of Oaxaca's people have rapidly brought **[10]** (*they, them*) out of poverty.

The Possessive Case

The personal pronouns in the possessive case—*my, mine, your, yours, his, her, hers, its, our, ours, their,* and *theirs*—are used to show ownership or possession.

6f. The possessive pronouns *mine, yours, his, hers, its, ours,* and *theirs* are used in the same ways that the pronouns in the nominative and the objective cases are used.

SUBJECT	Your car and **mine** need to be washed.
PREDICATE NOMINATIVE	This yearbook is **hers.**
DIRECT OBJECT	We ordered **ours** yesterday.
INDIRECT OBJECT	Ms. Kwan gave **theirs** a quick look.
OBJECT OF A PREPOSITION	Next to **yours,** my Siamese cat looks puny.

6g. The possessive pronouns *my, your, his, her, its, our,* and *their* are used to modify nouns.

EXAMPLES   **My** watch is broken.

His first public performance as a concert pianist was in 1998.

Do you know **their** address?

6h. A noun or pronoun that precedes a gerund should be in the possessive case.

A *gerund* is a verb form that ends in *–ing* and functions as a noun. Since a gerund acts as a noun, the noun or pronoun that comes before it must be in the possessive case in order to modify the gerund.

EXAMPLES   We were all thrilled by **Joetta's** scoring in the top 5 percent. [*Joetta's* modifies the gerund *scoring*. Whose scoring? Joetta's scoring.]

His parents objected to **his** working late on school nights. [*His* modifies the gerund *working*. Whose working? His working.]

Their winning the state championship led to a week-long celebration. [*Their* modifies the gerund *winning*. Whose winning? Their winning.]

Reference Note

For more about **gerunds,** see page 61.

┌ S T Y L E   T I P ┐

As a matter of courtesy, first-person pronouns are placed at the end of compound constructions.

NOMINATIVE CASE
Nia and **I** went to the hockey game.

OBJECTIVE CASE
My aunt Evanda met Nia and **me** outside the hockey arena.

POSSESSIVE CASE
Aunt Evanda bought Nia's ticket and **mine.**

USAGE

STYLE · TIP

The form of a noun or pronoun before an *–ing* word often depends on the meaning you want to express. If you want to emphasize the *–ing* word, use the possessive form. If you want to emphasize the noun or pronoun preceding the *–ing* word, do not use the possessive form. Notice the difference in meaning between the two sentences below.

EXAMPLES
The **pep squad's** dancing got the most applause. [emphasis on the gerund *dancing*]

The **pep squad** dancing got the most applause. [emphasis on *pep squad*, not on the participle *dancing*]

NOTE Do not confuse a gerund with a present participle, which is also a verb form that ends in *–ing*. A gerund acts as a noun; a present participle serves as an adjective. A noun or pronoun that is modified by a present participle should not be in the possessive case.

EXAMPLE We found him **sitting on a bench in the park.** [*Him* is modified by the participial phrase *sitting on a bench in the park.*]

Exercise 4 **Using Pronouns with Gerunds and Present Participles**

For each of the following sentences, identify the *–ing* word as either a *gerund* or a *present participle* and then choose the correct noun or pronoun in parentheses. Be prepared to explain your choices. [Hint: Some sentences may be correctly completed in more than one way.]

EXAMPLE 1. Jody saw (*us, our*) standing on the corner and waved.
1. present participle—us

1. Hao didn't see the huge, green wave until she felt (*it, its*) crashing over her shoulders.
2. I like my stepfather, but I just can't get used to (*him, his*) cooking.
3. The baby reached out to touch all the shiny (*ribbons, ribbon's*) decorating the gift.
4. (*He, His*) being sarcastic has ruined our chance to win the debate.
5. Do you mind (*me, my*) telling Dave that you entered the essay contest?
6. We could barely hear (*them, their*) singing over the music.
7. Pablo Neruda's political career didn't interfere with (*him, his*) writing.
8. Make (*you, your*) exercising a top priority.
9. Have you tasted the new (*chef, chef's*) cooking?
10. Several little (*boys, boys'*) dancing in traditional finery did their best to master the intricacies of the Zuni dance.

Special Pronoun Problems

Appositives

An ***appositive*** is a noun or a pronoun placed beside another noun or pronoun to identify or describe it.

6i. A pronoun used as an appositive is in the same case as the word to which it refers.

EXAMPLES   My best friends, **Raúl and she,** have been nominated for class treasurer. [*Raúl* and *she* are appositives identifying the subject *friends*. Since a subject is in the nominative case, an appositive identifying a subject is in the nominative case.]

My grandfather paid the two boys, **Mario** and **him,** for raking leaves. [*Mario* and *him* are appositives identifying the direct object *boys*. Since a direct object is in the objective case, an appositive identifying a direct object is in the objective case.]

To identify which pronoun form to use as an appositive, try each form in the position of the word to which it refers.

EXAMPLES   Two juniors, Erin and (*she, her*), conducted the survey. [*she conducted* or *her conducted?*]

Two juniors, Erin and **she,** conducted the survey.

The survey was conducted by two juniors, Erin and (*she, her*). [*by she* or *by her?*]

The survey was conducted by two juniors, Erin and **her.**

NOTE   Sometimes the pronoun *we* or *us* is followed by an appositive. To determine which pronoun form to use, try each form without the appositive.

EXAMPLES   (*We, Us*) students learned many interesting facts about our solar system. [*We learned* or *Us learned?*]

We students learned many interesting facts about our solar system.

The guidance counselor talked to (*we, us*) students. [*to we* or *to us?*]

The guidance counselor talked to **us** students.

Reference Note

For more information about **appositives,** see page 68.

MEETING THE CHALLENGE

"Just between you and I," personal pronouns do get misused. For a few days, be a pronoun spy. Listen to speakers around you, in the halls, at home, everywhere, and record the pronoun errors you hear. Back in the classroom, compile your findings with those of class-mates. Why do speakers make these mistakes? What common patterns do you find? For instance, the mis-use of *I* in "between you and I" might result from hypercorrection: Speakers think, "Wait, isn't it *you and I*, not *you and me*?"

USAGE

Exercise 5   Using Appositives in Sentences

For each item, write a sentence using the given word group in the way specified in parentheses. Supply a pronoun in the correct case for each blank.

EXAMPLE   **1.** my neighbors, _____ and Steven (*indirect object*)

1. We gave my neighbors, her and Steven, a ride to the football game.

1. the two star players, _____ and Kelly (*direct object*)

2. _____ and _____, the loudest fans (*subject*)

3. _____ Tigers boosters (*object of a preposition*)

4. _____ juniors (*predicate nominative*)

5. the world's best coaches, _____ and Mr. Gresham (*indirect object*)

6. _____ running backs (*predicate nominative*)

7. the head cheerleaders, _____ and _____ (*indirect object*)

8. _____ defensive linemen (*direct object*)

9. _____ and _____, the referees (*subject*)

10. Daniel and _____, the two band captains (*object of preposition*)

Pronouns in Elliptical Constructions

Reference Note

For more information about **elliptical constructions,** see page 84.

An *elliptical construction* is a word group, usually a clause, from which words have been omitted. The word *than* or *as* often begins an elliptical construction.

6j. A pronoun following *than* or *as* in an elliptical construction is in the same case as it would be if the construction were completed.

ELLIPTICAL   Jo said Ann was more frustrated **than he.**

COMPLETED   Jo said Ann was more frustrated **than he was frustrated.**

ELLIPTICAL   The assignment frustrated me as much **as him.**

COMPLETED   The assignment frustrated me as much **as it frustrated him.**

The pronoun form in an elliptical construction determines the meaning of the construction. Be sure to use the pronoun form that expresses the meaning you intend. Notice how the meaning of each of the following sentences depends on the pronoun form in the elliptical construction.

EXAMPLES   Dan misses New York more **than her.** [Dan misses New York more *than Dan misses her.*]

Dan misses New York more **than she.** [Dan misses New York more *than she misses New York.*]

Did Mr. Matsuda pay you as much **as I**? [Did Mr. Matsuda pay you as much *as I paid you?*]

Did Mr. Matsuda pay you as much **as me**? [Did Mr. Matsuda pay you as much *as he paid me?*]

Exercise 6 **Selecting Pronouns for Elliptical Constructions**

Add words to complete the elliptical construction in each of the following sentences. Include in the construction the appropriate pronoun form. Then, tell whether the pronoun is a *subject* or an *object*.

EXAMPLE 1. Jo works longer hours than (*I, me*).

1. *than I work—subject*

1. No one else in my class is as shy as (*I, me*).
2. The editors of our newspaper have written as much as (*they, them*).
3. Can you whistle as loudly as (*he, him*)?
4. If you want to sell more raffle tickets than Bradley, you should make more phone calls than (*he, him*).
5. My coach told me that I had more agility than (*she, her*).
6. We were all more eager than (*he, him*).
7. I am more interested in Spike Lee's films than (*she, her*).
8. Judges in the salsa dance contest presented Estella with a larger trophy than (*I, me*).
9. They sent Lois as many get-well cards as (*I, me*).
10. No one gave more time to good causes than (*she, her*).

HELP

Some of the elliptical constructions in Exercise 6 may be completed in more than one way; you need to give only one way of completing each.

Reflexive and Intensive Pronouns

Reflexive and intensive pronouns (sometimes called *compound personal pronouns*) have the same forms.

Reflexive and Intensive Pronouns		
	Singular	**Plural**
First Person	myself	ourselves
Second Person	yourself	yourselves
Third Person	himself, herself, itself	themselves

A *reflexive pronoun* refers to the subject of the verb and functions as a complement or an object of a preposition.

EXAMPLES Bill is not **himself** today. [*Himself* refers to *Bill* and functions as a predicate nominative.]

I hurt **myself.** [*Myself* refers to *I* and functions as a direct object.]

The cat gave **itself** a bath. [*Itself* refers to *cat* and functions as an indirect object.]

She would rather be by **herself.** [*Herself* refers to *she* and functions as the object of the preposition *by.*]

Reference Note

The words *hisself* and *theirselves* are nonstandard forms. See page 252.

┌HELP┐

Unlike a reflex-
ive pronoun, an intensive
pronoun may be omitted
from a sentence without
changing its basic meaning.

EXAMPLE
The children decorated
the gym themselves.
[*The children decorated
the gym* makes sense
without the pronoun.
Therefore, the pronoun
is intensive.]

┌HELP┐

If the sentence
is imperative, the subject
you may be understood.

An ***intensive pronoun*** emphasizes its antecedent and has no grammatical function in the sentence.

EXAMPLES   My grandfather and I restored the car **ourselves.**
[*Ourselves* emphasizes *grandfather* and *I.*]

The weather **itself** seemed to be our enemy. [*Itself*
emphasizes *weather.*]

6k. A pronoun ending in *–self* **or** *–selves* **should not be used in
place of a personal pronoun.**

NONSTANDARD	Rena and myself mow lawns in the summer.
STANDARD	Rena and **I** mow lawns in the summer.

NONSTANDARD	Did Rosa make lunch for herself and yourself?
STANDARD	Did Rosa make lunch for herself and **you**?

**Exercise 7   Using Reflexive and Intensive
Pronouns Correctly**

For each of the following sentences, identify the italicized pronoun as
intensive or *reflexive*. Then, give the word or words that the pronoun
refers to or emphasizes.

EXAMPLE   1. Ruthie taught *herself* how to make the special beads she
wanted for her beadwork.

1. *reflexive—Ruthie*

1. Will the president *himself* preside at the welcoming ceremony for
the foreign leaders?
2. Maria and Giorgio should be proud of *themselves.*
3. The store manager found the address of a lumberyard for us, but
we had to order the materials *ourselves.*
4. To celebrate their anniversary, Mom and Dad bought *themselves*
a couple of theater tickets.
5. I hurt *myself* building that fence.
6. Standing atop a hill all by *itself,* a full-grown stag can be a truly
impressive sight.
7. Imagine *yourself* setting sail across the Ionian Sea.
8. Muriel *herself* replaced the shingles on the roof.
9. After I yelled at my little brother, I felt ashamed of *myself* and
apologized.
10. The bear *itself* removed all the garbage from the dumpster and
tossed the litter all over the ground.

Who and Whom

Like most personal pronouns, the pronoun *who* (*whoever*) has different case forms.

Nominative Case	who	whoever
Objective Case	whom	whomever
Possessive Case	whose	whosever

These pronouns may be used to form questions and to introduce subordinate clauses.

NOTE When *who*, *whom*, and *whose* are used to introduce adjective clauses, they are called **relative pronouns.**

EXAMPLES   Anna is the woman **whom** we rely on to take care of our cats while we are away.

Is he the boy **who** gave you that beautiful bracelet?

Jalene is the girl **whose** parents are from Guatemala.

Yes, I am the one **who** wrote that poem.

In questions, *who* is used as a subject or as a predicate nominative. *Whom* is used as a direct object, an indirect object, or an object of a preposition.

NOMINATIVE   **Who** played this role on Broadway? [*Who* is the subject of the verb *played.*]

Who could it have been? [*Who* is a predicate nominative referring to the subject *it.*]

OBJECTIVE   **Whom** did the president recommend? [*Whom* is the direct object of the verb *did recommend.*]

Whom did you ask the question? [*Whom* is the indirect object of the verb *did ask.*]

For **whom** did E. E. Cummings write that poem? [*Whom* is the object of the preposition *For.*]

When choosing between *who* and *whom* in a subordinate clause, follow these steps:

STEP 1:   Find the subordinate clause.

STYLE   TIP

In informal English, the use of *whom* is gradually disappearing. In informal situations, it is acceptable to begin a question with *who* regardless of whether the nominative or objective form is grammatically correct. In formal speaking and writing, though, it is still important to distinguish between *who* and *whom*.

USAGE

STYLE   TIP

Frequently, *whom* is omitted from subordinate clauses but is still understood.

EXAMPLE

The boys [*whom*] you met are brothers.

Leaving out *whom* tends to make writing sound informal. In formal situations, it is generally better to include *whom*.

Reference Note

For more information about **subordinate clauses,** see page 77.

STEP 2: Decide how the pronoun is used in the clause—as a *subject, predicate nominative, direct object, indirect object,* or *object of a preposition.*

STEP 3: Determine the case for this use of the pronoun.

STEP 4: Select the correct case form of the pronoun.

EXAMPLE   Ms. Gonzalez, (*who, whom*) I greatly admire, operates a shelter for homeless people in our community.

STEP 1: The subordinate clause is (*who, whom*) *I greatly admire.*

STEP 2: The pronoun serves as the direct object of the verb *admire.* [I greatly admire (*who, whom*).]

STEP 3: A direct object is in the objective case.

STEP 4: The objective form of the pronoun is *whom.*

ANSWER: Ms. Gonzalez, **whom** I greatly admire, operates a shelter for homeless people in our community.

The case of a pronoun in a subordinate clause is not affected by any word outside the subordinate clause.

EXAMPLE   The prize goes to (*whoever, whomever*) is the first to solve the riddles.

STEP 1: The subordinate clause is (*whoever, whomever*) *is the first to solve the riddles.*

STEP 2: The pronoun serves as the subject of the verb *is,* not the object of the preposition *to.* (The entire clause is the object of the preposition *to.*)

STEP 3: A subject of a verb is in the nominative case.

STEP 4: The nominative form of the pronoun is *whoever.*

ANSWER: The prize goes to **whoever** is the first to solve the riddles.

NOTE   When choosing between *who* and *whom* to begin a question or a subordinate clause, do not be misled by an expression consisting of a subject and a verb, such as *I think, do you suppose, he feels,* or *they believe.* Select the pronoun form you would use if the expression were not in the sentence.

EXAMPLES   **Who** do you think will win the Super Bowl? [*Who* is the subject of the verb *will win.*]

She is the one **whom** we believe they will elect. [*Whom* is the direct object of the verb *will elect.*]

Ed is the student **who** I feel will be valedictorian. [*Who* is the subject of the verb *will be.*]

USAGE

Choose the correct form of the pronoun in parentheses in each of the following sentences. Then, tell how the pronoun is used in the sentence—as a *subject*, a *predicate nominative*, a *direct object*, an *indirect object*, or an *object of a preposition*.

EXAMPLE
1. Here are the names of some of the authors (*who, whom*) we will study this semester.

1. *whom—direct object*

1. Betty Smith, the author of *A Tree Grows in Brooklyn*, was an obscure writer (*who, whom*) became a celebrity overnight.
2. Her novel is an American classic about a young girl (*who, whom*) she called Francie Nolan.
3. Francie, (*who, whom*) we follow through girlhood to adulthood, has only one tree in her city backyard.
4. Carson McCullers, (*who, whom*) critics describe as a major American writer, also wrote a novel about a young girl's coming of age.
5. (*Who, Whom*) could not be moved by *The Member of the Wedding*?
6. Do you know (*who, whom*) the actor was that played Frankie in the Broadway production of *The Member of the Wedding*?
7. Pearl Buck is a novelist with (*who, whom*) most Americans are familiar.
8. Pulitzer Prizes are awarded to (*whoever, whomever*) is selected by the panel of judges.
9. Gwendolyn Brooks, (*who, whom*) you told me won the Pulitzer Prize for poetry, also wrote a book called *Maud Martha*.
10. (*Who, Whom*) did you ask the question about who Maud Martha really is?

Review B **Selecting Correct Forms of Pronouns**

Choose the correct form of the pronoun in parentheses in each sentence in the following paragraph.

EXAMPLE
Ms. Kent talked with Jordan and [1] (*I, me*) about the artwork of some famous Impressionists.

1. *me*

Jordan and [1] (*I, me*) had thought of Impressionism as a French style of painting, and for the most part, we were right. Every artist, however, is influenced by other artists, regardless of [2] (*their, theirs*) nationality. If you have heard of Edgar Degas, you might know that

COMPUTER TIP

You can use the search function of a word-processing program to find each use of *who* and *whom* in a document. Then, you can double-check to make sure that you have used the correct form of the pronoun in each instance.

USAGE

both [3] (*he, him*) and the American Impressionist Mary Cassatt were very much influenced by exhibitions of Japanese prints that came to Paris. At first glance, Impressionist paintings don't resemble Japanese works, but just look at [4] (*they, them*) placed side by side, and you can see strong parallels. This morning, Ms. Kent pointed out some of those stylistic similarities to Jordan and [5] (*me, myself*), using the paintings shown on this page. Neither of [6] (*we, us*) art lovers could possibly mistake the resemblance. "Just between you and [7] (*I, me*)," said Ms. Kent, "almost all of the Impressionists openly copied ideas from the Japanese." One of my favorite painters is Toulouse-Lautrec, [8] (*who, whom*) often used the Japanese technique of including a large object in the extreme foreground to lend a feeling of depth to a picture. Both Mary Cassatt and [9] (*he, him*) learned from the Japanese the principle of cutting figures at the edge of the canvas to achieve a snapshot-like quality. As you can see, the Japanese technique of juxtaposing different patterned fabrics appealed to Mary Cassatt, and this technique was used by Pierre Bonnard as well as by [10] (*she, her*).

Andro Hiroshige, *Branch of a Flowering Apple Tree*. Color woodcut. Paris, Galerie Janette Ostier/Giraudon/Art Resource, New York.

Toulouse-Lautrec, *Jane Avril* (1893). Albi, Musée Toulouse-Lautrec/Scala/Art Resource, New York.

Mary Cassatt, *The Letter*. The Metropolitan Museum of Art, Gift of Arthur Sachs, 1916.

Japanese woodcut, Victoria and Albert Museum, London/Art Resource, New York.

Review C **Proofreading Sentences for Correct Pronoun Forms**

For each of the following sentences that contains an incorrect pronoun form, identify the error and then give the correct form. If a sentence is already correct, write *C*.

EXAMPLE   **1.** Neither Karl nor myself could find the book.

       1. myself—I

1. I thought that Beth and her would make the best officers.
2. Both her father and herself have artistic talent.
3. I can't understand his dropping out of the marching band during his senior year.
4. The new exchange students from Switzerland, Michelle and her, already speak some English.
5. Robert's parents have no objection to him trying to get a job at the gas station after school.
6. Many farm workers voted for Cesar Chavez, who they knew would fight for their rights.
7. They have many more CDs than us.
8. The title of salutatorian goes to whomever has the second-highest grade-point average.
9. Who is supposed to sit in this empty seat between Lauren and I?
10. Who do you suppose won the traditional dance contest at the powwow?

Review D **Selecting Correct Forms of Pronouns**

Choose the correct form of each pronoun in parentheses in the following paragraph. Be prepared to explain your choices.

EXAMPLE   You have the same features in almost exactly the same positions as **[1]** (*I, me*), yet nearly anyone can easily tell our faces apart.

       1. I

[1] (*Whom, Who*) do you think the pictures on the next page represent? Reuben thought the one on the right was a woman, and I told him I was surprised at [2] (*him, his*) not recognizing [3] (*who, whom*) it is! You should give [4] (*yourself, you*) a round of applause if you guessed George Washington. Both of these pictures were created when a scientist named Leon D. Harmon asked [5] (*himself, him*) how much information people actually need to recognize a face. [6] (*He, Him*) and his

HELP

In the example sentence, the features *you have* are compared to the features *I* [have]. Adding the verb makes it clear that *I* is the subject and should be in the nominative case.

USAGE

colleagues took photographs of famous portraits, divided each photo into squares, and then averaged the color and brightness inside each square into a single tone. The computer-generated image gives you and [7] (*I, me*) very little information—there are no features and no outlines, only a pattern of colored blocks. Although we can't see the eyes, nose, and mouth, the chances of [8] (*us, our*) recognizing a particular human face are very high. For the picture on the left, Reuben was a better guesser than [9] (*I, me*), especially when I held the page a few feet from his eyes. Suddenly, he saw the [10] (*Mona Lisa, Mona Lisa's*) looking back at him!

Ed Manning, Blocpix, Stratford, CT.

Ed Manning, Blocpix, Stratford, CT.

Chapter Review

A. Selecting Correct Forms of Pronouns

Choose the correct form of the pronoun in parentheses in each of the following sentences. Base your answers on standard, formal usage.

1. Because of the impending storm, (*us, we*) three decided to postpone our plans for the picnic.
2. It's easy to write about someone (*who, whom*) you know well.
3. The most difficult task remained for Lisle and (*I, me*).
4. No one worked harder on the campaign than (*she, her*).
5. Mr. and Mrs. Sandoval had duplicate photographs made for themselves and for (*me, myself*).
6. Vince and (*I, me*) have been classmates since kindergarten.
7. I saw (*you, your*) helping Ignacio in the kitchen.
8. (*Who, Whom*) did Elissa see in front of the theater?
9. I am certain that the scholarship winner will be (*him, he*).
10. Did you ask (*who, whom*) was at the front door?
11. This afternoon the talent committee will audition Tina and (*myself, me*).
12. As I waited for the elevator, I heard the receptionist say, "(*Who, Whom*) shall I say is calling?"
13. The best tennis players in school are my cousin Adele and (*he, him*).
14. I helped Two Bear and (*she, her*) prepare for the powwow.
15. We have the same kind of blender in our kitchen as they do in (*their, theirs*).

B. Proofreading Sentences for Correct Pronoun Forms

Each of the following sentences contains incorrect pronoun usage. Identify each incorrect pronoun. Then, write the form that is correct according to standard, formal usage. Some sentences may have more than one error.

16. Neither Lee nor me lost the tools.

17. Kyoko and I are the students whom our teacher says will represent our class in the competition.
18. Just between you and I, I think he gave the wrong answer.
19. The two whom could win the award are Carlos and him.
20. Will Michael and him cut the lawn today?
21. She encouraged the rest of we students to work harder.
22. Aaron and Rene, who I rely upon, are both home sick today.
23. Grandma lent Martin and I enough money that we could go Christmas shopping.
24. Jimi and her always finish their math assignments sooner than me.
25. Do you think him leaving early will be a problem?
26. Because Alberto and them have taken dancing lessons, they were chosen to be in the chorus line.
27. Our math teacher strongly objects to us yelling out answers during class.
28. My great-grandmother taught we children about life in post-World War II Cuba.
29. Us student filmmakers should pool our resources and buy a camera.
30. When we were small, Ellie always got into more trouble than me.

C. Proofreading a Paragraph for Correct Pronoun Forms

The following paragraph contains errors in pronoun usage. Identify each incorrect pronoun form, and then write the form that is correct according to the rules of standard, formal usage. If a sentence is already correct, write *C*.

[31] Do you know whom won the Nobel Prize for literature in 1991? [32] The winner was Nadine Gordimer, my favorite writer. [33] She is a South African writer whose novels and short stories have brought herself much renown. [34] She winning the Nobel Prize helped to bring attention to the problem of apartheid in South Africa. [35] Few writers have been as skilled at exposing injustice as her. [36] In 1974, two writers, Stanley Middleton and her, won an important British literary award, the Booker Prize. [37] Her 1979 novel, *Burger's Daughter,* is the story of a young white woman and her activist father and how apartheid affects she as well as him. [38] After her father is imprisoned,

the daughter has mixed feelings about him opposing apartheid. **[39]** Gordimer's 1994 novel, *None to Accompany Me,* is about a woman who tries to achieve self-understanding through political activism in postapartheid South Africa. **[40]** Perhaps now you understand why my favorite writer is her.

Writing Application
Using Pronouns Correctly in a Letter

Who and Whom   Your school's newspaper is planning a special feature on outstanding students. Write a letter to the editor, describing a student at your school and explaining what makes him or her outstanding. In your letter, use *who* (or *whoever*) three times and *whom* (or *whomever*) twice.

Prewriting   Decide who you think is the most outstanding student at your school. Then, jot down some notes on the qualities and achievements that make this person special. Note a few specific examples of the person's behavior that illustrate these qualities.

Writing   Begin by naming the person and telling briefly why he or she should be featured in the newspaper. Then, give the examples you listed in your notes. You may also want to tell an anecdote that shows the person's special qualities.

Revising   Is your letter clear and convincing? If not, you will need to revise your examples or replace them with more engaging ones. Be sure each of your examples supports your description of the person.

Publishing   Does your letter follow one of the correct forms for a business letter? Proofread your paragraph carefully. Take extra care with pronouns, making sure that each of them is in the correct case. You and your classmates may want to create your own "Wall of Fame." Collect your letters and, perhaps, some photographs of the outstanding students about whom you have written, and arrange the letters and photos in a bulletin board display.

Clear Reference
Pronouns and Antecedents

Diagnostic Preview

A. Correcting Faulty Pronoun References

The following sentences contain examples of ambiguous, general, weak, and indefinite references. Revise each sentence, correcting the faulty pronoun reference.

EXAMPLE   1. My grandparents walk five miles every day. It is one of the best forms of exercise.

           1. *My grandparents walk five miles every day. Walking is one of the best forms of exercise.*

1. If the phone rings again this evening, ask them please not to call anymore.
2. The German shepherds chased deer until they were quite exhausted.
3. We hiked almost fourteen miles to the campsite, pitched our tents, arranged our sleeping bags, and then made our supper. This was so exhausting that we immediately went to sleep.
4. Many of our presidents began their political careers as minor public officials, which is a good thing.
5. Maria told Joan that her bicycle had a flat tire.
6. In *Mama's Bank Account,* it describes how a Norwegian American family lives in San Francisco.
7. When we saw the flock of geese during the guided tour, they told us that they had flown all the way from northern Canada.
8. Jan liked the Wynton Marsalis tape but was disappointed that it didn't include her favorite one.

9. The shipwrecked men paddled their raft with their hands day after day, but this brought them no closer to land.
10. In northern regions, far away from city lights, you can frequently see the aurora borealis.

B. Correcting Faulty Pronoun References

Most of the following sentences contain ambiguous, general, weak, or indefinite references. Revise each faulty sentence. If a sentence is already correct, write *C*.

EXAMPLE   1. Carl Sagan praised Stephen W. Hawking after he wrote *A Brief History of Time.*

1. *Carl Sagan praised Stephen W. Hawking after Hawking wrote* A Brief History of Time.

11. In Sagan's review of the book, it calls Hawking one of the greatest physicists of the twentieth century.
12. Hawking's 1988 book about physics and the universe became a bestseller, which was surprising.
13. Jaime told Rick that he should have read Hawking's chapter about black holes in space before writing his report.
14. Whenever Francine reads a good book about science, she always wants to become one of them.
15. According to Hawking, Galileo was a talented science writer. One of these was the work *Two New Sciences,* the basis of modern physics.
16. In this magazine article on Hawking, they tell about his personal battle with motor neuron disease.
17. Because the disease affects his speech and movement, Hawking wrote his book by using a voice synthesizer and a personal computer.
18. Even though Hawking carefully explains his theories on the thermodynamic and cosmological arrows of time, it still confuses some readers.
19. That Hawking apparently understands the applications of Einstein's theories to time and the universe does not seem astonishing.
20. One question Hawking has tried to answer is this: If you were to drop a book into a black hole, would the information in the book be destroyed?

USAGE

Pronouns and Their Antecedents

Reference Note

For more information about **pronouns and antecedents,** see page 5.

In most cases, a pronoun has no definite meaning in itself. Its meaning is clear only when the reader knows to which word or words the pronoun refers. This word or word group is called the *antecedent* of the pronoun.

7a. A pronoun should refer clearly to its antecedent.

In the following examples, arrows point from the pronouns to their antecedents.

EXAMPLES   Peg asked **Leonardo** to tell her what the surprise was, but **he** refused.

The math teacher gave **us** a problem that **we** couldn't solve.

After trying on the **dress,** Mary said, "**This** fits perfectly."

Ambiguous Reference

7b. Avoid an *ambiguous reference,* which occurs when any one of two or more words could be a pronoun's antecedent.

AMBIGUOUS	Colleen called Alicia while she was doing her homework. [The antecedent of *she* and *her* is unclear. Who was doing her homework, Colleen or Alicia?]
CLEAR	While Colleen was doing her homework, she called Alicia.
CLEAR	While Alicia was doing her homework, Colleen called her.
AMBIGUOUS	The ship's officer explained to the passenger the meaning of the regulation he had just read. [The antecedent of *he* is unclear. Who had just read the regulation?]
CLEAR	After the ship's officer read the regulation, he explained its meaning to the passenger.
CLEAR	After reading the regulation, the ship's officer explained its meaning to the passenger.
CLEAR	After the passenger read the regulation, the ship's officer explained its meaning to him.

Oral Practice   **Correcting Ambiguous References**

Read each of the sentences on the next page aloud. Then, re-read the sentence, correcting the ambiguous pronoun reference.

USAGE

EXAMPLE   **1.** When the ship struck the dock, it burst into flames.

     1. *When it struck the dock, the ship burst into flames.*

or

The dock burst into flames when the ship struck it.

1. The loyal forces fought the guerrillas until they were almost entirely destroyed.
2. The police officer told the sergeant that a button was missing from her uniform.
3. The guide explained to the tourist the value of the stone that she had found.
4. Leon told Carlos that his report would be better if he added more details about Cesar Chavez.
5. When Anna brought Lena to the conference, we asked her for her press credentials.
6. Since the show was scheduled for the same night as the intramural playoff game, it had to be postponed.
7. The manager told the dishwasher to be more careful because he would have to replace all the broken dishes.
8. When the ambassador joined the foreign minister, reporters thought he looked confident.
9. When the truck hit the wall, it was hardly damaged.
10. The Black History Month schedule was in my bag, but somebody took it.

General Reference

7c. Avoid a *general reference*, which is the use of a pronoun that refers to a general idea rather than to a specific antecedent.

The pronouns commonly used in making general references are *it, that, this,* and *which.*

GENERAL   The gusts grew stronger, and rain clouds began rolling in from the distant hills. This prompted the campers to seek shelter.
           [*This* has no specific antecedent.]

CLEAR   The gusts grew stronger, and rain clouds began rolling in from the distant hills. These ominous conditions prompted the campers to seek shelter.

CLEAR   As the gusts grew stronger and rain clouds began rolling in from the distant hills, the campers sought shelter.

HELP

Although sentences in the Oral Practice can be corrected in more than one way, you need to give only one revision for each.

USAGE

GENERAL	More than 20 percent of those who enter college fail to graduate, which is a shame. [*Which* has no specific antecedent.]
CLEAR	That more than 20 percent of those who enter college fail to graduate is a shame.

Exercise 1 **Correcting General References**

Revise each of the following sentences, correcting the general pronoun reference.

EXAMPLE 1. England invaded France in 1337. That began a series of wars known as the Hundred Years' War.

1. *England's invasion of France in 1337 began a series of wars known as the Hundred Years' War.*

or

When England invaded France in 1337, a series of wars known as the Hundred Years' War began.

1. On California's San Miguel Island, a ranger showed us around, and this made the visit especially interesting.
2. A great many young people have already left Hastings Corners to work in the city, which is unfortunate for this town.
3. My parents bought a new carpet and new curtains, and they hired someone to paint the walls and ceiling. That certainly improved the appearance of the room.
4. The guidance counselor asked me whether I wanted to take German, French, or Spanish, which was difficult to decide.
5. After the storm last weekend, the trail to the top of the mountain was washed out in some spots and was blocked in many places with fallen branches. It made the ascent nerve-racking.
6. The first part of the test will be on chemistry, the second on mathematics, the third on physics. This will make it very difficult.
7. Several of the eyewitnesses described the man as short, others said he was tall, and yet others said he was "about average." It confused the police investigators.
8. We hiked all morning and then went skiing at Gates of the Arctic National Park and Preserve, which made us all extremely tired.
9. The principal said that the play will have to be given in the old auditorium unless by some miracle the new auditorium can be completed ahead of schedule; that will surely be a blow to the Central High Drama Club.
10. I found out that three of my library books were overdue, which was a complete surprise.

Review A Correcting Ambiguous and General References

Most of the following sentences contain ambiguous or general pronoun references. Revise each faulty sentence. If a sentence is already correct, write *C*.

EXAMPLE
1. Some people still haven't heard about the Civil Rights Memorial, which is unfortunate.

1. *That some people still haven't heard about the Civil Rights Memorial is unfortunate.*

1. After Tonya saw the Civil Rights Memorial at the Southern Poverty Law Center in Montgomery, Alabama, she sent a postcard to Alice.
2. Morris S. Dees, cofounder of the Law Center, and other center officials wanted to find a top architect to create a special memorial. This led them to Maya Lin.
3. My mother remembers reading about Lin when she was chosen to design the Vietnam Veterans Memorial in Washington, D.C.
4. Before she made up her mind, Lin researched the history of the civil rights movement. That convinced her to accept the project.
5. As you can see here, the granite memorial consists of two distinct parts: a wall with an engraved quotation and a round, engraved tabletop. This makes a simple but striking effect.

┌─ **HELP** ─

Although sentences in Review A can be corrected in more than one way, you need to give only one revision for each.

USAGE

6. Whoever thought of engraving the events and names associated with the civil rights movement on the granite tabletop had an inspired idea.

7. Water flows down the wall and over the tabletop of the memorial, which adds a sense of calm and continuity.

8. Mrs. Bledsoe told Tamisha about some of the forty entries she had just read on the tabletop.

9. When the Law Center dedicated the memorial in 1989, it became a popular tourist attraction.

10. Nowadays, many people come to Montgomery especially to see the Civil Rights Memorial, which, of course, benefits the city.

Weak Reference

7d. Avoid a *weak reference,* which occurs when a pronoun refers to an antecedent that has been suggested but not expressed.

WEAK	Every time a circus came to town, my sister Erin wanted to become one of them. [The antecedent of *them* is not expressed.]
CLEAR	Every time a circus came to town, my sister Erin wanted to become one of the troupe.

WEAK	Kane is very talented musically. Two of these are singing harmony and playing the saxophone. [The antecedent of *these* is not expressed.]
CLEAR	Kane is very talented musically. Two of his talents are singing harmony and playing the saxophone.
CLEAR	Kane has many musical talents. Two of these are singing harmony and playing the saxophone.
CLEAR	Kane has many musical talents, two of which are singing harmony and playing the saxophone.

Exercise 2 Correcting Weak References

Revise each of the following sentences, correcting the weak pronoun reference.

EXAMPLE
1. Mom is very interested in psychiatry, but she does not believe they know all the answers.

1. *Mom is very interested in psychiatry, but she does not believe that psychiatrists know all the answers.*

—HELP—

Although some sentences in Exercise 2 can be corrected in more than one way, you need to give only one revision for each.

1. Sir Arthur Conan Doyle began his career as a doctor, and it explains his interest in careful observation.
2. She is a careful gardener, watering them whenever the soil gets dry.
3. They planned to eat dinner outdoors by candlelight, but a strong wind kept blowing them out.
4. For years after seeing the Alvin Ailey American Dance Theater perform, Leah dreamed of joining them.
5. Although rain was predicted on the night of the concert, Eric went because his favorite ones were scheduled to be played.
6. My brother has an anthology of Japanese literature for his college course, but he hasn't read any of them yet.
7. Although Bradley has always enjoyed reading poetry, he has never written one.
8. Sarah's uncle has a huge vegetable garden, and he keeps them supplied with fresh vegetables all summer long.
9. He spent more than an hour at the clothing store but did not try any on.
10. Deep-sea fishing isn't very enjoyable to me unless I catch at least one.

Indefinite Reference

7e. Avoid an *indefinite reference*—the use of a pronoun that refers to no particular person or thing and that is unnecessary to the meaning and structure of a sentence.

The pronouns commonly used in making indefinite references are *it, they,* and *you.* To correct an indefinite reference, revise the sentence to eliminate the unnecessary pronoun.

INDEFINITE	In the newspaper it reported that a volcano had erupted in the Indian Ocean. [*It* is not necessary to the meaning of the sentence.]
CLEAR	The newspaper reported that a volcano had erupted in the Indian Ocean.

INDEFINITE	At Yerkes Observatory in Wisconsin, they have the world's largest refracting telescope. [*They* does not refer to any specific persons.]
CLEAR	Yerkes Observatory in Wisconsin has the world's largest refracting telescope.

USAGE

INDEFINITE   In Shakespeare's time you could attend the performance of a play for a penny. [*You* does not refer to the reader or to any other particular antecedent.]

CLEAR   In Shakespeare's time a theatergoer could attend the performance of a play for a penny.

NOTE   The indefinite use of *it* in familiar expressions such as *it is snowing, it is early,* and *it seems* is acceptable.

Exercise 3   Correcting Indefinite Pronoun References

Revise each of the following sentences, correcting the indefinite use of *it, they,* or *you.*

EXAMPLE   1. In Japan they have the world's tallest roller coaster.

   1. *Japan has the world's tallest roller coaster.*

or

   The world's tallest roller coaster is in Japan.

1. In *The Diary of Anne Frank,* it shows a young Jewish girl's courage during two years of hiding from the Nazis.
2. I asked my aunt Shirley, who works for one of the largest architectural design firms in the city, what you have to do to become a licensed architect.
3. In some parts of Africa, they mine diamonds and sell them to jewelers to be cut.
4. In the sports sections of daily newspapers, it usually tells all about the previous day's events in sports.
5. When Grandpa was a child, you were supposed to be absolutely silent at the table.
6. In the movie guide, it states that *The Long Walk Home* is almost a documentary about civil rights.
7. On the book jacket, they say that the authors themselves had experienced these thrilling adventures.
8. The dancers, trying to keep up with the spirited pace of the music, had whirled so fast it made them dizzy.
9. One of the attractions of the tour was that they gave tour members free admissions to all the museums on the tour.
10. When the Neville Brothers come to town next week, it will be a sold-out show.

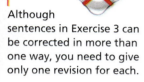

Correcting Weak and Indefinite Pronoun References

Most of the following sentences contain weak and indefinite pronoun references. Revise each faulty sentence. If a sentence is already correct, write *C*.

EXAMPLE
1. In the newspaper they ran an article about the late English actor Jeremy Brett, who played the detective Sherlock Holmes.

1. *The newspaper ran an article about the late English actor Jeremy Brett, who played the detective Sherlock Holmes.*

1. Every time I see Sherlock Holmes reruns on public television's *Mystery!* series, I want to read some more of them.
2. In the article, they talk about Brett's authentic Holmes wardrobe, an example of which can be seen in the picture below.
3. Holmes is a very theatrical person. One of these is using disguises, such as that of a priest in "The Final Problem."
4. In the *Mystery!* series, Brett was given the opportunity to play Holmes as Conan Doyle himself had created the character.

┌─**HELP**─

Although sentences in Review B can be corrected in more than one way, you need to give only one revision for each.

USAGE

5. Throughout Conan Doyle's fiction, they present Sherlock Holmes as confident, fair, and dramatic but also as restless, temperamental, and moody.

6. When we heard that Brett had starred as Sherlock Holmes on the London stage, we wished we had seen it.

7. In the reviews of *Mystery!* they state that Brett is still widely considered the best Sherlock Holmes ever.

8. I joined the local chapter of the Baker Street Irregulars, which is a kind of Sherlock Holmes fan club.

9. From 1887 to 1927, Conan Doyle chronicled the life of Holmes, writing more than fifty of them.

10. In England around the end of the nineteenth century, you could read Sherlock Holmes stories in the *Strand* magazine.

Chapter Review

A. Correcting Faulty Pronoun References

Most of the following sentences contain examples of ambiguous, general, weak, and indefinite references. Correctly rewrite each sentence that contains a faulty pronoun reference. Although sentences can be corrected in more than one way, you need to give only one revision for each. If a sentence is already correct, write *C.*

1. In the magazine article, they explain how microprocessors are used in the electrical stimulation of paralyzed muscles.
2. Lucia wrote to Sara every week while she was visiting her aunt and uncle in Guadalajara, Mexico.
3. The star of the play was sick, two other actors had not memorized their lines, and the stage manager was out of town. This caused the director to cancel rehearsals.
4. Zack likes to browse in music stores but seldom buys any of them.
5. In Massachusetts between 1659 and 1681, you could not legally celebrate Christmas.
6. The architect discussed with the contractor the changes she had just made on the blueprint.
7. We could not ride the mules to Phantom Ranch at the bottom of the Grand Canyon, which was disappointing.
8. Even though it is raining again, the state highway crew is working to repair the bridge.
9. When the ceramic bowl landed on the glass table, it shattered.
10. He told many of his own original jokes, one of which was about a penguin on its first visit to Times Square.
11. Aaron had not yet seen the new aerobics video, so he had a difficult time doing any of them.
12. On the radio program it gave the time for the rally.
13. Before buying a season ticket to the film society, Glenn checked the society's schedule for his favorite ones.
14. Annie revised the first two chapters of her novel. That made the development of the characters clearer.
15. At the skating rink they have ice skates for rent.

USAGE

┌─HELP─┐

Although
sentences in Parts B and C
of the Chapter Review can
be corrected in more than
one way, you need to give
only one revision for each.

B. Correcting Faulty Pronoun References

Most of the following sentences contain pronouns without clear antecedents. Revise each sentence to correct any unclear pronoun references. If a sentence is already correct, write *C*.

16. Ferris studied the poet T'ao Ch'ien in his world literature class.
17. T'ao Ch'ien loved to work in his garden, which is evident in his poetry.
18. T'ao Ch'ien's topics came from his own simple life. One of these was worrying about his five sons.
19. In our literature book it states that the Chinese consider Tu Fu to be their greatest poet.
20. Many people admire poetry, but most people don't think they can be used for medicinal purposes.
21. In this book, it has a story about Tu Fu suggesting that his poetry could cure malarial fever.
22. That more than a thousand of Tu Fu's poems survive is amazing.
23. The poet Li Po liked to travel and to enjoy nature. This gave him many subjects for his poetry but little family life.
24. Alicia explained the meaning of the Li Po poem she had read.
25. Jay liked Po Chu-i's poetry, and he wanted to memorize one.
26. Darnell described the tragic love story related in Po Chu-i's narrative poem *The Song of Everlasting Regret.* It went by very quickly.
27. The world literature course could only scratch the surface of Chinese literature, and Ferris wanted to read more of them.
28. Ms. Johnson said some famous Chinese works were available in translation, and this prompted Ferris to check the library for them.
29. Ferris met Darnell in the library, where he found a copy of *Dream of the Red Chamber.*
30. In *Dream of the Red Chamber* it tells the story of the decline of a family during the Ch'ing dynasty.

C. Revising a Paragraph to Correct Faulty Pronoun References

Revise the following paragraph to correct each unclear pronoun reference.

[31] The Millers went with the Ochoas to the Okefenokee Swamp when they were visiting. [32] The swamp covers a total area of about

684 square miles, which is amazing. [**33**] The Okefenokee is full of subtropical vegetation, and the two families saw quite a few of them. [**34**] In the information brochure, it stated that the swamp is a habitat for cypress trees, waterlilies, and brush vines. [**35**] The brochure also mentioned the swamp's connection to the Suwannee River and the Gulf of Mexico, into which it drains. [**36**] The Suwannee River has been an inspiration for many songwriters; two of these are Stephen Foster's "Old Folks at Home" and George Gershwin's "Swanee." [**37**] They say the name *Okefenokee* comes from an American Indian word meaning "trembling ground." [**38**] The Millers and Ochoas saw alligators in the water and flocks of birds flying overhead; they were delighted by this. [**39**] At one point, Lisa Ochoa called Suzette Miller's attention to a heron while she was looking into the distance. [**40**] The two families learned that most of the swamp has been designated as the Okefenokee National Wildlife Refuge to protect them.

Writing Application

Using Pronouns in Paragraphs

Clear Pronoun Reference   Your school's career counselor asks you to write about people you know who have different jobs. Making sure that your pronouns have clear and unambiguous references, write a paragraph about the jobs of three people you know.

Prewriting   Make a list of at least three people you know who have different sorts of jobs. Tell a little bit about each person, and describe what he or she does on the job.

Writing   While writing your first draft, be sure to include details that show how the jobs are different from each other.

Revising   Make sure that your rough draft shows a variety of jobs. If the jobs do not seem very different from each other, replace some examples or add new ones.

Publishing   Check for errors in grammar, usage, and mechanics. Make sure your pronoun references are clear. You and your classmates may want to read some of the paragraphs aloud in class and discuss how jobs differ from each other.

Using Verbs Correctly

Principal Parts, Tense, Voice, Mood

Diagnostic Preview

A. Proofreading Sentences for Verb Usage

Most of the following sentences contain awkward, informal, or incorrect verb usage. If a sentence has an awkward, informal, or incorrect usage, revise the sentence, using the verb form that is correct in formal, standard English. If a sentence is already correct, write *C*.

EXAMPLE **1.** If I would have seen the accident, I would certainly have reported it.

     1. If I had seen the accident, I would certainly have reported it.

1. According to this news article, the concert last Saturday night is "a resounding success."
2. According to the latest census, more than 39,000 American Indians had been currently living in Wisconsin.
3. How many of us possess the skills to have survived on our own without using store-bought items?
4. If you would have taken the nutrition class, you would have learned how to shop wisely for food.
5. Wacky, my pet hamster, was acting as if she were trying to tell me something.

6. Yesterday, Dad's pickup truck was washed and waxed by my brother.
7. If modern society was an agricultural one, more of us would know about farming and about the difficulties faced by farmers.
8. Last week's concert has broke all attendance records here.
9. Because of the excessive amount of rain this spring, the water in the dam has raised to a dangerous level.
10. Working in the garden earlier this morning, Jim is now laying down for a rest.

B. Proofreading Sentences for Verb Usage

Most of the following sentences contain errors in the use of verbs. If a sentence has a verb error, revise the sentence, using the correct verb form. If a sentence is already correct, write *C*.

EXAMPLE
   1. From our studies, we have concluded that women had played many critical roles in the history of our nation.

   1. From our studies, we have concluded that women have played many critical roles in the history of our nation.

11. In Daytona Beach, Florida, Mary McLeod Bethune founded a tiny school, which become Bethune-Cookman College.
12. Jane Addams founded Hull House in Chicago to educate the poor and to acquaint immigrants with American ways; for her efforts she had received the Nobel Prize for peace in 1931.
13. In 1932, Amelia Earhart flown solo across the Atlantic Ocean.
14. Pearl Buck, a recipient of the Nobel Prize for literature in 1938, seeked to bring understanding and peace to people all over the world.
15. In 1964, Margaret Chase Smith, a senator from Maine, received twenty-seven delegate votes for the presidential nomination.
16. Lorraine Hansberry wrote the successful play *A Raisin in the Sun*, which had already been translated into at least thirty languages.
17. Have you ever heard of Belva Lockwood, whose accomplishments paved the way for women in politics?
18. In 1879, a short time after Lockwood was admitted to the bar, she became the first female lawyer to argue a case before the United States Supreme Court.
19. Although her name is not well known now, Lockwood gotten more than four thousand votes for the presidency in 1884.
20. By the time you leave high school, you will learn many interesting facts about history.

Reference Note

Depending on how they are used, verbs may be classified as **transitive verbs** or **intransitive verbs,** as **action verbs** or **linking verbs,** and as **main verbs** or **helping verbs.** For a discussion of these different kinds of verbs, see page 13.

┌─**HELP**─┐

The words *is* and *have* are included in the chart to the right because the present participle and past participle verb forms require helping verbs (forms of *be* and *have*) to form tenses.

┌─**HELP**─┐

Sometimes the helping verb appears as part of a contraction.

EXAMPLES
He**'s** running late.
We**'ve** already ordered.

Reference Note

For more information on **infinitives,** see page 64.
For more information about **contractions,** see page 349.
For more about **passive voice,** see page 194.

The Principal Parts of Verbs

8a. The principal parts of a verb are the *base form,* the *present participle,* the *past,* and the *past participle.* All other verb forms are derived from these principal parts.

Base Form	Present Participle	Past	Past Participle
receive	[is] receiving	received	[have] received
join	[is] joining	joined	[have] joined
bring	[is] bringing	brought	[have] brought
sing	[is] singing	sang	[have] sung
hurt	[is] hurting	hurt	[have] hurt

NOTE Some teachers refer to the base form as the *infinitive.* Follow your teacher's directions when labeling this form.

When the present participle and past participle forms are used as verbs in sentences, they require helping verbs.

Helping Verb	+	Present Participle	=	Verb Phrase
forms of *be*	+	taking	=	am taking
		walking		was walking
		going		have been going

Helping Verb	+	Past Participle	=	Verb Phrase
forms of *have*	+	taken	=	have taken
		walked		has walked
		gone		had gone

NOTE Sometimes a past participle is used with a form of *be: was chosen, are known, is seen.* This use of the verb is called the *passive voice.*

All verbs form the present participle in the same way: by adding *−ing* to the base form. Not all verbs, however, form the past and past participle in the same way.

Regular Verbs

8b. A *regular verb* forms its past and past participle by adding –*d* or –*ed* to the base form.

Reference Note

Adding suffixes to the base forms of some verbs can pose spelling problems. For information on **adding suffixes,** see page 364.

Base Form	Present Participle	Past	Past Participle
use	[is] using	used	[have] used
revise	[is] revising	revised	[have] revised
outline	[is] outlining	outlined	[have] outlined
watch	[is] watching	watched	[have] watched
happen	[is] happening	happened	[have] happened
trim	[is] trimming	trimmed	[have] trimmed

A few regular verbs have alternative past and past participle forms ending in –*t*.

Base Form	Present Participle	Past	Past Participle
burn	[is] burning	burned *or* burnt	[have] burned *or* burnt
dream	[is] dreaming	dreamed *or* dreamt	[have] dreamed *or* dreamt
leap	[is] leaping	leaped *or* leapt	[have] leaped *or* leapt

NOTE The regular verbs *deal* and *mean* always form the past and past participle by adding –*t: dealt, (have) dealt; meant, (have) meant.*

When forming the past and past participle of regular verbs, avoid omitting the –*d* or –*ed* ending. Pay particular attention to the forms of the verbs *ask, attack, drown, prejudice, risk, suppose,* and *use.*

Reference Note

For a discussion of **standard and nonstandard English,** see page 241.

NONSTANDARD	The firefighter risk his life to save the valuable artifacts.
STANDARD	The firefighter **risked** his life to save the valuable artifacts.

NONSTANDARD	We should have ask for directions.
STANDARD	We should have **asked** for directions.

USAGE

8 a, b

Exercise 1 Using Regular Verbs

For each of the following sentences, give the correct past or past participle form of the verb in parentheses.

EXAMPLE 1. As a rule, electronic equipment should be (*clean*) regularly.

1. *cleaned*

1. Haven't you ever (*bake*) clams on the beach before?
2. The rangers had often (*walk*) the five miles from their station down to the lodge.
3. By the end of the carnival, we will have (*raise*) more than ten thousand dollars.
4. You should have (*stir*) that lime sauce; now it has lumps in it.
5. Henry Ossawa Tanner (*paint*) Biblical subjects as well as everyday scenes from African Americans' lives.
6. For our service project this semester, our club (*remove*) the graffiti from the park walls.
7. Because the dates of the holidays often are (*print*) in red on calendars, we have the expression "red-letter day."
8. My grades in speech went up after I (*tape*) myself and then played the tape back to study my delivery.
9. The Sioux leader Sitting Bull had (*emerge*) victorious at the Battle of Little Bighorn.
10. One of the American Dance Theater's artistic directors, José Arcadio Limón, was born in Mexico; he (*dance*) his way to success.

Irregular Verbs

8c. An *irregular verb* forms its past and past participle in some other way than by adding *–d* or *–ed* to the base form.

The best way to learn the principal parts of irregular verbs is to memorize them. No single usage rule applies to the different ways that these verbs form the past and past participle. However, there are some general guidelines that you can use. Irregular verbs form the past and past participle in one of these ways:

- changing vowels
- changing consonants
- changing vowels and consonants
- making no change

┌HELP──

When you are not sure whether a verb is regular or irregular, look it up in a dictionary. Entries for irregular verbs generally list the principal parts.

Base Form	Present Participle	Past	Past Participle
swim	[is] swimming	swam	[have] swum
bend	[is] bending	bent	[have] bent
teach	[is] teaching	taught	[have] taught
burst	[is] bursting	burst	[have] burst

When forming the past and the past participle of irregular verbs, avoid these common errors:

(1) using the past form with a helping verb

NONSTANDARD   I have never swam in this lake before.
STANDARD   I never **swam** in this lake before.

(2) using the past participle form without a helping verb

NONSTANDARD   She swum to shore to get help.
STANDARD   She **has swum** to shore to get help.

(3) adding –d, –ed, or –t to the base form

NONSTANDARD   We bursted into laughter as soon as we saw the comedian.
STANDARD   We **burst** into laughter as soon as we saw the comedian.

Common Irregular Verbs

Group I: Each of these irregular verbs has the same form for its past and past participle.

Base Form	Present Participle	Past	Past Participle
bind	[is] binding	bound	[have] bound
bring	[is] bringing	brought	[have] brought
build	[is] building	built	[have] built
buy	[is] buying	bought	[have] bought
catch	[is] catching	caught	[have] caught
creep	[is] creeping	crept	[have] crept
feel	[is] feeling	felt	[have] felt
fight	[is] fighting	fought	[have] fought

(continued)

STYLE TIP

Some verbs have two correct past or past participle forms. However, these forms are not always interchangeable.

EXAMPLES
He **shone** the candle into the cellar. [*Shined* would also be correct.]

I **shined** my shoes. [*Shone* would be incorrect in this usage.]

If you are unsure about which past participle to use, check an up-to-date dictionary.

(continued)

Common Irregular Verbs

Group I: Each of these irregular verbs has the same form for its past and past participle.

Base Form	Present Participle	Past	Past Participle
find	[is] finding	found	[have] found
fling	[is] flinging	flung	[have] flung
have	[is] having	had	[have] had
hear	[is] hearing	heard	[have] heard
hold	[is] holding	held	[have] held
keep	[is] keeping	kept	[have] kept
lay	[is] laying	laid	[have] laid
lead	[is] leading	led	[have] led
leave	[is] leaving	left	[have] left
lend	[is] lending	lent	[have] lent
light	[is] lighting	lit *or* lighted	[have] lit *or* lighted
lose	[is] losing	lost	[have] lost
make	[is] making	made	[have] made
meet	[is] meeting	met	[have] met
pay	[is] paying	paid	[have] paid
say	[is] saying	said	[have] said
seek	[is] seeking	sought	[have] sought
sell	[is] selling	sold	[have] sold
send	[is] sending	sent	[have] sent
sit	[is] sitting	sat	[have] sat
spend	[is] spending	spent	[have] spent
spin	[is] spinning	spun	[have] spun
stand	[is] standing	stood	[have] stood
sting	[is] stinging	stung	[have] stung
swing	[is] swinging	swung	[have] swung
teach	[is] teaching	taught	[have] taught
tell	[is] telling	told	[have] told
think	[is] thinking	thought	[have] thought
win	[is] winning	won	[have] won

Exercise 2 Using the Past and Past Participle Forms of Irregular Verbs

For each of the following sentences, give the correct past or past participle form of the verb in parentheses.

EXAMPLE **1.** Bob and Terri have (*lead*) our class in math scores for two years.

    1. led

1. The movie monster (*swing*) around and lurched into the woods.
2. Have you (*teach*) your little brother Stephano how to throw a curveball yet?
3. Mrs. Torres (*tell*) us yesterday that Mexican ballads are called *corridos*.
4. Ever since we met last year, Kitty and I have (*sit*) together in assembly.
5. When Larry and Dana got to the new video store at the mall, you had just (*leave*).
6. Unfortunately, Darlene has already (*spend*) most of her weekly allowance.
7. In an earlier scene, Tarzan had (*catch*) hold of a vine and used it to swing through the trees.
8. Those two paintings by Horace Pippin really (*hold*) our interest.
9. Not only had he juggled six oranges, but he had also (*spin*) two plates on sticks.
10. The tiger-striped cat (*creep*) down the hallway and into the room.

Exercise 3 Using the Past and Past Participle Forms of Irregular Verbs Correctly

Many people like to play with the English language. Some enjoy word games. Some, like the author of the following silly poem, break the rules of standard usage just for fun. Each couplet in the poem contains an incorrect past or past participle form of an irregular verb. For each incorrect form shown in italics, provide the correct form.

EXAMPLE   Bake, baked; make, **[1]** *maked*? Hold it—not so fast!
    Verbs that rhyme in the present may not rhyme in the past!

    1. made

Today we fling the same old ball that yesterday we flung;
Today we bring the same good news that yesterday we **[1]** *brung*.

And we still mind our parents, the folks we've always minded;
And I may find a dime, just like the dime you **[2]** *finded*.

┌─ H E L P ─
The poem in Exercise 3 will no longer rhyme when it is corrected.

I smell the crimson rose, the very rose you smelled;
I tell a silly joke today, the same joke you once [3] *telled.*

You grin to hear me tell it now, just as last week you grinned;
You win our game of checkers, just as last week you [4] *winned.*

I peek into your closet now, and yesterday I peeked;
I seek my birthday present, as every year I've [5] *seeked.*

You reach to take my hand in yours; it was not I who reached;
You teach me to be friendly, as always you have [6] *teached.*

I beep my horn to warn you; I'm sure my horn just beeped;
I keep all my appointments, the ones I should have [7] *keeped.*

I scream all day, I yell all night, I've screamed and I have yelled
To sell all my newspapers, and today's batch I have [8] *selled.*

I wink my eye at you today, as yesterday I winked;
I think I like you very much, as yesterday I [9] *thinked.*

I lose my train of thought sometimes; my train of thought I've [10] *losed.*
But I can use my verbs with care; just see the ones I've used!

HELP

Notice that several of these verbs have alternate past or past participle forms.

Common Irregular Verbs

Group II: Most of these irregular verbs have different forms for their past and past participles.

Base Form	Present Participle	Past	Past Participle
arise	[is] arising	arose	[have] arisen
be	[is] being	was, were	[have] been
bear	[is] bearing	bore	[have] borne *or* born
beat	[is] beating	beat	[have] beaten *or* beat
become	[is] becoming	became	[have] become
begin	[is] beginning	began	[have] begun
bite	[is] biting	bit	[have] bitten *or* bit
blow	[is] blowing	blew	[have] blown
break	[is] breaking	broke	[have] broken
choose	[is] choosing	chose	[have] chosen
come	[is] coming	came	[have] come
dive	[is] diving	dove *or* dived	[have] dived

Common Irregular Verbs

Group II: Most of these irregular verbs have different forms for their past and past participles.

Base Form	Present Participle	Past	Past Participle
do	[is] doing	did	[have] done
draw	[is] drawing	drew	[have] drawn
drink	[is] drinking	drank	[have] drunk
drive	[is] driving	drove	[have] driven
eat	[is] eating	ate	[have] eaten
fall	[is] falling	fell	[have] fallen
fly	[is] flying	flew	[have] flown
forbid	[is] forbidding	forbade *or* forbad	[have] forbidden *or* forbid
forget	[is] forgetting	forgot	[have] forgotten *or* forgot
forgive	[is] forgiving	forgave	[have] forgiven
forsake	[is] forsaking	forsook	[have] forsaken
freeze	[is] freezing	froze	[have] frozen
get	[is] getting	got	[have] gotten *or* got
give	[is] giving	gave	[have] given
go	[is] going	went	[have] gone
grow	[is] growing	grew	[have] grown
hide	[is] hiding	hid	[have] hidden *or* hid
know	[is] knowing	knew	[have] known
lie	[is] lying	lay	[have] lain
ride	[is] riding	rode	[have] ridden
ring	[is] ringing	rang	[have] rung
rise	[is] rising	rose	[have] risen
run	[is] running	ran	[have] run
see	[is] seeing	saw	[have] seen
shake	[is] shaking	shook	[have] shaken
show	[is] showing	showed	[have] showed *or* shown
shrink	[is] shrinking	shrank *or* shrunk	[have] shrunk

USAGE

(continued)

Common Irregular Verbs

Group II: Most of these irregular verbs have different forms for their past and past participles.

Base Form	Present Participle	Past	Past Participle
sing	[is] singing	sang	[have] sung
sink	[is] sinking	sank *or* sunk	[have] sunk
slay	[is] slaying	slew	[have] slain
speak	[is] speaking	spoke	[have] spoken
spring	[is] springing	sprang *or* sprung	[have] sprung
steal	[is] stealing	stole	[have] stolen
strike	[is] striking	struck	[have] struck *or* stricken
strive	[is] striving	strove *or* strived	[have] striven *or* strived
swear	[is] swearing	swore	[have] sworn
swim	[is] swimming	swam	[have] swum
take	[is] taking	took	[have] taken
tear	[is] tearing	tore	[have] torn
throw	[is] throwing	threw	[have] thrown
wake	[is] waking	waked *or* woke	[have] waked *or* woken
wear	[is] wearing	wore	[have] worn
weave	[is] weaving	wove *or* weaved	[have] woven *or* weaved
write	[is] writing	wrote	[have] written

Exercise 4   Using the Past and Past Participle Forms of Irregular Verbs

For each of the following sentences, give the correct past or past participle form of the verb in parentheses.

EXAMPLE   **1.** Aunt Barbara (*freeze*) fourteen pints of corn.

     1. *froze*

1. Your friends have (*come*) to see you.
2. He (*do*) his best on the PSAT last Saturday.

3. Elizabeth has finally (*begin*) to understand the value of proofreading.
4. One of the poems I had (*choose*) to read was "Out of the Cradle Endlessly Rocking."
5. The tour group had (*see*) the ancient Pueblo dwellings.
6. Strong winds (*drive*) the Dutch galleon off its course.
7. The silence was (*break*) by a sudden clap of thunder.
8. West Side High's team easily (*beat*) its opponents.
9. Miguel (*blow*) up balloons and made decorations for his sister's *quinceañera* party, the celebration of her fifteenth birthday.
10. How long had the treasure (*lie*) undiscovered?

Review A **Using the Past and Past Participle Forms of Irregular Verbs Correctly**

In the following paragraph, decide whether each italicized verb form is correct. If it is not, give the correct verb form. If a verb form is correct, write *C*.

EXAMPLE   Even as a child, Midori never **[1]** *shrinked* from an audience.
            1. *shrank*

If you have [1] *seen* the maturity and intensity of performances by the young woman shown to the right, you know firsthand that she has [2] *stealed* the hearts of many music lovers. More than once, excited fans [3] *brung* down the house with applause and [4] *throwed* bouquets of roses at her feet. In fact, Midori has [5] *knew* the joys and struggles of being a professional concert violinist ever since she was a young girl. Whenever she has [6] *spoke* to the press, Midori has always [7] *showed* an out-going and unaffected personality. Her violin teacher at the Juilliard School, Dorothy DeLay, also [8] *taught* such stars as Itzhak Perlman and Joshua Bell. When Midori was eleven, the famous conductor Zubin Mehta [9] *lead* her onstage as a surprise guest soloist with the New York Philharmonic. Ever since, Midori has [10] *finded* the concert hall a wonderful place; in fact, she says that she loves being there, whether she is on the stage by herself or with an orchestra.

Common Irregular Verbs			
Group III: Each of these irregular verbs has the same form for its base form, past, and past participle.			
Base Form	**Present Participle**	**Past**	**Past Participle**
burst	[is] bursting	burst	[have] burst
cost	[is] costing	cost	[have] cost
cut	[is] cutting	cut	[have] cut
hit	[is] hitting	hit	[have] hit
hurt	[is] hurting	hurt	[have] hurt
let	[is] letting	let	[have] let
put	[is] putting	put	[have] put
read	[is] reading	read	[have] read
set	[is] setting	set	[have] set
spread	[is] spreading	spread	[have] spread

Exercise 5 **Using the Past and Past Participle Forms of Irregular Verbs Correctly**

Most of the following sentences contain an incorrect verb form. If a verb form is incorrect, give the correct form. If a sentence is already correct, write *C*.

EXAMPLE   1. The concert ticket costed thirty dollars.

    1. cost

1. The crowded roots of the plant had bursted the ceramic flowerpot.
2. Nancy carefully sat the antipasto salad in the center of the dining table.
3. After we've cut the grass, we'll weed the garden.
4. The angry hornet stung me right on the end of my nose, and it hurted all afternoon.
5. Hasan spreaded his pita bread with a thick layer of tasty hummus.
6. Where have I putted my notebook?
7. You must have read the assignment too quickly.
8. As soon as the robin was well, we letted it go free.
9. How much money has owning a car costed you this year?
10. Both Felina and Fernanda hitted home runs in last week's game.

The following paragraph contains ten numbered blanks. For each blank, choose an appropriate verb from the box below and give the correct past or past participle form of the verb.

become	creep	make	spin
begin	find	see	spread
bring	let	seek	think

EXAMPLE   Suppose you were a farmer, and one morning you went out to your fields and **[1]** _____ a 300-foot-long pattern of circles and lines in the middle of your crops!

1. *found*

Many circular flattened areas like these **[1]** _____ to appear in fields across southern England in the late 1970s. The phenomenon soon **[2]** _____ one of the most popular mysteries the world had ever known. People calling themselves "cereologists" insisted that no human being could have **[3]** _____ these unusual patterns. The idea quickly **[4]** _____ that the circles were the landing spots of UFOs that had **[5]** _____ visitors from space. Respected scientists **[6]** _____ that the weird designs resulted from ball lightning, whirling columns of air, or other strange weather conditions. When it was reported that circle researchers had **[7]** _____ public funding, two British landscape painters came forward with the truth. David Chorley and Douglas Bower confessed that they had **[8]** _____ into the fields at night with a ball of twine and a wooden plank and had **[9]** _____ the plank in a circle to create the flattened areas of grain. Before Chorley and Bower spoke up, millions of people had **[10]** _____ themselves believe that the crop circles were formed by extraterrestrials—and even now, thousands of diehards still do.

Review C **Using the Past and Past Participle Forms of Irregular Verbs**

For each of the sentences on the next page, give the correct past or past participle form of the verb in parentheses.

USAGE

EXAMPLE   1. The pitcher (*strike*) out eleven batters in a row.

   1. struck

 1. Has Chelsea ever (*read*) anything by Gwendolyn Brooks, the poet laureate of Illinois?
 2. We (*drink*) tomato juice with last night's dinner.
 3. How many of you (*see*) Fernando Valenzuela pitch?
 4. I thought my skates had been (*steal*), but then I finally found them.
 5. He had (*write*) a play about his experience in Vietnam.
 6. Garrett's dad has (*sing*) in a barbershop quartet for years.
 7. If they had not (*cost*) so much, we would have bought one for everyone in the family.
 8. Some of the authors who had been scorned ten years earlier had (*become*) quite popular.
 9. Don't you think that the dough for the bread has (*rise*) enough to bake?
10. Mary says she has never (*ride*) on a roller coaster.
11. Have you ever (*fly*) a Japanese dragon kite?
12. I shivered and (*shake*) after I dented the front fender of Mom's car.
13. When Mrs. Isayama called my name, I (*swing*) around.
14. Have you (*forgive*) Christy for playing that practical joke on Marcia and you?
15. Wanda (*burst*) into the room to greet her friends.
16. Yesterday, Nguyen and I each (*hit*) about two hundred tennis balls.
17. Darius had (*fall*) as he went in for the layup.
18. The government class has (*go*) to observe the city council in session.
19. I was not aware that the telephone had (*ring*).
20. Have you (*have*) a taste of that delicious pea soup yet?

Review D   Using the Past and Past Participle Forms of Irregular Verbs Correctly

For each of the following sentences, decide whether the italicized verb form is correct. If it is not, give the correct verb form. If a sentence is already correct, write *C*.

EXAMPLE   1. When the bagger at the supermarket asked me whether I wanted paper or plastic bags, I *telled* her, "Paper, please."

   1. told

 1. American shoppers have certainly *grew* accustomed to the convenience of paper grocery bags.

2. In recent years, many Americans have *went* right on using them—at the rate of forty billion bags a year!

3. Have you ever *thinked* about the history of the standard flat-bottomed grocery bag with pleated sides?

4. Someone must have *cutted* out and pasted together the first flat-bottomed paper bag.

5. Actually, I have *read* that the inventor of these bags was a man named Charles Stilwell.

6. After he had *fighted* in the Civil War, he returned home and began to tinker with inventions.

7. He created a machine to fold and glue brown paper into bags, a job that had previously been *did* by hand.

8. Earlier bags had V-shaped bottoms, which meant that they had not *standed* up by themselves.

9. I have certainly *putted* Charles Stilwell's bags to good use in my after-school supermarket job.

10. Many other everyday items that we have always *took* for granted, such as safety pins and eyeglasses, have interesting histories, too.

Review E **Proofreading Sentences for Correct Verb Forms**

For the following sentences, give the correct form for each incorrect verb form. If a sentence is already correct, write *C*.

EXAMPLE
1. When my art class went to the Museum of African American Art, I seen some collages that Romare Bearden had maked.

1. *saw; made*

1. Seeing the unusual medium of collage has leaded me to think about art in a new way.

2. Bearden growed up in North Carolina and then spended time studying in New York, Pittsburgh, and Paris.

3. His art career begun in the 1930s, and he soon gotten a reputation as a leading abstract artist.

4. Instead of specializing in painting or drawing, Bearden finded his niche in the somewhat unusual medium of collage.

Blue Interior, Morning by Romare Bearden, 1968. Collage on board, 44" x 56". Collection of the Chase Manhattan Bank / Courtesy the Estate of Romare Bearden.

5. He fashioned his works of art out of pieces of colored paper that had been cutted or teared into small shapes.

6. Often, he gave his collages more variety by using pieces from black-and-white or color photographs.

7. If you examine his *Blue Interior, Morning,* you can see that Bearden built this composition around a family eating breakfast.

8. The materials that he assembled were chose for their textural harmony and for their ability to be woven into the color scheme.

9. In his work, Bearden often depicted universal human figures whose complex nature is clearly showed by their different-colored fingers or legs.

10. I could have swore it was nearly impossible to create a pleasing composition with all the figures way down in one corner, but Bearden certainly succeeded.

Review F Proofreading a Paragraph for the Correct Use of Irregular Verbs

Most of the sentences in the following paragraph contain an error in the use of irregular verbs. If a verb form is incorrect, give the correct form. If a sentence is already correct, write *C.*

EXAMPLE   [1] Thanks to James Beckwourth, crossing the Sierra Nevada becomed easier for wagon trains traveling to California.

   1. became

[1] Pioneers on their way to California had always losed much time when they hit the rugged Sierra Nevada. [2] Wagon trains had turned and drived many miles out of their way, searching for a trail their oxen and horses could take through these mountains. [3] Then James Beckwourth, a frontiersman and explorer, finded an important route between the forbidding peaks. [4] Beckwourth Pass is shown on the map on this page. [5] Other routes, including Donner Pass, had already been discovered, but soon wagonmasters seen that Beckwourth Pass was the lowest in elevation and, therefore, the easiest to cross. [6] James Beckwourth was a versatile man; he been a trapper, trader, explorer, and mountain man. [7] He even fighted in the Second Seminole War as an army scout. [8] During the Gold Rush, he caught gold fever and spended some time prospecting in California. [9] Beckwourth always gotten along quite well with many American Indians—especially the Crow people, who adopted him. [10] By the end of his life, he had became such a good friend to the Crow that they gave him the chance to be a chief!

Most of the sentences in the following paragraph have one or more errors in verb usage. For each error, write the correct form of the verb. If a sentence is already correct, write *C*. Be prepared to explain your answers.

EXAMPLE
[1] As a child, Frida Kahlo often thinked she would become an explorer.

1. *thought*

┌─**HELP**─
In the example, the past tense of *think* is *thought*.

[1] You have probably saw pictures of murals painted by Diego Rivera, the famous Mexican painter. [2] However, you may have never came across paintings by Frida Kahlo, his wife. [3] Kahlo was a powerful painter in her own right, although she often standed in the shadow of her more renowned husband. [4] She taked up painting during her recovery from a streetcar accident in which she had broke several bones. [5] Other medical problems arised from time to time throughout her life, and though sometimes she had to paint from her wheelchair, Kahlo always painted straight from her heart. [6] In fact, she gave this figure of speech literal expression in one of her paintings, in which she portrays herself using a heart as her palette. [7] Kahlo never forgetted her childhood dream of exploration, and, instead of seas and mountains, she explored the territory of the human spirit.[8] Frida Kahlo striked people who met her as an elegant, intense, and talented woman. [9] Although she sometimes found life painful, she was full of fun, high spirits, and love. [10] Kahlo is especially noted for her self-portraits, in which she sometimes choosed to paint herself with a tiny portrait of Rivera on her forehead, as in the painting shown here.

Frida Kahlo (1907–54), *Self Portrait as a Tehuana (Diego on my mind)*. Oil on canvas (29 ⅞" x 24") (76 cm x 61 cm). Private collection, Mexico City. Photo courtesy of The Metropolitan Museum of Art.

Six Troublesome Verbs

Lie and Lay

The verb *lie* means "to rest," "to recline," or "to be in a place." *Lie* does not take an object. The verb *lay* means "to put [something] in a place." *Lay* generally takes an object.

STYLE · TIP

The verb *lie* has definitions other than the ones given here. One common definition is "to tell an untruth."

EXAMPLE
Don't **lie** to them, Irena.

In this use, *lie* does not take an object.

Base Form	Present Participle	Past	Past Participle
lie	[is] lying	lay	[have] lain
lay	[is] laying	laid	[have] laid

EXAMPLES   The printout **is lying** there next to the computer. [no object]

The secretary **is laying** a copy of the printout next to the computer. [*Copy* is the object of *is laying*.]

The holiday decorations **lay** in the box. [no object]

Martha carefully **laid** the holiday decorations in the box. [*Decorations* is the object of *laid*.]

My basset hound **has lain** in front of the fireplace since early this morning. [no object]

My basset hound **has laid** my slippers in front of the fireplace. [*Slippers* is the object of *has laid*.]

Exercise 6   **Choosing the Forms of *Lie* and *Lay***

For each of the following sentences, choose the correct verb form in parentheses. Be prepared to explain your choices.

EXAMPLE   1. The workers are (*laying, lying*) the planks down.

1. *laying*

HELP

The meaning of the verb in the example sentence is "to put"; therefore, the correct verb is *lay*, and the answer is *laying*.

1. The old stereoscope had (*lain, laid*) in the attic for years.
2. The interstate you want to take (*lays, lies*) north of town.
3. The rake is (*laying, lying*) in a pile of leaves.
4. Where has Roger (*laid, lain*) the keys this time?
5. Judy and Adrian (*lay, laid*) their books on the table.
6. She read *The Awakening* as she (*laid, lay*) in the hammock.
7. The key to success (*lays, lies*) in determination.
8. (*Lie, Lay*) here and relax before going on.
9. Ms. Collins (*laid, lay*) the study guides on the table.
10. I was (*laying, lying*) my beach towel on the sand just then.

Exercise 7   **Writing Sentences Using the Forms of *Lie* and *Lay***

For each numbered item, use the given subject and verb form to write a correct sentence. Be sure to add an object for forms of *lay*. For participle forms, you will need to give helping verbs. When two forms are spelled the same, the information in parentheses tells you which form and meaning to use.

EXAMPLE

SUBJECT	VERB FORM
1. package	lying

1. *The package was lying on the doormat when we got home.*

SUBJECT	VERB FORM
1. detectives	lay (base form meaning "put")
2. sparrow	laid (past form meaning "placed [something]")
3. father	laying
4. dog	lain
5. children	lie
6. butler	laid (past participle meaning "placed [something]")
7. Mr. Hill	lay (past form meaning "rested or reclined")
8. books	lying
9. Miami	lies
10. mechanic	lays

Sit and Set

The verb *sit* means "to be in a seated, upright position" or "to be in a place." *Sit* seldom takes an object. The verb *set* means "to put [something] in a place." *Set* generally takes an object.

Base Form	Present Participle	Past	Past Participle
sit	[is] sitting	sat	[have] sat
set	[is] setting	set	[have] set

EXAMPLES

May I **sit** here? [no object]

May I **set** the chair here? [*Chair* is the object of *May set.*]

The candles **sat** on the piano, where Karen left them. [no object]

Karen **set** the candles on the piano. [*Candles* is the object of *set.*]

The squirrel **has sat** on the sill awhile. [no object]

The squirrel **has set** a pecan on the sill. [*Pecan* is the object of *has set.*]

STYLE TIP

The verb *set* has definitions other than the one given here.

EXAMPLE

The sun **sets** in the west.

In this use, *set* does not take an object.

Exercise 8 Using the Forms of *Sit* and *Set*

Complete each of the following sentences by using the correct form of *sit* or *set*.

EXAMPLE
1. Carrie is _____ in the rocking chair and reading the newspaper.

1. *sitting*

1. I _____ in the doctor's waiting room for an hour yesterday morning.
2. Yesterday, we _____ the seedlings on a table on the back porch.
3. _____ the carton down near the door.
4. We were _____ so high up in the theater that the stage looked no bigger than a postage stamp.
5. If we had _____ any longer, we would have been late for class.
6. Let's _____ that pot of hot-and-sour soup on the buffet.
7. Jonathan is _____ aside five dollars each week to buy a CD player.
8. You shouldn't _____ on the damp ground.
9. I hope that Trish and Brandon haven't _____ those plants too close to the radiator.
10. We have _____ around the campfire a long while.

Rise and *Raise*

The verb *rise* means "to go up" or "to get up." *Rise* does not take an object. The verb *raise* means "to lift up" or "to cause [something] to rise." *Raise* generally takes an object.

Base Form	Present Participle	Past	Past Participle
rise	[is] rising	rose	[have] risen
raise	[is] raising	raised	[have] raised

EXAMPLES
She **rose** from the chair uncertainly. [no object]

She **raised** herself from the chair uncertainly. [*Herself* is the object of *raised.*]

The prices of fresh fruit and vegetables **have risen** considerably because of the drought. [no object]

The grocer **has raised** the price of fresh fruit and vegetables. [*Price* is the object of *has raised.*]

STYLE TIP

The verb *raise* has definitions other than the one given here. Another common definition is "to grow" or "to bring to maturity."

EXAMPLES
They **raise** sorghum.

She **raised** two foster children.

Notice that both of these uses also take an object.

Exercise 9 Using *Rise* and *Raise* Correctly

For each of the following sentences, decide whether the italicized verb form is correct. If it is not, give the correct verb form. If a sentence is already correct, write *C*.

EXAMPLE 1. Everyone *raised* for the pledge of allegiance.
    1. *rose*

1. The cost of a ticket to see a LeAnn Rimes concert *has raised*.
2. The student council president *had risen* the new flag.
3. The Bunsen burner flame *has raised* too high.
4. While fishing with my uncle Etienne in Louisiana, I saw an alligator slowly *raise* out of the mud.
5. The curling smoke *risen* from the pile of leaves.
6. The campers *had rose* early to climb Pikes Peak.
7. The woman who *is rising* now to address the audience has been nominated for vice-president.
8. *Has* the price of gasoline *raised*?
9. The price of a dozen eggs *has been raised*, but you can use this coupon.
10. *Has* the popularity of video games *risen*?

Review H Choosing the Forms of *Lie* and *Lay*, *Sit* and *Set*, and *Rise* and *Raise*

For each of the following sentences, choose the correct verb form in parentheses. Be prepared to explain your choices.

EXAMPLE 1. I think I will (*lay, lie*) here and rest awhile.
    1. *lie*

1. They (*sit, set*) the yearbooks in Mr. Cohen's office.
2. The thermostat should have kept the temperature from (*rising, raising*).
3. Where was Emily (*sitting, setting*) at the end of *Our Town*?
4. Has the number of traffic fatalities (*raised, risen*)?
5. San Francisco (*lays, lies*) southwest of Sacramento.
6. Let's (*set, sit*) down and talk about the problem.
7. The price of citrus fruit (*rises, raises*) after a freeze.
8. Hours of driving (*lay, laid*) ahead of us.
9. A replica of Rodin's *The Thinker* had (*set, sat*) there.
10. The helium-filled balloon (*rose, raised*) into the air.

HELP
The meaning of the verb in the example is "to recline"; therefore, the correct verb is *lie*.

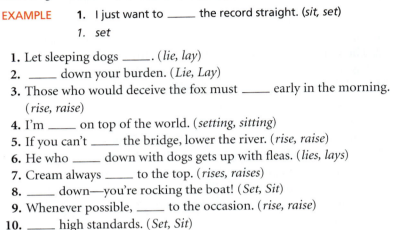

Choosing the Forms of *Lie* and *Lay*, *Sit* and *Set*, and *Rise* and *Raise*

Many familiar expressions and sayings include a form of *lie, lay, sit, set, rise,* or *raise.* Read aloud each expression below, and complete it by choosing the correct form from the pair given.

EXAMPLE   **1.** I just want to _____ the record straight. (*sit, set*)

    1. set

1. Let sleeping dogs _____. (*lie, lay*)
2. _____ down your burden. (*Lie, Lay*)
3. Those who would deceive the fox must _____ early in the morning. (*rise, raise*)
4. I'm _____ on top of the world. (*setting, sitting*)
5. If you can't _____ the bridge, lower the river. (*rise, raise*)
6. He who _____ down with dogs gets up with fleas. (*lies, lays*)
7. Cream always _____ to the top. (*rises, raises*)
8. _____ down—you're rocking the boat! (*Set, Sit*)
9. Whenever possible, _____ to the occasion. (*rise, raise*)
10. _____ high standards. (*Set, Sit*)

Tense

8d. The ***tense*** of a verb indicates the time of the action or of the state of being expressed by the verb.

The tenses are formed from the verb's principal parts. Verbs in English have the six tenses shown on the following time line:

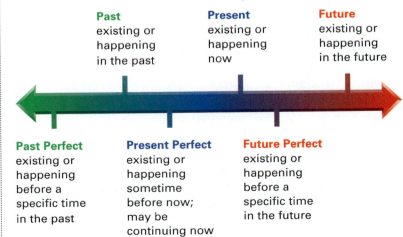

Past
existing or happening in the past

Present
existing or happening now

Future
existing or happening in the future

Past Perfect
existing or happening before a specific time in the past

Present Perfect
existing or happening sometime before now; may be continuing now

Future Perfect
existing or happening before a specific time in the future

Verb Conjugation

Listing all of the forms of a verb according to tense is called *conjugating* a verb.

Conjugation of the Verb *See* in the Active Voice	
Present Tense	
Singular	**Plural**
I see	we see
you see	you see
he, she, it sees	they see
Past Tense	
Singular	**Plural**
I saw	we saw
you saw	you saw
he, she, it saw	they saw
Future Tense	
Singular	**Plural**
I will (shall) see	we will (shall) see
you will (shall) see	you will (shall) see
he, she, it will (shall) see	they will (shall) see
Present Perfect Tense	
Singular	**Plural**
I have seen	we have seen
you have seen	you have seen
he, she, it has seen	they have seen
Past Perfect Tense	
Singular	**Plural**
I had seen	we had seen
you had seen	you had seen
he, she, it had seen	they had seen

(continued)

Reference Note

For a **conjugation of *see* in the passive voice,** see page 194.

STYLE TIP

Traditionally, the helping verbs *shall* and *will* were used to mean different things. Now, however, *shall* can be used almost interchangeably with *will*.

(continued)

Conjugation of the Verb *See* in the Active Voice	
Future Perfect Tense	
Singular	**Plural**
I will (shall) have seen	we will (shall) have seen
you will (shall) have seen	you will (shall) have seen
he, she, it will (shall) have seen	they will (shall) have seen

MEETING THE CHALLENGE

Today, *shall* and *will* are nearly interchangeable. You probably use *shall* only in the most formal situations or perhaps when you want to mimic elevated diction for comic effect. In the past, however, *shall* was used in many situations. Using the library or the Internet, find out what rules used to govern *shall* and *will*. Write a few sample sentences using the old rules. Why, in your opinion, did these rules die out?

The Progressive Form

Each of the tenses has an additional form, called the **progressive form,** which expresses continuing action or state of being. It consists of the appropriate tense of *be* plus the present participle of a verb. The progressive form is not a separate tense but another form of each of the six tenses.

Present Progressive	am, is, are seeing
Past Progressive	was, were seeing
Future Progressive	will (shall) be seeing
Present Perfect Progressive	has been, have been seeing
Past Perfect Progressive	had been seeing
Future Perfect Progressive	will (shall) have been seeing

The Emphatic Form

The present and past tenses have another form, called the **emphatic form,** which shows emphasis. In the present tense, the emphatic form of a verb consists of *do* or *does* plus the base form. In the past tense, the emphatic form consists of *did* plus the base form.

Present Emphatic	do, does see
Past Emphatic	did see

S T Y L E   T I P

The emphatic form is also used in questions and in negative statements. These uses do not place any special emphasis on the verb.

QUESTION
Do you **know** him?

NEGATIVE STATEMENT
They **don't** [**do** not] **have** any.

The Verb *Be*

The verb *be* is the most irregular verb in English. The chart on the following pages gives the conjugation of *be*.

Conjugation of the Verb *Be*

Present Tense

Singular	Plural
I am	we are
you are	you are
he, she, it is	they are

Present Progressive: am, are, is being

Past Tense

Singular	Plural
I was	we were
you were	you were
he, she, it was	they were

Past Progressive: was, were being

Future Tense

Singular	Plural
I will (shall) be	we will (shall) be
you will (shall) be	you will (shall) be
he, she, it will (shall) be	they will (shall) be

Present Perfect Tense

Singular	Plural
I have been	we have been
you have been	you have been
he, she, it has been	they have been

Past Perfect Tense

Singular	Plural
I had been	we had been
you had been	you had been
he, she, it had been	they had been

(continued)

(continued)

Conjugation of the Verb *Be*	
Future Perfect Tense	
Singular	**Plural**
I will (shall) have been	we will (shall) have been
you will (shall) have been	you will (shall) have been
he, she, it will (shall) have been	they will (shall) have been

The conjugation of the verb *be* differs from that of any other verb. The progressive form of *be* is rarely used in any tenses other than the present and past tenses, and none of the tenses have the emphatic form.

The Uses of the Tenses

8e. Each of the six tenses has its own uses.

(1) The *present tense* expresses an action or a state of being that is occurring now, at the present time.

EXAMPLES Martina **races** down the court and **shoots** the ball. [present]

The fans **are cheering** wildly. [present progressive]

Martina and her teammates **do look** confident. [present emphatic]

The present tense is also used

- to show customary or habitual action or state of being
- to convey a general truth—something that is always true
- to summarize the plot or subject matter of a literary work (such use is called *literary present*)
- to make a historical event seem current (such use is called *historical present*)
- to express future time

EXAMPLES On Saturdays I usually **go** to the tennis court and **practice** my serve. [customary action]

The gravity of the moon **pulls** on the earth's oceans and **causes** the tides. [general truth]

USAGE

The Dark Child **relates** the experiences of a boy growing up in an African village. [literary present]

In a surprise move, the Greeks **construct** a huge wooden horse and **leave** it outside the walls of Troy. [historical present]

The tournament that **starts** next Thursday **continues** for two weeks. [future time]

(2) The *past tense* expresses an action or a state of being that occurred in the past and did not continue into the present.

EXAMPLES   In the last lap the runner **fell** and **injured** his knee. [past]

He **was trying** to break the record for that event. [past progressive]

The injury **did prevent** him from competing in the relay race. [past emphatic]

NOTE   A past action or state of being may also be shown by using *used to.*

EXAMPLE   I **used to hate** spicy food.

(3) The *future tense* expresses an action or a state of being that will occur. The future tense is formed with the helping verb *shall* or *will*.

EXAMPLES   The president **will** not **return** to Washington today. [future]

We **will** (or **shall**) **be holding** a press conference at noon. [future progressive]

A future action or state of being may also be expressed by using

- the present tense of *be* followed by *going to* and the base form of a verb
- the present tense of *be* followed by *about to* and the base form of a verb
- the present tense of a verb with a word or phrase that expresses future time

EXAMPLES   My cousins **are going to visit** Japan in July.

Ms. Scheirer **is about to announce** the winners.

The boxer **defends** his title **next Friday night.**

BORN LOSER reprinted by permission of Newspaper Enterprise Association, Inc.

Reference Note

For more information about using **past perfect in "if" clauses,** see Rule 8g on page 191.

(4) The ***present perfect tense*** expresses an action or a state of being that occurred at an indefinite time in the past. The present perfect tense is formed with the helping verb *have* or *has.*

EXAMPLES   Miguel and Tim **have** already **entered** the information into the computer. [present perfect]

                  Who **has been using** this computer? [present perfect progressive]

     The present perfect tense is also used to express an action or a state of being that began in the past and that continues into the present.

EXAMPLES   Mr. Steele **has taught** school for twenty-one years. [present perfect]

                  He **has been coaching** soccer since 1996. [present perfect progressive]

NOTE   Do not use the present perfect tense to express a specific time in the past. Use the past tense.

NONSTANDARD   They have bought a computer last week. [*Last week* indicates a specific time in the past.]

STANDARD   They **bought** a computer last week. [past tense]

(5) The ***past perfect tense*** expresses an action or a state of being that ended before some other past action or state of being. The past perfect tense is formed with the helping verb *had.*

EXAMPLES   Paul **had traveled** several miles before he realized his mistake. [past perfect]

                  He discovered that he **had been misreading** the road map. [past perfect progressive]

NOTE   Use the past perfect tense in an *"if"* clause that expresses the earlier of two past actions.

EXAMPLE   If I **had used** the spellchecker, I would have corrected the spelling errors.

(6) The ***future perfect tense*** expresses an action or a state of being that will end before some other future occurrence. The future perfect tense is formed with the helping verbs *shall have* or *will have.*

By the time school begins in August, you **will have saved** enough money to buy the car. [future perfect]

By then, you **will have been working** here a year. [future perfect progressive]

Exercise 10 Identifying the Six Tenses

Identify the tenses of the italicized verbs in each of the following pairs of sentences. Be prepared to explain how these differences in tense alter the meanings of the sentences.

EXAMPLE   **1. a.** Mr. Olmos *taught* Spanish for thirty years.
   b. Mr. Olmos *has taught* Spanish for thirty years.

   1.   a—past tense; b—present perfect tense

1. a. Channel 5 News *has reported* on how successfully Asian immigrants have adjusted to life in the United States.
   b. Channel 5 News *is reporting* on how successfully Asian immigrants have adjusted to life in the United States.

2. a. I *took* piano lessons for three years.
   b. I *have taken* piano lessons for three years.

3. a. We *will do* our research on Friday.
   b. We *will have done* our research on Friday.

4. a. Jane *has studied* recent fossil discoveries.
   b. Jane *had studied* recent fossil discoveries.

5. a. *Do* you *know* that voting by secret ballot originated in Australia?
   b. *Did* you *know* that voting by secret ballot originated in Australia?

6. a. We *did send* out invitations.
   b. We *are sending* out invitations.

7. a. I *will make* a time line of the Middle Ages before this weekend.
   b. I *will have made* a time line of the Middle Ages before this weekend.

8. a. Ms. Wong *was* the club sponsor for five years.
   b. Ms. Wong *has been* the club sponsor for five years.

9. a. *Did* the jury *reach* a verdict?
   b. *Has* the jury *reached* a verdict?

10. a. I *think* that I *have seen* her somewhere before.
   b. I *thought* that I *had seen* her somewhere before.

┌─HELP─

The meaning of the first sentence is that Mr. Olmos used to teach but no longer does. The second sentence means that Mr. Olmos is still teaching now.

USAGE

Exercise 11 Changing Tenses

For each of the following sentences, change the tense of the verb according to the instructions in italics.

EXAMPLE
1. Do those blue jays still nest in the hedge? (*Change to present progressive tense.*)

1. Are those blue jays still nesting in the hedge?

1. Ivy roots made their way into the bricks. (*Change to present progressive tense.*)
2. By next June, Xavier will have studied piano for ten years. (*Change to future perfect progressive tense.*)
3. He runs for thirty minutes every morning. (*Change to past perfect progressive tense.*)
4. These scissors had been needing sharpening. (*Change to present emphatic tense.*)
5. A true samurai always follows *bushido,* a code of honor. (*Change to past emphatic tense.*)
6. A cool layer of air is holding the thermal inversion layer in place. (*Change to future perfect tense.*)
7. The heady scent of Mexican tuberoses filled the air. (*Change to past perfect tense.*)
8. Are you calling about the tickets? (*Change to past progressive tense.*)
9. By my birthday, I will have visited relatives in Arizona. (*Change to future progressive tense.*)
10. We were singing "Home on the Range." (*Change to present perfect progressive tense.*)

Special Problems in the Use of Tenses

Sequence of Tenses

8f. Use tense forms correctly to show relationships between verbs in a sentence. Do not change needlessly from one tense to another.

(1) When describing events that occur at the same time, use verbs in the same tense.

EXAMPLES   The coach **blows** the whistle as the swimmers **dive** into the pool. [present tense]

The coach **blew** the whistle as the swimmers **dived** into the pool. [past tense]

(2) When describing events that occur at different times, use verbs in different tenses to show the order of events.

EXAMPLES She **plays soccer** now, but last year she **played** field hockey. [Because her soccer playing is occurring now, the present tense form *plays* is the correct form. Her field hockey playing occurred at a specific time in the past and preceded her soccer playing; therefore, the past tense form *played* is the correct form.]

Since the new band director **took** over, our band **has won** all of its contests. [Because the new director took over at a specific time in the past, the past tense form *took* is correct. The winning has taken place over a period of time and continues into the present; therefore, the present perfect tense form *has won* is used.]

The tense you use depends on the meaning that you want to express.

EXAMPLES I **think** I **have** a B average in math. [Both verbs are in the present tense to indicate that both actions are occurring now.]

I **think** I **had** a B average in math. [The change to the past tense in the second verb implies that I had a B average sometime in the past.]

Lia **said** that she **lived** near the park. [Both verbs are in the past tense to indicate that both actions happened in the past.]

Lia **said** that she **lives** near the park. [The change to the present tense in the second verb indicates that Lia still lives near the park.]

8g. Do not use *would have* in "if" clauses that express the earlier of two past actions. Use the past perfect tense.

NONSTANDARD If she would have handed in her application, she would have gotten the job.

STANDARD If she **had handed** in her application, she would have gotten the job.

NONSTANDARD If Felita would have asked her parents, she probably could have gone with us.

STANDARD If Felita **had asked** her parents, she probably could have gone with us.

Exercise 12 Using Tenses Correctly

Each of the following sentences contains an error in the use of tenses. Identify the error, and give the correct form of the verb.

EXAMPLE   1. The holidays will begin by the time we arrive in Miami.

   1. *will begin—will have begun*

1. Would you still have told that joke if we said we had already heard it?
2. Who found that the earth revolved around the sun?
3. By the time we get to the picnic area, the rain will stop.
4. In July my parents will be married for twenty-five years.
5. If the books have been cataloged last week, why haven't they been shelved?
6. I would have agreed if you would have asked me sooner.
7. Val claims that cats made the best pets.
8. After Sam had answered, Mr. Catalano says, "There were no rabbits."
9. Before leaving the house, we have closed the windows.
10. As a witness to the accident, Pam told the police what happened.

The Present Infinitive and the Present Perfect Infinitive

Reference Note

For more about **infinitives** and their uses, see page 64.

Infinitives have present and present perfect forms.

Present Infinitive	to see	to be	to change
Present Perfect Infinitive	to have seen	to have been	to have changed

8h. The ***present infinitive*** **expresses an action or a state of being that follows another action or state of being.**

EXAMPLES   Latrice hopes **to attend** the Super Bowl. [The action expressed by *to attend* follows the action expressed by *hopes*.]

   Latrice had planned **to go** to the game with her brother. [The action expressed by *to go* follows the action expressed by *had planned*.]

8i. The ***present perfect infinitive*** **expresses an action or a state of being that precedes another action or state of being.**

EXAMPLES   The divers claim **to have located** an ancient sailing vessel. [The action expressed by *to have located* precedes the action expressed by *claim*.]

They claimed **to have spent** three weeks exploring the ship. [The action expressed by *to have spent* precedes the action expressed by *claimed*.]

The Present Participle, the Past Participle, and the Present Perfect Participle

Participles have present, past, and present perfect forms.

Present Participle	seeing	being	changing
Past Participle	seen	been	changed
Present Perfect Participle	having seen	having been	having changed

8j. When used as a verbal, the *present participle* or *past participle* expresses an action or a state of being that occurs at the same time as another action or state of being.

EXAMPLES **Gazing** through the telescope, I saw the rings around Saturn. [The action expressed by *Gazing* occurs at the same time as the action expressed by *saw*.]

Committed to the recycling project, the students work tirelessly to see it through. [The action expressed by *Committed* occurs at the same time as the action expressed by *work*.]

8k. When used as a verbal, the *present perfect participle* expresses an action or a state of being that precedes another action or state of being.

EXAMPLES **Having completed** her outline, Kate wrote the first draft of her research paper. [The action expressed by *Having completed* precedes the action expressed by *wrote*.]

Having proofread her research paper, Kate is typing the final draft. [The action expressed by *Having proofread* precedes the action expressed by *is typing*.]

Review I **Using Tenses Correctly**

Most of the sentences on the following page contain an error in the use of verbs and verbals. Identify each error, and give the correct form of the verb or verbal. If a sentence is already correct, write *C*.

Reference Note

For more about **verbals,** see page 58.

Reference Note

For more information about **participles** and their uses, see page 58.

USAGE

1. I would have taken more money on my trip to Japan if
       I would have known what the exchange rate was.

   1. *would have known—had known*

1. When you charge the battery in the car, be sure to have protected
   your eyes and hands from the sulfuric acid in the battery.
2. Deciding to attend the concert at Boyer Hall, we bought four
   tickets for Saturday night.
3. By the time Friday is over, we will hear some great music.
4. If I would have known about the free offer, I would have sent in
   a coupon.
5. My old skates are lying in my closet for the past two years.
6. I had hoped to have gone swimming yesterday.
7. Having sung the aria, Jessye Norman received a standing ovation.
8. If I had the address, I would have been able to deliver the package.
9. Dave goes to the dentist three months ago when his tooth began
   to hurt.
10. The volcano sent up a huge cloud of ash and smoke that will have
    closed the nearby airport for several hours.

Active Voice and Passive Voice

Voice is the form a verb takes to indicate whether the subject of the
verb performs or receives the action. When the subject of a verb performs the action, the verb is in the *active voice.* When the subject
receives the action, the verb is in the *passive voice.*

The verb in a passive construction always includes a form of *be*
and the past participle of a verb. Notice in the following conjugation
of the verb *see* in the passive voice that the form of *be* determines the
tense of the passive verb.

Reference Note

For more discussion of
transitive verbs, see
page 16.

Reference Note

The **conjugation of *see*
in the active voice** is on
page 183.

Conjugation of the Verb *See* in the Passive Voice	
Present Tense	
Singular	**Plural**
I am seen	we are seen
you are seen	you are seen
he, she, it is seen	they are seen
Present Progressive: am, are, is being seen	

USAGE

Conjugation of the Verb *See* in the Passive Voice

Past Tense

Singular	Plural
I was seen	we were seen
you were seen	you were seen
he, she, it was seen	they were seen

Past Progressive: was, were being seen

Future Tense

Singular	Plural
I will (shall) be seen	we will (shall) be seen
you will (shall) be seen	you will (shall) be seen
he, she, it will (shall) be seen	they will (shall) be seen

Present Perfect Tense

Singular	Plural
I have been seen	we have been seen
you have been seen	you have been seen
he, she, it has been seen	they have been seen

Past Perfect Tense

Singular	Plural
I had been seen	we had been seen
you had been seen	you had been seen
he, she, it had been seen	they had been seen

Future Perfect Tense

Singular	Plural
I will (shall) have been seen	we will (shall) have been seen
you will (shall) have been seen	you will (shall) have been seen
he, she, it will (shall) have been seen	they will (shall) have been seen

USAGE

STYLE TIP

Choosing between the active voice and the passive voice is a matter of style, not correctness. In general, however, the passive voice is less direct, less forceful, and less concise than the active voice. In fact, the passive voice may produce an awkward effect.

AWKWARD PASSIVE
Last night, the floor was scrubbed by my father, and the faucet was fixed by my mother.

ACTIVE
Last night, my father **scrubbed** the floor, and my mother **fixed** the faucet.

As the following examples show, transitive verbs in the active voice have direct objects, and transitive verbs in the passive voice do not.

ACTIVE VOICE	Gloria Naylor **wrote** *The Women of Brewster Place.* [*The Women of Brewster Place* is the direct object.]
PASSIVE VOICE	*The Women of Brewster Place* **was written** by Gloria Naylor. [no direct object]
ACTIVE VOICE	The optometrist **adjusted** the eyeglasses. [*Eyeglasses* is the direct object.]
PASSIVE VOICE	The eyeglasses **were adjusted** by the optometrist. [no direct object]
ACTIVE VOICE	Carol **has adopted** the two puppies. [*Puppies* is the direct object.]
PASSIVE VOICE	The two puppies **have been adopted** by Carol. [no direct object]
PASSIVE VOICE	The two puppies **have been adopted.** [no direct object]

From the examples above, you can see how an active construction can become a passive construction. The verb from the active construction becomes a past participle preceded by a form of *be.* The object of the verb becomes the subject of the verb in a passive construction. The subject in an active construction may become the object of the preposition *by* in a passive construction. (As the last example shows, a prepositional phrase beginning with *by* is not always necessary.)

The Retained Object

A transitive verb in the active voice often has both an indirect object and a direct object. When such a verb is put in the passive voice, either object can become the subject. The other object then serves as a complement called a *retained object.*

	S	V	IO	DO
ACTIVE VOICE	Ms. Ribas	gave	each student	a thesaurus.

S	**V**	**RO**

PASSIVE VOICE   Each student was given a thesaurus (by Ms. Ribas).

S	**V**	**RO**

PASSIVE VOICE   A thesaurus was given each student (by Ms. Ribas).

As you can see, the indirect object *student* in the active construction becomes the subject in the first passive construction, and the direct object *thesaurus* remains a complement. In the second passive construction, *thesaurus* is the subject, and *student* is the complement. Remember, a complement in a passive construction is a retained object, not a direct object or an indirect object.

The Uses of the Passive Voice

8I. The passive voice should be used sparingly. Use the passive voice in the following situations:

(1) when you do not know the performer of the action

EXAMPLES   Asbestos **was used** for making fireproof materials.

              An anonymous letter **had been sent** to the police chief.

(2) when you do not want to reveal the performer of the action

EXAMPLES   Several flat notes **were hit** during the opening number.

              The missing paintings **have been returned** to the museum.

(3) when you want to emphasize the receiver of the action

EXAMPLES   Penicillin **was discovered** accidentally.

              This book **has been translated** into more than one hundred languages.

Exercise 13   **Revising Sentences in the Passive Voice**

Revise the sentences on the following page by changing the passive voice to active voice wherever the change is desirable. If you think the passive voice is preferable, write *C*. Be prepared to explain your answers.

EXAMPLE   **1.** A variety of cooking methods and utensils were invented by early humans.

              1. *Early humans invented a variety of cooking methods and utensils.*

COMPUTER TIP

If you use a computer when you write, you may want to find out more about the different kinds of style-checking software programs that are available. At least one such program checks for overuse of passive voice. Remember, though, that the computer can highlight the passive-voice verbs it finds, but it cannot determine whether they are used for a particular reason.

USAGE

─HELP─

In the example, the active voice is preferable because we know and want to reveal the performer of the action.

1. At first, roots and berries were gathered and eaten by these people.
2. The discovery that certain foods can be improved by cooking may have accidentally been made by them.
3. Slaughtered animals or piles of edible roots may have been left near the fire by hunters and gatherers.
4. It was noticed by them that when food was cooked, it tasted better.
5. The first ovens were formed from pits lined with stones and hot coals.
6. It wasn't long before ovens were built above the ground with some kind of chimney to carry away the smoke.
7. Primitive kettles were made by early humans by smearing clay over reed baskets and drying them in the sun.
8. Liquid foods could then be kept in such a basket for short periods without leaking out.
9. When a clay-coated basket was placed near the flames by a prehistoric cook to heat its contents, sometimes the clay was baked by the high temperature into a pottery shell.
10. Once the basic skill of making pottery was mastered by early people, they learned to create the pottery shell without the basket.

Mood

Reference Note

For examples of all of the **tense forms in the indicative mood,** see the conjugations on pages 183 and 194.

Mood is the form a verb takes to indicate the attitude of the person using the verb. Verbs in English may be in one of three moods: the *indicative,* the *imperative,* or the *subjunctive.*

8m. The *indicative mood* expresses a fact, an opinion, or a question.

EXAMPLES   Andrei Sakharov **was** the nuclear physicist who **won** the Nobel Peace Prize in 1975.

All of us **think** that this baseball team **is** the best one in the entire state.

Can you **explain** the difference between a meteor and a meteorite?

8n. The *imperative mood* expresses a direct command or request.

The imperative mood of a verb has only one form. It is the same as the verb's base form.

	S	**V**	**RO**

USAGE

EXAMPLES   **Explain** the difference between a meteor and a meteorite.

Please **fasten** your seat belt.

Stop!

8o. **The *subjunctive mood* expresses a suggestion, a necessity, a condition contrary to fact, or a wish.**

Only the present and past tenses have distinctive subjunctive forms. The following partial conjugation of *be* shows how the present and past tense forms in the subjunctive mood differ from those in the indicative mood.

Present Indicative		Present Subjunctive	
Singular	**Plural**	**Singular**	**Plural**
I am	we are	(that) I be	(that) we be
you are	you are	(that) you be	(that) you be
he, she, it is	they are	(that) he, she, it be	(that) they be

Past Indicative		Past Subjunctive	
Singular	**Plural**	**Singular**	**Plural**
I was	we were	(if) I were	(if) we were
you were	you were	(if) you were	(if) you were
he, she, it was	they were	(if) he, she, it were	(if) they were

┌**HELP**──
The use of *that* and *if* in the chart is explained on the next page.

USAGE

Notice in the above conjugation that the present subjunctive form of a verb is the same as the base form. For verbs other than *be*, the past subjunctive form is the same as the past tense form. The verb *be* has two past tense forms. As you can see, however, the past tense form *was* in the indicative mood becomes *were* in the subjunctive mood. Therefore, *were* is the only past subjunctive form of *be*.

GREETING CARDS · all occasions ·

I NEED A GET-WELL CARD FOR MY OLD ENGLISH TEACHER. DO YOU HAVE ONE THAT CAJOLES IN THE INDICATIVE MOOD RATHER THAN COMMANDS IN THE IMPERATIVE?

FRANK & ERNEST reprinted by permission of Newspaper Enterprise Association, Inc.

STYLE TIP

Although the use of the subjunctive mood is declining in informal situations, you should use it in formal, standard English.

(1) The *present subjunctive* expresses a suggestion or a necessity.

Generally, the verb in a subordinate clause beginning with *that* is in the subjunctive mood when the independent clause contains a word indicating a suggestion (such as *ask, request, suggest,* or *recommend*) or a word indicating a necessity (such as *necessary* or *essential*).

EXAMPLES Ms. Chávez suggested that he **apply** for the job.

The moderator at the convention requested that the state delegates **be seated.**

It is necessary that she **attend** the convention.

It is required that you **be** here on time.

(2) The *past subjunctive* expresses a condition contrary to fact or expresses a wish.

In general, a clause beginning with *if, as if,* or *as though* expresses a condition contrary to fact—something that is not true. In such a clause, use the past subjunctive. Remember that *were* is the only past subjunctive form of *be.*

EXAMPLES If I **were** you, I'd have those tires checked.

If he **were** older, he would be allowed to stay up later.

Because of the bad telephone connection, Gregory sounded as though he **were** ten thousand miles away.

Similarly, use the past subjunctive to express a wish—a condition that is desirable.

EXAMPLES I wish I **were** more patient than I am.

Reiko wishes that the summer **were**n't so hot.

Exercise 14 Identifying the Mood of Verbs

For each of the following sentences, identify the mood of the italicized verb as *indicative, imperative,* or *subjunctive.*

EXAMPLE 1. I wish I *were* going with you to the Bahamas.
  1. subjunctive

1. Theo, *stand* back a safe distance while I try again to start this lawn mower.

2. Did you know that Tamisha's mother *is* the new manager at the supermarket?
3. Bradley says that if he *were* president, he would take steps to increase the minimum wage.
4. I suggest that these young maple trees *be* planted quickly, before they wilt.
5. *Were* you and your two brothers excited about visiting your birthplace in Mexico?
6. This Lenni-Lenape moccasin *was* found near Matawan, New Jersey.
7. Stay there and *be* a good dog while I go into the bakery, Molly.
8. When my dad saw the dented fender, he looked as if he *were* ready to explode.
9. "I wish that you *were* not moving so far away," muttered my best friend, Bao.
10. Mr. Darwin said that you *will be* the bus monitor on our next class trip.

Modals

8p. A ***modal*** **is a helping, or auxiliary, verb that is joined with a main verb to express an attitude toward the action or state of being of the main verb.**

The helping verbs *can, could, may, might, must, ought, shall, should, will,* and *would* are modals.

(1) The modals *can* and *could* are used to express ability.

EXAMPLES   **Can** you **repair** this necklace?

I **could** not **have solved** the problem without your help.

(2) The modal *may* is used to express permission or possibility.

EXAMPLES   **May** I **use** your computer? [permission]

You **may want** to add a little more garlic to the pasta sauce. [possibility]

(3) The modal *might,* like *may,* is used to express possibility.

Often, the possibility expressed by *might* is less likely than the possibility expressed by *may.*

EXAMPLE   The jury **might reach** its verdict today, but I doubt that it will.

Reference Note

For more about **helping (auxiliary) verbs** and **main verbs,** see page 15.

STYLE TIP

Can is often used to express permission in informal situations. In formal situations, you should use *may.*

INFORMAL   Can I borrow your book?

FORMAL   **May** I borrow your book?

(4) The modal *must* is used most often to express a requirement.

Sometimes, *must* is used to express an explanation.

EXAMPLES   Antonio and I **must be** home by 7:00 P.M. [requirement]

You **must have overwatered** this plant, for many of its leaves have turned yellow. [explanation]

(5) The modal *ought* is used to express obligation or likelihood.

EXAMPLES   You **ought** to send her a thank-you note. [obligation]

The rehearsal **ought** to be over by 8:00 P.M. [likelihood]

(6) The modals *shall* and *will* are used to express future time.

EXAMPLES   I **will** (or **shall**) **be** eighteen years old next month.

When **will** the election results **be announced**?

(7) The modal *should* is used to express a recommendation, an obligation, or a possibility.

EXAMPLES   My guidance counselor told me that I **should take** the Scholastic Aptitude Test in October. [recommendation]

You **should have called** Ms. Langley as soon as you heard the news. [obligation]

Should you **decide** to go to the ceremony, please let me know. [possibility]

(8) The modal *would* is used to express the conditional form of a verb.

A conditional verb form usually appears in an independent clause that is joined with an *"if"* clause. The *"if"* clause explains *under what condition(s)* the action or state of being of the conditional verb takes place.

EXAMPLE   If I had known you were interested in the job, I **would have offered** it to you.

Would is used also to express future time in a subordinate clause when the verb in the independent clause is in the past tense.

EXAMPLE   Calista said that she **would meet** us at the restaurant at 6:00 P.M.

Additionally, *would* is used to express an action that was repeated in the past, an invitation, or a request.

EXAMPLES Every summer, my family and I **would go** camping in the Blue Ridge Mountains. [repeated past action]

Would you **like** to attend the arts and crafts festival? [invitation]

Would you please **help** Damon program the VCR? [request]

Exercise 15 Writing Appropriate Modals

For each of the following sentences, supply an appropriate modal.

EXAMPLE 1. Provided that the agreement is acceptable to all parties, I _____ draw up the contract.

1. *will*

1. Oops, the board is too short; I _____ have measured more carefully.
2. No, class, you certainly _____ not leave twenty minutes early today.
3. "I definitely _____ call you tomorrow," Eleanor promised.
4. It _____ rain; then again, it _____ not.
5. There are no exceptions: All students _____ complete two semesters of American government classes.
6. We were so close to the stage that we _____ touch the microphone.
7. Although the rules allowed a substitute, the judges _____ not allow it.
8. Explain this spreadsheet to me; I simply _____ not figure it out.
9. The committee _____ not have chosen anyone better than Esteban.
10. The word *kosher* denotes food that _____ be eaten according to Jewish dietary laws; these laws exclude shellfish and pork.

Review J Proofreading Sentences for Correct Verb Usage

Most of the following sentences contain informal or incorrect verb usage. Identify each informal or incorrect usage, and give the correct verb form. If a sentence is already correct according to the rules of formal, standard usage, write *C*.

EXAMPLE 1. After he had passed the jewelry store, he wished he went into it.

1. *went—had gone*

1. Do you think that she volunteer to help the victims of the flood?
2. The rock group had finished the concert, but the audience called for another set.
3. If Sherrie would not have missed the printer's deadline, the yearbook delivery would have been on time.

HELP

Although more than one response may be possible for each item in Exercise 15, you need to give only one answer for each.

4. Although I thought I planned my trip down to the last detail, there was one thing I had forgotten.
5. If you would have remembered to bring along something to read, you would not have been so bored.
6. The smell from the paper mill laid over the town like a blanket.
7. Stephanie says she enjoyed working on the kibbutz in Israel last summer, but she hardly got a chance to set down the whole time.
8. By the time they had smelled the smoke, the flames had already begun to spread.
9. I hope to have the opportunity to revise my essay.
10. If Emiliano Zapata would have known the invitation was a trap, he would not have been ambushed.

Review K Proofreading a Paragraph for Correct Use of Verbs

Most of the following sentences contain awkward, informal, or incorrect verb usage. If a sentence has an awkward, informal, or incorrect usage, revise the sentence, using the verb form that is correct in formal, standard English. If a sentence is already correct, write *C*.

EXAMPLE   [1] After he had lit the candle, Dad begun to recite the first principle of Kwanzaa.

1. *begun—began*

[1] Kwanzaa is celebrated by African Americans for more than a quarter of a century. [2] This holiday has been created in 1966 by Maulana Karenga, who is a professor of black studies at California State University. [3] Dr. Karenga wished that there was a nonreligious holiday especially for black Americans. [4] If he has not treasured his own background, we would not have this inspiring celebration to enjoy. [5] Professor Karenga has long believed that people's heritage should be celebrated by them. [6] Recently, more and more African Americans have began to reserve the seven-day period immediately following Christmas for Kwanzaa. [7] If you would have joined my family for Kwanzaa last year, you would have heard my grandfather's talk about family values and about African Americans who have fought for freedom and honor. [8] We all wore items of traditional African clothing and displayed a red, black, and green flag to symbolize Africa. [9] Mom lay out a wonderful feast each night, and we lit a candle and talked about one of the seven principles of Kwanzaa. [10] I wish I asked you to our house last year for Kwanzaa, and I will definitely invite you this year.

Chapter Review

A. Using Irregular Verbs Correctly

For each of the following sentences, identify the verb form in parentheses that is correct in standard, formal English.

1. These gloves have (*lay, laid, lain*) on the bureau all week.
2. If I (*knew, had known, would have known*) about the team tryouts, I would have signed up for them.
3. Only after I (*had went, had gone, went*) home did I remember my dental appointment.
4. My younger brother (*has took, taken, has taken*) my notebook.
5. The book (*laid, lay, lied, lain*) open at page 35.
6. Even though the sun had not yet (*rose, risen, raised*), my uncles were out fishing on the lake.
7. I suddenly knew what I had wanted (*saying, to say, to have said*).
8. I didn't notice that my pocket had (*teared, torn, tore*).
9. I would be careful with that if I (*had been, were, was*) you.
10. By this time next year, Lupe (*has began, will have begun, will begin*) classes at the University of Colorado.

B. Proofreading Sentences for Verb Usage

In each of the following sentences, identify the incorrect verb form, and then write the correct form. If a sentence is already correct, write *C*.

11. A beautiful oak tree raises above the meadow.
12. If you would have visited Mexico City, you might have seen the great pyramids of Tenochtitlán.
13. Sara wishes that she had went to the beach yesterday.
14. Edmundo ought to go to the Diez y Seis party yesterday.
15. One of the statues has fell off its base.
16. How long did it lie on the floor?
17. Since last September I missed only one day of school.
18. I predict that by next year Lorenzo will grow taller than his sister.
19. Fortunately, I have never been stinged by a bee.
20. The unusual pattern in this wool material was woven by Seamus MacMhuiris, an artist who uses bold geometric designs.

C. Proofreading Sentences for Verb Usage

Identify each incorrect verb form in the following sentences, and then write the verb form that is correct in standard, formal English. If a sentence is already correct, write *C*.

21. Sit this pitcher of lemonade on the table, please.

22. If Maya would have listened to the instructor, she wouldn't have made that mistake.

23. The mural *Sky Above Clouds* was painted by Georgia O'Keeffe.

24. Martin's teacher has suggested that Martin learns more about the history of his town before writing the essay.

25. When Maritza left the lecture, she knew she wanted to have studied the gray wolf.

26. Mr. Huang looked as if he was about to faint.

27. Mount Etna erupted in Sicily in 1669, and approximately 20,000 people are killed.

28. The Koslowski family use to have a Dalmatian.

29. By this time next month, the software company will ship a hundred thousand copies of its new game.

30. Bette studied economics for two years before she realized that she really wanted to make documentary films.

D. Revising Sentences in the Passive Voice

Revise the following sentences by changing the passive voice to active voice.

31. The rules of the game were explained to me by the coach.

32. The half-time show was enjoyed by the crowd.

33. It was noticed by the choir that Linda was quite a good singer.

34. The quilt that was made by me won second prize.

35. The ball that was thrown by me was caught by the dog.

E. Identifying the Mood of Verbs

For each of the following sentences, identify the mood of the italicized verb as *indicative, imperative,* or *subjunctive.*

36. What *is* the distance between the earth and the moon?

37. Mimi wishes that the winters in Michigan *were* not so long.

38. *Remember* to remove your shoes in a Japanese restaurant.

39. I strongly recommend that you *see* a doctor about that cough.

40. The members of the football team played as if they *were* unaware of the driving rain.

Writing Application
Using Verbs in a Story

Active Voice and Passive Voice   A writers' club is holding a contest to find the most exciting opening of an adventure story. To enter the contest, write a two- or three-paragraph opening for an adventure story. Use active-voice verbs to make your sentences lively and concise. Use passive-voice verbs wherever they are needed for style or for emphasis.

Prewriting   Brainstorm some ideas for an exciting conflict. Then, create a brief plot outline for a story based on the conflict you think would lead to the greatest adventure. Think of a way to begin your story. You may want to begin at an exciting point in the middle of the action, or you may want to tell the story as a flashback.

Writing   Use your prewriting notes to help you write a first draft. Expand on your original ideas, adding details as you think of them. Remember that you are telling an exciting story and that you want to hold the reader's interest.

Revising   Ask a friend to read your story opener. Is the opening interesting and exciting? Can your friend predict what will happen next? Write down any revision suggestions. Have you used active voice and passive voice effectively?

Publishing   Check carefully for mistakes in grammar, usage, spelling, and punctuation. Be sure that you have used the correct forms of irregular verbs. Take turns reading your story openings aloud in front of the class. After everyone has read their openings, the class might vote on which story or stories they would like to hear continued.

Using Modifiers Correctly

Forms and Uses of Adjectives and Adverbs; Comparison

Diagnostic Preview

A. Using Modifiers Correctly

Most of the following sentences contain errors in the use of modifiers. If a sentence is incorrect, revise it to eliminate the error. If it is already correct, write *C*.

EXAMPLE   1. Steve is the most brightest student in the physics class.
            1. *Steve is the brightest student in the physics class.*

1. After listening to The Battle of the Bands, we thought that the jazz band performed even more better than the rock group.
2. When the treasurer presented the annual report, the statistics showed that the company had done badder this year than last.
3. Megan shoots free throws so good that she has already made the varsity team.
4. The more even you distribute the workload among the group members, the more satisfied everyone will be.

5. In 1949, Jackie Robinson was voted the Most Valuable Player in the National League.
6. Last night the weather forecaster announced that this has been the most wet spring season the area has had in the past decade.
7. This is the most tastiest piece of sourdough bread I have ever eaten.
8. After receiving a rare coin for my birthday, I began to take coin collecting more seriously.
9. Before taking a computer course, I couldn't program at all, but now I program very good.
10. When she danced at the Paris Opera, American ballet star Maria Tallchief was received enthusiastic by French audiences.

B. Proofreading for the Correct Use of Modifiers

Proofread the following paragraph, correcting any errors in the use of modifiers. If a sentence is already correct, write *C*.

EXAMPLE **[1]** When in doubt, dress conservative rather than stunningly for a job interview.

 1. *conservatively*

[11] No matter whether three or three hundred candidates apply for a job, a smart employer tries to find the more qualified applicant. [12] If you heed the following simple guidelines, you will likely create a more favorable general impression than any candidate in your job market. [13] First, a well-prepared résumé always helps to make a better impression before the interview. [14] Second, a proper dressed candidate appears neat and well groomed during the interview. [15] Your clothes do not have to be fancier or more expensive than any other candidate's clothes, but they should look professional. [16] Third, before your interview, you should try to imagine the most common asked questions for your field. [17] There is no worst way to make a lasting impression than to provide poorly thought-out answers to an interviewer's questions. [18] Finally, learning all you can about a company is one of the effectivest ways to impress a future employer. [19] When two equally well-qualified candidates apply for the same position, often the one with the greatest knowledge of the company is hired. [20] If you follow these guidelines and still don't get the job, try not to feel too bad; instead, set your sights on succeeding at your next job interview.

USAGE

Forms of Modifiers

A *modifier* is a word or word group that makes the meaning of another word or word group more specific. The two kinds of modifiers are *adjectives* and *adverbs*.

Reference Note

For more information on **adjectives,** see page 9. For more information on **adverbs,** see page 17.

An *adjective* makes the meaning of a noun or a pronoun more specific.

EXAMPLES   **strong** wind   **an** alligator   **two** cubes

               a loud voice   **the painted** one   **this** bit

An *adverb* makes the meaning of a verb, an adjective, or another adverb more specific.

EXAMPLES   drives **carefully**   **suddenly** stopped   **too** hot

               extremely low   **rather** quickly   **not** here

Most modifiers with an *–ly* ending are used as adverbs. In fact, many adverbs are formed by adding *–ly* to adjectives.

Adjectives	Adverbs
perfect	perfect**ly**
clear	clear**ly**
quiet	quiet**ly**
abrupt	abrupt**ly**
handy	handi**ly**

However, some modifiers ending in *–ly* are used as adjectives.

EXAMPLES   a **daily** lesson   an **early** breakfast   a **lively** discussion

A few modifiers have the same form whether used as adjectives or as adverbs.

Adjectives	Adverbs
a **hard** job	works **hard**
a **late** start	started **late**
an **early** arrival	arriving **early**
a **fast** walk	to walk **fast**

USAGE

Phrases Used as Modifiers

Like one-word modifiers, phrases can also be used as adjectives and adverbs.

EXAMPLES   It was a monument **to peace.** [The prepositional phrase *to peace* acts as an adjective that modifies the noun *monument*.]

Sweeping through the gulch, the wind scattered leaves and branches. [The participial phrase *Sweeping through the gulch* acts as an adjective that modifies the noun *wind*.]

She is the one **to invite today.** [The infinitive phrase *to invite today* acts as an adjective that modifies the pronoun *one*.]

Drive **to the lakefront in the morning.** [The prepositional phrases *to the lakefront* and *in the morning* act as adverbs that modify the verb *Drive*.]

This is easy **to do well.** [The infinitive phrase *to do well* acts as an adverb that modifies the adjective *easy*.]

Reference Note

For more about different kinds of **phrases,** see Chapter 3.

Clauses Used as Modifiers

Like words and phrases, clauses can also be used as modifiers.

EXAMPLES   Toni Morrison is the author **who wrote *Beloved.*** [The adjective clause *who wrote Beloved* modifies the noun *author*.]

Because winter was coming, the butterflies flew south. [The adverb clause *Because winter was coming* modifies the verb *flew*.]

Reference Note

For more about **clauses,** see Chapter 4.

Uses of Modifiers

9a. Use an adjective to modify the subject of a linking verb.

The most common linking verbs are the forms of *be: am, is, are, was, were, be, been,* and *being.* A linking verb is often used to connect its subject to a **predicate adjective**—an adjective that is in the predicate and that modifies the subject.

EXAMPLES   Our new computer system is **efficient.**

The governor's comments on the controversial issue were **candid.**

Reference Note

For more about **predicate adjectives,** see page 43.

USAGE

9b. Use adverbs to modify action verbs.

Action verbs are often modified by adverbs—words that tell *how, when, where,* or *to what extent* an action is performed.

EXAMPLES   Our new computer system is operating **efficiently.**

The governor **candidly** expressed her point of view on the controversial issue.

Some verbs may be used as linking verbs or as action verbs. Notice the kinds of modifiers used after the verbs in the following examples.

EXAMPLES   Carmen looked **frantic.** [*Looked* is a linking verb. *Frantic* is an adjective modifying *Carmen.*]

Carmen looked **frantically** for her class ring. [*Looked* is an action verb. *Frantically* is an adverb modifying *looked.*]

Like verbs, verbals may be modified by adverbs.

EXAMPLES   Barking **loudly,** the dog frightened the burglar. [The adverb *loudly* modifies the participle *Barking.*]

Not fastening the bracket **tightly** will enable you to adjust it **later.** [The adverbs *Not* and *tightly* modify the gerund *fastening.* The adverb *later* modifies the infinitive *to adjust.*]

Reference Note

For more information about **linking verbs** and **action verbs,** see page 13.

Reference Note

For more about **verbals,** see page 58.

TIPS & TRICKS

To help you determine whether a verb is a linking verb or an action verb, replace the verb with a form of *seem.* If the substitution sounds reasonable, the original verb is a linking verb. If the substitution sounds absurd, the original verb is an action verb.

EXAMPLES
Carmen looked frantic. [Since *Carmen seemed frantic* sounds reasonable, *looked* is a linking verb.]

Carmen looked frantically for her class ring. [Since *Carmen seemed frantically for her class ring* sounds absurd, *looked* is an action verb.]

USAGE

Exercise 1   Selecting Modifiers to Complete Sentences

Select the correct modifier in parentheses in each of the following sentences.

EXAMPLE   **1.** When you look (*careful, carefully*) at the pots shown on the next page, you can see how tiny they are compared to the kernels of corn.

1. *carefully*

1. Rosemary Apple Blossom Lonewolf is an artist whose style remains (*unique, uniquely*) among American Indian potters.

2. Lonewolf combines (*traditional, traditionally*) and modern techniques to create her miniature pottery.

3. In crafting her pots, Lonewolf uses dark red clay that is (*ready, readily*) available around the Santa Clara Pueblo in New Mexico, where she lives.

4. These miniatures have a detailed and (*delicate, delicately*) etched surface called sgraffito.

5. Because of the (*extreme, extremely*) intricate detail on its surface, a single pot may take many months to finish.

6. The subjects for most of Lonewolf's pots combine ancient Pueblo myths and traditions with (*current, currently*) ideas or events.

7. One of her pots (*clear, clearly*) depicts a Pueblo corn dancer walking down a city street lined with skyscrapers.

8. Lonewolf uses such images to show that American Indians can and do adapt (*real, really*) well to new ways.

9. At first known only in the Southwest, Lonewolf's work is now shown throughout the United States because the appeal of her subjects is quite (*broad, broadly*).

10. Rosemary Lonewolf's father, grandfather, and son also are (*high, highly*) skilled potters.

COMPUTER TIP

Some word-processing software packages include a thesaurus. You can use the thesaurus to help you find precise modifiers to use in your writing. To make sure, however, that a modifier you choose from the thesaurus has exactly the meaning you intend, you should look up the word in the dictionary.

USAGE

Eight Troublesome Modifiers

Bad and Badly

Bad is an adjective. *Badly* is an adverb. In standard English, only the adjective form should follow a sense verb or other linking verb.

| NONSTANDARD | If the meat smells badly, don't eat it. |
| STANDARD | If the meat smells **bad,** don't eat it. |

| NONSTANDARD | This shade of green looks badly on me. |
| STANDARD | This shade of green looks **bad** on me. |

Good and Well

Good is an adjective. *Well* may be used as an adjective or as an adverb. Avoid using *good* to modify a verb. Instead, use *well* as an adverb, meaning "capably" or "satisfactorily."

| NONSTANDARD | The school orchestra played good. |
| STANDARD | The school orchestra played **well.** |

| NONSTANDARD | Although she was extremely nervous, Aretha performed quite good. |
| STANDARD | Although she was extremely nervous, Aretha performed quite **well.** |

| NONSTANDARD | Did you do good on the quiz? |
| STANDARD | Did you do **well** on the quiz? |

Feel good and *feel well* mean different things. *Feel good* means "to feel happy or pleased." *Feel well* means "to feel healthy."

EXAMPLES   Donating some of my time at the children's ward at the hospital makes me feel **good.**

Frank went home because he didn't feel **well.**

Slow and Slowly

Slow is used as both an adjective and an adverb. *Slowly* is used as an adverb. In most adverb uses, it is better to use *slowly* than to use *slow.*

| ADJECTIVE | Are sloths always that **slow**? |
| ADVERB | Do sloths always move that **slowly**? |

| ADJECTIVE | Take a few **slow,** deep breaths. |
| ADVERB | Breathe **slowly** and deeply. |

Real and Really

Real is an adjective. *Really* is an adverb meaning "truly" or "actually." Informally, *real* is used as an adverb meaning "very."

INFORMAL	Jamaal's report was real interesting.
FORMAL	Jamaal's report was **really** interesting.

INFORMAL	Most of the students seemed real eager to return to school after the winter break.
FORMAL	Most of the students seemed **really** eager to return to school after the winter break.

MEETING THE CHALLENGE

Remembering how to use the eight troublesome modifiers listed in your handbook is a matter of remembering how they function and what part of speech they are. *Good,* for example, is an adjective, while *well* is usually an adverb. Choose three pairs of the troublesome modifiers. For each pair, write a sentence that explains each word's use while using it—for instance, "It's a *good* idea to use adjectives *well.*" Working with your classmates, compile a list of helpful hints that you can copy and give to the class.

Oral Practice   **Using *Bad* and *Badly, Well* and *Good, Slow* and *Slowly,* and *Real* and *Really***

Read aloud each of the following sentences. If the italicized modifier is used incorrectly or informally, re-read the sentence, giving the form that is correct according to the rules of formal, standard English. If the modifier is already correct, say *correct.*

EXAMPLE   1. When I painted the house, I fell off the ladder and hurt my right arm *bad.*

      1. *badly*

1. The renowned conductor Leonard Bernstein led the New York Philharmonic Orchestra *well* for many years.
2. Despite the immense size and tremendous power of this airplane, the engines start up *slow.*
3. I can hit the ball *good* if I keep my eye on it.
4. Before Uncle Chet's hip replacement surgery, his gait was *real* painful and slow.
5. After studying French for the past three years in high school, we were pleased to discover how *good* we spoke and understood it on our trip to Quebec.
6. Some of the experiments that the chemistry class has conducted have made the corridors smell *badly.*
7. During the Han dynasty in China, candidates who did *bad* on civil service tests did not become government officials.
8. Whenever I watch the clock, the time seems to go *slowly.*
9. The movie's special effects are *real* spectacular.
10. After hearing how her Navajo ancestors overcame many problems, Anaba felt *well* about her situation.

USAGE

Determining the Correct Use of Modifiers

Proofread the following paragraph, correcting any informal or incorrect uses of modifiers. If a sentence is already correct, write *C.*

EXAMPLES   **[1]** Some volcanoes rest quiet for many years.

    1. quietly

    [2] When they erupt, however, they can be extremely violent.

    2. C

    [1] More than five hundred actively volcanoes exist on land, and thousands more are found in the sea. **[2]** Eruptions of these volcanoes are often spectacularly violent. **[3]** Hugely reddish clouds rise from the volcano, while bright rivers of lava pour down the mountainside. **[4]** Beyond the eerie, beautiful spectacle that the eye sees, however, is the tremendous destructive force of the volcano. **[5]** A volcano begins as magma, a river of rock melted by the extreme heat inside the earth. **[6]** The rock melts slow, forming a gas that, together with the magma, causes the volcano to erupt. **[7]** Lava flows from the eruption site, sometimes quite rapid, destroying everything in its path. **[8]** After a volcano erupts, observers usually feel badly because the heat and ash created by the eruption can seriously threaten not only the environment but also the lives and property of people nearby. **[9]** On the other hand, volcanoes can also have a positively effect on the environment. **[10]** Lava and volcanic ash gradually mix with the soil to make it wonderful rich in minerals.

Comparison of Modifiers

9c. Modifiers change form to show comparison.

There are three degrees of comparison: the *positive*, the *comparative*, and the *superlative.*

USAGE

	Positive	Comparative	Superlative
Adjectives	large	larger	largest
	careful	more careful	most careful
	courageous	less courageous	least courageous
	good	better	best
Adverbs	soon	sooner	soonest
	clearly	more clearly	most clearly
	commonly	less commonly	least commonly
	well	better	best

Regular Comparison

(1) Most one-syllable modifiers form the comparative degree by adding –er and the superlative degree by adding –est.

Positive	Comparative	Superlative
soft	soft**er**	soft**est**
clean	clean**er**	clean**est**
fast	fast**er**	fast**est**
long	long**er**	long**est**
big	bigg**er**	bigg**est**

(2) Two-syllable modifiers may form the comparative degree by adding –er and the superlative degree by adding –est, or they may form the comparative degree by using more and the superlative degree by using most.

Positive	Comparative	Superlative
simple	simpl**er**	simpl**est**
funny	funni**er**	funni**est**
angry	angri**er**	angri**est**
cautious	**more** cautious	**most** cautious
freely	**more** freely	**most** freely
certain	**more** certain	**most** certain

 S T Y L E T I P

Most two-syllable modifiers can form their comparative and superlative forms either way. If adding –er or –est makes a word sound awkward, use more or most instead.

AWKWARD
specialer, specialest

SMOOTH
more special, most special

(3) Modifiers that have three or more syllables form the comparative degree by using *more* and the superlative degree by using *most.*

Positive	Comparative	Superlative
efficient	**more** efficient	**most** efficient
punctual	**more** punctual	**most** punctual
frequently	**more** frequently	**most** frequently
skillfully	**more** skillfully	**most** skillfully

(4) To show a decrease in the qualities they express, modifiers form the comparative degree by using *less* and the superlative degree by using *least.*

Positive	Comparative	Superlative
proud	**less** proud	**least** proud
honest	**less** honest	**least** honest
patiently	**less** patiently	**least** patiently
reasonably	**less** reasonably	**least** reasonably

Irregular Comparison

The comparative and superlative degrees of some modifiers are not formed by the usual methods.

Positive	Comparative	Superlative
bad	worse	worst
ill	worse	worst
good	better	best
well	better	best
little	less	least
many	more	most
much	more	most
far	farther *or* further	farthest *or* furthest

┌**HELP**──
A dictionary will tell you when a word forms its comparative or superlative form in some way other than by adding –*er* or –*est* or *more* or *most.* Look in a dictionary if you are not sure whether a word has irregular comparative or superlative forms or whether you need to change the spelling of a word before adding –*er* or –*est.*

┌**HELP**──
The word *little* also has regular comparative and superlative forms: *littler, littlest.* These forms are used to describe physical size (the **littlest** piglet). The forms *less* and *least* are used to describe an amount (**less** lemonade).

Exercise 2 Writing the Comparative and Superlative Forms of Modifiers

Write the comparative and the superlative forms of each of the following modifiers.

EXAMPLE   **1.** stubborn

     1. more (less) stubborn; most (least) stubborn

1. anxious
2. hard
3. cheerful
4. eager
5. quick
6. well
7. cold
8. stealthily
9. expensive
10. enthusiastically
11. late
12. safely
13. colorful
14. dangerously
15. jealous
16. fresh
17. clearly
18. silly
19. bravely
20. responsibly

FRANK & ERNEST reprinted by permission of Newspaper Enterprise Association, Inc.

Uses of Comparative and Superlative Forms

9d. Use the comparative degree when comparing two things. Use the superlative degree when comparing more than two things.

COMPARATIVE   Both sisters are athletic, but the **younger** one works **harder.** [comparison of two sisters]

After reading *King Lear* and *A Winter's Tale,* I can understand why *King Lear* is **more widely** praised. [comparison of two plays]

SUPERLATIVE   Of the careers I have researched, I think marine biology is the **most appealing.** [comparison of many careers]

I sat in the front row because it provided the **best** view of the chemistry experiment. [comparison of many views]

S T Y L E   **T I P**

In formal English the words *farther* and *farthest* are used to compare physical distance. The words *further* and *furthest* are used to compare amounts, degrees, and abstract concepts.

EXAMPLES
    The campers hiked **farther** up the mountain than they had planned. [physical distance]

    Excavation of the ancient ruins may provide **further** understanding of the reasons for the decline of the ancient civilization. [abstract concept]

S T Y L E   **T I P**

In informal situations the superlative degree is sometimes used to compare only two things. Avoid such uses of the superlative degree in formal speaking and writing.

INFORMAL
    Which was hardest to learn, French or Spanish?

FORMAL
    Which was **harder** to learn, French or Spanish?

The superlative degree is also used to compare two things in some idiomatic expressions.

EXAMPLE
    Put your **best** foot forward.

USAGE

Problems Using Modifiers

Double Comparisons

9e. **Avoid using double comparisons.**

A *double comparison* is the use of two comparative forms (usually *–er* and *more*) or two superlative forms (usually *–est* and *most*) to modify the same word.

NONSTANDARD	This week's program is more funnier than last week's.
STANDARD	This week's program is **funnier** than last week's.

NONSTANDARD	In our school the most furthest you can go in math is Calculus II.
STANDARD	In our school the **furthest** you can go in math is Calculus II.

Comparison Within a Group

9f. **Include the word *other* or *else* when comparing one member of a group with the rest of the group.**

ILLOGICAL	Anita has hit more home runs this season than any member of her team. [Anita is a member of the team. Logically, Anita could not have hit more home runs than she herself did.]
LOGICAL	Anita has hit more home runs this season than any **other** member of her team.

ILLOGICAL	I think Jean-Pierre Rampal plays the flute better than anyone. [The pronoun *anyone* includes Jean-Pierre Rampal. Logically, Rampal cannot play better than he himself plays.]
LOGICAL	I think that Jean-Pierre Rampal plays the flute better than anyone **else.**

Exercise 3 Using the Comparative and Superlative Forms of Modifiers

Revise the following sentences by correcting the errors in the use of the comparative and superlative forms of modifiers.

EXAMPLE	**1.** It seems I spend more time doing my biology homework than anyone in my class.
	1. It seems I spend more time doing my biology homework than anyone else in my class.

1. Which is the most famous Russian ballet company, the Kirov or the Bolshoi?
2. When Barbara Rose Collins served as a state representative in Michigan, my aunt thought that Collins fought harder than anyone for key legislation to help minorities.
3. I read that Hurricane Andrew, which hit Florida in 1992, did more damage than any hurricane in the 1990s.
4. Both cars appear to be well constructed; I think that the most desirable one is the one that gets better gas mileage.
5. Which of these two hotels is farthest from the airport?
6. I know this shade of blue is a closer match than that one, but we still haven't found the better match.
7. In the dance marathon, Anton and Inez managed to stay awake and keep moving more longer than any other couple on the dance floor.
8. Of all the female singers of the 1960s and 1970s, Joan Baez may have participated in more peace rallies than anyone.
9. Lucinda has the most uncommonest hobby I've ever heard of— collecting insects.
10. The newscaster said that the pollen count this morning was more higher than any other count taken in the past ten years.

Clear Comparisons

9g. Be sure comparisons are clear.

When making comparisons, clearly indicate which items you are comparing.

ILLOGICAL	Katie's arguments in the debate were more persuasive than her opponent. [The sentence makes an illogical comparison between arguments and an opponent.]
LOGICAL	Katie's arguments in the debate were more persuasive than her **opponent's [arguments].** [The sentence logically compares Katie's arguments with her opponent's arguments.]
ILLOGICAL	The ears of the African elephant are larger than the Asian elephant. [The sentence makes an illogical comparison between ears and the Asian elephant.]
LOGICAL	The ears of the African elephant are larger than **those of** the Asian elephant. [By including *those of,* the sentence logically compares the ears of the two elephants.]

Use a complete comparison if there is any chance that an incomplete one could be misunderstood.

UNCLEAR   I baby-sit them more often than anyone else. [The comparison is unclear because the elliptical construction *than anyone else* may be completed in more than one way.]

CLEAR   I baby-sit them more often than **anyone else does.**

CLEAR   I baby-sit them more often than **I baby-sit anyone else.**

UNCLEAR   The director admired the stage crew as highly as the cast members.

CLEAR   The director admired the stage crew as highly as **the cast members did.**

CLEAR   The director admired the stage crew as highly as **she admired the cast members.**

Include all the words that are necessary to complete a *compound comparison,* which uses both the positive and the comparative degrees of a modifier. Avoid the common error of omitting the second *as* in the positive degree.

INCORRECT   The meteorologist predicted, "The temperature tomorrow will be as high, if not higher than, it was today."

CORRECT   The meteorologist predicted, "The temperature tomorrow will be as high **as,** if not higher than, it was today."

Absolute Adjectives

A few adjectives have no comparative or superlative forms; they do not vary in degree. Such adjectives are called *absolute adjectives.* In formal situations, avoid using absolute adjectives in comparisons.

Common Absolute Adjectives		
complete	eternal	round
correct	full	square
dead	impossible	true
endless	infinite	unique
equal	perfect	

INFORMAL	Lena's design was more unique than any of the other designs.
FORMAL	Lena's design was **more unusual** than any of the other designs.
FORMAL	Lena's design was **unique** among all of them.
INFORMAL	Of all the gymnasts' performances, Kyle's was the most perfect!
FORMAL	All of the gymnasts' performances were excellent, but Kyle's was **perfect**!

An absolute adjective may be used in a comparison if the adjective is accompanied by *more nearly* or *most nearly.*

| INCORRECT | Yolanda's answer was more correct than mine. |
| CORRECT | Yolanda's answer was **more nearly** correct than mine. |

Review B   Making Correct Comparisons

The following sentences contain errors in the use of comparisons. Identify and revise each error.

EXAMPLE   1. Does Column A or Column B give the best estimate?

1. *best—better*

1. For many years, the observatory at Mount Palomar was larger than any in the world.
2. Macros make using a computer program more simpler.
3. Sound quality from a CD is generally most acute than that from a cassette tape.
4. Among these writers, Amy Tan certainly has the most unique point of view.
5. When Mrs. Garr decided between the two designs, she chose the one with the best access for wheelchairs.
6. Wow! Your brother Ricardo certainly handles a skateboard better than anyone!
7. This edition of the encyclopedia features the most complete index of subjects.
8. You always have the bestest ideas, Wendy.
9. Athens is older than any European capital.
10. The Bentley was the better of all the British racing cars manufactured between World War I and World War II.

USAGE

Proofread the following paragraph, correcting any informal or incorrect uses of modifiers. If a sentence is already correct, write *C*.

EXAMPLE [1] Of the two forts, this one is the oldest.

1. *older*

[1] St. Augustine, Florida, is the home of Castillo de San Marcos, the most oldest standing fort in the United States. [2] Earlier wooden forts were extremely difficult to defend, but Castillo de San Marcos was built of stone. [3] Before the construction of this fort, Spain had no strong military base that could withstand a real fierce enemy assault. [4] In fact, previous battles with the British had proved that of the two countries, Spain had the least defensible forts. [5] Begun in 1672, the building of Castillo de San Marcos went slow, taking several decades to complete. [6] Replacing the existing nine wooden forts in St. Augustine, the new stone fort fared good against attacks. [7] Today, no one is sure which fort was easiest to protect, Spain's Castillo de San Marcos or the British fort in Charleston, South Carolina. [8] However, Castillo de San Marcos, with its 16-foot-thick walls and 40-foot-wide moat, proved to be one of the most strongest forts in the South and was never taken by force. [9] When Florida finally did come under British control, the Spanish felt especially badly about leaving their impressive fort in the hands of their old enemies. [10] Castillo de San Marcos is now a national monument and stands today as a memorial to all those who fought so courageous to guard St. Augustine long ago.

USAGE

CHAPTER

Chapter Review

A. Using Modifiers Correctly

For each of the following sentences, identify the modifier in parentheses that is correct according to the rules of formal, standard English.

1. When Rosa and I had the flu, Rosa was (*sicker, sickest*).
2. Emilia watched the demonstration (*careful, carefully*).
3. As you approach the next intersection, drive (*cautious, cautiously*).
4. Our new car is roomier than (*any, any other*) car we have ever had.
5. The leaders of the Underground Railroad acted (*quick, quickly*) to help runaway slaves.
6. The smaller kitten is the (*healthier, healthiest*) one.
7. The candidate had prepared his answers (*well, good*).
8. That was a (*real, really*) bad movie.
9. You will drive more (*steady, steadily*) if you focus on the road.
10. Mr. Yan thinks that Jacinto Quirarte is the (*better, best*) of all authorities on Mexican American and pre-Columbian art.

B. Revising Sentences to Correct Modifier Errors

Most of the following sentences contain an awkward, informal, or incorrect use of a modifier. Revise the sentences to correct each such usage. If a sentence is already correct, write *C*.

11. I don't think this suitcase is any more heavier than yours.
12. After comparing my air conditioner with the one on sale, I decided that mine was most efficient.
13. Antonia cooks so bad that I was hesitant to taste her stew.
14. "I predict," said Gretchen, "that the backgammon final between Pearly and Katina will be won by the player with the better strategy."
15. The Indian physicist's theory about supernovas turned out to be more accurate than the Russian astronomer.
16. What is the most scariest movie you have ever seen?
17. She feels badly after losing the chess tournament.
18. After the game, Ian said that his team had played terrible.
19. Lena is the candidest and least pretentious person in our class.
20. Paco is quieter than any member of his debating team.

USAGE

C. Correcting Modifier Errors

Most of the following sentences contain at least one error in the use of modifiers. Identify each error, and then write the correct form. If a sentence is already correct, write *C*.

21. Mrs. Chiang seemed doubtfully when I promised to repair the damage right after dinner.
22. The house on the corner is the less attractive of all the houses on the block, but with a few repairs it could be the nicer.
23. Her perfume smelled even sweeter when she came nearer.
24. My aunt treats uninvited guests rather rude.
25. Dr. Black seems most capable than the other doctor in the clinic.
26. Though the car was in the repair shop for two days, it still does not run real good.
27. When Davis gave his speech, his tone was clearer than that of any other speaker in the class.
28. Your excuse sounds very convincingly.
29. Carry these dishes cautious.
30. Raul seemed even more nervouser about the test than I.

D. Proofreading a Paragraph for the Correct Use of Modifiers

Proofread the following paragraph, and identify any errors in the use of modifiers. Then, write the correct form of the modifier. If a sentence is already correct, write *C*.

[31] Malcolm and I went to visit Chicago's interestingest museum, the Museum of Science and Industry. [32] The museum houses more than two thousand displays, so we knew it would be totally impossible to see all the exhibits in one day. [33] To see certain special displays, we planned our day careful. [34] First, we walked through a really incredible model of a beating heart. [35] The thumping and swishing of the heart were the most greatest sound effects we had ever heard. [36] Next, Malcolm went to play computer games while I decided to explore more livelier happenings at the farm exhibit. [37] When we met later for lunch, I asked him which computer game was hardest to win, tic-tac-toe or solitaire. [38] As we headed for the Omnimax Theater to view the most advanced film projection system in the world, Malcolm admitted that he had not done good at either game. [39] We spent the

rest of the day looking at a submarine, a lunar module, and—the funniest thing of all—ourselves on television! **[40]** We both agreed that the Museum of Science and Industry is the better museum we have ever visited.

Writing Application
Using Modifiers in a Letter

Comparative Forms   Write one of the major television networks a letter pointing out how producers can better address the interests and concerns of teenage viewers. To support your opinion, draw a comparison between two current television shows—one that you and your friends like and one that you do not like. In your letter, use at least five comparative forms of modifiers.

Prewriting   Start by listing several current TV programs aimed at teenage audiences. Ask a few friends to tell you what they like or dislike about each show. Jot down your friends' responses along with your own opinions. Use your notes to help you identify the kinds of characters, situations, and themes that do and do not appeal to teenage viewers.

Writing   Begin your draft by explaining the reason for your letter and clearly stating your opinion. Then, use your notes to help you give specific examples to support your opinion. Be sure that you use the proper form for a business letter.

Revising   Revise your letter to make it as concise and direct as you can. Make sure your comparisons are organized in a clear and logical order.

Publishing   Proofread your letter for any errors in grammar, spelling, and punctuation. Pay special attention to modifiers, and revise any double comparisons. Mail your revised letter to a television network. First, find out the address of the network and, if possible, the name of the person to whom you should write. Then, retype or recopy the letter neatly. You and your classmates may want to collect your letters and send them all together, along with a cover letter.

Placement of Modifiers
Misplaced and Dangling Modifiers

HELP

Sentences in the Diagnostic Preview may be correctly revised in more than one way.

Diagnostic Preview

A. Revising Sentences by Correcting Faulty Modifiers

The following sentences contain errors in the use or placement of modifiers. Revise each sentence so that its meaning is clear and correct.

EXAMPLE   1. Attached to my application, you will find a transcript of my grades.

   1. *You will find a transcript of my grades attached to my application.*

1. Having eaten the remains of the zebra, we watched the lion lick its chops contentedly.
2. To reach the barrier island, the bridge must be crossed.
3. Snowing heavily, we couldn't see the road in front of us.
4. To do well on examinations, good study habits should be used.
5. We have almost seen every painting on the third floor of the modern art museum.

6. The leader of the photo safari promised in the morning we would see a herd of eland.
7. While running for the bus, my wallet must have dropped out of my pocket.
8. Catching the line drive with her usual skill, the crowd rose to their feet and cheered.
9. She traveled to Paris especially to see the *Venus de Milo* on the train last week.
10. After crumbling for hundreds of years, we hardly recognized the ruins as a castle.

B. Using Modifiers Correctly

Most of the following sentences contain errors in the use or placement of modifiers. Revise each faulty sentence so that its meaning is clear and correct. If a sentence is already correct, write *C*.

EXAMPLE   1. Using computer technology, last-minute changes in newspaper layout can be made more easily.

1. *Using computer technology, people who lay out newspaper pages can make last-minute changes more easily.*

11. Computer expert Kim Montgomery claimed in the computer resource center anyone can learn to master basic desktop publishing.
12. To prove Kim's point, we asked Terri, the editor of the school newspaper, to give desktop publishing a try.
13. Kim led Terri, a novice computer user, to an unoccupied terminal with an encouraging smile.
14. In a short tutorial session, Kim emphasized the need to practice adding, deleting, and moving paragraphs.
15. Enthusiastic, page layout was what Terri wanted to learn next.
16. Terri asked Kim to review the session's major points after a short break.
17. Creating illustrations, the sample pages looked terrific to Terri.
18. "To prepare professional-quality illustrations, a graphics package is what is needed," Kim said.
19. Finishing the tutorial, it was clear that desktop publishing would make the school paper even better than last year's.
20. Kim was pleased to see Terri confidently keyboarding information on the way to helping another student.

Misplaced Modifiers

A modifying word, phrase, or clause that seems to modify the wrong word or word group in a sentence is a *misplaced modifier.*

10a. Avoid using misplaced modifiers.

To correct a misplaced modifier, place the modifying word, phrase, or clause as close as possible to the word or words you intend it to modify.

MISPLACED   Undaunted, the storm did not prevent the crew from setting sail as planned. [misplaced word]

CORRECT   The storm did not prevent the **undaunted** crew from setting sail as planned.

MISPLACED   Uncle Carmine saw a deer bounding across a meadow on his way to work. [misplaced prepositional phrases]

CORRECT   **On his way to work,** Uncle Carmine saw a deer bounding across a meadow.

MISPLACED   They were delighted to see a field of daffodils climbing up the hill. [misplaced participial phrase]

CORRECT   **Climbing up the hill,** they were delighted to see a field of daffodils.

MISS PEACH courtesy of Mell Lazarus and Creators Syndicate. © 1991, Mell Lazarus.

USAGE

MISPLACED	The coach praised his players for playing their best as he gave out the trophies. [misplaced adverb clause]
CORRECT	**As he gave out the trophies,** the coach praised his players for playing their best.

Reference Note

For more about **phrases and clauses used as modifiers,** see Chapter 3, The Phrase, and Chapter 4, The Clause.

MISPLACED	A few years ago, a resident of our town bequeathed her entire estate to the animal shelter, which was valued at two million dollars. [misplaced adjective clause]
CORRECT	A few years ago, a resident of our town bequeathed her entire estate, **which was valued at two million dollars,** to the animal shelter.

Squinting Modifiers

10b. Avoid misplacing a modifying word, phrase, or clause so that it seems to modify either of two words. Such a misplaced modifier is often called a *squinting,* or a *two-way, modifier.*

MISPLACED	The prime minister said yesterday her opponent spoke honestly. [Did the prime minister speak yesterday or did her opponent?]
CORRECT	**Yesterday,** the prime minister said her opponent spoke honestly.
CORRECT	The prime minister said her opponent spoke honestly **yesterday.**

MISPLACED	The manager told the two rookies after the game to report to the dugout. [Did the manager talk to the rookies after the game or were the rookies to report to the dugout after the game?]
CORRECT	**After the game** the manager told the two rookies to report to the dugout.
CORRECT	The manager told the two rookies to report to the dugout **after the game.**

MISPLACED	The mayor said when the city council met he would discuss the proposed budget. [Did the mayor make his statement when the council met or would he discuss the budget when the council next met?]
CORRECT	**When the city council met,** the mayor said he would discuss the proposed budget.
CORRECT	The mayor said he would discuss the proposed budget **when the city council met.**

USAGE

Exercise 1 **Revising Sentences by Correcting Misplaced Modifiers**

The following sentences contain misplaced modifiers. Revise each sentence so that its meaning is clear and correct.

EXAMPLE 1. To get some exercise during our vacation last summer, we almost played tennis every day.

1. *To get some exercise during our vacation last summer, we played tennis almost every day.*

1. Louise projected the photographs on a large screen that she had taken at the zoo.
2. Mr. Martínez promised in the morning he would tell an American Indian trickster tale.
3. I pointed to the fish tank and showed my friends the baby angelfish, swelling with pride.
4. Ralph Ellison said during an interview Richard Wright inspired him to become a writer.
5. I talked about the problem I had in writing my first draft with Megan, and she said she had the same problem.
6. My aunt had finally mastered the art of upholstering furniture, filled with pride.
7. Rested and refreshed, a night's sleep had energized them.
8. Mrs. Jennings sang some folk songs about working on the railroad in the auditorium.
9. There is a bracelet in the museum that is four thousand years old.
10. I found a good book about Virginia Woolf written by her husband Leonard at a garage sale.

Dangling Modifiers

A modifying word, phrase, or clause that does not clearly and sensibly modify any word or word group in a sentence is a ***dangling modifier.***

10c. Avoid using dangling modifiers.

To correct a dangling modifier, add or replace words to make the meaning of the sentence clear and sensible.

DANGLING Determined, Christy Haubegger's plan was to publish a bilingual magazine for Hispanic women. [Was the plan determined?]

| CORRECT | **Determined, Christy Haubegger planned** to publish a bilingual magazine for Hispanic women. |

| CORRECT | **Christy Haubegger was determined** to publish a bilingual magazine for Hispanic women. |

| DANGLING | Having selected a college, a trip to the campus was planned. [Who selected a college?] |

| CORRECT | **Having selected a college, my friend and I** planned a trip to the campus. |

| CORRECT | **After we selected a college, my friend and I** planned a trip to the campus. |

| DANGLING | After researching the African American oral tradition in Florida, the book *Mules and Men* was written. [Who was researching?] |

| CORRECT | **After researching the African American oral tradition in Florida, Zora Neale Hurston** wrote the book *Mules and Men.* |

| CORRECT | **After Zora Neale Hurston researched the African American oral tradition in Florida, she** wrote the book *Mules and Men.* |

| DANGLING | While wrapping the gifts, Murphy, my pet terrier, kept trying to untie the bows. [Was the terrier wrapping the gifts?] |

| CORRECT | **While I was wrapping the gifts,** Murphy, my pet terrier, kept trying to untie the bows. |

| CORRECT | **While wrapping the gifts, I** noticed that Murphy, my pet terrier, kept trying to untie the bows. |

Reference Note

For information about using a **comma after an introductory word, phrase, or clause,** see page 309.

USAGE

Exercise 2 Revising Sentences by Correcting Dangling Modifiers

The following sentences contain dangling modifiers. Revise each sentence so that its meaning is clear and correct.

EXAMPLE 1. Waiting at the bus stop, my older brother drove by in his new car.

1. *While I was waiting at the bus stop, my older brother drove by in his new car.*

HELP

Sentences in Exercise 2 may be correctly revised in more than one way.

1. Noticing the fresh lettuce, the rabbit's ears perked up and its nose twitched.
2. To interpret this poem, a knowledge of mythology is helpful.
3. All bundled up in a blanket, the baby's first outing was a brief one.
4. When performing onstage, the microphone should not be placed too near the speaker cones.

5. To be a good opera singer, clear enunciation is extremely important.

6. To help colonial soldiers during the Revolutionary War, Haym Solomon's efforts raised money to buy food and clothing.

7. Before moving to Sacramento, Pittsburgh had been their home for ten years.

8. While reaching into his pocket for change, the car rolled into the side of the tollbooth.

9. Alone, the peace and quiet that followed the busy weekend was a welcome relief.

10. When discussing colonial American writers, the contributions of the African American poet Phillis Wheatley should not be forgotten.

Review A   Identifying and Correcting Dangling and Misplaced Modifiers

Most of the following sentences contain a dangling or misplaced modifier. Revise each sentence so that it is clear and correct. If a sentence is already correct, write *C*.

EXAMPLE   1. Please put the grocery bags in the car on the counter.

1. *Please bring the grocery bags in from the car and put them on the counter.*

1. Puzzled by the philosopher's statements, a forest of hands rose in the audience.

2. A painting of horses prancing around a stream by that artist hangs in our living room.

3. Vinnie, who had just turned three years old, saw his grandfather for the first time.

4. Before being admitted to the university, numerous forms must be completed and returned.

5. Having met the Dalai Lama in person, the memory would always be treasured.

6. Surprised, the announcement of the award left Heidi speechless.

7. Did you see a video about polar bears at summer camp?

8. To make accurate calculations, using a computer is helpful but not necessary for accountants.

9. Balloons flew to the ceiling above the children carried by helium.

10. While cleaning my room, a number of lost items appeared—a charm from my bracelet, my favorite socks, and my old journal from fourth grade.

┌**HELP**┐

Sentences in Review A may be correctly revised in more than one way.

┌**STYLE**   **TIP**┐

A dangling modifier may occur when a sentence is in the passive voice. Rewriting sentences in the active voice not only eliminates many dangling modifiers but also makes your writing more interesting and lively.

PASSIVE VOICE
To improve your writing, good books must be read. [*To improve your writing* is a dangling modifier.]

ACTIVE VOICE
To improve your writing, you must read good books. [*To improve your writing* modifies *you.*]

The following sentences contain misplaced and dangling modifiers. Read each sentence aloud, and revise it so that its meaning is clear and correct.

EXAMPLES
1. Taylor told me at tonight's concert Nicoletta would be singing a solo part in Prokofiev's cantata *Alexander Nevsky*.

1. *Taylor told me Nicoletta would be singing a solo part in Prokofiev's cantata* Alexander Nevsky *at tonight's concert.*

or

1. *At tonight's concert, Taylor told me Nicoletta would be singing a solo part in Prokofiev's cantata* Alexander Nevsky.

2. After washing and peeling the carrots, they were sliced lengthwise and added to the stew.

2. *After washing and peeling the carrots, I sliced them lengthwise and added them to the stew.*

1. Having deposited her paycheck at the bank branch in the supermarket, her checkbook could not be found until she looked in her shopping cart.

2. Afraid that the strong wind and enormous waves of the hurricane were going to sink his ship, the freighter was deliberately driven aground just south of the lighthouse by its captain.

3. To prepare us for the test on Monday, our English teacher encouraged us to watch the film version of *Much Ado About Nothing* directed by Kenneth Branagh at some point during the weekend.

4. Having admired the young pianist's first two recordings of Duke Ellington's tunes, the music critic's wish was that the artist would record a version of Ellington's "Take the A Train."

5. Ms. Beckinsale always ordered whatever new dish was placed on the menu of the Thai restaurant downtown before anyone else had tried it.

6. Kendra announced after reading through all the college and university catalogs she had decided to apply to three schools: the University of Michigan, the University of Texas, and Stanford University.

7. While trying to write a short story at my computer, my cat Sam insisted on walking back and forth across the keyboard.

MEETING THE CHALLENGE

The Style Tip on page 234 notes that sentences containing passive-voice verbs are prone to dangling modifiers in a way that sentences containing active-voice verbs are not. Go through the textbook's examples of sentences with dangling modifiers, copying any that are in passive voice. Then, analyze the sentences: Why are passive-voice sentences prone to dangling modifiers? Discuss your thoughts with your classmates.

USAGE

Reference Note

For more about **active voice** and **passive voice,** see page 194.

8. The research ship from the oceanographic institute discovered the wreck of an old Spanish galleon in the waters of the Gulf of Mexico that had sunk over three hundred years ago.
9. Concerned about the heat and the humidity, the annual marathon was canceled to protect the health of the runners.
10. Looking everywhere, even under the bed and at the back of the closet, the red shoes could not be found in time for the dance recital.

Review B   Revising Sentences by Correcting Faulty Modifiers

Most of the following sentences contain errors in the use of modifiers. Revise each faulty sentence so that its meaning is clear and correct. If a sentence is already correct, write *C*.

EXAMPLE
1. I showed all my friends the terrific photos I had taken on my trip to Hawaii when I got back.

1. *When I got back, I showed all my friends the terrific photos I had taken on my trip to Hawaii.*

1. Visitors soon learn how important one person can be on vacation in Hawaii.
2. Born in the mid-1700s, the Hawaiian people were united under one government by Kamehameha I.
3. After capturing Maui, Molokai, and Lanai, the island of Oahu soon became another of Kamehameha's conquests.
4. Kamehameha assured the Hawaiian people when he became the ruler of the entire island they would see peace.
5. Kamehameha was certain by 1810 his conquest of the islands would be successful.
6. United, Kamehameha's victory over Kauai and Niihau brought prosperity to the Hawaiian Islands.
7. A hero to his people, Kamehameha's government ruled Hawaii for many years.
8. Thomas Gould crafted a statue honoring the great ruler.
9. While being transported by sea, the Hawaiian people lost their beloved statue.
10. Still resting at the bottom of the ocean, the sculptor made the duplicate shown here.

┌HELP┐

Sentences in Review B may be correctly revised in more than one way.

USAGE

KAMEHAMEHA I

Chapter Review

A. Revising Sentences by Correcting Misplaced Modifiers

The following sentences contain misplaced modifiers. Revise each sentence so that its meaning is clear and correct.

1. Min Li happened to see an albino squirrel on the way to school.
2. The teacher told Meg during the class to present her book report.
3. The race car driver said earlier his crew had performed well.
4. I saw an organ grinder and his monkey perform on a crowded sidewalk while sitting in a café on the Champs Élysées in Paris.
5. In costume, Elizabeth thought the dancer looked stunning.
6. The speaker of the house said after the final vote was taken he would speak to the press.
7. Tony was fascinated by a school of dolphins on the excursion boat.
8. Fearless, the bomb was defused by the special squad.
9. Ava counted the moons of Jupiter looking through the telescope.
10. The literary agent promised for the author to negotiate a fair royalty when the book was accepted.

B. Revising Sentences by Correcting Dangling Modifiers

The following sentences contain dangling modifiers. Revise each sentence so that its meaning is clear and correct.

11. When planning a vacation, Brownsville, Texas, is an interesting destination to consider.
12. Serving as a tourist gateway from the U.S. to Mexico, two bridges lead to Matamoros, Tamaulipas.
13. Located near South Padre Island, you can visit the best beaches in Texas without driving far from there.
14. To attend the Charros Days festival hosted by Brownsville and Matamoros, February is the time to go.
15. Before leaving the area, the Sabal Palm Grove Wildlife Sanctuary should be explored.

C. Revising Sentences by Correcting Faulty Modifiers

Most of the following sentences contain errors in the placement and use of modifiers. Revise each faulty sentence so that its meaning is clear. If a sentence is already correct, write *C*.

16. The Alvarezes decided to visit the historic town of Williamsburg, Virginia, which has been painstakingly restored on the spur of the moment.
17. Decorated in colonial style, the family registered at a quaint inn.
18. After resting for an hour or so, the Governor's Palace and the Capitol were visited.
19. Joel snapped a shot of a candlemaker quickly focusing his camera.
20. A tour guide at DeWitt Wallace Decorative Arts Gallery explained how eighteenth-century costumes were sewn.
21. The tour guide said when the family asked she would be happy to go into greater detail.
22. Dressed in colonial garb, a woman at the Raleigh Tavern asked the family to imagine how eighteenth-century residents may have spread news.
23. Having seen enough for the day, a quiet dinner at the inn was enjoyed by the Alvarez family.
24. Kevin dipped his spoon into a bowl of peanut-butter soup filled with great apprehension.
25. With fond memories and many photographs, the trip to Williamsburg will not soon be forgotten.

D. Revising Sentences by Correcting Faulty Modifiers

Most of the following sentences contain errors in the use of modifiers. Revise each faulty sentence so that its meaning is clear. If a sentence is already correct, write *C*.

26. Racing across the screens, computer programmers use animation programs to show cartoon characters.
27. Grant and Lee rode to Appomattox Court House to make an agreement that ended the Civil War on horses.
28. To honor the inventor Jan Ernst Matzeliger, the U.S. Postal Service issued a new stamp in the Black Heritage Series.

29. Lue Gim Gong developed a type of orange that could resist frost in his laboratory.

30. Attacking at dawn, the Battle of Hastings was won by William the Conqueror in 1066.

31. The detective writer said on page one he would introduce a new villain.

32. In all departments of Huntsville's Marshall Space Flight Center, scientists have planned carefully to ensure that the International Space Station will soon be completed.

33. When proofreading on a computer, screen format should be checked as well as spelling.

34. The mayoral candidate said in a full-page newspaper advertisement an apology would be forthcoming.

35. Did you know that Navajo advisors helped to develop a system of codes that the U.S. Army used while fighting World War II in New Mexico?

Writing Application

Using Modifiers in a Restaurant Review

Making Comparisons   You are the restaurant critic for a food magazine. Write a paragraph describing, evaluating, and comparing one meal at each of your two favorite restaurants. Make sure your modifiers are correctly placed.

Prewriting   Think of two restaurants, either real or imaginary. Compare the restaurants in several categories—food, atmosphere, price, service. Read several columns by a magazine or newspaper restaurant critic to see how a professional writes about food.

Writing   Use your prewriting notes to help you describe the meals as you write your first draft.

Revising   Ask a classmate to read your paragraph. Are your descriptions clear? Did you include factual details to support your opinions? Revise any confusing or unclear sentences.

Publishing   Check your paragraph for errors in grammar, usage, and mechanics. Your class may want to assemble your paragraphs and put together a guide to local restaurants.

CHAPTER

11

A Glossary of Usage
Common Usage Problems

Diagnostic Preview

A. Correcting Errors in Usage

Most of the following sentences contain errors in the use of standard English. If a sentence contains an error, revise the sentence. If a sentence is already correct, write *C*.

EXAMPLE   **1.** Did we do alright, Terry?
            1. Did we do all right, Terry?

1. They said it was a awfully serious issue.
2. I inferred from what Julio said that he has excepted my apology.
3. Over eighty years ago my great-grandfather immigrated from Mexico.
4. The Seminoles of Florida piece together colorful fabrics to create striking dresses, shirts, skirts, and etc.
5. He talked persuasively for an hour, but his words had no affect.
6. The amount of hours I have spent studying lately has really helped my grades.
7. Are you implying that you noticed nothing unusual in the cafeteria today?
8. When Ruth, Tamisha, and I ate at the new Ethiopian restaurant, the food was served in communal bowls, and we divided it between ourselves.

9. The reason the book was so difficult to understand was because the writing was unclear.
10. If you kept less fish in your tank, they would live longer.

B. Correcting Errors in Usage

Each of the sentences in the following paragraph contains at least one error in the use of standard, formal English. Identify the error(s) in each sentence, and then write the correct form(s).

EXAMPLE   [1] In-line skates provide such a smooth, fast ride that they give the allusion of ice-skating.

1. allusion—illusion

[11] Almost no one could of predicted the revolution that took place in skating equipment a few years ago. [12] Surprisingly, the very first in-line roller skates were invented somewheres in the Netherlands in the 1700s. [13] I read in the newspaper where in 1769 a London instrument maker and mechanic wore in-line skates with metal wheels to a party. [14] Playing a violin, he came gliding into the room on the skates, but he made a crash landing because he didn't have no idea how to stop. [15] Maybe that's why nobody really excepted the newfangled skates in them days. [16] Later, an American inventor devised the four-wheeled skate, which became popular, and it looked like in-line skates weren't never going to succeed. [17] Finally, in 1980, two Minneapolis brothers noticed that hockey players hated being off of the ice during the summer. [18] Being as in-line skates would be a perfect cross-training tool to help keep hockey players in shape all year, the brothers started making the new skates in their basement. [19] The idea might of stopped right there if other people hadn't found out that beside being a good training tool, in-line skating is just plain fun. [20] In-line skating offers a great low-impact aerobic workout, and it's safe—as long as skaters wear the right type protective gear and learn how to stop!

About the Glossary

This chapter provides a compact glossary of common problems in English usage. A *glossary* is an alphabetical list of special terms or expressions with definitions, explanations, and examples.

You will notice that some examples in this glossary are labeled *nonstandard, standard, formal,* or *informal.* The label **nonstandard** identifies usage that does not follow the guidelines of standard English usage. *Standard* English is language that is grammatically correct and appropriate in formal and informal situations. *Formal* identifies usage that is appropriate in serious writing and speaking, such as in compositions for school and in speeches. The label *informal* indicates standard English that is generally used in conversation and in everyday writing, such as in personal letters.

The following are examples of formal and informal English.

Reference Note

For a list of **words often confused,** see page 375. Use the index at the back of the book to find discussions of other usage problems.

Reference Note

For more about **articles,** see page 10.

Formal	Informal
unpleasant	yucky
agreeable	cool
very impressive	totally awesome

a, an   These *indefinite articles* refer to a member of a general group. *A* is used before words beginning with a consonant sound. *An* is used before words beginning with a vowel sound.

EXAMPLES   "New African" is **a** poignant story about **a** young African American girl growing up in Philadelphia during the early 1960s.

Orchard Avenue is **a** one-way street. [The *o* in *one-way* is pronounced as if it were preceded by a *w;* therefore, the word begins with a consonant sound.]

The teacher read from the novel **an** excerpt that describes the grandfather as **an** honorable man. [The *h* in *honorable* is silent; therefore, the word begins with a vowel sound.]

accept, except   *Accept* is a verb meaning "to receive." *Except* may be used as a verb or as a preposition. As a verb, *except* means "to leave out." As a preposition, *except* means "excluding."

EXAMPLES   Dawn is always eager to **accept** a challenge.

Ms. Liu will not **except** anyone from the deadline. [verb]

She typed everything **except** the bibliography. [preposition]

affect, effect   *Affect* is a verb meaning "to influence." *Effect* may be used as a verb or as a noun. As a verb, *effect* means "to bring about [a desired result]" or "to accomplish." As a noun, *effect* means "the result [of an action]."

USAGE

Decisions of the United States Supreme Court **affect** the lives of many people.

Some of the decisions **effect** great social change. [verb]

Did you study the **effects** of the *Brown* v. *Board of Education of Topeka, Kansas,* decision? [noun]

ain't *Ain't* is nonstandard. Avoid using *ain't* in speech and in all writing other than dialogue.

all ready, already See page 375.

all right *All right* means "satisfactory," "unhurt," "safe," "correct," or, in reply to a question or to preface a remark, "yes." Although the spelling *alright* is sometimes used, it has not become accepted as standard usage.

EXAMPLES   There has been an accident, but everyone is **all right.**

All right, now save the document on your hard drive.

all the farther, all the faster Avoid using these expressions. Instead, use *as far as* and *as fast as.*

NONSTANDARD   Eight miles is all the farther we can hike in one day.
STANDARD   Eight miles is **as far as** we can hike in one day.

allusion, illusion An *allusion* is an indirect reference to something. An *illusion* is a mistaken idea or a misleading appearance.

EXAMPLES   The phrase *the golden touch* is an **allusion** to the myth of King Midas.

Illusions of being invincible can lead to tragedy.

The 3-D glasses created the **illusion** of depth.

a lot With the article *a, lot* may be used as a noun or as an adverb. As a noun, *a lot* means "a large number or amount." As an adverb, *a lot* means "a great deal" or "very much." Both uses are informal; avoid them in formal speaking and writing situations. *Alot* is a misspelling of the expression in either use.

INFORMAL   A lot [not *Alot*] of movies have been adapted from the works of Shakespeare. [noun]

They arrived a lot [not *alot*] earlier than I did. [adverb]

FORMAL   **Many** movies have been adapted from the works of Shakespeare. [adjective]

They arrived **much** earlier than I did. [adverb]

alumni, alumnae   *Alumni* (pronounced ə·lum´·nī) is the plural of *alumnus* (a male graduate). *Alumnae* (pronounced ə·lum´·nē) is the plural of *alumna* (a female graduate). Considered as a single group, the graduates of a coeducational school are referred to as *alumni*.

EXAMPLES   The **alumni** I mentioned are both Eagle Scouts.

Did the administration ask the **alumnae** how they felt about admitting men to the school?

Men and women from the first graduating class attended the **alumni** reunion.

NOTE   In informal usage the graduates from a women's college are sometimes called *alumni*. In formal situations, however, the plural *alumnae* should be used.

among   See **between, among.**

amount, number   Use *amount* to refer to uncountable nouns. Use *number* to refer to countable nouns.

EXAMPLES   Pearl has a large **amount** of homework today. [*Amount* refers to the word *homework*.]

She must study for a **number** of quizzes. [*Number* refers to the word *quizzes*.]

STYLE   TIP

In formal situations, it is generally best to avoid using *etc.*

and etc.   *Etc.* is an abbreviation of the Latin words *et cetera*, meaning "and others" or "and so forth." Since *and* is included in the definition of *etc.*, using *and* with *etc.* is redundant.

EXAMPLE   Arthur has already learned several dances: the two-step, the waltz, the grapevine, the mazurka, **etc.** [not *and etc.*]

anyways, anywheres   These words and similar words, such as *everywheres*, *somewheres*, and *nowheres*, should have no final *s*.

EXAMPLES   I couldn't take both band and art **anyway** [not *anyways*].

Are your grandparents going camping **anywhere** [not *anywheres*] this summer?

as   See **like, as.**

as if   See **like, as if, as though.**

at   Avoid using *at* after a construction beginning with *where.*

NONSTANDARD   Where is the Crow Canyon Archaeological Center at?

STANDARD   Where is the Crow Canyon Archaeological Center?

a while, awhile   Used with the article *a, while* is a noun meaning "a period of time." *Awhile* is an adverb meaning "for a short time."

EXAMPLES   It's been **a while** since we've taken a vacation.

Michael Jordan played professional baseball for **a while.**

Let's rest **awhile;** I'm tired.

Exercise 1   Identifying Correct Usage

For each of the following sentences, choose the word or word group that is correct according to the rules of standard, formal English.

EXAMPLE   **1.** My mother and Ms. Wang, both (*alumnae, alumni*) of Pratt Institute, went there to see an exhibition of paintings.

1. alumnae

1. In 1988, the artist Chuck Close suffered spinal-artery collapse, and even though he never fully recovered, he kept painting (*anyway, anyways*).

2. Partially paralyzed, he learned to work from a wheelchair, with (*a, an*) handy arrangement of straps to hold his brush in place.

3. As he had done before his illness, Close painted large portraits of friends, fellow artists, (*and etc., etc.*)

4. The picture here is an example of how Close generally painted before 1988, dividing a photograph of a person into a large (*amount, number*) of tiny squares.

5. He would first rule the canvas or paper into a grid, and then he would copy the photo's colors, bit by bit, into the small squares to create the type of (*allusion, illusion*) you see here.

6. A single painting might contain (*anywhere, anywheres*) from a few hundred to several thousand squares.

7. This explanation was perfectly clear to everyone (*accept, except*) me.

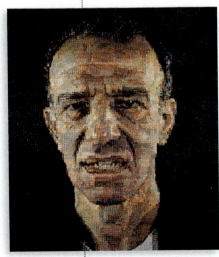

Chuck Close, *Alex* (1987). Oil on canvas (100" x 84"). John Back. Photo courtesy of The Pace Gallery, New York.

USAGE

8. The photograph here shows Close in 1991 working on a self-portrait that has a similar (*affect, effect*); you can see that his style is bolder and more colorful.

9. At first glance, you may be surprised by his newer paintings and wonder where that computerlike quality (*is, is at*)!

10. However, you soon realize that Close had never really gone (*all the farther, as far as*) he could with his grid technique and that his recent paintings are a logical extension of his earlier style.

Chuck Close in his studio painting *Self Portrait* (1991). Oil on canvas (100"x 84"). Bill Jacobson Studio. Photograph courtesy of The Pace Gallery, New York.

bad, badly See page 214.

because In formal writing and speaking, do not use the construction *reason . . . because.* Instead, use *reason . . . that.*

INFORMAL   One reason to use mulch on your garden is because it helps keep the weeds down.

FORMAL   One reason to use mulch on your garden is **that** it helps keep the weeds down.

being as, being that Avoid using either of these expressions for *because* or *since.*

EXAMPLE   **Because** [not *Being as*] Flora is a good carpenter, she will be a great asset to the stage crew.

beside, besides *Beside* is a preposition meaning "by the side of." *Besides* may be used as a preposition or as an adverb. As a preposition, *besides* means "in addition to." As an adverb, *besides* means "moreover."

EXAMPLES   He set the plate of sandwiches **beside** the bowl of fruit punch.

Besides fringe benefits, the job offered a high salary. [preposition]

I am not really hungry for popcorn; **besides,** the movie is about to start. [adverb]

between, among Use *between* when referring to only two items or to more than two when each item is being compared to each other item.

EXAMPLES   The photography assignments for the next issue have been divided **between** Tanaki and Jeffrey.

Ms. Murray explained the differences **between** a neutron, a proton, and an electron.

Use *among* when you are referring to more than two items and are not considering each item in relation to each of the others.

EXAMPLE The mother divided the broccoli casserole equally **among** the three children.

borrow, lend *Borrow* means "to take [something] temporarily." *Lend* means "to give [something] temporarily." Its principal parts are *lend, (is) lending, lent, (have) lent.*

EXAMPLES May I **borrow** your calculator?

I'll be glad to **lend** you the money if you want to buy the tickets.

bring, take *Bring* means "to come carrying something." *Take* means "to go carrying something."

EXAMPLES Please **bring** the results of your survey when you come to our next class meeting.

Please **take** the model of the Globe Theatre to the library tomorrow.

You may **take** my softball glove to school today, but please **bring** it home this afternoon.

bust, busted Avoid using these words as verbs. Use a form of *break* or *burst*, or *catch* or *arrest*, depending on the meaning you intend.

EXAMPLES One of the headlights on the van is **broken** [not *busted*].

A pipe in the apartment above ours **burst** [not *busted*].

I tried to sneak past Charley, but I got **caught** [not *busted*].

The police **arrested** [not *busted*] two burglars.

but, only See **The Double Negative,** page 261.

can, may See page 201.

can't hardly, can't scarcely See **The Double Negative,** page 261.

could of See **of.**

discover, invent *Discover* means "to learn of the existence of [something]." *Invent* means "to bring [something new] into existence."

EXAMPLES In 1610, Galileo Galilei **discovered** Jupiter's four large moons: Io, Europa, Ganymede, and Callisto.

The compact disc was **invented** in 1972.

STYLE   **TIP**

Loan, a noun in formal language, is often used in place of *lend* in informal situations.

INFORMAL
I'll be glad to loan you the money if you want to buy the tickets.

FORMAL
I will be glad to **lend** you the money if you want to buy the tickets.

USAGE

done *Done* is the past participle of *do*. Avoid using *done* for *did*, which is the past form of *do* and does not require a helping verb.

NONSTANDARD   He done all of his homework over the weekend.
STANDARD   He **did** all of his homework over the weekend.
STANDARD   He **had done** all of his homework over the weekend.

STYLE   TIP

Some people consider contractions informal. Therefore, in formal speech and writing, it is generally best to spell out words instead of using contractions.

Reference Note

For more information about **contractions,** see page 349.

don't, doesn't *Don't* is the contraction of *do not*. *Doesn't* is the contraction of *does not*. Use *doesn't*, not *don't*, with singular subjects except *I* and *you*.

EXAMPLES   She **doesn't** [not *don't*] like seafood.

The bookstore **doesn't** [not *don't*] have any copies of Faith Ringgold's *Tar Beach* in stock.

effect See **affect, effect.**

emigrate, immigrate *Emigrate* is a verb meaning "to leave a country or region to settle elsewhere." *Immigrate* is a verb meaning "to come into a country or region to settle there."

EXAMPLES   Thousands of people **emigrated** from Germany during the 1870s.

Most of the German refugees **immigrated** to the United States.

NOTE The nouns that correspond to *emigrate* and *immigrate* are *emigrant* (one who goes away from a country or region) and *immigrant* (one who comes into a country or region).

etc. See **and etc.**

everywheres See **anyways, anywheres.**

except See **accept, except.**

fewer, less Use *fewer*, which tells "how many," to modify a countable noun. Use *less*, which tells "how much," to modify an uncountable noun.

EXAMPLES   **Fewer** students are going out for football this year.

I find that I have much more fun now that I spend **less** time watching TV.

good, well See page 214.

Oral Practice · Choosing Correct Usage

Read aloud each of the following sentences, choosing the word or word group that is correct according to the rules of standard, formal English.

EXAMPLE 1. I need to (*bring, take*) these books back to the library.

1. *I need to take these books back to the library.*

1. There isn't one state that (*doesn't, don't*) have numerous place names derived from American Indian words.
2. You will make (*fewer, less*) mistakes if you proofread your paper.
3. The assignments on classical Greek philosophers were divided (*among, between*) the juniors in the humanities class.
4. Please (*borrow, lend*) me your notes from yesterday.
5. Will you (*bring, take*) these books to Jonah when you go to his house?
6. (*Being that, Since*) she has passed all the tests, she should be a likely candidate for the military academy.
7. The reason the can burst is (*because, that*) water expands when it freezes.
8. Chen Rong was a famous Chinese artist who (*did, done*) many beautiful paintings of dragons.
9. (*Beside, Besides*) *The Scarlet Letter* and *The Red Badge of Courage*, we read *The Joy Luck Club*.
10. During the middle of the nineteenth century, many Asians (*emigrated, immigrated*) to the United States.

Review A · Completing Sentences with Correct Usage

Choose an item from the colored box to complete each of the following sentences correctly.

except	accept	held at	number
being as	busted	that	because
immigrate	alumni	alumnae	took
anywheres	held	amount	anywhere
brought	emigrate	since	broke

HELP

Be careful! Some of the items in the box in Review A are nonstandard usages.

EXAMPLE 1. Two years ago, my uncle Koichi decided to _____ to this country.

1. *immigrate*

1. Fortunately, he _____ along his marvelous kite-making skills and his keen business sense.

2. At first it was hard for Uncle Koichi to _____ the fact that kite flying isn't as popular here as it is in Japan.

3. I did some research for him and found out where the big kite festivals are _____.

4. He decided to settle right here in Southern California _____ plenty of kite enthusiasts live here year-round.

5. First, Uncle Koichi built a small _____ of beautiful kites, and then he started giving kite-flying lessons.

6. All three of my older brothers are enthusiastic _____ of Koichi's Kite College.

7. The reason that Uncle Koichi's shop is successful is _____ he loves his work and is very good at it.

8. My first kite _____ into pieces when I crashed it into a tree, but Uncle Koichi built me another one.

9. I took this photograph of his magnificent dragon kite, which takes _____ from three to five people to launch, depending on wind conditions.

10. My uncle's customers and friends all hope that he will never _____ from the United States and take his glorious kites back to Japan.

Review B Correcting Errors in Usage

Most of the following sentences contain errors in the use of standard, formal English. If a sentence contains an error or an informal usage, revise the sentence. If a sentence is already correct, write *C*.

EXAMPLE **1.** The five starting players have twenty fouls between them.

1. *The five starting players have twenty fouls among them.*

1. It don't look as if the rain will stop this afternoon.
2. Sometimes I can get so absorbed in a movie that I forget where I am at.
3. Would you bring your guitar when you come to visit us?
4. The drought seriously effected the lettuce crop.
5. You must learn to except criticism if you want to improve.
6. Being as the Black History Month essay contest ends next week, we need to submit our entries soon.
7. The reason that many Irish people moved to France and Argentina after the unsuccessful Irish rebellion in 1798 is because they refused to live under English rule.
8. Who discovered computer chips?
9. The title of James Baldwin's *Notes of a Native Son* is an illusion to Richard Wright's famous novel *Native Son.*
10. Beside you and me, who is going on the hike?

Review C **Proofreading a Paragraph for Correct Usage**

Most of the sentences in the following paragraph contain an error in the use of standard English. Identify the error in each sentence, and then write the correct form. If a sentence is already correct, write *C.*

EXAMPLE   [1] If you like to jump rope alot, find out if there's a branch of the American Double Dutch League near you.

    1. *alot—a lot*

    [1] Double Dutch is a fast-action rope-jumping style that has been popular on U.S. playgrounds for anywhere from fifty to a hundred years. [2] In Double Dutch, turners twirl two ropes alternately in opposite

directions, creating an eggbeater effect. [3] Being that the two ropes are going so fast, jumpers have to jump double-fast. [4] Their feet fly at over three hundred steps a minute—about half that number is all the faster I can go! [5] To make things even more interesting, two jumpers often perform together to rhymes or music, doing flips, twists, cartwheels, and etc. [6] Besides competing in local meets, jumpers can participate in competitions organized by the American Double Dutch League, the sport's official governing body. [7] In competition, all teams must undergo the same amount of tests, including the speed test, the compulsory-tricks test, and the freestyle test. [8] The photo on the previous page isn't an optical allusion—the two jumpers are twins as well as a Double Dutch doubles team! [9] These girls not only won their divisional title in the American Double Dutch League World Championships but also were chosen to bring their sport to the Moscow International Folk Festival. [10] The late Olympic athlete Florence "Flo-Jo" Joyner enthusiastically supported Double Dutch, and it don't surprise me at all that she liked to jump Double Dutch herself!

had of See **of.**

had ought, hadn't ought Do not use *had* or *hadn't* with *ought.*

NONSTANDARD	Your rough draft had ought to be finished by now.
STANDARD	Your rough draft **ought** to be finished by now.

NONSTANDARD	She hadn't ought to have turned here.
STANDARD	She **ought not** to have turned here.

hardly See **The Double Negative,** page 261.

he, she, it, they Avoid using a pronoun along with its antecedent as the subject of a verb. Such an error is sometimes called a ***double subject.***

NONSTANDARD	The computer system it is down today.
STANDARD	The **computer system** is down today.

NONSTANDARD	Fay Stanley and Diane Stanley they wrote a biography of the Hawaiian princess Ka'iulani.
STANDARD	**Fay Stanley and Diane Stanley** wrote a biography of the Hawaiian princess Ka'iulani.

hisself, theirself, theirselves *Hisself, theirself,* and *theirselves* are nonstandard. Avoid using these forms in speech and in all writing other than dialogue. Instead, use *himself* and *themselves.*

hopefully *Hopefully* means "in a hopeful manner" or "it is to be hoped."

EXAMPLES   When the fog lifted, the mountain climbers **hopefully** resumed their ascent.

We will leave early, **hopefully** by six.

illusion See **allusion, illusion.**

immigrate See **emigrate, immigrate.**

imply, infer *Imply* means "to suggest." *Infer* means "to interpret" or "to draw as a conclusion."

EXAMPLES   The governor **implied** in her speech that she would support a statewide testing program.

I **inferred** from the governor's speech that she would support a statewide testing program.

in, into *In* means "within." *Into* means "from the outside to the inside." In formal situations, avoid using *in* for *into*.

INFORMAL   He threw the scraps of paper in the litter basket.
FORMAL   He threw the scraps of paper **into** the litter basket.

invent See **discover, invent.**

it See **he, she, it, they.**

its, it's See page 378.

kind of, sort of In formal situations, avoid using *kind of* or *sort of* for the adverb *somewhat* or *rather*.

INFORMAL   Jackie was kind of disappointed when she did not make the basketball team.
FORMAL   Jackie was **somewhat** [or *rather*] disappointed when she did not make the basketball team.

kind of a, sort of a In formal situations, omit the *a*.

INFORMAL   What kind of a car do you drive?
FORMAL   What **kind of** car do you drive?

kind(s), sort(s), type(s) With the singular form of each of these nouns, use *this* or *that*. With the plural form, use *these* or *those*.

EXAMPLES   **This kind** of gas is dangerous; **those kinds** are harmless.

These types of reading assignments are always challenging.

STYLE   TIP

Some authorities disapprove of the use of *hopefully* to mean "it is to be hoped." Avoid using *hopefully* in this sense in formal speech and writing.

INFORMAL
We will leave early; hopefully, we will leave by six.

FORMAL
We will leave early; **we hope to** leave by six.

USAGE

learn, teach *Learn* means "to gain knowledge." *Teach* means "to provide with knowledge."

EXAMPLES   I would like to **learn** how to play chess.

Will you **teach** me the fundamental rules of chess?

leave, let *Leave* means "to go away." *Let* means "to permit" or "to allow." Do not use *leave* for *let.*

EXAMPLES   Please **let** [not *leave*] them stay where they are.

They **let** [not *left*] Jaime have the flag that flew over the capitol.

lend   See **borrow, lend.**

less   See **fewer, less.**

lie, lay   See page 177.

like, as   *Like* is a preposition. In formal situations, do not use *like* for the conjunction *as* to introduce a subordinate clause.

INFORMAL   The stir-fry did not turn out like I had hoped it would.
FORMAL   The stir-fry did not turn out **as** I had hoped it would.

like, as if, as though   In formal situations, avoid using the preposition *like* for the conjunction *as if* or *as though* to introduce a subordinate clause.

INFORMAL   That guitar sounds like it is out of tune.
FORMAL   That guitar sounds **as if** [or *as though*] it is out of tune.

may, can   See page 201.

might of, must of   See **of.**

Reference Note

For more information about **prepositions,** see page 20. For more about **subordinate clauses,** see page 77.

Exercise 2   Identifying Correct Usage

For each of the following sentences, choose the word or word group in parentheses that is correct according to the rules of standard, formal English.

EXAMPLE   **1.** What (*kind of, kind of a*) computer do you have?

1. kind of

1. (*These, This*) kinds of questions require more thought than (*that, those*) kind.
2. I (*had ought, ought*) to check out a good library book.
3. It looks (*like, as if*) we'll be able to attend the powwow.

4. Will the coach (*leave, let*) you skip soccer practice today?
5. He serves the ball exactly (*as, like*) the coach showed him.
6. I (*implied, inferred*) from Dad's remark about "slovenliness" that my sister and I ought to clean our room.
7. When Jay Gatsby walked (*in, into*) the room, everyone stared at him.
8. (*Leave, Let*) Rosetta explain the trigonometry problem.
9. Did Mr. Stokes (*imply, infer*) that he was pleased with my research paper on Mexican American authors?
10. What sort (*of, of a*) culture did the Phoenicians have?

no, none, nothing   See **The Double Negative,** page 261.

nor   See **or, nor.**

nowheres   See **anyways, anywheres.**

number   See **amount, number.**

number of, a/the   See page 103.

of   *Of* is a preposition. Do not use *of* in place of *have* after verbs such as *could, should, would, might, must,* and *ought to.*

| NONSTANDARD | He could of had a summer job if he had applied earlier. |
| STANDARD | He **could have** had a summer job if he had applied earlier. |

| NONSTANDARD | You ought to of taken a foreign language. |
| STANDARD | You **ought to have** taken a foreign language. |

Also, do not use *of* after *had.*

| NONSTANDARD | If I had of known the word *raze,* I could have completed the crossword puzzle. |
| STANDARD | If I **had** known the word *raze,* I could have completed the crossword puzzle. |

Avoid using *of* after other prepositions such as *inside, off,* and *outside.*

| EXAMPLE | Meet me **outside** [not *outside of*] the auditorium at six o'clock. |

off, off of   Do not use *off* or *off of* in place of *from.*

| NONSTANDARD | You can get a program off of the usher. |
| STANDARD | You can get a program **from** the usher. |

MEETING THE CHALLENGE

The Glossary of Usage chapter lists many pairs and trios of words that speakers and writers often confuse. Review these words, and copy the information on the two sets of words that give you the most trouble when you write. Study the information on the words; then, write a personalized rule for each usage issue on separate index cards. Ask a classmate to use these cards to quiz you, so that you will never again confuse the words you found troublesome.

USAGE

or, nor Use *or* with *either;* use *nor* with *neither.*

EXAMPLES Edwina will make **either** vegetable stew **or** bean burritos for the potluck dinner.

Before 1959, **neither** Alaska **nor** Hawaii was officially part of the United States.

ought to of See **of.**

raise, rise See page 180.

reason . . . because See **because.**

scarcely See **The Double Negative,** page 261.

she See **he, she, it, they.**

should of See **of.**

sit, set See page 179.

slow, slowly See page 214.

some, somewhat In formal situations, avoid using *some* to mean "to some extent." Instead, use *somewhat.*

INFORMAL Wyatt's TV viewing has decreased some during the past month.

FORMAL Wyatt's TV viewing has decreased **somewhat** during the past month.

somewheres See **anyways, anywheres.**

sort(s) See **kind(s), sort(s), type(s)** and **kind of a, sort of a.**

sort of See **kind of, sort of.**

supposed to, used to When writing the past form of *suppose* or *use,* especially before the word *to,* avoid omitting the *–d* ending.

EXAMPLES Juan is **supposed to** [not *suppose to*] meet us at the restaurant at 6:00 P.M.

I **used to** [not *use to*] live on a farm in Nebraska.

take See **bring, take.**

teach See **learn, teach.**

than, then *Than* is a subordinating conjunction used in comparisons. *Then* is an adverb telling *when.*

EXAMPLES He is a better cook **than** I am.

Reference Note

For information about forming the past tense of **regular verbs,** see page 163.

Reference Note

For information about **subordinating conjunctions,** see page 84. For more about **adverbs,** see page 17.

USAGE

Let the sauce simmer for ten minutes, and **then** stir in two cups of cooked mixed vegetables.

that   See **who, which, that.**

theirs, there's   See page 383.

theirself, theirselves   See **hisself, theirself, theirselves.**

their, there, they're   See page 383.

them   Do not use *them* as an adjective. Use *those.*

EXAMPLE   All of **those** [not *them*] paintings are by Carmen.

they   See **he, she, it, they.**

this here, that there   Avoid using *here* or *there* after the demonstrative adjective *this* or *that.*

EXAMPLE   **This** [not *This here*] story tells about the Hmong people of Laos.

this, that, these, those   See **kind(s), sort(s), type(s).**

try and, try to   Use *try to,* not *try and.*

EXAMPLE   Let me **try to** [not *try and*] repair the pipes before you call a plumber.

type(s)   See **kind(s), sort(s), type(s).**

type, type of   Avoid using *type* as an adjective. Add *of* after *type.*

NONSTANDARD   The trainer recommended a new type shoe.

STANDARD   The trainer recommended a new **type of** shoe.

used to   See **supposed to, used to.**

ways   In formal situations, you should use *way,* not *ways,* in referring to distance.

INFORMAL   We had to travel a long ways when we moved from Virginia to New Mexico.

FORMAL   We had to travel a long **way** when we moved from Virginia to New Mexico.

well, good   See page 214.

what   Use *that,* not *what,* to introduce an adjective clause.

EXAMPLE   One of the books **that** [not *what*] he recommended was Langston Hughes's novel *Not Without Laughter.*

Reference Note

For more about **adjective clauses,** see page 78.

when, where Unless you are defining a time or a place, do not use *when* or *where* to begin a definition.

| NONSTANDARD | A spoonerism is when the beginning sounds of two words are switched. |
| STANDARD | A spoonerism is **a slip of the tongue in which the beginning sounds of two words are switched.** |

| NONSTANDARD | Claustrophobia is where you have an abnormal fear of enclosed spaces. |
| STANDARD | Claustrophobia is **an abnormal fear of enclosed spaces.** |

where Do not use *where* for *that*.

EXAMPLE I read **that** [not *where*] Demosthenes learned to enunciate by practicing with pebbles in his mouth.

where . . . at See **at.**

who, which, that *Who* refers to persons only. *Which* refers to things only. *That* may refer to either persons or things.

EXAMPLES Isn't Nora the runner **who** [or ***that***] won the gold medal?

The movie *La Bamba,* **which** was written and directed by Luis Valdez, received popular and critical acclaim.

Emily Dickinson is the poet **that** [or ***who***] wrote "Tell all the Truth but tell it slant."

Is this the film version of *Macbeth* **that** stars Orson Welles?

who, whom See page 137.

who's, whose See page 384.

would of See **of.**

your, you're See page 384.

Exercise 3 Identifying Correct Usage

For each of the following sentences, choose the word or word group that is correct according to the rules of standard, formal English.

EXAMPLE 1. Where did you get (*that, that there*) poster?
   1. *that*

1. I read in a newspaper article (*that, where*) some dogs are being trained to help people who have hearing impairments.

2. The first female novelist in United States literature who wrote frankly about women's concerns was neither Willa Cather (*or, nor*) Edith Wharton, but Kate Chopin.

3. Jack London must (*of, have*) led an adventurous life.

4. Our teacher assigned us (*this, this here*) chapter to read.

5. Joe had the flu last week, but he's feeling (*some, somewhat*) better.

6. As we passed Shreveport and crossed the Texas line, El Paso seemed a long (*way, ways*) away.

7. For advice, I go to Ms. Sanchez, (*which, who*) is a very understanding guidance counselor.

8. This (*type, type of*) short story has appealed to readers for many years.

9. Pass me (*them, those*) notes on the experiment, please.

10. He jumped (*off, off of*) the edge of the porch.

Review D Identifying Correct Usage

Each sentence in the following paragraphs contains at least one pair of italicized items. From each pair, choose the item that is correct according to the rules of standard, formal English.

EXAMPLE [1] While we were driving through the Appalachian Mountains, (*my father, my father he*) suddenly started chuckling and pulled over to the side of the road.

1. my father

[1] Dad said that we really (*had ought, ought*) to get out of the car and see the amazing mailbox that somebody had built. [2] Neither Ivy nor I was especially interested in mailboxes, but when we saw the fanciful metal figure that Dad was pointing to, we both smiled just (*as, like*) he had. [3] We jumped out to take the photo shown on this page, and while we were standing (*beside, besides*) the road, a man came out of the house. [4] He introduced himself as Charlie Lucas and said he had built the mailbox man by welding together scraps from (*broken, busted*) machinery. [5] We started chatting with him, and the next thing we knew, he had invited us (*in, into*) the house to see more of his figures. [6] The house was (*kind of, rather*) like an art museum: There were dinosaurs made from colorful twisted wire, a fiddle player with a head made from a shovel, and an alligator whose body (*might have, might of*) once been a crankshaft.

[7] "Dad, are these figures art?" Ivy whispered, and Dad's answer

Charlie Lucas, *Old Buddy*. Photo: Paul Rocheleau.

(*inferred, implied*) that they were. [**8**] He said that art (*don't, doesn't*) have to be stuffy and serious or made from bronze or marble and that true artists aren't always (*alumna, alumni*) of famous art schools. [**9**] (*Mr. Lucas he, Mr. Lucas*) agreed with Dad that (*these kind, these kinds*) of sculptures and all other kinds of folk art are of great value. [**10**] Folk art comes straight from the heart; it often recycles castoff materials that most people (*would have, would of*) considered junk; it offers a different perspective on life; and it makes people smile!

Review E Identifying Correct Usage

Each sentence in the following paragraphs contains at least one pair of italicized items. From each pair, choose the item that is correct according to the rules of standard, formal English.

EXAMPLE [1] Have you read (*where, that*) Vietnamese refugees are working hard to succeed in the United States?

1. *that*

[1] When Vietnamese immigrants stepped (*off, off of*) the planes that had brought them from refugee camps all over Asia, they didn't know what to expect in America. [2] However, like previous immigrants, they were people (*which, who*) managed to succeed against all odds. [3] Many of them neither spoke English (*or, nor*) knew much about life in the United States. [4] Often grateful just to be alive, they could (*of, have*) contented themselves with simple survival. [5] Instead, many of (*them, those*) Vietnamese families have encouraged their children to achieve academic excellence. [6] According to one study, half of the refugee children earn a B average overall and half also receive A's in math; (*that, that there*) study also places these students near the national average in English.

[7] One reason Vietnamese students do so well is (*because, that*) many believe that success comes from hard work, not from luck or natural aptitude. [8] Consequently, rather (*than, then*) watch television or go to the mall, many families spend weeknights doing homework together. [9] Parents who do not speak English well sometimes help by assigning (*less, fewer*) chores on weeknights. [10] Younger children get extra instruction (*from, off of*) older brothers and sisters, and all this effort is helping the Vietnamese become one of the most successful immigrant groups in the United States.

The Double Negative

A *double negative* is a construction in which two negative words are used to express a single negative idea. Although acceptable until Shakespeare's time and common in other languages, double negatives are now considered nonstandard English.

NONSTANDARD	She has not read none of Nadine Gordimer's books.
STANDARD	She has **not** read **any** of Nadine Gordimer's books.
STANDARD	She has read **none** of Nadine Gordimer's books.

NONSTANDARD	I do not know nothing about the Peloponnesian War.
STANDARD	I do **not** know **anything** about the Peloponnesian War.
STANDARD	I know **nothing** about the Peloponnesian War.

NONSTANDARD	Grandma said that she hadn't never seen another pumpkin that was as large as this one.
STANDARD	Grandma said that she **hadn't ever** seen another pumpkin that was as large as this one.
STANDARD	Grandma said that she had **never** seen another pumpkin that was as large as this one.

Common Negative Words		
barely	never	not (n't)
but (meaning "only")	no	nothing
	nobody	nowhere
hardly	none	only
neither	no one	scarcely

NOTE Avoid the common error of using *–n't*, the contraction of *not*, with another negative word, especially *barely, hardly,* or *scarcely*.

NONSTANDARD	The film is so long that we couldn't scarcely see all of it in one class period.
STANDARD	The film is so long that we could **scarcely** see all of it in one class period.

The words *but* and *only* are considered negative words when they are used as adverbs meaning "no more than." In such cases, the use of another negative word with *but* or *only* is considered informal.

INFORMAL	Whenever I see you, I can't help but smile.
FORMAL	Whenever I see you, **I can't help smiling.**

"Confounded Double Negatives!"

© 1993 by Sidney Harris.

USAGE

HELP

Although the sentences in Exercise 4 can be corrected in more than one way, you need to give only one revision for each.

Exercise 4 **Correcting Double Negatives**

Revise each of the following sentences to correct the double negative.

EXAMPLE 1. He hadn't no pencils on his desk.

1. *He had no pencils on his desk.*

1. Tom didn't have no time to buy the books.
2. Haven't none of you seen the dog?
3. Isn't nobody else interested in going to visit the pueblo at Tesuque this morning?
4. We haven't but one day to visit the fair.
5. She didn't contribute nothing to the project.
6. The lights were so dim that we couldn't barely see.
7. They said that they didn't have no time to go to the post office before tomorrow.
8. In the mountains you can't help but feel calm.
9. Can't none of them come to the party?
10. José Martí was sentenced to six years in prison, and he hadn't done nothing but write a letter that the Spanish government didn't like.

Review F **Correcting Errors in Usage**

Most of the following sentences contain errors in the use of standard, formal English. If a sentence contains an error, revise the sentence. If a sentence is already correct, write *C*.

EXAMPLE 1. Can't none of the staff sort the yearbook pictures?

1. *Can't any of the staff sort the yearbook pictures?*

1. A New Year's Eve Watch is when African Americans join together to welcome the new year by singing, chanting, and shouting.
2. We divided the confetti between the four children.
3. We should of paid closer attention to the instructions.
4. I wonder how many Americans realize the importance of the Minutemen, which were true champions of freedom during the American Revolution.
5. Being as my parents prefer CDs, they don't hardly ever play their tapes anymore.
6. A large amount of people contributed to the charity drive.
7. Swimming is a type of sport that requires daily training.
8. I don't think he knows where he is at.

9. Did Mr. Jackson mean to infer that we might have a pop quiz tomorrow, or was he just ~~kidding~~?

10. Some speakers make il~~lusi~~ons to the "good old days."

Nonsexist ~~La~~nguage

Nonsexist ~~la~~nguage ~~is~~ language that applies to people in general, both male and ~~f~~emale. For example, the nonsexist terms *humanity, human beings,* ~~and people~~ can substitute for the gender-specific term *mankind.*

~~Man~~y skills and occupations were generally closed to ~~wom~~en, ~~or to~~ men. Expressions like *seamstress, stewardess,* and ~~so on reflect~~ those limitations. Since most jobs can now be held by ~~eith~~er ~~men or~~ women, language is adjusting to reflect this change.

~~When yo~~u are referring generally to people, use nonsexist expres-~~sions rathe~~r than gender-specific ones. Following are some widely ~~used non~~sexist terms that you can use to replace the older, gender-~~specific~~ ones.

Gender-specific	Nonsexist
businessman	executive, businessperson
chairman	chairperson, chair
deliveryman	delivery person
fireman	firefighter
foreman	supervisor
housewife	homemaker
mailman	mail carrier
man-made	synthetic, manufactured
manpower	workers, human resources
policeman	police officer
salesman	salesperson, salesclerk
seamstress	needleworker
steward, stewardess	flight attendant

If the antecedent of a pronoun may be either masculine or feminine, use both masculine and feminine pronouns to refer to it.

EXAMPLES   **Anyone** who wants to apply should bring **his or her** application.

               Any **applicant** may bring a résumé with **him or her.**

STYLE TIP

Avoid using the awkward expressions *s/he* and *wo/man.*

You can often avoid the awkward *his or her* construction (or the alternative *his/her*) by substituting an article (*a, an,* or *the*) for the construction. You can also rephrase the sentence using the plural forms of both the pronoun and its antecedent.

EXAMPLES   Any interested **worker** may submit ~~~~

All interested **workers** may submit th~~~ation.

~~~~~tions.

Exercise 5   Using Nonsexist Language

Rewrite each of the following sentences to avoid using ge~~~ terms.

EXAMPLE   1. I had to stay home all afternoon to wait for the deliveryman.

1. *I had to stay home all afternoon to wait for the delivery person.*

1. Some of the visitors felt that the man-made objects detracted fro~ the natural beauty.
2. Make sure those letters are ready to go by the time the mailman gets here.
3. The first business before the committee was to elect a chairman.
4. Among the speakers at career day were doctors, lawyers, and businessmen.
5. Are you certain we have enough manpower to get this project done on time?
6. If anyone wants to join us at the movie tonight, he should meet us out front at 7:15.
7. The salesman never stood a chance of convincing Father to buy a more expensive car.
8. If you need the stewardess, just press that button above your head.
9. Jaime's uncle was one of those few who followed through on his childhood dream of becoming a policeman.
10. Johnny's summer job involved calling housewives and asking them questions about laundry detergent.

Chapter Review

A. Identifying Correct Usage

For each of the following sentences, choose the word or word group in parentheses that is correct according to the rules of standard, formal English.

1. The Polar Bear Club jumped (*in, into*) the icy lake.

2. The clap of thunder almost (*burst, busted*) my eardrums.

3. After hearing my grandmother's stories about World War II, I realized that she was more daring (*than, then*) I had ever imagined.

4. Rochelle read (*where, that*) flood waters reached the rooftops.

5. Leticia's temperature rose (*somewhat, some*) before noon.

6. Many students felt that the date for the prom should (*have, of*) been set in early June rather than in May.

7. Mr. Cronin wants to raise cattle (*like, as*) his grandfather did.

8. A large (*amount, number*) of students in my computer class are unfamiliar with spreadsheets.

9. Chan repeated that he preferred that (*type, type of*) backpack.

10. Alex thought the workshop on handcrafting paper was (*kind of, somewhat*) interesting.

B. Correcting Errors in Usage

Most of the following sentences contain errors in the use of standard, formal English. If a sentence contains an error or an informal usage, revise the sentence. If a sentence is already correct, write *C*.

11. All of the members of the budget committee accept, I believe, Representative Carpenter voted to retain the present tax structure.

12. The generosity of my grandparents has effected all of us.

13. I couldn't hardly believe my eyes when I saw a 90 on my paper.

14. This here paper glider was designed by Dr. Yasuaki Ninomiya.

15. Does this poem make an illusion to the *Iliad*?

16. Being that Jennifer had never learned to swim, she was afraid to go on the boat ride.

17. Two of my great-grandparents emigrated from Ireland and came to the United States.

18. When the singer recorded the CD of folk songs, he didn't have no way of knowing that it would sell thousands of copies.

19. Can't anybody see that she is doing her best?

20. The Gallaghers they have lived in this town for years.

C. Identifying Correct Usage

For each of the following sentences, choose the word or word group in parentheses that is correct according to the rules of standard, formal English.

21. Just (*like, as*) Devin had thought, the library was closed.

22. The lifeguard got down (*off of, from*) his high seat to help us.

23. The reason she was late was (*because, that*) the roads were blocked.

24. All of the teachers will (*bring, take*) their students to the park on the last day of school.

25. The new legislation attempts to (*effect, affect*) a change in the behavior of the stock market.

26. The trucker (*could of, could have*) avoided the accident.

27. Jahi and Aritha don't like (*those kinds, those kind*) of concerts.

28. He was so tired that he (*couldn't hardly, could hardly*) move.

29. (*Less, Fewer*) than fifty people attended the lecture.

30. (*Among, Between*) those invited to the governor's inauguration were Mr. and Mrs. Jackson.

D. Identifying Correct Usage

Each sentence in the following paragraph contains at least one pair of italicized items. From each pair, choose the item that is correct according to the rules of standard, formal English.

Whenever I walk into Montsho Books, I can't help **[31]** (*feeling, but feel*) proud to be black. Do you want to know where this bookstore **[32]** (*is at, is*)? I should have mentioned that it's in Orlando, Florida, just a short **[33]** (*way, ways*) from the Orlando Arena. Ms. Perkins, **[34]** (*which, who*) runs the store, told me **[35]** (*where, that*) *montsho* means "black" in an African language. **[36]** (*Anyways, Anyway*), when Ms. Perkins was a schoolteacher, she noticed that there **[37]** (*were, weren't*) hardly any children's books that featured African Americans. Ms. Perkins decided she **[38]** (*had ought, ought*) to open a store that sold books exclusively by blacks and about blacks.

[39] (*Beside, Besides*) poetry and fiction by African Americans, the shop offers all kinds of nonfiction selections. Montsho Books has become a **[40]** (*kind of, kind of a*) cultural center for Orlando's black community.

Writing Application

Using Standard English in a Letter

Writing a Local History   Dr. Yolanda Washington, a professor at the nearby community college, is compiling an informal history of your area. Write a letter to Dr. Washington, telling a true story about your block, your neighborhood, or your town. You may use dialect in direct quotations, but be sure to use standard English in the rest of your letter.

Prewriting   First, think of some of the stories you may have heard about your community. Then, choose the best story to send to Dr. Washington. Jot down as many concrete details as you can. Record a few good quotations and paraphrases that capture the local flavor of the story.

Writing   Begin your draft by greeting Dr. Washington and explaining that you would like to contribute to her local history project. Then, set the scene for your story by indicating the time period and setting. Write down the events of the story in a clear, straightforward order.

Revising   Have a classmate read your draft. Does the letter flow logically? Do the details and quotations capture the local flavor of your area? Add or revise details to make the story clear and vivid.

Publishing   Proofread your letter carefully for errors in grammar, usage, and mechanics. Be sure you have used the correct form for business letters. Check words and expressions in the Glossary of Usage to make sure that they are formal, standard English. If you have included quotations, check them for correct punctuation. You and other members of your class may want to compile an informal history of your community. You can publish your stories by collecting them in a booklet.

Reference Note

For more information about **punctuating quotations,** see page 333.

Capitalization
Rules of Standard Usage

Diagnostic Preview

Capitalizing Words Correctly

For each of the following sentences, correctly write the word or words that should be capitalized. If a sentence is already correct, write *C*.

EXAMPLE 1. The rotary club has invited congressman William Bashone to speak tonight at the annual banquet.

1. *Rotary Club; Congressman*

1. According to Zack Johnson, the company's representative, you should not buy just any car; you should buy a neptune.
2. One of the earliest cars made by Henry Ford was called the Model T; it had a four-cylinder, twenty-horsepower engine.
3. On our vacation we toured several states in the south.
4. Ridgewood bake shop and deli is just north of park ridge street on highway 143.
5. Before you can take this computer course, you must pass algebra II.
6. Aren't they planning a parade and party to celebrate Dr. Martin Luther King, jr.'s, birthday?
7. Because we cheered so loudly at the special olympics, ms. Andrews made us honorary cheerleaders for her special-education class.
8. In a nationally televised press conference, the president warned that he would veto any tax increase.

9. The british poet Ted Hughes was married to Sylvia Plath, who was an american writer.

10. The only man in American history who was not elected Vice-President or President—yet held both positions—is ex-president Gerald Ford.

11. My mother asked me to walk to the supermarket and buy a quart container of farmingbury milk and two pounds of dried beans.

12. When we toured eastern Tennessee, we visited the Oak Ridge National Laboratory, where atomic research was carried out during World War II.

13. The Spanish-american Club has planned a festival for late summer; it will be held at the north end of the city.

14. If you are looking for the best apples in the state, follow route 14 until you see the signs for Peacock's Orchard.

15. In a controversial debate over the Panama canal, the United States voted to relinquish its control of the canal to the government of Panama.

16. When aunt Janice visited England last summer, she toured buckingham palace and tried to catch a glimpse of queen Elizabeth.

17. Mayor-elect Sabrena Willis will speak to the public about her proposals to expand the city's literacy program.

18. Earl and Jamie were lucky to get tickets to see the garth brooks concert at freedom hall.

19. When spring arrives, I know it is time to start thinking about where to look for a summer job.

20. Although the east room of the White house is now used mainly for press conferences, it was once a place where Abigail Adams aired president Adams's laundry.

Using Capital Letters Correctly

In your reading, you will notice variations in the use of capital letters. Most writers, however, follow the rules presented in this chapter. In your own writing, following these rules will help you communicate clearly with the widest possible audience.

12a. Capitalize the first word in every sentence.

EXAMPLE   **I**n 1985, Lynette Woodard became the first woman to play for the Harlem Globetrotters.

The first word of a quoted sentence should begin with a capital letter, whether or not the quotation comes at the beginning of your sentence.

EXAMPLE   Plutarch once said, "**T**he mind is not a vessel to be filled but a fire to be lighted."

When quoting only part of a sentence, capitalize the first word of the quotation if (1) the person you are quoting capitalized it or (2) it is the first word of your sentence.

EXAMPLES   What does the image "**a** fire to be lighted" suggest about the mind?

"**A** fire to be lighted" suggests the mind's potential.

NOTE Capitalize the first word of a sentence fragment used in dialogue.

EXAMPLE   Selena asked, "Have you read Toni Morrison's new novel?"
Bradley said, "**N**o, not yet."

Traditionally, the first word of each line of a poem is capitalized.

EXAMPLE   **I** peeled my orange
That was so bright against
The gray of December
That, from some distance
Someone might have thought
I was making a fire in my hands.

Gary Soto, "Oranges"

12b. Capitalize the first word in both the salutation and the closing of a letter.

EXAMPLES   **D**ear Mr. Ramirez: **M**y dear Sasha,

Sincerely yours,   **Y**ours truly,

12c. Capitalize the pronoun *I* and the interjection *O*.

The interjection *O* is usually used only for invocations and is followed by the name of the person or thing being addressed. Don't confuse it with the common interjection *oh*, which is generally not capitalized and which is followed by punctuation.

EXAMPLES   Walt Whitman's tribute to Abraham Lincoln begins, "**O** Captain! my Captain!"

What **I** meant was—**o**h, never mind.

Reference Note

For more information on using **capital letters** in **quotations,** see page 334.

┌HELP─
Some writers do not follow traditional capitalization rules. When you quote from a writer's work, use capital letters exactly as the writer uses them.

12d. Capitalize proper nouns and proper adjectives.

A *common noun* names any one of a group of persons, places, things, or ideas. A *proper noun* names a particular person, place, thing, or idea. A *proper adjective* is formed from a proper noun.

Common nouns are capitalized only if they

- begin a sentence (also, in most cases, a line of poetry)
  or
- begin a direct quotation
  or
- are part of a title

Reference Note

For more information on **proper nouns** and **common nouns,** see page 3. For more on **proper adjectives,** see page 11.

Common Nouns	Proper Nouns	Proper Adjectives
a **w**riter	**D**ickens	**D**ickensian characters
a **c**ountry	**C**hina	**C**hinese coastline
a **p**resident	**L**incoln	**L**incolnesque ideals
an **i**sland	**H**awaii	**H**awaiian climate
a **l**anguage	**A**rabic	**A**rabic letters
a **p**oet	**S**hakespeare	**S**hakespearean sonnet
a **r**egion	**N**ew England	**N**ew England chowder

Articles, coordinating conjunctions, and short prepositions (those with fewer than five letters) are generally not capitalized in proper nouns made up of two or more words.

EXAMPLES   Queen **o**f Spain

"Ebony **a**nd Ivory"

"Tales **f**rom **t**he Vienna Woods"

American Society **f**or **t**he Prevention **o**f Cruelty **t**o Animals

NOTE   Proper nouns and proper adjectives may lose their capitals after long usage.

EXAMPLES   **m**adras   **s**andwich   **w**att   **p**uritan

quisling   **b**oycott   **p**latonic   **h**amburger

When you're not sure whether to capitalize a word, look it up in a dictionary.

MECHANICS

Reference Note

For information on **abbreviations** such as *Dr.* and *Jr.,* see page 297.

(1) Capitalize the names of persons and animals. Capitalize initials in names and abbreviations that either precede or follow names.

Persons	Animals
Toshio Williams	Socks
Heitor Villa-Lobos	Secretariat
W.E.B. DuBois	Lassie
Dr. Aretha Ozawa	Shamu
Brian Goldblum, Jr.	White Fang

COMPUTER TIP

The spellings of personal names can challenge even the best spellchecking software. However, you may be able to customize the spellchecker you use. If the software allows, add to it any frequently used names that you have difficulty spelling or capitalizing.

NOTE Some names contain more than one capital letter. Usage varies in the capitalization of *van, von, du, de la,* and other parts of multiword names. When possible, verify the spelling of a name with the person whose name it is, or check in a reference source.

EXAMPLES La Fontaine McEwen O'Connor Van Doren

De la Mer Ibn Ezra Smith-Tyson van Gogh

(2) Capitalize geographical names.

Type of Name	Examples	
Towns, Cities	New Orleans Tokyo	Portage la Prairie San Jose
Counties, Parishes	Marion County	Lafayette Parish
Townships, Provinces	Saskatchewan Province	Lawrence Township
States	Wisconsin New Hampshire	Oklahoma North Carolina
Regions	the South the Sunbelt the West Coast	the Middle East the Northern Hemisphere

Reference Note

The abbreviations of names of states are capitalized. For information on using and punctuating such **abbreviations,** see page 298.

NOTE Words such as *north, western,* and *southeast* are not capitalized when they indicate direction.

EXAMPLES east of the river driving south western Iowa

MECHANICS

Type of Name	Examples	
Countries	India	United States
	Ivory Coast	of America
Continents	Australia	South America
	Africa	Europe
Islands	Dauphin Island	Isle of Wight
	Greater Antilles	Florida Keys
Mountains	Blue Ridge Mountains	Mount McKinley
	Sierra Nevada	Humphreys Peak
Bodies of Water	Pacific Ocean	Rio de la Plata
	Gulf of Mexico	Saint Lawrence Seaway
Parks, Forests	Point Reyes National Seashore	Lowden Memorial State Park
Streets, Roads, Highways	County Road 16	Downing Street
	Interstate 10	Euclid Avenue
	Lancaster Turnpike	Avenida de Mayo
Other Geographical Names	Cape Canaveral	Isthmus of Suez
	Perce Rock	Crater of Diamonds
	Mississippi Valley	Point Sur

STYLE TIP

Since *rio* is Spanish for "river," *Rio de la Plata River* is redundant. Use only *Rio de la Plata*.

Other terms to watch for are

- *sierra*, Spanish for "mountain range" [Use only *Sierra Nevada*, not *Sierra Nevada Mountains*.]

- *yama*, Japanese for "mountain" [Use only *Fujiyama* or *Mount Fuji*, not *Mount Fujiyama*.]

- *sahara*, Arabic for "desert" [Use only *Sahara*, not *Sahara Desert*.]

- *gobi*, Mongolian for "desert" [Use only *Gobi*, not *Gobi Desert*.]

MECHANICS

NOTE The second word in a hyphenated number begins with a lower-case letter.

EXAMPLE Twenty-fifth Street

A word such as *city, island, street,* or *park* is capitalized only when it is part of a proper noun.

Proper Nouns	Common Nouns
a rodeo in Carson City	a rodeo in a nearby city
a ferry to Block Island	a ferry to a resort island
swimming in Clear Lake	swimming in the lake
along Canal Street	along a neighborhood street

Reference Note

In addresses, abbreviations such as *St., Ave., Dr.,* and *Blvd.* are capitalized. For information on **abbreviations,** see page 298.

Exercise 1　Capitalizing Words and Names Correctly

If one or more words in an item should be capitalized, write the entire item correctly. If an item is already correct, write *C*.

EXAMPLE　　**1.** south american countries

　　　　　　1.　South American countries

1. living in the west
2. a city north of louisville
3. bonneville salt flats
4. the cape of good hope
5. chris o'malley
6. hoover dam
7. southern illinois
8. lock the door!
9. the kalahari desert
10. the northeast
11. gulf of Alaska
12. mary mcleod bethune
13. a mountain people
14. tom delaney, jr.
15. hawaiian volcanoes state park
16. north american actor
17. san francisco bay
18. skiing on the lake
19. turned west at the corner
20. he said, "i am, too."
21. mexican gold
22. and, o Zeus, save us
23. west indian curry
24. decatur street
25. fifty-sixth street

(3) Capitalize the names of planets, stars, constellations, and other heavenly bodies.

EXAMPLES　　

Saturn	**R**igel
Centaurus	**Little D**ipper
Comet **K**ohoutek	**P**luto
Pisces	**C**anis **M**inor
Betelgeuse	**P**roxima **C**entauri
the **G**reat **N**ebula	**I**o
Antares	**V**ega
Sirius	**A**rcturus

NOTE　The word *earth* is not capitalized unless it is used along with the name of another heavenly body that is capitalized. The words *sun* and *moon* are generally not capitalized.

EXAMPLES　Recycling is just one way to help preserve the **e**arth.

　　　　　The planet **J**upiter takes almost twelve **E**arth years to orbit the **s**un.

　　　　　The **m**oon reflects light from the **s**un.

(4) Capitalize the names of organizations, teams, government bodies, and institutions.

Type of Name	Examples	
Organizations	League of Women Voters Habitat for Humanity	American Dental Association Franklin Key Club
Teams	St. Louis Cardinals Karr Cougars	Miami Dolphins Seattle Sounders
Government Bodies	Department of State National Institute on Aging	Congress North Carolina State Senate
Institutions	Duke University Newcomb College United States Air Force Academy	St. Jude's Children's Research Hospital Smithsonian Institution

Do not capitalize words such as *democratic, republican,* and *socialist* when they refer to principles or forms of government. Capitalize these words only when they refer to specific political parties.

EXAMPLES   The citizens demanded **d**emocratic reforms.

Who will be the **R**epublican nominee for governor?

(5) Capitalize the names of businesses and the brand names of business products.

Businesses	De Havilland, Ltd.	Motorola, Inc.	Kelley's Hardware
Product Names	Toyota Tercel® Kraft® cheese	Apple Macintosh® Quaker® oatmeal	Sanford Pink Pearl®

Notice that a common noun that follows a brand name is not capitalized.

(6) Capitalize the names of particular buildings and other structures.

EXAMPLES   Rialto Theater   Columbia Seafirst Center

Moore High School   Clark Memorial Hospital

STYLE   **TIP**

The names of organizations, businesses, and government bodies are often abbreviated to a series of capital letters.

EXAMPLE
American **T**elephone & **T**elegraph   **AT&T**

STYLE   **TIP**

The word *party* in the name of a political party may or may not be capitalized; either way is correct. However, you should be consistent within any piece of writing.

EXAMPLE
Democratic **p**arty
or
Democratic **P**arty

MECHANICS

HELP

Do not capitalize a word such as *building, monument,* or *award* unless it is part of a proper noun.

Reference Note

For more on the differences between **common nouns** and **proper nouns,** see pages 3 and 271.

(7) **Capitalize the names of monuments, memorials, and awards.**

EXAMPLES

Navajo National Monument

Craters of the Moon National Monument

Mount Rushmore National Memorial

Civil Rights Memorial

Presidential Medal of Freedom

National Society of Film Critics Award

(8) **Capitalize the names of historical events and periods, special events, holidays, and other calendar items.**

Type of Name	Examples	
Historical Events and Periods	Great Depression Reformation Pax Romana Reign of Terror	the American Revolution Renaissance Middle Ages
Special Events	Career Day 2002 New York City Marathon Special Olympics	Texas State Fair Pan American Games
Holidays and Other Calendar Items	Monday September Kwanzaa	Cinco de Mayo Memorial Day Mother's Day

NOTE Do not capitalize the name of a season unless the season is being personified or it is used as part of a proper noun.

EXAMPLES This has been a rainy spring.

Finally, Spring tiptoed in and kissed the chill away.

This year's Spring Festival will feature folk dancing and arts and crafts.

STYLE TIP

The words *black* and *white* may or may not be capitalized when they refer to races; either way is correct. However, you should be consistent within any piece of writing.

EXAMPLES
Black-owned businesses
or
black-owned businesses

(9) **Capitalize the names of nationalities, races, and peoples.**

EXAMPLES

Lithuanian	Haitian	Jewish	Asian
Caucasian	Hispanic	Bantu	Serbo-Croatian

(10) Capitalize the names of religions and their followers, holy days and celebrations, sacred writings, and specific deities.

Type of Name	Examples	
Religions and Followers	Christianity	Buddhist
	Hinduism	Muslim
	Judaism	Presbyterian
Holy Days and Celebrations	Epiphany	Easter
	Ramadan	Passover
	Rosh Hashanah	Yom Kippur
Sacred Writings	the Holy Bible	Rig-Veda
	the Koran	Genesis
	the Talmud	the Pentateuch
Specific Deities	Allah	God
	Brahma	the Holy Spirit

The words *god* and *goddess* are not capitalized when they refer to deities of ancient mythology. However, the names of specific mythological gods and goddesses are capitalized.

EXAMPLE   The Greek **g**od of the sea was **P**oseidon.

NOTE   Some writers capitalize all pronouns that refer to a deity. Other writers capitalize such pronouns only if necessary to prevent confusion.

EXAMPLE   Through Moses, God commanded the pharaoh to let **H**is people go. [The capitalization of *His* shows that the pronoun refers to God, not to Moses or the pharaoh.]

(11) Capitalize the names of ships, trains, aircraft, spacecraft, and any other vehicles.

Type of Name	Examples	
Ships	*Monitor*	**R.M.S.** *Titanic*
Trains	*Zephyr*	*Orient Express*
Aircraft	*Flyer*	*Enola Gay*
Spacecraft	*Skylab*	*Columbia*

Reference Note

For information on when to **italicize names,** see page 332.

MECHANICS

The names of the make and model of a vehicle are capitalized.

EXAMPLES   **T**oyota **C**elica®   **F**ord **R**anger®   **C**essna **C**onquest®

TIPS & **TRICKS**

As a rule, a singular noun identified by a number or letter is capitalized.

EXAMPLES
Room 22   **F**igure A
Chapter 18   **E**xample B
Channel 11   **A**pt. 3C

However, the word *page* is not usually capitalized, nor is a plural noun followed by two or more numbers or letters.

EXAMPLE
Look at **m**aps A and B on **p**age 315.

12e. **Do not capitalize the names of school subjects, except course names that include a number and the names of language classes.**

EXAMPLES   **h**istory   **a**rt   **p**hysics   **g**eometry

             Spanish   **L**atin   **A**lgebra I   **C**hemistry II

NOTE   Do not capitalize the class name *senior, junior, sophomore,* or *freshman* unless it is part of a proper noun.

EXAMPLES   The **j**uniors are planning a surprise for **S**enior **D**ay.

               The **F**reshman **F**ollies was a big success.

Oral Practice   **Capitalizing Words Correctly**

Read aloud the following word groups, saying where capital letters are needed. If an item is already correct, say "correct."

EXAMPLE   **1.** tropicana® orange juice

           1. *Tropicana® orange juice—the T should be capitalized.*

1. two juniors and a senior
2. north atlantic treaty organization
3. st. patrick's cathedral
4. *city of new orleans* (train)
5. the federal reserve bank
6. the normandy invasion
7. classes in auto mechanics
8. the world cup
9. the washington monument
10. cherokee history
11. midtown traffic
12. jones and drake, inc.
13. spaceflight to mars
14. on labor day
15. the boat *ariadne*
16. at holiday inn®
17. the louisiana world exposition
18. early summer
19. gold medal® flour
20. an american history class

Review A   **Proofreading a Paragraph for Correct Capitalization**

For each sentence in the following paragraph, correctly write the word or words containing incorrect capital or lowercase letters. If a sentence is already correct, write *C*.

MECHANICS

EXAMPLE **[1]** Even if you don't know much about Horses, you likely can appreciate the beauty of the arabian horse shown below.

　1.　*horses; Arabian*

[1] Perhaps no other breed of horses can conjure up such images of romance as these beautiful animals from Northern Africa. [2] Their distinctive and colorful trappings bring to mind the nomadic lives of wandering peoples and the exciting exploits of their bedouin chieftains. [3] Smaller and lighter than many other breeds, with relatively large hooves, these horses are perfectly suited to the hot sands of the Sahara or the Arabian desert. [4] Some evidence suggests that african peoples may have been breeding these horses as long ago as seven thousand years. [5] Arabians characteristically have elegant heads and necks as well as large, lustrous eyes, features that have been prized by breeders all over the Earth. [6] These horses have played a part in many historical events far from the Continent of Africa. [7] During the Revolutionary war, for instance, George Washington rode a gray horse said to be the offspring of a famous Arabian stallion. [8] America's love affair with the Arabian horse has continued from the early days of our nation right through to the Present. [9] Today, the Arabian Horse International association has thousands of names on its roster. [10] Some importers include W. R. Brown of Berlin, New Hampshire, and Spencer Bade of Fall river, Massachusetts.

Using Capital Letters Correctly　**279**

12f. Capitalize titles.

(1) Capitalize a person's title when the title comes before the person's name.

EXAMPLES   **M**ajor Malone   **D**r. Ramírez   **P**resident Carter

Mrs. Wilson   **P**rofessor Cho   **M**r. Scott

Generally, a title used alone or following a person's name is not capitalized. Some titles, however, are by tradition capitalized. If you are not sure whether to capitalize a title, look it up in a dictionary.

EXAMPLES   The city elected a new **m**ayor today.

Sherian Grace Cadoria was the first African American woman in the U.S. armed forces to achieve the rank of **b**rigadier **g**eneral.

The **S**peaker of the **H**ouse rose to greet the **Q**ueen of England.

Also, for special emphasis or clarity, writers sometimes capitalize a title used alone or following a person's name.

EXAMPLES   I recently met Frank Sanchez, our local **B**usiness **L**eader of the **Y**ear.

Did the **P**resident veto the bill?

Titles used alone in direct address are generally capitalized.

EXAMPLES   Can you discuss your strategy, **G**eneral?

We're honored to welcome you, **M**s. **M**ayor.

Please come in, **S**ir [or *sir*].

NOTE   Do not capitalize *ex–*, *–elect, former,* or *late* when using it with a title.

EXAMPLES   **ex**-Governor Walsh   President-**e**lect Chan

(2) Capitalize a word showing a family relationship when the word is used before or in place of a person's name, unless the word is preceded by a possessive.

EXAMPLES   **A**unt Amanda   **U**ncle Hector   **G**randmother Ross

my **a**unt Amy   your **c**ousin   Thelma's **n**ephew

MECHANICS

(3) Capitalize the first and last words and all important words in titles and subtitles.

Unimportant words in a title include

- articles: *a, an, the*
- short prepositions (fewer than five letters), for example: *of, to, in, for, from, with*
- coordinating conjunctions: *and, but, for, nor, or, so, yet*

Type of Name	Examples
Books	*The Way to Rainy Mountain* *Edgar Allan Poe: The Man Behind the Legend*
Chapters and Other Parts of Books	"Empires of the Americas" "Glossary of Literary Terms"
Periodicals	*Popular Science* *Louisville Courier-Journal & Times*
Poems	"Tonight I Can Write" "Most Satisfied by Snow"
Short Stories	"In Another Country" "The Catch in the Shadow of the Sunrise"
Plays	*Watch on the Rhine* *The Importance of Being Earnest*
Historical Documents	the Magna Carta Treaty of Versailles
Works of Art	*Woman Before a Mirror* *Prelude to Farewell*
Movies	*Lost in Space* *Free Willy*
Television and Radio Programs	*Adventures in Good Music* *Discovery: Barrier Reef* *Third Rock from the Sun*

(continued)

MEETING THE CHALLENGE

One kind of word puzzle is the acrostic, in which each letter in a word begins a line that describes the word. Using your first name (and your last name, if you have a very short first name), create an acrostic in which each line describes you. Include such details as your favorite performers, movies, and books, as well as descriptive modifiers. Be sure to capitalize any proper nouns and adjectives. Share your acrostic with a partner, and learn more about him or her. If you're looking for a real challenge, make your acrostic rhyme.

MECHANICS

(continued)

Type of Name	Examples
Videos, Video Games	*The Adventures of Mowgli* *Super Mario Brothers*
Musical Works	"Bridge over Troubled Water" *La Traviata*
Audiotapes, Compact Discs	*Celtic Twilight* *One Step at a Time*
Computer Games and Programs	*Titanic: Adventure Out of Time* *Microsoft Word*
Comic Strips	*For Better or Worse* *Wizard of Id*

Reference Note

For information about **which titles should be italicized and which should be enclosed in quotation marks,** see pages 331 and 338.

NOTE Capitalize an article (*a, an,* or *the*) at the beginning of a title or subtitle only if it is the first word of the official title or subtitle.

EXAMPLES **A** *Christmas Carol*   **t**he *Austin American-Statesman*

        "**A**n *Acre of Grass*"   **T**he *New Yorker*

The official title of a book is found on the title page. The official title of a newspaper or other periodical is found on the masthead, which usually appears on the editorial page or in the table of contents.

Exercise 2   Capitalizing Correctly

Write the following items, using capital and lowercase letters where they are needed. If an item is already correct, write *C.*

EXAMPLE   1. the story "the kind of light that shines on texas"

          1. the story *"The Kind of Light That Shines on Texas"*

1. *the washington post*

2. ex-senator Margaret Chase Smith

3. the television program *soul train*

4. emancipation proclamation

5. the first chapter in *the grapes of wrath*

6. the painting *Holy Family On The Steps*

7. my poem "Black my Midnight Sight"

8. Secretary of State Colin Powell

MECHANICS

9. the song "Blowin' In The Wind"
10. for my Aunt Mary

Review B **Proofreading Paragraphs for Correct Capitalization**

For each sentence in the following paragraphs, change lowercase letters to capitals and capital letters to lowercase as necessary. If a sentence is already correct, write *C*.

EXAMPLE **[1]** Did mr. Lebowski explain the process of Vulcanization?

1. *Did Mr. Lebowski explain the process of vulcanization?*

[1] Among the many unusual scenes that captain Christopher Columbus witnessed in the Americas was that of the Tainos playing games with balls made of latex, a white liquid produced by plants like the rubber tree, guayule, milkweed, and dandelion. [2] Latex balls were also used by the maya, but unlike the ball games that you may have played with your Brother or Sister, many Mayan games were sacred rituals. [3] According to the *Book Of counsel,* an ancient Mayan document, some games reenacted the story of twins who became immortal. [4] Ball games were so important to the Mayan culture that, along with stately masks of their gods, Mayan artists rendered statues of ball players, and builders erected large stone stadiums for the games. [5] Besides columbus, other European explorers observed how the maya used latex; in fact, one explorer reported what is shown in the scene here—the Mayan practice of coating their feet with a protective layer of Latex.

[6] Latex does not hold up well in extreme temperatures, and it was used in europe only for erasing pencil marks until Charles Goodyear became fascinated with the substance and declared that "elastic gum" glorified god. [7] Goodyear's invention of vulcanization enabled the successful commercial production of rubber and earned him the public admiration of emperor Napoleon III. [8] In the next

decades, Brazil increased its rubber production thousands of times over, as Eric R. Wolf points out in *Europe And The People Without History*. [9] Indeed, rubber became such an essential part of our lives that the U.S. army once asked a young Major named Eisenhower to study the matter. [10] Wisely, the Future President Eisenhower advised the military to maintain its own source of this valuable commodity.

Abbreviations

12g. Generally, abbreviations are capitalized if the words that they stand for are capitalized.

An ***abbreviation*** is a shortened form of a word or phrase. Notice how capital letters are used in abbreviations in the following examples.

Personal Names

Abbreviate given names only if the person is most commonly known by the abbreviated form of the name. Capitalize initials.

EXAMPLES   Ida **B.** Wells   **T. H.** White

NOTE Leave a space between two initials, but not between three or more.

EXAMPLES   **J.R.R.** Tolkien   **W.E.B.** DuBois

Titles

(1) Abbreviate and capitalize most titles whether used before the full name or before the last name alone.

EXAMPLES   **Mr.** Chris Evans   **Ms.** Sue Aiello   **Mrs.** Dupont

Sr. (Señor) Cadenas   **Sra.** (Señora) Garza   **Dr.** O'Nolan

(2) You may abbreviate civil and military titles used before full names or before initials and last names. Spell them out before last names alone. Capitalize the title whether or not is it abbreviated.

EXAMPLES   **Sen.** Kay Bailey Hutchison   **Senator** Hutchison

Prof. E. M. Makowski   **Professor** Makowski

Brig. Gen. Norman Schwarzkopf   **Brigadier General** Schwarzkopf

STYLE TIP

Only a few abbreviations are appropriate in the text of a formal paper written for a general audience. In tables, notes, and bibliographies, abbreviations are used more freely in order to save space.

Reference Note

For information on **forming the plurals of abbreviations,** see page 351.

(3) Abbreviate and capitalize titles and academic degrees that follow proper names.

EXAMPLES   Hank Williams, **Jr.**   Peter Garcia, **M.D.**

> **NOTE** Do not include the titles, *Mr., Mrs., Ms.,* or *Dr.* when you use an abbreviation for a degree after a name.
>
> EXAMPLE   **Dr.** Joan West *or* Joan West, **M.D.** [not *Dr. Joan West, M.D.*]

Agencies, Organizations, and Acronyms

In formal writing, the names of agencies, organizations, and other things commonly known by their initials should be spelled out the first time the name is mentioned but may be abbreviated in later references.

EXAMPLE   My older sister encouraged me to sign up for the **Preliminary Scholastic Aptitude Test (PSAT).** She said that taking the **PSAT** is good practice for the standardized tests I will face in the next few years.

An *acronym* is a word formed from the first (or first few) letters of a series of words. Acronyms are written without periods. The abbreviations for many agencies and organizations are acronyms.

Abbreviations	Names
AMA	American Medical Association
IRS	Internal Revenue Service
NASA	National Aeronautics and Space Administration
UN	United Nations
USAF	United States Air Force

Geographical Terms

In regular text, spell out names of states and other political units whether they stand alone or follow other geographical terms.

EXAMPLES   Willa Cather spent her early years in **Winchester, Virginia,** and **Red Cloud, Nebraska.**

On our vacation in **Canada,** we visited **Edmonton,** the capital of **Alberta.**

---HELP---

Many common abbreviations are capitalized even though the spelled-out words are not. If you are not sure whether to capitalize an abbreviation, check a dictionary.

---HELP---

A few acronyms, such as *radar, laser,* and *scuba,* are now considered common nouns. They do not need to be spelled out on first use and are no longer capitalized. When you're not sure whether an acronym should be capitalized, check a recent dictionary.

MECHANICS

STYLE **TIP**

In regular text, include the traditional abbreviation for the District of Columbia, *D.C.,* with the city name *Washington* to show that you are not referring to the state of Washington.

Reference Note

For more information on **geographical terms,** see page 298.

COMPUTER TIP

Publishers usually set time abbreviations as small capital letters—uppercase letters of a smaller font size. If you use a computer, your word-processing software may offer small capitals as a style option. If it does not, or if you are writing by hand, you may use either uppercase or lowercase letters for time abbreviations as long as you are consistent within each piece of writing.

Abbreviate the terms in tables, notes, and bibliographies. Generally, you should use the same capitalization rules for the abbreviations as you use for the full words.

TABLE

| London, **U.K.** | Tucson, **Ariz.** |
| Victoria, **B.C.** | Fresno, **Calif.** |

FOOTNOTE ³The Public Library in Annaville, **Mich.,** has an entire collection of Smyth's folios.

BIBLIOGRAPHY ENTRY "The Last Hurrah." Editorial. *Star-Ledger* [Newark, **NJ**] 29 Aug. 1991:30.

In regular text, spell out every word in an address.

EXAMPLE We live at 413 **West** Maple **Street.**

Send the package to Holmstead **Drive,** Santa Fe, **New Mexico.**

Such words should be abbreviated in letter and envelope addresses and may be abbreviated in tables and notes.

ENVELOPE 413 **W.** Maple **St.**

TABLE

Holmstead **Dr.**
Santa Fe, New **Mex.**

NOTE Two-letter state abbreviations without periods are used only when the ZIP Code is included.

EXAMPLE Cincinnati, **OH 45233-4234**

Time

Abbreviate the two most frequently used era designations, A.D. and B.C. The abbreviation A.D. stands for the Latin phrase *anno Domini,* meaning "in the year of the Lord." It is used with dates in the Christian era. When used with a specific year, A.D. precedes the number. When used with the name of a century, it follows the name.

EXAMPLES In **A.D.** 476, the last Western Roman emperor, Romulus Augustulus, was overthrown.

The legends of King Arthur may be based on the life of a real British leader of the sixth century **A.D.**

The abbreviation B.C., which stands for "before Christ," is used for dates before the Christian era. It follows either a specific year number or the name of a century.

EXAMPLES Homer's epic poem the *Iliad* was probably composed between 800 and 700 **B.C.**

The poem describes battles that occurred around the twelfth century **B.C.**

In regular text, spell out the names of months and days whether they appear alone or in dates. Both types of names may be abbreviated in tables, notes, and bibliographies.

TEXT Please join us on **Thursday, March 21,** to celebrate Grandma and Grandpa's anniversary.

FOOTNOTE **Thurs. Mar.** 21

Abbreviate the designations for the two halves of the day measured by clock time. The abbreviation A.M. stands for the Latin phrase *ante meridiem*, meaning "before noon." The abbreviation P.M. stands for *post meridiem*, meaning "after noon." Both abbreviations follow the numerals designating the specific time.

EXAMPLE My mom works four days a week, from 8:00 **A.M.** until 6:00 **P.M.**

Units of Measurement

In regular text, spell out the names of units of measurement whether they stand alone or follow a spelled-out number or a numeral. Such names may be abbreviated in tables and notes when they follow a numeral.

TEXT Dad prefers to drive at a steady sixty-five **miles per hour** [not *mph*].

The cubicle measured ten **feet** [not *ft*] by twelve.

TABLE

| 1 **tsp** pepper, 2 **tbsp** olive oil | 97°**F** |
| 12 **ft** 6 **in.** | 2 **oz** flour |

Notice that the abbreviation for the word *inch* is followed by a period to avoid confusion with the preposition *in*.

HELP

In your reading, you may come across the abbreviations C.E. and B.C.E. These abbreviations stand for *Common Era* and *Before Common Era*. These abbreviations are used in place of A.D. and B.C., respectively, and are always used after the date.

EXAMPLES
Constantinople fell to the Turks in 1453 **C.E.**

Pharaoh Ramses the Great died in 1213 **B.C.E.**

MECHANICS

Rewrite the following sentences, correcting errors in the use and capitalization of abbreviations.

EXAMPLE   1. Charles Demuth was born in Lancaster, PA.

        1. Pennsylvania

1. Tomorrow, the flight for NY departs at 11:15 A.M.
2. Julius Caesar was assassinated in the Roman Forum in B.C. 44.
3. Harun ar-Rashid, whose reign is associated with the Arabian Nights, ruled as caliph of Baghdad from 786 to 809 A.D.
4. The Mississippi River flows from Lake Itasca, MN, all the way to the Gulf of Mexico at Port Eads, la.
5. The letter was addressed to Mr. Nugent on Elm st. in New London, WI.
6. G. Washington was our country's first president.
7. The keynote speaker was dr. Matthew Villareal, Ph.D.
8. Congress has designated holidays to honor the memory of such great Americans as Abraham Lincoln and Dr. Martin Luther King, jr.
9. Gen. de Gaulle became president of France in 1958.
10. I think sr. Martinez is waiting for you in the front lobby.

"After working all day on my MBA, I hop into my BMW and race home to watch PBS on my VCR—OK?"

© 1990; reprinted courtesy of Bunny Hoest and Parade magazine.

MECHANICS

Chapter Review

A. Capitalizing Words and Names Correctly

If a word group in the following items has an error in capitalization, write the entire word group correctly. If an item is already correct, write *C*.

1. *The Return Of The Native*
2. Yellowstone National park
3. the Federal bureau of investigation
4. temple Beth Israel
5. a bar of Ivory soap
6. a hindu temple
7. *A Day in the Life: the Music and the Artistry of the Beatles*
8. the constellation cassiopeia
9. on Fifty-first Avenue
10. the Rocky mountains

B. Revising Sentences to Correct Capitalization

Rewrite the following sentences, correcting errors in capitalization.

11. My Uncle Roger sailed on the *star of India* from London to Cyprus and Turkey.
12. the film was in spanish, and english subtitles were provided.
13. Was Artemis the Greek Goddess of the hunt?
14. Pablo's favorite movie is *2001: a Space Odyssey.*
15. Have you seen *A raisin in the sun* yet?
16. Leora went to the store during her lunch hour and chose just the right card for Valentine's day.
17. My cat bartinka often chases my dog piper through the yard and into the garden.
18. Lucinda's new brother was born at Sparrow hospital.
19. Come see our fantastic selection of top-quality stereo equipment at thompson electronics, at our new location just south of interstate 4 and River road!
20. Name the country located to the North of Zambia.

MECHANICS

C. Correcting Errors in Capitalization

Identify and correct the capitalization errors in the following sentences. If a sentence is already correct, write *C*.

21. The committee included Mrs. Alaria, dean Roget, and Mr. Wilson.

22. Last Winter, she took a short course in Psychology at the University of southern California.

23. After Labor day I will return to the West and continue my work.

24. The delegates stayed at the Conrad Hilton Hotel on Forty-seventh Street during the Democratic National Convention last August.

25. My Sister Francesca enjoyed reading "A Rose For Emily."

D. Using Abbreviations and Correct Capitalization

Rewrite the following sentences, correcting errors in the use of abbreviations and capitalization.

26. The author of the play *Twelfth night* is Wm. Shakespeare.

27. The first structures at Stonehenge, the ancient monument near Salisbury, eng., were constructed about B.C. 3100.

28. I'm proud to be able to address my aunt as dr. Lauren Wigen, m.d.

29. My family comes from the little town of dime box, TX.

30. Sen. Baxter went to the hospital and visited her mother in the icu.

E. Proofreading a Paragraph for Correct Capitalization

Proofread the following paragraph for errors in capitalization. Identify each error, and then write the correct form.

[**31**] Last year, in a special Ecology course at Charlotte High School, I found out about some endangered North American animals. [**32**] I learned that conservationists here in the south are particularly concerned about the fate of the Florida panther. [**33**] All of that classroom discussion didn't have much impact on me, however, until early one Saturday morning last Spring, when I was lucky enough to sight one of these beautiful creatures. [**34**] My Uncle and I were driving to Big Bass Lake for some fishing when I saw what looked like a large dog crossing

MECHANICS

the road some distance ahead of us. **[35]** Suddenly, Uncle Billy stopped his old ford truck and reached for the field glasses in the glove compartment. **[36]** As he handed them to me, he said, "look closely, Chris. You probably won't see a panther again any time soon." **[37]** Standing in the middle of Collingswood avenue, the cat turned and looked straight at us. **[38]** When those brown eyes met mine, I knew I had the title for my term paper—"Hello And Goodbye." **[39]** Then the big cat leisurely turned and crossed the road and loped off into the woods east of Sunshine mall. **[40]** As the panther disappeared back into the wilds of Charlotte county, Uncle Billy said, "Good luck to you, pal."

Writing Application
Using Capitalization in a Letter

Proper Nouns and Proper Adjectives   You have just started corresponding with a teenager in Japan. Write a letter to your pen pal describing some custom or practice that is unique to American culture or special to your family. In your letter, follow the rules of capitalization given in this chapter.

Prewriting   List some typically American holidays, customs, and practices. For each item on your list, brainstorm as many descriptive details as you can. Choose one item from your list to describe.

Writing   As you write your draft, organize your information clearly. Add facts, examples, and details as you think of them. Use clear, straightforward language, and try to avoid colloquialisms and idioms that your friend may not recognize. Make sure you include at least three proper nouns and three proper adjectives, all correctly capitalized.

Revising   Be sure that you have followed the guidelines for writing personal letters. Also, make sure your description paints a vivid picture of American customs.

Publishing   Proofread your letter for errors in grammar, usage, and mechanics. Take special care with capitalization of proper nouns. You and your classmates may want to display your letters on a bulletin board or collect them in a binder.

Punctuation

End Marks and Commas

Diagnostic Preview

A. Using End Marks and Commas

Rewrite the following sentences, adding, deleting, or reordering end marks and commas as necessary. If a sentence is already correct, write *C*.

EXAMPLE   1. Sally asked, "Where do you want to go after the recital"?

          1. *Sally asked, "Where do you want to go after the recital?"*

1. Who said, "I only regret that I have but one life to give for my country?"
2. Startled, we heard a high-pitched, whining, noise just outside the living room window.
3. Any student, who has not signed up for the contest by three o'clock, will not be eligible to participate.
4. My friend Esteban, running up the stairs two at a time, yelled out the good news.
5. "Why does the telephone always ring just as soon as I sit down to work," she asked?
6. My parents are trading in their car a two-door model with a sunroof four-wheel drive and air conditioning.
7. I have drilled practiced trained and exercised for weeks.
8. "Well Coach I can promise you that I'll be ready for the game next week," Kit said.

9. James King an Iroquois guide used to conduct tours of the Somers Mountain Indian Museum in Somers Connecticut.

10. He answered, "The abbreviation for *California* is *Cal.*".

B. Proofreading a Letter for the Correct Use of End Marks and Commas

Add, delete, or replace end marks or commas to correct each numbered word group in the following letter.

EXAMPLE   **[1]** Dear Toni

           1.   *Dear Toni,*

Dear Toni,

    [11] As she promised our friend Takara, and her family were waiting for us at the Osaka airport on Monday June 16. **[12]** I am very glad that you introduced us and that I could come to visit such a kind generous, and friendly family

    [13] Wow I love their house; it's quite different from any home that I've ever seen before and my favorite part of it is the garden **[14]** In the middle of the house and down one step a large rectangular courtyard lies open to the sun and air. **[15]** Rocks not plants and trees fill the space, and clean white sand not grass covers the ground **[16]** I wonder who carefully rakes the sand every day leaving small rows of lines covering the ground? **[17]** Takara told me that the sand represents the ocean the lines are like waves, and the rocks stand for islands. **[18]** I believe she is right for the garden is as peaceful as any deserted beach.

    [19] My flight by the way will be arriving in Portland in ten short days; if you're free would you please meet me at the airport.

        [20] Sincerely yours.

        Ramona

MECHANICS

End Marks

End marks—periods, question marks, and exclamation points—are used to indicate the purpose of a sentence.

13a. A statement (or *declarative sentence*) is followed by a period.

EXAMPLES   The blue whale is the largest animal that has ever lived.

September 15 to October 15 is Hispanic Heritage Month in the United States.

The keyboardist showed us how she uses the synthesizer to create a wide range of sounds.

NOTE In a sentence ending with a direct quotation, the period at the end of a sentence should be placed inside the closing quotation marks.

EXAMPLE   The teacher explained, "Hoping to learn the secret of everlasting life, Gilgamesh, the epic's hero, searches for Utnapishtim."

13b. A question (or *interrogative sentence*) is followed by a question mark.

EXAMPLES   Did you get the leading role?

When is your first performance?

Can you name the Seven Wonders of the Ancient World?

NOTE In a sentence ending with a direct quotation, a question mark should be placed inside the closing quotation marks when the quotation itself is a question. Otherwise, it should be placed outside the quotation marks.

EXAMPLES   To avoid answering a personal question, simply reply, "Why do you ask?" [The quotation is a question.]

Did Mr. Shields actually say, "Your reports are due in three days"? [The quotation is not a question, but the sentence as a whole is.]

Do not use a question mark after a declarative sentence containing an indirect question.

EXAMPLE   Katie wondered who would win the award.

Reference Note

For information on how **sentences** are **classified according to structure,** see page 87.

S T Y L E   **T I P**

Some requests and commands are put in question form even though they are not actually questions. In informal writing, such requests and commands may be followed by either a question mark or a period.

EXAMPLES

Will you please complete this brief questionnaire?

or

Will you please complete this brief questionnaire.

MECHANICS

13c. An exclamation (or *exclamatory sentence*) is followed by an exclamation point.

EXAMPLES   I can't believe that!

What an exciting race that was!

We're so happy for you!

NOTE In a sentence ending with a direct quotation, an exclamation point should be placed inside the closing quotation marks when the quotation itself is an exclamation. Otherwise, it should be placed outside the quotation marks.

EXAMPLES   "Down in front!" yelled the crowd.

Ms. Chen couldn't have said, "No homework"!

STYLE   **TIP**

Do not overuse exclamation points. Use an exclamation point only when a statement or an interjection is obviously emphatic.

At the beginning of a sentence, an interjection is generally followed by a comma or an exclamation point.

EXAMPLES   Hey, you're a great dancer! [mild exclamation]

Hey! Don't do that again! [strong exclamation]

Instead of a comma or an exclamation point, another mark of punctuation—period, question mark, dash, or ellipsis points—can be used after an interjection, depending on the meaning of the sentence.

EXAMPLES   "Oh. Are you sure that's what Carmen said?" inquired César.

"Well? What do you think of my painting?" Gillian asked.

"Hey—never mind," said Kevin.

"Wow . . . I don't know what to say," Myron stammered.

13d. A request or command (or *imperative sentence*) is generally followed by either a period or an exclamation point.

Generally, a request or mild command is followed by a period; a strong command is followed by an exclamation point.

EXAMPLES   Close the door, please. [request]

Close the door. [mild command]

Close the door! [strong command]

Reference Note

For more information about **interjections,** see page 25.

Reference Note

For more about **dashes** and **ellipsis points,** see pages 328 and 342.

MECHANICS

Reference Note

For more about the **placement of end marks and quotation marks,** see Chapter 14.

S T Y L E   T I P

Sometimes (usually in dialogue) a writer will use more than one end mark to express intense emotion or a combination of emotions.

EXAMPLES
The panicked passenger kept shouting, "Help‼"
[intense emotion]

"You told them what⁈" Mary Ann exclaimed.
[combination of curiosity and surprise]

Using double end punctuation is acceptable in most informal writing. However, in formal writing, use only one end mark at a time.

NOTE In a sentence ending with a direct quotation, a period at the end of an imperative sentence or interjection should be placed inside the closing quotation marks.

EXAMPLE   The announcer requested, "Please stand for the singing of the national anthem**.**"

An exclamation point should be placed inside the quotation marks when the quotation is a strong command or interjection. Otherwise, it should be placed outside the quotation marks.

"Hey**!**" exclaimed Mark. "I just can't believe the referee said 'Foul'**!**"

ANIMAL CRACKERS ©
Tribune Media Services, Inc.
All rights reserved.
Reprinted with permission.

Exercise 1   Correcting Sentences by Adding End Marks

Write each word that should be followed by an end mark in the following sentences; then, add an appropriate end mark. If quotation marks should precede or follow the end mark, write them in the proper place.

EXAMPLES   **1.** Mom asked, "When did you receive the letter

1. letter?"

2. Terrific What a throw you made

2. Terrific!; made!

1. When do you want to take your vacation
2. Andrew didn't think he had enough money to go to the movies
3. Wow Did you see that liftoff
4. Willie, are you ready to give your report on Thurgood Marshall
5. Carefully set the Ming vase on the display stand

MECHANICS

6. Mom wants to know why you did not buy a newspaper on your way home
7. What a downpour we had last night
8. Leave the theater immediately
9. He yelled across the field, "Hurry
10. Didn't you hear her say "I'm not ready yet

Abbreviations

13e. Use a period after certain abbreviations.

An *abbreviation* is a shortened form of a word or phrase. Notice how periods are used with abbreviations in the examples in this part of the chapter.

Personal Names

Abbreviate given names only if the person is most commonly known by the abbreviated form of the name.

EXAMPLES   Daniel **P.** Moynihan   **P. J.** O'Rourke   **J.R.R.** Tolkien

NOTE   Leave a space between two such initials but not between three or more.

Titles

Abbreviate social titles whether used before the full name or before the last name alone.

EXAMPLES   **Mr.** Ted Evans   **Mrs.** Anne Frears   **Ms.** Agnello

Sr. (Señor) Cadenas   **Sra.** (Señora) Garza   **Dr.** Kostas

You may abbreviate civil and military titles used before full names or before initials and last names. Spell them out before last names used alone.

EXAMPLES   **Gen.** Douglas MacArthur   **General** MacArthur

Sen. Margaret Chase Smith   **Senator** Smith

Prof. E. M. Makowski   **Professor** Makowski

Abbreviate titles and academic degrees that follow proper names.

EXAMPLES   Ken Griffey, **Jr.**   Joe Sears, **M.D.**

─ H E L P ─

If a statement ends with an abbreviation, do not use an additional period as an end mark. However, do use a question mark or an exclamation point if one is needed.

EXAMPLES

Mrs. Cuellar visited her relatives in Edison, N.J.

How long did she stay in Edison, N.J.?

NOTE Do not include the title *Mr., Mrs., Ms.,* or *Dr.* when you use a professional title or degree after a name.

EXAMPLE **Dr.** Jack Profumo *or* Jack Profumo, **M.D.** [not *Dr. Jack Profumo, M.D.*]

Agencies, Organizations, and Acronyms

An *acronym* is a word formed from the first (or first few) letters of a series of words. Acronyms are written without periods.

AMA, American Medical Association

NASA, National Aeronautics and Space Administration

FSA, Farm Service Agency

NFL, National Football League

USAF, United States Air Force

UN, United Nations

PBS, Public Broadcasting Service

DOC, Department of Commerce

After spelling out the first use of the names of agencies and organizations, abbreviate these names and other things commonly known by their acronyms.

EXAMPLE Tamara is interested in working for the **United Nations Educational, Scientific, and Cultural Organization (UNESCO).** She says that **UNESCO** promotes international cooperation.

Geographical Terms

In regular text, spell out names of states and other political units whether they stand alone or follow other geographical terms. You may abbreviate them in tables, notes, and bibliographies.

TEXT Karen Blixen spent her early years in Copenhagen, **Denmark,** and in East Africa.

On our vacation in Mexico, we visited Guadalajara, the capital of **Jalisco.**

TABLE

Copenhagen, **Den.**	Tucson, **Ariz.**
Vancouver, **B.C.**	Guadalajara, **Jal.**

FOOTNOTE [3]The Public Library in Setauket, **N.Y.,** has an entire collection of Smyth's folios.

STYLE TIP

A few acronyms, such as *radar, laser,* and *sonar,* are now considered common nouns. They do not need to be spelled out on first use and are no longer capitalized. When you are not sure whether an acronym should be capitalized, look it up in a recent dictionary.

Reference Note

For more information about **geographical terms,** see page 272.

STYLE TIP

Include the traditional abbreviation for the District of Columbia, *D.C.,* with the city name, *Washington,* to distinguish it from the state of Washington.

BIBLIOGRAPHY ENTRY	Wilson, E.O. <u>The Diversity of Life</u>. Cambridge, **Mass.:** Harvard University Press, 1992.

In regular text, spell out every word in an address. Such words should be abbreviated in letter and envelope addresses and may be abbreviated in tables and notes.

TEXT	We live at 413 **West Maple Street.**
	Send the package to **Holmstead Avenue, Santa Fe, New Mexico.**
ENVELOPE	413 **W. Maple St.**
TABLE	Holmstead **Ave.,** Santa Fe, **New Mex.**

NOTE Two-letter state abbreviations without periods are used only when the ZIP Code is included.

EXAMPLE   Golden, **CO** 80401-0029

Time

Abbreviate the frequently used era designations. The abbreviation *A.D.* stands for the Latin phrase *anno Domini,* meaning "in the year of the Lord." It is used with dates in the Christian era. When used with a specific year number, *A.D.* precedes the number. When used with the name of a century, it follows the name.

EXAMPLES   Between **A.D.** 61 and **A.D.** 63, Queen Boadicea led a war against the Roman invaders in Britain.
The Romans finally defeated her and controlled Britain until the sixth century **A.D.**

The abbreviation *B.C.*, which stands for *before Christ*, is used for dates before the Christian era. It follows either a specific year number or the name of a century.

EXAMPLES   In 343 **B.C.,** Aristotle tutored a thirteen-year-old boy who would later be known as Alexander the Great.
Aristotle, one of the great philosophers of ancient Greece, wrote over 400 literary works during the fourth century **B.C.**

In regular text, spell out the names of months and days whether they appear alone or in dates. Both types of names may be abbreviated in tables, notes, and bibliographies.

STYLE TIP

Only a few abbreviations are appropriate in the text of a formal paper written for a general audience. In tables, notes, and bibliographies, abbreviations are used more freely in order to save space.

STYLE TIP

In your reading, you may see the abbreviations *B.C.E.* (Before the Common Era) and *C.E.* (Common Era). These abbreviations should be placed after the year.

EXAMPLES
The famous Roman orator Cicero died on December 7, 43 **B.C.E.**

The Ottoman Turks took Constantinople in 1453 **C.E.**

MECHANICS

TEXT	Please join us on **Thursday, March 21,** to celebrate Grandma and Grandpa's anniversary.
FOOTNOTE	**Thurs., Mar.** 21
BIBLIOGRAPHY ENTRY	Bower, B. "Domesticating an Ancient 'Temple Town.'" <u>Science News</u> 15 **Oct.** 1988: 246.

Abbreviate the designations for the two halves of the day measured by clock time. The abbreviation *A.M.* stands for the Latin phrase *ante meridiem,* meaning "before noon." The abbreviation *P.M.* stands for *post meridiem,* meaning "after noon." Both abbreviations follow the numerals designating the specific time.

EXAMPLE	The dentist's office is open five days a week, from 7:00 **A.M.** until 4:30 **P.M.**

Units of Measurement

In regular text, spell out the names of units of measurement whether they stand alone or follow a spelled-out number or a numeral. Such names may be abbreviated in tables and notes when they follow a numeral. Abbreviations for units of measurement are usually written without periods. However, do use a period with the abbreviation for inch (*in.*) to prevent confusing it with the word *in.*

TEXT	Dad prefers to drive at a steady sixty-five **miles per hour** [not *mph*].
	The sinkhole measured ten **feet** [not *ft*] by twelve.

TABLE	1 **tsp** salt	2 **tbsp** vinegar	79° **F**
	2 **ft** 6 **in.**	1 1/2 **c** water	2 **oz** dried beans

Exercise 2 Using Abbreviations

Rewrite the following sentences, correcting errors in the use of abbreviations.

EXAMPLE	1. Mom was born in Waukesha, WI.
	1. *Mom was born in Waukesha, Wisconsin.*

1. Tomorrow, the flight for Cincinnati departs at 11:15 A.M. in the morning.
2. The Athenian statesman Alcibiades died in B.C. 404.
3. Charlemagne ruled the Holy Roman Empire from 800 to 814 A.D.

STYLE TIP

Do not use *A.M.* or *P.M.* with numbers spelled out as words or as substitutes for the words *morning, afternoon,* or *evening.*

EXAMPLE
The walkathon will begin at **8:00 A.M. (or eight o'clock in the morning)** Saturday [not *eight A.M. Saturday*].

Also, do not use the words *morning, afternoon,* or *evening* with numerals followed by *A.M.* or *P.M.*

EXAMPLE
The next bus for Bangor leaves at **1:30 P.M. (or one-thirty in the afternoon)** [not *1:30 P.M. in the afternoon*].

4. The Mississippi River flows from Lake Itasca, MN, all the way to the Gulf of Mexico at Port Eads, LA.

5. The letter was addressed to Mr. Schenk on Pine St. in Boise, ID.

6. Juan hopes to fly jets for the United States AF.

7. The keynote speaker was Dr. David Hoyt, Ph.D.

8. Congress has designated holidays to honor the memory of such great Americans as Abraham Lincoln, George Washington, and Martin Luther King, Junior.

9. R. Reagan was the fortieth president of the United States.

10. The table on page 13 gives the measurement as "6 ft, 3 in deep."

Review A **Correcting Sentences by Adding Periods, Question Marks, and Exclamation Points**

Write the following sentences, adding periods, question marks, and exclamation points as needed.

EXAMPLE   1. Does Pete come from New York City

         1. *Does Pete come from New York City?*

1. What a car that is

2. Whose car is that

3. I went to Washington, DC., to visit Patrick.

4. We asked who owned that boat

5. By AD. 1100, Moscow was already an important city

6. George Washington Carver, Jr, received the Spingarn Medal in 1923

7. Why do so many dogs enjoy playing fetch

8. Please explain why so many dogs enjoy playing fetch

9. When did Bill Bradley run for president

10. Terrific Here's another coin for my collection

COMPUTER TIP

Publishers usually print time abbreviations as small capitals—uppercase letters that are slightly smaller than standard uppercase letters. Your word processor may offer small capitals as a style option. If it does not or if you are writing by hand, you may use either uppercase or lowercase letters for time abbreviations, as long as you are consistent within each piece of writing.

Commas

Items in a Series

13f. Use commas to separate items in a series.

EXAMPLES   The basketball coach recommended that Désirée practice dribbling, shooting, weaving, and passing. [words in a series]

         We can meet before English class, during lunch, or after school. [phrases in a series]

After school I must make sure that my room is clean, that my little brother is home from his piano lesson, and that the garbage has been emptied. [clauses in a series]

When *and*, *or*, or *nor* joins the last two items in a series, the comma is sometimes omitted before the conjunction if a comma is not needed to make the meaning of the sentence clear.

UNCLEAR   Phyllis, Ken and Matt formed a rock band. [It looks as though Phyllis is being addressed.]

CLEAR   Phyllis, Ken, and Matt formed a rock band. [Phyllis is clearly a member of the band.]

NOTE Some words—such as *bread and butter* and *law and order*—are paired so often that they may be considered a single item.

EXAMPLE   For lunch we had soup, salad, **bread and butter,** and milk.

(1) If all the items in a series are joined by *and, or,* or *nor,* do not use commas to separate them.

EXAMPLES   Tyrone **and** Earlene **and** Lily won awards for their sculptures.

Should we walk **or** ride our bikes **or** take the bus?

(2) Generally, a comma should not be placed before or after a series.

INCORRECT   I enjoy, gymnastics, basketball, and wrestling.

CORRECT   I enjoy gymnastics, basketball, and wrestling.

INCORRECT   I'll meet Mr. Catalano, Mr. Lawson, and Mr. Liu, tomorrow afternoon.

CORRECT   I'll meet Mr. Catalano, Mr. Lawson, and Mr. Liu tomorrow afternoon.

(3) Short independent clauses in a series may be separated by commas.

EXAMPLE   I came, I saw, I conquered.

Julius Caesar

13g. **Use commas to separate two or more adjectives preceding a noun.**

EXAMPLE   Lucia is an intelligent, thoughtful, responsible student.

STYLE **TIP**

For clarity, some writers prefer always to use the comma before the conjunction in a series. Follow your teacher's instructions on this point.

STYLE **TIP**

The abbreviation *etc.* (meaning "and so forth") at the end of a series should be followed by a comma unless it falls at the end of a sentence.

EXAMPLES

Al bought hamburger, buns, onions, etc., for the French Club's cookout.

For the French Club's cookout, Al bought hamburger, buns, onions, etc.

Reference Note

Independent clauses in a series can be separated by semicolons. For more about this use of the **semicolon,** see page 322.

Do not use a comma before the final adjective preceding a noun if that adjective is thought of as part of the noun.

EXAMPLES   Let's play this new video game. [not *new, video game*]

I've finally found a decent, affordable used car. [not *affordable, used car*]

NOTE   An adverb may modify an adjective preceding a noun. Do not use a comma between the adverb and the adjective.

EXAMPLE   I think you should wear the **bright blue** shirt with that suit.

Independent Clauses

13h. Use a comma before a coordinating conjunction (*and, but, for, nor, or, so,* or *yet*) when it joins independent clauses.

EXAMPLES   I read a review of Charles Frazier's *Cold Mountain,* and now I want to read the book.

Amy followed the recipe carefully, for she had never made paella before.

NOTE   Always use a comma before *for, so,* or *yet* joining independent clauses. The comma may be omitted before *and, but, nor,* or *or* if the independent clauses are very short and if the sentence is not awkward or unclear without it.

CLEAR   The phone rang and I answered it.
We can go in the morning or we can leave now.

AWKWARD   The teacher called on Maria and John began to answer.

CLEAR   The teacher called on Maria, and John began to answer.

Do not confuse a compound sentence with a simple sentence that has a compound verb.

SIMPLE
SENTENCE   My stepsister had been accepted at Howard University but decided to attend Grambling State University instead. [one independent clause with a compound verb]

COMPOUND
SENTENCE   My stepsister had been accepted at Howard University, but she decided to attend Grambling State University instead. [two independent clauses]

TIPS & TRICKS

A compound noun such as *video game* or *used car* is considered a single noun. You can use two tests to determine whether an adjective and a noun form a unit.

TEST 1
Change the order of the adjectives. If the order of the adjectives can be reversed sensibly, use a comma. *Affordable, decent used car* makes sense, but *used decent car* and *video new game* do not.

TEST 2
Insert the word *and* between the adjectives. If *and* fits sensibly between the adjectives, use a comma. *And* cannot be logically inserted between *new* and *video game*. *And* sounds sensible between *decent* and *affordable* but not between *affordable* and *used*.

MECHANICS

Also, keep in mind that compound subjects and compound objects are generally not separated by commas.

EXAMPLES What he is saying today and what he said yesterday are two different things. [two subordinate clauses serving as a compound subject]

Television crews covered the women's triathlon and the awards ceremony. [compound object]

Reference Note

For more about **compound subjects** and **compound verbs,** see page 35. For more about **compound sentences,** see page 88.

Oral Practice Using Commas Correctly

Read aloud each of the following sentences, and say where commas should be added or deleted. If a sentence is already correct, say *correct.*

EXAMPLE 1. Salvatore is an eager, willing, and able, young man.
1. *The comma after* able *should be deleted.*

1. Soon both coasts would be connected by huge coal-black "iron horses" traveling along the rails.
2. I'll draw the plans Clay will get the supplies and Kerry will build the fountain.
3. I can't decide what to order but I'm sure that I'll have something spicy, mild or sweet-and-sour.
4. I enjoy, guitar music, *Zarzuelas,* and light opera.
5. Dad had sent away for the new coat but then changed his mind and canceled the order.
6. The tenor sang his solo and the soprano sang hers.
7. The watch has been ordered from Europe, but will not be delivered until next month.
8. They will visit museums, shops, and art galleries, this week.
9. You'll be writing many addresses in your life so learn to use commas now and you won't have many problems later.
10. Blanche Kelso Bruce took a seat in the U.S. Senate in 1875 served six years, and so became the first African American to serve a full term as senator.

Exercise 3 Correcting Sentences by Adding Commas

For the following sentences, write each word that should be followed by a comma, and add the comma. If a sentence is already correct, write *C.*

EXAMPLE 1. Taylor Greer is the strong-minded unpredictable heroine of Barbara Kingsolver's novel *The Bean Trees.*
1. *strong-minded,*

MECHANICS

1. The photograph showed a happy mischievous good-natured boy.
2. Barbara will bring potato salad to the picnic and Marc will bring the cold cuts and the volleyball net.
3. Alain Locke taught philosophy created one of the foremost collections of African art and mentored many African American writers.
4. We studied the following authors in English class this semester: F. Scott Fitzgerald Lorraine Hansberry and Rudolfo Anaya.
5. The introduction of the hardy sweet potato helped the Chinese to alleviate the famines that plagued them.
6. The committee has suggested that the cafeteria serve a different selection daily that classes not be interrupted by announcements and that pep rallies always be held during sixth period.
7. Students will receive paper pencils rulers etc. at the beginning of the test.
8. April looked on the desk, under the chair, and in her purse.
9. Last winter was abnormally cold icy and snowy.
10. The concert consisted of African American music and featured jazz rhythm and blues spirituals and several gospel songs.

Review B **Proofreading for the Correct Use of End Marks and Commas**

Rewrite the sentences in the following paragraph, adding, deleting, or reordering end marks and commas as necessary.

EXAMPLE [1] Do you know the name of the famous structure shown in the photograph on the next page

1. *Do you know the name of the famous structure shown in the photograph on the next page?*

[1] Known as Stonehenge, this great circle of stones is located in England, and remains one of the most mysterious structures of the ancient world. [2] Much of the riddle of Stonehenge concerns the transport of the awesome massive stones that stand in the monument's inner circle. [3] These rocks are indigenous to Wales and many people have asked, "How did these huge stones travel two hundred miles to England" [4] Do you remember Merlin from the stories of King Arthur's legendary court [5] This wily, and powerful sorcerer is said to have moved the stones by magic. [6] The story of Merlin may be fascinating but modern astronomers anthropologists, and other scientists are searching for a more rational explanation. [7] Some theorists believe that many of the incredibly heavy gigantic monoliths were shipped by raft through dangerous tidal waters, but other scientists

scoff and exclaim, "That's impossible"! [8] Still other theorists wonder whether glaciers may have lifted moved, and deposited the stones so far from their home? [9] Visitors to Stonehenge are no longer allowed within the monument and venturing inside the protected area will draw a polite but authoritative, "Will you please step back" [10] So far, Stonehenge has not yielded a solution to the mystery of the stones yet a section of the site remains unexplored and may contain clues as to how they got there.

Nonessential Clauses and Phrases

13i. Use commas to set off nonessential subordinate clauses and nonessential participial phrases.

Reference Note

For more about **subordinate clauses,** see page 77. For more about **participial phrases,** see page 59.

A *nonessential* (or *nonrestrictive*) subordinate clause or participial phrase adds information that is unnecessary to the basic meaning of the sentence.

NONESSENTIAL CLAUSES   Marie Curie**, who studied radioactivity,** won the Nobel Prize for chemistry in 1911.

Did the 1998 Senate hearings**, which were televised,** attract a large audience?

NONESSENTIAL PHRASES   Monique**,** **carrying the heaviest load,** lagged far behind the others.

     Willie Herenton**,** **defeating the incumbent in 1991,** became the first African American mayor of Memphis.

Notice that the nonessential clause or phrase from each of the examples above can be left out without changing the basic meaning of the sentence.

EXAMPLES   Marie Curie won the Nobel Prize for chemistry in 1911.

     Did the 1998 Senate hearings attract a large audience?

     Monique lagged far behind the others.

     Willie Herenton became the first African American mayor of Memphis.

An *essential* (or *restrictive*) subordinate clause or participial phrase is not set off by commas because it contains information that cannot be left out without changing the basic meaning of the sentence.

ESSENTIAL CLAUSES   The juniors **who were selected for Boys State and Girls State** were named.

     Should material **that is quoted verbatim** be placed in quotation marks?

ESSENTIAL PHRASES   Those **participating in the food drive** should bring their donations by Friday at the latest.

     The election **won by Willie Herenton** was in October 1991.

Notice how leaving out the essential clause or phrase changes the basic meaning of each of the examples above.

EXAMPLES   The juniors were named. [Which juniors?]

     Should material be placed in quotation marks? [Which material?]

     Those should bring their donations by Friday at the latest. [Which those?]

     The election was in October 1991. [Which election?]

Some subordinate clauses and participial phrases may be either essential or nonessential. The presence or absence of commas tells the reader how the clause or phrase relates to the main idea of the sentence.

TIPS & TRICKS

A subordinate clause or a participial phrase that modifies a proper noun is generally nonessential.

EXAMPLES
The Eiffel Tower, **which Alexandre-Gustave Eiffel designed,** is in Paris.

Skipper, **barking at the mail carrier,** would not calm down.

MECHANICS

TIPS & TRICKS

Adjective clauses beginning with *that* are nearly always essential.

EXAMPLE
The platypus and the spiny anteater are the only mammals **that** lay eggs.

How do you know when
a descriptive clause is
essential and when it is
nonessential? The differ-
ences in meaning can be
subtle. Write three sen-
tence pairs that contain
descriptive clauses. These
clauses should make sense
in the sentence whether or
not commas set them off.

EXAMPLE
The couple who were
sitting at the table celebrated their anniversary.

The couple, who were
sitting at the table, celebrated their anniversary.

Then, trade with a partner
and examine his or her sentences. How do they differ
in meaning? Which sen-
tence contains the essential
clause and which the
nonessential? Can you
create a rule that tells you
when to set off the clause
with commas?

NONESSENTIAL CLAUSE	Una's cousin, **who wants to be an astronaut,** attended a space camp in Huntsville, Alabama, last summer. [Una has only one cousin, and that cousin attended the space camp.]
ESSENTIAL CLAUSE	Una's cousin **who wants to be an astronaut** attended a space camp in Huntsville, Alabama, last summer. [Una has more than one cousin. The one who wants to be an astronaut attended the space camp.]
NONESSENTIAL PHRASE	Your cat, **draped along the back of the couch,** seems contented. [You have only one cat, and it seems contented.]
ESSENTIAL PHRASE	Your cat **draped along the back of the couch** seems contented. [You have more than one cat. The one draped along the back of the couch seems contented.]

Exercise 4   Using Commas Correctly

Rewrite the following sentences, adding or deleting commas as necessary. If a sentence is already correct, write *C.*

EXAMPLE **1.** The movie which is one of my favorites is about a
friendly extraterrestrial.

1. *The movie, which is one of my favorites, is about a
friendly extraterrestrial.*

1. Students, going on the trip tomorrow, will meet in the auditorium.
2. The White River Bridge which closed today for resurfacing will not
be open for traffic until mid-October.
3. The symphony, that Beethoven called the *Eroica,* was composed to
celebrate the memory of a great man.
4. From the composer's letters, we learn that the "great man" whom
he had in mind was Napoleon Bonaparte.
5. Natalie Curtis Burlin always interested in the music of American
Indians recorded their songs in the early 1900s.
6. The driver stopped on the side of the road had a flat tire.
7. The musician, who founded the annual music festival in Puerto
Rico, was Pablo Casals.
8. Semantics which is concerned with the meanings of words is an
interesting subject of study for high school students.
9. My parents' station wagon which is more than seven years old simply refuses to start on cold mornings.
10. All contestants, submitting photographs, must sign a release form.

Introductory Elements

13j. Use a comma after certain introductory elements.

(1) Use a comma to set off a mild exclamation such as *well*, *oh*, or *why*. Other introductory words such as *yes* and *no* are also set off by commas.

EXAMPLES   **Well,** I guess so.

              Yikes, are we late!

              Yes, I heard your question.

(2) Use a comma after an introductory participle or participial phrase.

EXAMPLES   **Exhausted,** the scouts took a break.

              Looking poised and calm, Jill walked to the podium.

NOTE Do not confuse a gerund phrase used as the subject of a sentence with an introductory participial phrase.

EXAMPLES   **Following directions** can sometimes be difficult. [*Following directions* is a gerund phrase used as the subject of the sentence.]

              Following directions, I began to assemble the bike. [*Following directions* is an introductory participial phrase modifying *I*.]

(3) Use a comma after two or more introductory prepositional phrases or after one long one.

EXAMPLES   **In the first round of the golf tournament,** I played against one of the best golfers in the state.

              In the secret chamber called "the crystal keep," the heroine found the missing map.

    A single short introductory prepositional phrase does not require a comma unless the sentence is awkward to read without one or unless the phrase is parenthetical.

EXAMPLES   **At the track,** meet me in front of the snack bar. [The comma is needed to avoid reading "track meet."]

              By the way, I need to borrow a quarter. [The comma is needed because *by the way* is parenthetical.]

13
j

STYLE **TIP**

Make sure that an introductory participial phrase modifies the subject of the sentence; otherwise, the phrase may be misplaced.

MISPLACED
Cracking and eating the seeds from the bird feeder, we enjoyed watching the playful cardinals.

REVISED
Cracking and eating the seeds from the bird feeder, the playful cardinals were a joy to watch.

Reference Note

For information on **participial phrases** and **gerund phrases,** see pages 59 and 62. For information on **prepositional phrases,** see page 54.

MECHANICS

(4) Use a comma after an introductory adverb clause.

An introductory adverb clause may appear at the beginning of a sentence or before any independent clause in the sentence.

EXAMPLES **After I had locked the car door,** I remembered that the keys were still in the ignition.

I had a spare set of keys with me; **if I hadn't,** I would have had to walk home.

NOTE An adverb clause that follows an independent clause is generally not set off by a comma.

EXAMPLE Thousands of homes in the Philippines were destroyed **when Mount Pinatubo erupted in 1991.**

Review C **Using Commas in a Paragraph**

For the sentences in the following paragraph, write each word that should be followed by a comma, and add the comma. If a sentence is already correct, write *C*.

EXAMPLE **[1]** Well what do you think the clocks in the painting shown on the opposite page symbolize?

1. *Well,*

[1] Have you ever had a dream that seemed absolutely real; then, as you awoke you realized how outlandish it was? [2] An artist painting a surrealistic picture can sometimes generate that same dreamlike feeling in an audience. [3] For example, this painting which is one of many surreal landscapes by Salvador Dali conveys the strange experience of a dream. [4] In a dream time has a different meaning, and the bizarre can seem ordinary. [5] While only five minutes may actually have passed events requiring hours or days may have taken place in a dream. [6] Dali's clocks drooping as limply as a sleeper show that the rigid march of time can relax in a dream. [7] In the liquid time and unearthly space of dreams not even solid reality can be certain.

[8] Objects far more fantastic and incredible than the creature who reclines on the sand can seem in dreams to be as familiar as your own face. [9] Sleeping peacefully Dali's strange creature does not seem to realize that it is saddled with the burden of time. [10] Well until the alarm clock wakes you from your own dreams you probably don't realize it either.

MECHANICS

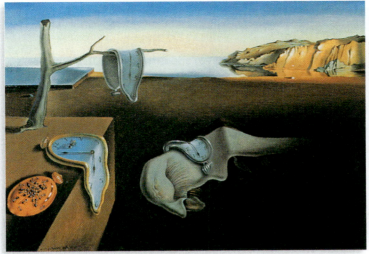

Salvador Dalí, *The Persistence of Memory* (Persistence de la memoire) (1931). Oil on canvas (9½" x 13") (24.1 cm x 33 cm). The Museum of Modern Art, New York, given anonymously. © 1996 Demart Pro Arte®, Geneva/Artists Rights Society (ARS), New York.

Interrupters

13k. Use commas to set off an expression that interrupts a sentence.

(1) Nonessential appositives and appositive phrases are set off by commas.

An *appositive* is a noun or pronoun placed beside another noun or pronoun to identify or describe it. An *appositive phrase* consists of an appositive and its modifiers.

A *nonessential* (or *nonrestrictive*) appositive or appositive phrase adds information that is unnecessary to the meaning of the sentence. In other words, the basic meaning of the sentence is clear and complete with or without the appositive or appositive phrase.

EXAMPLES   Ron Arias's first novel, **The Road to Tamazunchale,** was nominated for the National Book Award.

Tylan, **my oldest nephew,** plays the accordion.

Is that he, **the young man with the red hair**?

Notice that the basic meaning of each of the examples above remains clear and complete without the appositive or appositive phrase.

EXAMPLES   Ron Arias's first novel was nominated for the National Book Award.

Reference Note

For more about **appositives** and **appositive phrases,** see page 68.

Tylan plays the accordion.

Is that he?

NOTE An **essential** (or **restrictive**) appositive or appositive phrase is not set off by commas because it adds information that is necessary to the meaning of the sentence. In other words, the basic meaning of the sentence is unclear or incomplete without the appositive or appositive phrase.

EXAMPLES Does your friend **Joshua** have a part in the play, too?

The old saying **"Haste makes waste"** certainly applies to this situation.

Notice that without the appositive the meaning of each of the examples above is unclear or incomplete.

Reference Note

For information on **correcting misplaced modifiers,** see page 230.

(2) Words used in direct address are set off by commas.

EXAMPLES **Mom,** have you called Mrs. Johnson yet?

Your painting, **Andy,** is very original.

Will you answer the question, **Monica**?

(3) Parenthetical expressions are set off by commas.

A *parenthetical expression* is a side remark that adds information or shows a relationship between ideas.

Reference Note

Some parenthetical expressions, such as *consequently, however, moreover,* and *therefore,* are **conjunctive adverbs.** For more information, see page 88.

Reference Note

Parentheses and **dashes** can also be used to set off parenthetical expressions. See page 327.

Commonly Used Parenthetical Expressions		
after all	I believe (hope, *etc.*)	naturally
at any rate	incidentally	nevertheless
by the way	in fact	of course
consequently	in general	on the contrary
for example	in the first place	on the other hand
for instance	meanwhile	that is
however	moreover	therefore

EXAMPLES **Incidentally,** I won't be home for supper.

Exercise makes the heart and lungs more efficient, and, **moreover,** it contributes to an overall sense of well-being.

It's too late to call now, **I believe.**

Sometimes the expressions in the preceding chart are not used parenthetically. When they are not, do not set them off with commas.

EXAMPLES   **By the way,** she is in my vocal music class. [parenthetical, meaning "incidentally"]

You can tell **by the way** she sings that she enjoys the class. [not parenthetical, meaning "by the manner in which"]

NOTE A contrasting expression introduced by *not* is parenthetical and is set off by commas.

EXAMPLES   Margaret Walker, **not Alice Walker,** wrote the novel *Jubilee.*

COMPUTER TIP

If you use a computer to write, you may want to create a file of the parenthetical expressions listed on page 312. Refer to this file as you proofread your writing, and be sure that you have punctuated these expressions correctly. Use the word-processing software's search function to speed up your proofreading. The computer will search for and highlight each occurrence of whatever expression you select.

Exercise 5   Correcting Sentences by Adding Commas

For each of the following sentences, write each word that should be followed by a comma, and add the comma. If a sentence is already correct, write C.

EXAMPLE   1. Hania one of my cousins from Poland sent me a copy of our family tree.

1. *Hania, Poland,*

1. As a matter of fact your lateness is your own fault since you knew what time the bus would be leaving.
2. Have you seen Mr. Welch our new accounting teacher?
3. Zimbabwe's stone ruins once a stronghold for an ancient empire attest to the skill of those early stonemasons.
4. Please listen class while Jim makes an announcement.
5. Our friend Mrs. Kirby gets our mail when we are away.
6. Texans have a right to be proud of Sergeants José Mendoza López and Macario García Texan citizens who earned the Congressional Medal of Honor.
7. Daniel my twin brother just got a new job.
8. It is the pressure of getting work in on time not the work itself that gets on my nerves.
9. Mr. Beck the yearbook photographer always tries I think to place each person in the most flattering pose.
10. It's the phone that's ringing Suzanne not the doorbell.
11. Incidentally the green revolution a few decades ago was the direct result of improved technology and better seed.
12. Doesn't the word *aerobic* after all simply refer to an increase in the body's oxygen intake?

MECHANICS

13. The Van Allen belt is to the best of my knowledge a layer of electrically charged particles over the earth's atmosphere.

14. My friend your accounting figures are on the contrary an oasis of certainty in a desert of unreliability.

15. This unproved theory moreover has formed the basis of much of modern thought.

16. We may have a vacancy late tomorrow evening however.

17. Tyler had been in first place not second for most of the race.

18. What are the employment possibilities in alternative energy industries for example geothermal energy?

19. In general mosquitoes seem to thrive in warm climates wherever there is standing water.

20. Actually, Stan, I'm not planning to enter the race; I'd be happy if this old jalopy ran at any rate at all.

Conventional Uses

13l. **Use commas in certain conventional situations.**

(1) **Use a comma to separate items in dates and addresses.**

EXAMPLES   On Monday, December 1, 1999, I bought my pet parakeet.

Contact the postmaster at 108 Griffith Lane, Bethesda, MD 20814-9997, if you need more information.

Notice in each example above that a comma separates the last item in a date or an address from the words that follow it.

Do not use commas to set off

- the month from the day

  EXAMPLE   My grandparents celebrated their fiftieth wedding anniversary on **January 17,** 2000.

- the day from the month when the day is given before the month

  EXAMPLE   On **15 June** 1924, Congress granted U.S. citizenship to all American Indians.

- the month from the year when no day is given

  EXAMPLE   Will the new high school be open by **August 2004?**

- a house number from a street name

  EXAMPLE   The Espinozas' address is **236 Meadowlark Lane,** Omaha, NE 68108-0335.

- a state abbreviation from a ZIP Code

   EXAMPLE   Is 1410 Azalea Drive, Alpharetta, **GA 30005-9725,** the
              correct address?

- items joined by prepositions

   EXAMPLE   The play is at the Majestic Theater **on** Broad Avenue **in**
              Midland Heights.

**(2) Use a comma after the salutation of a personal letter and after
the closing of any letter.**

EXAMPLES   Dear Dale and Amy**,**   Sincerely yours**,**

(NOTE) Use a colon after the salutation of a business letter.

   EXAMPLE   Dear Dr. Wong**:**

**(3) Use commas to set off a title, such as *Jr., Sr.,* or *M.D.,* that
follows a person's name.**

EXAMPLES   Coretta Jones **,** M.D.

            Isaiah Walker**,** Sr.**,** makes animated films.

Unnecessary Commas

13m. Do not use unnecessary commas.

Use a comma only if a rule requires one or if the meaning is unclear
without one.

INCORRECT   The teacher in the room across the hall, is Cameron's aunt.
             [There is no rule requiring a comma to separate the subject,
             teacher, from the verb, *is.*]

   CORRECT   The teacher in the room across the hall is Cameron's aunt.

**Review D   Correcting Sentences by Adding Periods,
Question Marks, Exclamation Points,
and Commas**

Rewrite each of the following sentences, adding periods, question
marks, exclamation points, and commas where they are needed.

EXAMPLE   1. Gina can you tell us how many American astronauts have
               walked on the moon

           1. *Gina, can you tell us how many American astronauts
               have walked on the moon?*

MECHANICS

1. Wow Rob who taught you to draw a bow like that
2. First performed on March 11 1959 on Broadway in New York City Lorraine Hansberry's most famous play *A Raisin in the Sun* was awarded the New York Drama Critics Circle Award
3. Grinning Dad said that if we all helped put away toys and books picked up all the clothes lying around dusted the furniture and vacuumed the rug the house might very well look presentable by the time Grandma arrived
4. After all you could look at the map to see whether there is an exit from Interstate 70 to a state road that will take us south to Greenville Illinois instead of just complaining because I don't know the way
5. On her way to work each morning she saw young people on their paper routes children waiting for school buses mail carriers beginning their deliveries and the inevitable joggers puffing along on their morning workouts
6. Why do buses run so infrequently and when they do arrive why are they in bunches of three or four or more
7. Gen Benjamin O Davis Jr the first African American who was promoted to the rank of lieutenant general in the U.S. Air Force was the grandson of a slave
8. If you are going to paint window frames cover the panes of glass with masking tape which will protect the glass from being spattered
9. On a beautiful fall day in New England it is wise to go for a walk play a game outdoors or go for a drive; for it won't be long until everything is bleak cold and dreary
10. If I had my way I would live in a climate where it would be warm not hot in the daytime and cool in the evening all year round

Chapter Review

A. Using Periods, Question Marks, Exclamation Points, and Commas Correctly

For each of the following sentences, write each word, numeral, or letter that should be followed by a punctuation mark. Then, add the correct punctuation. If a sentence is already correct, write *C*.

1. If you sign up as a volunteer for the Special Olympics you will find that you receive as much as you give

2. The task before us was challenging but we felt prepared to meet it

3. Because the dentist's office was decorated in subtle warm earth tones I felt very relaxed during my visit

4. Oh I didn't know we have the same birthday

5. Trailing in the fourth quarter, our school's football team won the game in the last ten seconds of play.

6. In fact on August 9 1974 Richard M Nixon made history by resigning from his position as president of the United States

7. Ms Rizzo wasn't W Averell Harriman one of the world's foremost experts on Russian society

8. Read *The Hobbit* one of my favorite books

9. When I began this science project I knew that I would have to spend hours researching the subject

10. Joe Croce Gina Jackson and Sonya Shavatski are all candidates in the primary so expect the vote to be very close

11. Everyone wanted to know who he was what he wanted and how long he intended to stay

12. Maria who is a lively enthusiastic worker began her job as an electrician yesterday

13. By running all the way to school Suke arrived at basketball practice on time

14. We need more volunteers I believe if we are going to finish on time

15. Kareem did you enjoy your sightseeing trip through Maine Vermont and New Hampshire

16. Wait until Saturday before you write the letter for the package will surely have arrived by then

MECHANICS

17. The student who maintains the highest average in school will receive the scholarship.
18. Watch out Lana
19. Having completed the painting I asked Dad whether I could go to the movie
20. According to the records Joseph Hardwicke Barrymore Jr. is the baby's full name

B. Using Periods, Question Marks, Exclamation Points, and Commas Correctly

Write the following sentences, adding, deleting, replacing, or reordering periods, question marks, exclamation points, and commas as necessary. If a sentence is already correct, write *C*.

21. Do you think that it will rain today Brian.
22. Before the start of the concert the musicians tuned their instruments.
23. When I joined the staff of the newspaper I was taught to write short powerful headlines
24. The essay, that Ms Hughes assigned yesterday, is due next Monday.
25. Lisette would you send me a postcard from Hawaii while you're there on vacation
26. Bravo What a great performance
27. Geometry which I took last year was not an easy subject for me.
28. Peg asked, "For example have you read *Animal Farm*"?
29. Please send this package to 116 East Elm Street, Allentown, PA 18001.
30. The letter was dated June 16 2000 and was mailed from Washington D.C..
31. Governor Jameston a Democrat does not plan to run.
32. Dear Rosaline

    How are you. Drop me a line.

    Yours

    Viola
33. In 1998 NASA. sent Sen. John Glenn back into space on the shuttle *Discovery.*
34. Preston asked Callie if she had seen the play yet.
35. My father enjoyed a visit with Uncle John, Aunt Dee, and my cousin Nora, yesterday afternoon.

MECHANICS

36. Will you be asking Dean to come to the movies with us.

37. The meadow was covered with tiny delicate flowers.

38. We told the man who brought us the menus that we wanted a pitcher of lemonade.

39. Vincente said, "Wait would you like to come with us."

40. The play by Oscar Wilde was witty, and also serious.

Writing Application
Using Commas in an Essay

Punctuating Interrupters   Next Friday, your English class will celebrate Literary Heroes Day. Your teacher has asked you to write a brief essay (two or three paragraphs long) about your favorite fictional character. Describe the character, and explain why the character is your hero. In your essay, use at least two appositives and three parenthetical expressions. Be sure to use commas correctly with each interrupter.

Prewriting   First, you will need to decide on a character. Choose the one that impressed or entertained you the most. In your notes, be sure to include the character's strongest and most interesting traits.

Writing   Use your notes to help you write your first draft. Begin by describing the character and noting some of the most important traits that make this person your hero. Illustrate these traits by giving at least two examples of things the character does or says.

Revising   Ask a friend or relative to read your essay. Does your description give a vivid picture of the character? Is it clear why this character is your hero? If not, add or revise details to make your point more clearly. Be sure that you have used at least two appositives and three parenthetical expressions.

Publishing   Proofread your essay for any errors in grammar, usage, and mechanics. Pay special attention to commas before and after parenthetical expressions. You and your classmates may want to celebrate Literary Heroes Day by creating a bulletin board display. Place a typed or neatly written copy of each essay on the bulletin board along with illustrations of the different characters.

14

Punctuation
Other Marks of Punctuation

Diagnostic Preview

A. Proofreading Sentences for Correct Punctuation

The following sentences contain errors in the uses of semicolons, colons, dashes, parentheses, brackets, italics (underlining), quotation marks, ellipses, apostrophes, and hyphens. Rewrite the sentences, correcting the errors. If a sentence is already correct, write *C*.

EXAMPLE   1. Did you say "that you want to join us"?

          1. Did you say that you want to join us?

1. Ed's and Jim's essays were both titled Kwanzaa A Special Time for African Americans.
2. Heres my phone number, call me if you decide to see the movie.
3. The circus audience loudly applauded and cheered as the acro bats performed the perfectly-timed stunt.
4. Paula said in a desperate tone, "I know Sue's directions stated, "Turn right when you get to the gas station; but, unfortunately, I'm not sure which gas station she meant.
5. William Butler Yeats 1865–1939, an Irish poet and playwright who won the Nobel Prize in literature, was once a member of the Irish parliament.
6. At the end of the play, Macbeth concludes that life is only "a tale . . . . . signifying nothing."
7. Oh no, I think my driver's license has no, it says here it wo'nt expire for another two weeks.

8. "Well, I dont know," Lauren said. "Where do you think all this soot comes from?"

9. Several people whom I respect think Raintree County by Ross Lockridge, Jr., is a fantastic novel, I plan to read it soon.

10. "Among the writers in America today, he Galway Kinnell has earned his reputation as an outstanding poet," noted the critic in Newsweek.

B. Proofreading a Dialogue for Correct Punctuation

The following dialogue contains errors in the uses of semicolons, colons, dashes, parentheses, italics (underlining), quotation marks, apostrophes, and hyphens. Rewrite the dialogue, correcting the errors.

EXAMPLE [1] "You may like mystery, comedy, and science fiction movies, but, you know, my favorite movies are those about real peoples lives, Ben said."

1. *"You may like mystery, comedy, and science fiction movies; but, you know, my favorite movies are those about real people's lives," Ben said.*

[11] Tell me we've got time some of your all time favorites," Tani replied to Ben.

[12] "I recently saw Mountains of the Moon for the first time I learned about the life of Sir Richard Burton from it," Ben replied.

[13] Whats his claim to fame"? Tani asked.

[14] "Sir Richard Burton was a man of many talents he was an explorer, an author, a scholar, a linguist, and a diplomat."

[15] "Did the movie try to show all his talents?" Tani asked. Doing so would be difficult."

[16] "The movie is mostly an African adventure its about Burtons search for the source of the Nile," Ben said. [17] "Some of my other favorites include: Gandhi, about the Indian independence leader, Amadeus, about Mozart's life, and The Spirit of St. Louis, a really old film about Charles Lindbergh."

[18] "I'll bet three-fourths of our friends have never heard of most of the movies youve seen," Tani said.

[19] "The downtown video store the one owned by Ross's brother has them all," Ben said.

[20] "Biographical movies well researched ones, anyway are a good way to learn about famous people," Tani said.

Semicolons

14a. Use a semicolon between independent clauses that are closely related in thought and that are not joined by a coordinating conjunction (*and, but, for, nor, or, so, or yet.*)

Reference Note

For more information about **coordinating conjunctions,** see page 23.

EXAMPLES   The rain had finally stopped; a few rays of sunshine were pushing their way through breaks in the clouds.

Owning a dog is a big responsibility; a dog requires training, grooming, and regular exercise.

Do not use a semicolon to join independent clauses unless there is a close relationship between the main ideas of the clauses.

INCORRECT   For Ramón, oil painting is a difficult medium to master; when he was younger, he had quite enjoyed taking photographs.

CORRECT   For Ramón, oil painting is a difficult medium to master. When he was younger, he had quite enjoyed taking photographs.

14b. Use a semicolon between independent clauses joined by a conjunctive adverb or a transitional expression.

Reference Note

For more information on **conjunctive adverbs** and **transitional expressions,** see page 88.

A *conjunctive adverb* or a *transitional expression* indicates the relationship of the independent clauses that it joins.

EXAMPLES   The snowfall made traveling difficult; **nevertheless,** we arrived home safely.

Denisa plays baseball well; **in fact,** she would like to try out for a major-league team.

Commonly Used Conjunctive Adverbs		
accordingly	however	moreover
besides	indeed	nevertheless
consequently	instead	otherwise
furthermore	meanwhile	therefore

Commonly Used Transitional Expressions		
in other words	for instance	as a result
for example	in fact	that is

MECHANICS

NOTE Use a comma after a conjunctive adverb or a transitional expression that is used directly after a semicolon joining independent clauses. When used within a clause, a conjunctive adverb or a transitional expression is set off by commas.

EXAMPLES   Most members of Congress favor the new tax bill**;** **however,** the president does not support it.

Most members of Congress favor the new tax bill; the president**,** **however,** does not support it.

Most members of Congress favor the new tax bill; the president does not support it**,** **however.**

14c. A semicolon (rather than a comma) may be needed before a coordinating conjunction to join independent clauses that contain commas.

EXAMPLES   Some monarch butterflies migrate all the way from Canada to California**,** to Florida**,** or to Mexico**;** and then**,** come spring**,** they head north again.

I wanted to register for biology**,** volleyball**,** and conversational Spanish**;** but only calculus**,** golf**,** and intermediate German were available during late registration.

14d. Use a semicolon between items in a series if the items contain commas.

EXAMPLES   The club's president has appointed the following people to chair the standing committees: Richard Stokes**,** planning**;** Rebecca Hartley**,** membership**;** Salvador Berrios**,** financial**;** and Ann Jeng**,** legal.

The collection of short stories includes "The Circuit**,**" by Francisco Jiménez**;** "The Iguana Killer**,**" by Alberto Ríos**;** and "Everybody Knows Tobie**,**" by Daniel Garza.

Exercise 1   **Using Semicolons Correctly**

For the following sentences, write each word or numeral that should be followed by a semicolon, and add the semicolon. If a sentence is already correct, write *C*.

EXAMPLE   1. The great American humorist Will Rogers was proud of his Cherokee heritage he often referred to it in his talks and writings.

    1. *heritage;*

STYLE   **TIP**

In cases covered by Rule 14c, use semicolons only to prevent misreading. If a sentence is clear without a semicolon, do not add one just because the clauses contain commas.

EXAMPLE
Lana, you are the best musician I know, and you're a great dancer, too. [clear without semicolon]

MECHANICS

HELP

Some of the sentences in Exercise 1 require more than one semicolon. Also, in some of the sentences, you will need to change another punctuation mark to a semicolon.

1. William Penn Adair Rogers was born in 1879 in Oologah, Indian Territory, which is now Oklahoma, and he spent his childhood on his father's ranch, a rather prosperous holding of about sixty thousand acres.

2. As a youth, Will Rogers liked to learn and practice rope tricks he often could be found roping instead of attending to his chores.

3. Rogers was captivated by professional roping performers at the Chicago World's Fair in 1893; in fact, that experience probably marked the start of his interest in show business.

4. He went on to do some roping and humorous speaking at fairs and other public gatherings however, his actual show business debut came in 1902.

5. That year, Rogers joined Texas Jack's Wild West Show as a lasso artist he also rode horses and performed in various Western skits in the show.

6. Notice how confident the young Rogers appears in this publicity photo his expression, stance, and costume suggest an accomplished performer.

7. Rogers greatly enjoyed earning his living by doing what he most loved—roping consequently, he decided to take his act to New York City's vaudeville theaters.

8. Rogers's stage shows, combining his roping with humorous comments, were popular they led to starring roles in musicals, in the legendary Ziegfeld Follies, and in movies.

9. In Hollywood, Rogers made such films as *The Ropin' Fool,* in which he performed fifty-three rope tricks, *Steamboat 'Round the Bend,* directed by John Ford, and *A Connecticut Yankee in King Arthur's Court,* based on the Mark Twain novel.

10. From 1922 until his death in 1935, Rogers wrote a syndicated newspaper column that Sunday column featured his unique and humorous insights into national and international news.

Colons

14e. Use a colon to mean "note what follows."

(1) Use a colon before a list of items, especially after expressions such as *as follows* and *the following*.

EXAMPLES   Prior to 1722, the Iroquois Confederation consisted of five American Indian nations**:** Mohawk, Oneida, Onondaga, Cayuga, and Seneca.

My brother is working on a multimedia presentation featuring the following women**:** Mary Baker Eddy, Clara Barton, Maria Mitchell, Mary Church Terrell, Susan B. Anthony, and Sarah Winnemucca.

NOTE Do not use a colon between a verb and its complement(s) or between a preposition and its object(s).

INCORRECT	The emergency kit included: safety flares, jumper cables, and a flashlight.
CORRECT	The emergency kit included safety flares, jumper cables, and a flashlight.
INCORRECT	Each student taking the math test was provided with: two sharpened pencils, some paper, and a ruler.
CORRECT	Each student taking the math test was provided with two sharpened pencils, some paper, and a ruler.

(2) Use a colon before a long, formal statement or quotation.

EXAMPLE   Abraham Lincoln's Gettysburg Address begins with these famous words**:** "Fourscore and seven years ago our fathers brought forth on this continent a new nation, conceived in liberty, and dedicated to the proposition that all men are created equal."

(3) Use a colon between independent clauses when the second clause explains or restates the idea of the first.

EXAMPLES   Lois felt that she had done something worthwhile**:** She had designed and sewn her first quilt.

Thomas Jefferson had many talents**:** He was a writer, a politician, an architect, and an inventor.

NOTE Notice that the first word of a complete sentence following a colon is capitalized.

14f. Use a colon in certain conventional situations.

(1) Use a colon between the hour and the minute.

EXAMPLES   7**:**30 P.M.   8**:**45 in the morning

MEETING THE CHALLENGE

Create a list of titles that use colons. (You may need to go to a library or access the Internet.) Compare your list with other students' findings, and then discuss these questions: How does the function of colons in titles differ from the function of colons in sentences? What sort of impression does a colon in a title make? What kinds of information are given on the two sides of a colon in a title?

MECHANICS

Reference Note

For more about **using long quotations,** see page 336.

(2) Use a colon between chapter and verse when referring to a passage from the Bible.

EXAMPLES   Proverbs 10**:**12   Luke 17**:**1–4

(3) Use a colon between a title and subtitle.

EXAMPLES   *Another View***:** *To Be Black in America* [book]

             *Superman IV***:** *The Quest for Peace* [movie]

             *Impression***:** *Sunrise* [painting]

(4) Use a colon after the salutation of a business letter.

EXAMPLES   Dear Mrs. Rodríguez**:**   To Whom It May Concern**:**

             Dear Sir or Madam**:**   Dear Service Manager**:**

Reference Note

For more about **using commas in letters,** see page 315.

NOTE   Use a comma after the salutation of a personal letter.

EXAMPLE   Dear Mom and Dad**,**

Oral Practice   Using Colons Correctly

Read aloud each of the following sentences, indicating where colons should be inserted or deleted as necessary.

EXAMPLE   1.   Did he mean 8 00 P.M. or 8 00 A.M.?

            1.   *Insert a colon between the hour and minute in* 8:00 *both times* 8:00 *appears.*

1. The word *zone* is a multipurpose word that can be found in many disciplines It is used in mathematics, ecology, anatomy, geology, computer science, city planning, and also slang.
2. We stared dumbfounded, for never had we read such wordy prose "Due to the fact that consumers may now avail themselves of many forms of energy from both traditional and alternative sources, revenue from governmentally established sites has in the local vicinity been decreasing although provider costs have tended to rise; consequently, this has made it incumbent upon your local site to warrant a slight increase in concurrent fees for said service. We thank you for your continued cooperation."
3. Do you have a book called *Sarajevo The Road to Destiny*?
4. The following items should be included in any first-aid kit bandages, antibacterial ointment, and disinfectant.
5. In the Bible, the story of how God creates light appears in Genesis 1 1.

MECHANICS

he contents of my little
follows broken marble, a hunk
of varying lengths, three cents, a
ninum oil, and a large pebble.

6. When I did the laundry yester... follows
brother's pockets proved to... Mr. Engstrom Thank you for
of moss, a live beetle, f...
quantity of dirt, a... esaurus entries for *money scratch, moola,*
7. I began my le... lettuce.
your ass... ers with: Pakistan, Afghanistan, Tibet, Nepal,
mar, and Bhutan.
8. Wo... out Pancho Villa on PBS tonight at 9 00.

eses

...rentheses to enclose informative or explanatory
material of minor importance.

EXAMPLES   Amelia Earhart **(**1897– c.1937**)** was the first woman to pilot
an airplane alone across the Atlantic Ocean.

A *roman* à *clef* **(**literally, "novel with a key"**)** is a novel
about real people to whom the novelist has assigned
fictitious names.

NOTE Be sure that the material enclosed in parentheses can be omitted
without losing important information or changing the basic meaning
and construction of the sentence.

IMPROPER USE   George Eliot (whose real name was Mary Ann
OF PARENTHESES   Evans) was one of many women in nineteenth-
century England who wrote under a masculine
pseudonym. [The information in parentheses
clarifies that George Eliot was a woman. The
parentheses should be replaced by commas.]

Follow these guidelines for capitalizing and punctuating parenthetical sentences.

(1) A parenthetical sentence that falls within another sentence

- should not begin with a capital letter unless it begins with a word
that should be capitalized

- should not end with a period but may end with a question mark or
an exclamation point

EXAMPLES   The Malay Archipelag⟨
includes the Philippines. ⟨e the map on page 350)

Legendary jazz musician Lou⟨
you heard of him?) was bo⟨

When parenthetical material falls within a ⟨strong (have
should not come before the opening parenthesis ⟨
closing parenthesis.

INCORRECT   The first professional baseball team, the Cinci⟨
Stockings, (the Reds) was formed in 1869.

CORRECT   The first professional baseball team, the Cincinnati ⟨
Stockings **(**the Reds**)**, was formed in 1869.

(2) A parenthetical sentence that stands by itself

- should begin with a capital letter
- should end with a period, a question mark, or an exclamation
  point before the closing parenthesis

EXAMPLES   The Malay Archipelago includes the Philippines. **(See the
map on page 350.)**

Legendary jazz musician Louis "Satchmo" Armstrong was
born in Louisiana. **(Have you heard of him?)**

Dashes

Sometimes words, phrases, and sentences are used *parenthetically;*
that is, they break into the main thought of a sentence.

EXAMPLES   Ann, **however,** does not agree with him.

The decision **(which player should he choose?)** weighed
on Coach Johnson's mind.

Most parenthetical elements are set off by commas or parentheses.
Sometimes, however, parenthetical elements are such an interruption
that a stronger mark is needed. In such cases, a dash is used.

14h. Use a dash to indicate an abrupt break in thought or speech.

EXAMPLES   The team's leading scorer——I can't remember her
name——is also an excellent defensive player.

The real villain turns out to be——but I don't want to
spoil the ending for those of you who have not yet seen
the movie.

map

o mean *namely, in other words,* or *that is* before

ass
ain

anda joined the chorus for only one reason——she loves
ng.

s

few people in this class——three, to be exact——have
completed their projects.

o

n

ts to enclose an explanation within quoted or
aterial.

e newspaper article stated, "At the time of that
mocratic National Convention **[in Chicago in 1968]** there
re many protest groups operating in the United States."
Chicago in 1968 is in brackets to show that it is not part
the original quotation.]

hink that Hilda Doolittle (more commonly known as H. D.
886–1961]) is best remembered for her imagist poetry.
886–1961 is in brackets because it is within parenthetical
aterial.]

Using Parentheses, Dashes, and Brackets Correctly

sentences have been punctuated incorrectly. Write each
ing incorrect punctuation and inserting correct dashes,
nd brackets as necessary. Make sure that any parentheti-
s properly capitalized and punctuated.

1. One, no, two, fawns are with the doe.

1. One——no, two——fawns are with the doe.

n like this, a bank will need collateral something of value
at or a car.

e, which is a common treatment for malaria, comes from
k of the cinchona (a name said to honor the Countess of
ón (1576–1639).

-faire pronounced les-ay-FAIR is a French phrase that
"let do"; it is often used to describe a system of government
w or no controls on business.

not a broken lamp; it's a sculpture oops, now it's broken;
e we can make a lamp out of it.

STYLE ✏️ **TIP**

Do not overuse dashes.
When you evaluate your
writing, check to see that
you have not used dashes
carelessly for commas,
semicolons, and end marks.
Saving dashes for instances
in which they are most
appropriate will make
them more effective.

COMPUTER TIP

Some computer programs
are capable of setting
dashes, and others are not.
If your computer program
does not set dashes, type
two hyphens to represent a
dash. Do not use a space
before, between, or after
the hyphens.

MECHANICS

5. The focal point of the Byzantine Empire, Constantinople [See on page 781] is now Istanbul.
6. I think we got here just in time hey, the curtain's going up.
7. The article continued, "Once the material reaches its critical m the minimum amount of pressure required for a reaction, a ch reaction occurs."
8. There must have been a million well, at least a few hundred ca stopped on the highway.
9. As the joker is to a modern deck of cards, so a blank card was the French hence the phrase, *carte blanche,* "a blank card."
10. The black history movement, which owes much to Melville Jea Herskovits he was my grandpa's professor at Northwestern University in 1951 began fifty years ago.

Reference Note

For examples of **titles** that are not italicized but are enclosed **in quotation marks,** see page 338.

COMPUTER TIP

If you use a personal computer, you may be able to set words in italics. Most word-processing software and printers can produce italic type.

Italics

Italics are printed characters that slant to the right—*like this.* To indicate italics in handwritten or typewritten work, use underlinin

PRINTED   *The Heart Is a Lonely Hunter* was written by Carson McCullers.

HANDWRITTEN   *The Heart Is a Lonely Hunter was written by Carson Mc Cullers.*

MECHANICS

14k. Use italics (underlining) for the titles and subtitles of books, plays, long poems, periodicals, works of art, movies, radio and TV series, videos, video games, long musical works and recordings, computer games, and comic strips.

Type of Title	Examples
Books	*The Princess Bride* *Aké: The Years of Childhood* *The Innocents Abroad*
Plays	*A Doll's House* *Death of a Salesman* *Harvey*
Long Poems	*Rubáiyát* *The Rime of the Ancient Mariner* *Don Juan*
Periodicals	*U.S. News & World Report* *The Dallas Morning News* *Sports Illustrated*
Works of Art	*Mona Lisa* *Nocturne in Black and Gold: The Falling Rocket*
Movies	*Hank Aaron: Chasing the Dream* *Antz*
Radio and TV Series	*Midnight Mystery Theatre* *Star Trek: Voyager*
Videos, Video Games	*Working Out at Home* *Moonwalker*
Long Musical Works and Recordings	*Rhapsody in Blue* *The Sounds of Nature*
Computer Games	*Raceway U.S.A.* *Flight Simulator*
Comic Strips	*Dennis the Menace* *Jumpstart* *Rose Is Rose*

TIPS & TRICKS

Long poems are poems that are long enough to be published as separate volumes. Such poems are usually divided into titled or numbered sections, such as cantos, parts, or books. Long musical works include operas, symphonies, ballets, oratorios, and concertos.

STYLE **TIP**

Generally, do not use italics for the title of your own paper. However, if your title contains a title that belongs in italics, you will need to use italics for that part of the title.

EXAMPLES
Rafe Buenrostro: A Soldier Comes Home [contains no title that belongs in italics]

Nathaniel Hawthorne's Use of Gothic Elements in *The Scarlet Letter* [contains a title that belongs in italics]

Be creative when giving your paper a title. Avoid using the title of another work as the complete title of your paper.

MECHANICS

Reference Note

For more information on **capitalizing titles,** see page 281.

STYLE **TIP**

Writers sometimes use italics (underlining) for emphasis, especially in written dialogue. The italic type shows how the sentence is supposed to be spoken. Read the following sentences aloud. Notice that by italicizing different words, the writer can change the meaning of the sentence.

EXAMPLE

"Did you read *that* book by Mark Twain?" asked Jennifer. [Did you read that book or some other book?]

"Did *you* read that book by Mark Twain?" asked Jennifer. [Did you read the book or did someone else?]

Italicizing (underlining) words for emphasis is a handy technique that should not be overused. It can quickly lose its impact.

NOTE An article (*a, an,* or *the*) before a periodical's title is not italicized or capitalized unless it is part of the official title, which is usually found on the editorial page or in the table of contents. The official title of a book appears on the title page of the book.

EXAMPLE   I found this information in **T**he New York Times, not in **t**he New York Post.

Do not use italics for titles of religious texts or for titles of legal or historical documents.

RELIGIOUS TEXTS	Old Testament
	Talmud
LEGAL OR HISTORICAL DOCUMENTS	Treaty of Guadalupe Hidalgo
	United States Constitution

14l. Use italics (underlining) for the names of trains, ships, aircraft, and spacecraft.

Type of Title	Examples
Trains, Ships	*Sunset Express*
	Andrea Doria
Aircraft, Spacecraft	*Graf Zeppelin*
	Voyager 2

14m. Use italics (underlining) for words, letters, symbols, and numerals referred to as such, and for foreign words that have not been adopted into English.

EXAMPLES   Make sure to use the words **emigrate** and **immigrate** correctly in your essay.

I like the basic design of the poster, but the **$** looks too much like an **S.**

Is that an **8** or a **3**?

The man waved and said, "More water, please, **garçon.**"

NOTE If you are not sure whether to italicize a foreign word, look it up in an up-to-date dictionary.

Exercise 3 Correcting Sentences by Adding Underlining

Underline all the words and word groups that should be italicized in the following sentences.

EXAMPLE   **1.** I try to watch Sixty Minutes every week.

        1. *Sixty Minutes*

1. According to tradition, The Red Vineyard is the only painting Vincent van Gogh ever sold during his lifetime.
2. The Fantasticks is the longest-running musical in history.
3. Jesse's birthday present was a subscription to Rolling Stone magazine.
4. The theater club will present Arsenic and Old Lace in the fall.
5. My sister missed the word xeriscape in the spelling bee.
6. Arlene reads Peanuts in the newspaper every day.
7. My uncle Bob remembers when the USSR first launched Sputnik 1 into orbit.
8. That last episode of Babylon 5 kept me on the edge of my seat!
9. In American literature, we are studying Stephen Crane's novel The Red Badge of Courage.
10. I get a little better at it every time I play Escape Velocity on my computer.

Quotation Marks

14n. Use quotation marks to enclose a *direct quotation*—a person's exact words.

Be sure to place quotation marks both before and after a person's exact words.

EXAMPLES   In his speech to the Virginia House of Burgesses in 1765, Patrick Henry said, "If this be treason, make the most of it."

               "The track meet is canceled because of the unusually cold weather," announced Coach Griffey.

Do not use quotation marks to enclose an *indirect quotation*—a rewording of a direct quotation.

| DIRECT QUOTATION | Aaron said, "I can type seventy-five words per minute." |
| INDIRECT QUOTATION | Aaron said that he can type seventy-five words per minute. |

MECHANICS

(1) A direct quotation generally begins with a capital letter.

EXAMPLE   The poet Emily Dickinson wrote in a letter to Thomas Wentworth Higginson, her literary advisor, "**If** I feel physically as if the top of my head were taken off, I know *that* is poetry."

However, when the quotation is obviously only a fragment of the original quotation, it generally begins with a lowercase letter.

EXAMPLE   In her essay "On the Mall," Joan Didion describes shopping malls as "**t**oy gardens in which no one lives."

(2) When an expression identifying the speaker divides a quoted sentence, the second part begins with a lowercase letter.

EXAMPLE   "If you like board games," said Tyrone, "**y**ou should come to the party." [Notice that each part of a divided quotation is enclosed in quotation marks.]

When the second part of a divided quotation is a complete sentence, it begins with a capital letter.

EXAMPLE   "English and French are recognized as official languages of Canada," explained Ms. Hawkins. "**T**he French Canadians, most of whom live in Quebec, speak French and observe many of the customs of their French ancestors."

NOTE   When a direct quotation of two or more sentences is not divided, only one set of quotation marks is used.

EXAMPLE   "English and French are recognized as official languages of Canada. The French Canadians, most of whom live in Quebec, speak French and observe many of the customs of their French ancestors."

(3) A direct quotation can be set off from the rest of the sentence by a comma, a question mark, or an exclamation point, but not by a period.

EXAMPLES   "I nominate Pilar for class president**,**" said Erin.

Erin said**,** "I nominate Pilar for class president."

"What is the capital of Thailand**?**" asked Mr. Klein.

"This chili is too spicy**!**" exclaimed Brian.

(4) When used with quotation marks, other marks of punctuation are placed according to the following rules:

- Commas and periods are placed inside the closing quotation marks.

EXAMPLE   "By the way," he said, "we decided to go to the play."

- Semicolons and colons are placed outside the closing quotation marks.

EXAMPLES   Winona said, "I need to study my lines tonight"; she has a major role in the community theater's next play.

Gina Berriault uses several types of figurative language in her short story "The Stone Boy": simile, metaphor, and personification.

- Question marks and exclamation points are placed inside the closing quotation marks if the quotation itself is a question or an exclamation. Otherwise, they are placed outside.

EXAMPLES   "Dad, will you please call the doctor tomorrow morning?" I asked.

"Move those feet double-time!" ordered the drum major.

Did Langston Hughes write the line "My soul has grown deep like the rivers"?

I'm tired of hearing "This is boring"!

Notice in the last two examples given above that the end mark belonging with each quotation has been omitted. When a sentence ends with a quotation, only one end mark is necessary.

(5) When quoting a passage that consists of more than one paragraph, put quotation marks at the beginning of each paragraph and at the end of only the last paragraph of the passage.

EXAMPLE   "The water was thick and heavy and the color of a mirror in a dark room. Minnows broke the surface right under the wharf. I jumped. I couldn't help it.

"And I got to thinking that something might come out of the water. It didn't have a name or a shape. But it was there."

Shirley Ann Grau, "The Land and the Water"

NOTE A long passage quoted from a printed source is often set off from the rest of the text. The entire passage may be indented and double-spaced. When a quotation is set off, quotation marks are used only if they appear in the printed source. Otherwise, quotation marks are unnecessary.

EXAMPLE

In Sabine Ulibarrí's story "My Wonder Horse," the young narrator, a fifteen-year-old boy, finally captures Mago, the legendary horse, and proudly brings him home. The following passage shows the reaction of the boy's father:

> My father saw me coming and waited for me without a word. A smile played over his face, and a spark danced in his eyes. He watched me take the rope from Mago, and the two of us thoughtfully observed him move away. My father clasped my hand a little more firmly than usual and said, "That was a man's job." That was all. Nothing more was needed. We understood one another very well.

(6) When writing *dialogue* (a conversation), begin a new paragraph every time the speaker changes, and enclose each speaker's words in quotation marks.

EXAMPLE

"But what kind of authentic and valuable information do you require?" asked Klapaucius.

"All kinds, as long as it's true," replied the pirate. "You never can tell what facts may come in handy. I already have a few hundred wells and cellars full of them, but there's room for twice again as much. So out with it; tell me everything you know, and I'll jot it down. But make it snappy!"

"A fine state of affairs," Klapaucius whispered in Trurl's ear. "He could keep us here for an eon or two before we tell him everything we know. Our knowledge is colossal!!"

"Wait," whispered Trurl, "I have an idea."

Stanislaw Lem, "The Sixth Sally"

(7) Use single quotation marks to enclose a quotation within a quotation.

EXAMPLES   Mr. Laveau said, "Please tell us what is meant by Benjamin Franklin's maxim 'Lost time is never found again.'" [Notice that the period is placed inside the single quotation mark.]

Mr. Laveau asked, "Can anyone tell us what is meant by Benjamin Franklin's maxim 'Lost time is never found again'?" [The question mark is placed inside the double quotation marks, not the single quotation mark, because the entire quotation of Mr. Laveau's words is a question.]

Exercise 4 **Using Quotation Marks with Other Marks of Punctuation**

Add quotation marks and other punctuation marks where they are needed in the following dialogue. Also, correct any errors in the use of capitalization, and begin a new paragraph each time the speaker changes.

EXAMPLE   [1] You can tell from this picture Lloyd said that people have a lot of fun during the Juneteenth holiday, but I don't get it.

   1.   *"You can tell from this picture," Lloyd said, "that people have a lot of fun during the Juneteenth holiday, but I don't get it."*

[1] Do you mean Janelle asked that you don't understand having fun or you don't understand Juneteenth [2] Lloyd, who didn't like being misunderstood, quickly replied stop joking around [3] Janelle said I'll be glad to tell you what Juneteenth is; she hadn't meant to tease

S T Y L E   **T I P**

Be sure to reproduce quoted material exactly as it appears in the original. If the original contains an error, write the Latin word *sic,* which means "thus so," in brackets directly after the error.

EXAMPLE
The writer continued, "The film is an excelent [*sic*] adaptation of a novel by Tom Clancy." [Notice that *sic* is italicized.]

MECHANICS

Lloyd. [**4**] Juneteenth is celebrated every year on June 19 she continued To mark the day in 1865 when a Union general proclaimed the slaves in Texas to be free. [**5**] It's celebrated not only in Texas but also throughout the rest of the South [**6**] Lloyd interrupted why were the Texas slaves proclaimed free so long after Lincoln's Emancipation Proclamation [**7**] Remember that Lincoln made his proclamation in 1863, but the Civil War continued until April 9, 1865 Janelle replied and then it took a while for news to spread [**8**] Janelle thought that her explanations had satisfied Lloyd, but then he asked Well, how is Juneteenth celebrated [**9**] Now that's a question you don't need to ask she replied Because you go to the Juneteenth parade every year. [**10**] It's celebrated much the same everywhere she added With families enjoying picnics, parades, games, and music.

14o. **Use quotation marks to enclose titles (including subtitles) of short works such as short stories, poems, essays, articles and other parts of periodicals, songs, episodes of radio and TV series, and chapters and other parts of books.**

Type of Title	Examples
Short Stories	"The Open Boat" "The Necklace"
Poems	"The Dance" "Mending Wall"
Essays	"Of Friendship" "Self-Reliance"
Articles and Other Parts of Periodicals	"Choices: Careers in Graphic Arts" "Talk of the Town"
Songs	"Georgia on My Mind" "Wind Beneath My Wings"
Episodes of Radio and TV Series	"Phantom Footsteps: A Ghost Tale" "Arctic Encounter"
Chapters and Other Parts of Books	"The Civil War: The Eastern Campaign" "Epilogue"

Reference Note
The titles of long poems and long musical works are italicized. For examples of these titles and of other **titles that are italicized,** see page 331.

NOTE Use single quotation marks for the titles of short works within quotations.

EXAMPLE   "Class, please read 'Child of the Americas' by tomorrow."

Do not use quotation marks for titles of religious texts or for titles of legal or historical documents.

| RELIGIOUS TEXTS | Holy Bible |
| | Koran |

| LEGAL OR HISTORICAL DOCUMENTS | Treaty of Medicine Lodge |
| | Declaration of Independence |

14p. Use quotation marks to enclose slang words, invented words, technical terms, dictionary definitions of words, and any expressions that are unusual in standard English.

EXAMPLES   Chloe reached for a high note and hit a "clinker."

Deanna calls Tyler's incessant punning "punishment"; he calls it "punnology."

Although I am not familiar with computer jargon, I do know that "to boot" a disk does not mean to kick it.

The verb *recapitulate* means "to repeat briefly" or "to summarize."

NOTE Avoid using slang words in formal speaking and writing. Also, when using technical terms, be sure to explain their meanings. If you are not sure whether a word is appropriate or whether its meaning is clear, consult an up-to-date dictionary.

Review A **Correcting Sentences by Adding Quotation Marks, Other Punctuation Marks, and Capitalization**

Revise the following sentences by correcting errors in the use of quotation marks, other marks of punctuation, and capitalization.

EXAMPLE   1. Mark Twain wrote it is easier to stay out than get out.

1. *Mark Twain wrote, "It is easier to stay out than get out."*

1. The section called People in the News in this book has some interesting facts about celebrities.

STYLE   TIP

On the cover page or title page of a paper of your own, do not use quotation marks for the title of your paper. However, if your title contains a title that belongs in quotation marks, you will need to use quotation marks for that part of your title.

EXAMPLE
Miss Lottie in "Marigolds": A Character Sketch
[contains a title that belongs in quotation marks]

Be creative when giving your paper a title. Avoid using the title of another work as the complete title of your paper.

MECHANICS

2. Are you going to the Greek Festival asked Mr. Doney or didn't you know that it's scheduled for this weekend

3. Our teacher quoted Willa Cather's words there are only two or three human stories, and they go on repeating themselves as fiercely as if they had never happened before.

4. How do I find out who wrote the poem Dream Deferred Jill asked her English teacher.

5. The expression icing on the cake is not literally about dessert it refers to something additional that is a pleasant surprise.

6. I'm still hungry complained Donna that baked apple looks tempting

7. When faced with a frightening situation, I often recite Psalm 23 4, which begins as follows Yea, though I walk through the valley of the shadow of death, I will fear no evil.

8. Perhaps the finest memorial to Abraham Lincoln is Walt Whitman's poem When Lilacs Last in the Dooryard Bloom'd.

9. Are you saying that I don't know the answer or that I don't understand the question

10. Ms. Hammer warned us that the movie was, to use her words, a parody of the novel furthermore, she advised us not to waste our money and time by seeing it.

11. Did she say guess or yes?

12. My older brother said that my new shoes were fly, meaning that they looked cool or stylish.

13. Please don't make me sing Jingle Bells another time, I begged my little sister.

14. One of the geologists pointed out chatter marks that indicated glacial action, and I asked her what the term meant.

15. Woody Guthrie wrote one of my favorite songs—This Land Is Your Land.

16. Did you read Cody's essay on dress codes, Shoelaces, Foolaces?

17. Here's the way I figure it: We're teaching the baby new words, so it's only fair that he teaches us new words like abot and fa-fa.

18. Why did she say, It's jake with me?

19. Are we supposed to read the story All Summer in a Day out loud? we asked.

20. The phrase ad hominem is Latin for to the man; the phrase refers to an argument that attacks one's opponent, not the issue.

21. The phrase putting the cart before the horse can be traced back to 61 B.C.

22. I'm sorry I couldn't talk on the phone last night Chris said but I was washing dishes.
23. Stephen Crane's poem War Is Kind is as topical today as it was one hundred years ago.
24. Who said To err is human, to forgive divine?
25. When Mr. Wilson said Put down your pencils, everyone sighed with relief.

Review B **Proofreading a Dialogue for Correct Punctuation**

Correct any errors in the use of quotation marks and other marks of punctuation in the following dialogue. Also, correct any errors in the use of capitalization, and begin a new paragraph each time the speaker changes.

EXAMPLE   **[1]** I think The Weeping Woman would be a good title for my new song Jim told Tomás. can you guess what it is about

1.   *"I think 'The Weeping Woman' would be a good title for my new song," Jim told Tomás. "Can you guess what it is about?"*

[1] Well, I once read a magazine article titled *La Llorona* The Weeping Woman. It was about a popular Mexican American legend, Tomás replied. [2] That's the legend I'm talking about! Jim exclaimed I first heard it when I was a little boy growing up in southern California. [3] I think commented Tomás, People in the music business would call the song a tear-jerker because it tells a sad story. [4] I'll say it's sad Jim replied it's about a poor, wronged woman who goes crazy, drowns her children, and kills herself; then she returns as a ghost to look for them forever. [5] The legend is frightening to hear when you're young because *La Llorona* is usually described as a headless woman dressed all in white. [6] Isn't she usually seen around water Tomás asked. [7] Yes, Jim said but you didn't mention one of the scariest things: Her fingernails look like knives [8] Didn't your mother ever say, Don't believe ghost stories, son asked Tomás [9] Oh, sure Jim replied. to tell the truth, I never did really believe them. They are great stories, though. [10] Well, maybe, but give me a humorous story like The Catbird Seat any day Tomás said.

Ellipsis Points

14q. **Use ellipsis points (. . .) to mark omissions from quoted material.**

ORIGINAL   Sitting here tonight, many years later, with more time than money, I think about those faces that pass before my eyes like it was yesterday. They remind me of the chances and temptations to become an outlaw. I sure came through a tough mill. I see those men as they stood in those old days of the Golden West—some of them in the springtime of their manhood, so beautiful and strong that it makes you wonder, because their hearts are as black as night, and they are cruel, treacherous and merciless as a man-eating tiger of the jungle.

Andrew García, *Tough Trip Through Paradise*

(1) When you omit words from the middle of a sentence, use three spaced ellipsis points.

EXAMPLE   In his autobiography, *Tough Trip Through Paradise,* Andrew García reflects, "Sitting here tonight, **. . .** I think about those faces that pass before my eyes like it was yesterday."

NOTE Be sure to include space before and after each ellipsis point.

(2) When you omit words at the beginning of a sentence within a quoted passage, keep the previous sentence's end punctuation and follow it with the ellipsis points.

EXAMPLE   García writes, "They remind me of the chances and temptations to become an outlaw. I sure came through a tough mill**. . . .** [T]heir hearts are as black as night, and they are cruel, treacherous and merciless as a man-eating tiger of the jungle."

NOTE Do not begin a quoted passage with ellipsis points.

INCORRECT   ". . . They remind me of the chances and temptations to become an outlaw. I sure came through a tough mill."

CORRECT   "They remind me of the chances and temptations to become an outlaw. I sure came through a tough mill."

(3) When you omit words at the end of a sentence within a quoted passage, keep the sentence's end punctuation and follow it with the ellipsis points.

┌─HELP─

Notice in the quotation to the right that *their* has been capitalized because it now begins the sentence. The *T* is in brackets to show that it was not capitalized in the original passage.

MECHANICS

EXAMPLE   García writes, "I think about those faces that pass before my eyes. . . . They remind me of the chances and temptations to become an outlaw."

(4) When you omit one or more complete sentences from a quoted passage, keep the previous sentence's end punctuation and follow it with the ellipsis points.

EXAMPLE   Recalling his youth, Andrew García writes, "Sitting here tonight, many years later, with more time than money, I think about those faces that pass before my eyes like it was yesterday. . . . I sure came through a tough mill."

(5) To show that a full line or more of poetry has been omitted, use an entire line of spaced periods.

COMPLETE   A single flow'r he sent me, since we met.
POEM   All tenderly his messenger he chose;
             Deep-hearted, pure, with scented dew still wet—
                  One perfect rose.

             I knew the language of the floweret;
                  "My fragile leaves," it said, "his heart enclose."
             Love long has taken for his amulet
                  One perfect rose.

             Why is it no one ever sent me yet
                  One perfect limousine, do you suppose?
             Ah no, it's always just my luck to get
                  One perfect rose.

                                 Dorothy Parker, "One Perfect Rose"

POEM WITH   A single flow'r he sent me, since we met.
OMISSION   All tenderly his messenger he chose;

             . . . .
             Why is it no one ever sent me yet
                  One perfect limousine, do you suppose?
             Ah no, it's always just my luck to get
                  One perfect rose.

14r. Use three ellipsis points (. . .) to indicate a pause in dialogue.

EXAMPLE   "Well . . . I can't really say," hedged the company's representative.

—HELP—

Notice that the line of ellipsis points showing an omission in a poem is as long as the line of poetry above it.

MECHANICS

┌HELP┐

In Exercise 5,
you may need to keep or
omit punctuation, such as
commas within a sentence,
depending on whether
that punctuation is necessary to the meaning or
clarity of the sentence with
the omission.

Exercise 5   Using Ellipsis Points Correctly

Omit the italicized parts of the following passages. Use ellipsis points
to punctuate each omission correctly.

EXAMPLE   1. In those days, *which is to say when the world was green,*
a baseball was the core of my universe, and a bat its axis.

    1. *In those days . . . a baseball was the core of my uni-
verse, and a bat its axis.*

1. Today's marathon runners race for a little more than twenty-six
miles. *Why not twenty-five miles or thirty?* The distance commemo-
rates the length of the plain of Marathon, where, as legend has it, a
long-distance runner once carried the news of the Athenian defeat
of the Persian army.

2. The software, to my mind, is cumbersome at best, *a little like
wearing an exceedingly large backpack on top of another backpack.*
However, it may have some limited use for animation professionals
and other high-resolution graphics users.

3. A globe, *translucent magenta and dotted with unfamiliar aqua-blue
continents,* sat on his desk and spun slowly, powered by some
unseen force.

4. She said, "Who am I?"
I say, "Fie."
I'm the pie in the sky of a dragon's eye.
So, bye-bye, small fry.

5. How could I have known? *Could I have even guessed?* The events
were so startling that even as I experienced them, they did not
seem real.

6. The new highway, *which will reduce inner-city traffic,* will bypass the
city by routing traffic to the west. This new freeway is scheduled to
be completed in 2007. Residents who wish to comment on the proposed path may obtain a copy of the plans at the courthouse.

7. Movie fans, save your summer cash and skip this movie. The
young actress Maisie Mills, *who plays the romantic lead, is very
pretty but* is painfully unfunny and no friend to our friend
the camera.

8. Persuasive essays demand a point of view; they require the writer
to take a position and defend it. There is no place for objective
reports or evenhanded considerations in a persuasive essay, *except
insofar as they might reinforce the position being advanced.* The
approach is entirely subjective.

9. The tension between freedom and responsibility powers the plot of this novel, *as, indeed, it drives the lives of most readers.* Duty's demands conflict directly with Lei Lei's wish to become a doctor. To achieve her dreams, she must sacrifice her family; to help her family, she must sacrifice her dreams.

10. Myles lived in a plain one-story house of the kind known as a bungalow, *with the word's lingering nostalgia for horizons on which the sun never set.* It was at the bottom end of The Parade and commanded a view, *through the stone crosses of St. Colm's churchyard,* of the white sails of sailboats on the English Channel.

Apostrophes

Possessive Case

The *possessive case* of a noun or a pronoun shows ownership or possession.

EXAMPLES

the **performers'** costumes   Mr. **Elders'** dog

Grandmother's recipe   ten **dollars'** worth

the **team's** coach   **your** responsibility

my best **friend's** sister   **our** cousins

14s. Use an apostrophe to form the possessive forms of nouns and indefinite pronouns.

(1) To form the possessive of most singular nouns, add an apostrophe and an *s*.

EXAMPLES

a **bird's** nest   Louis's opinion

the **principal's** office   a leader's responsibility

NOTE   When forming the possessive of a singular noun ending in an *s* sound, add only an apostrophe if the noun has two or more syllables and if the addition of an apostrophe and an *s* will make the noun awkward to pronounce. Otherwise, add an apostrophe and an *s*.

EXAMPLES   for conscience' sake   Ms. Schwartz's car

Xerxes' army   the witness's testimony

Reference Note

Do not confuse **the pronouns *its, your, their, theirs,* and *whose*** with **the contractions *it's, you're, they're, there's,* and *who's*.** See "Words Often Confused" in Chapter 15 for more about these words. For more about **possessive pronouns,** see pages 124 and 131.

MECHANICS

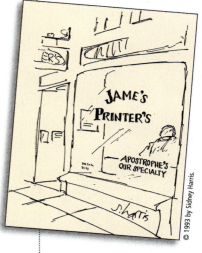

© 1993 by Sidney Harris.

JAME'S
PRINTER'S

APOSTROPHE'S
OUR SPECIALTY

(2) To form the possessive of a plural noun ending in *s*, add only the apostrophe.

EXAMPLES   the girls' gym   the Joneses' house

               the players' uniforms   the volunteers' efforts

The few plural nouns that do not end in *s* form the possessive by adding an apostrophe and an *s*.

EXAMPLES   women's fashions   children's toys

               geese's squawking   mice's nests

Reference Note

For information about using **apostrophes to form plurals of numerals, symbols, letters, and words referred to as words,** see page 350.

NOTE In general, you should not use an apostrophe to form the plural of a noun.

INCORRECT   How many Olympic medal's did Carl Lewis win?

CORRECT   How many Olympic **medals** did Carl Lewis win?

(3) Do not use an apostrophe with possessive personal pronouns or with the possessive pronoun *whose*.

Possessive Personal Pronouns		
First Person	my, mine	our, ours
Second Person	your, yours	your, yours
Third Person	his, her, hers, its	their, theirs

INCORRECT   The leopard can't change it's spots.

CORRECT   The leopard can't change **its** spots.

INCORRECT   Marjorie is the girl who's mother I met.

CORRECT   Marjorie is the girl **whose** mother I met.

(4) To form the possessive of an indefinite pronoun, add an apostrophe and an *s*.

Indefinite Pronouns in the Possessive Case			
another's	each's	nobody's	other's
anybody's	everybody's	no one's	somebody's
anyone's	everyone's	one's	someone's

MECHANICS

EXAMPLES   One runner got in the other**'s** way.

He seems to need everybody**'s** attention.

> **NOTE** The correct possessive forms of *anyone else* and *somebody else* are *anyone else***'s** and *somebody else***'s.**

Exercise 6   Proofreading for Correct Possessive and Plural Forms

Most of the following items contain an incorrect possessive or plural form. For each error, give the correct form of the word. If an item is already correct, write *C*.

EXAMPLE   1. Chris' tapes
              1. Chris's tapes

1. It is her's.
2. womens' department
3. that boys' radio
4. leaves' color
5. a fly's wings
6. four dog's in a line
7. that spacecrafts' air lock
8. childrens' program
9. no ones' fault
10. the Harlem Globetrotters's game
11. San Jose's industries
12. a Buddhist's beliefs
13. Who's is it?
14. It is somebody's else.
15. a pair of shoe's
16. it's shiny surface
17. That is their's.
18. a churches' spire
19. mice's tails
20. a horses' hooves

(5) Generally, in compound nouns, in names of organizations and businesses, and in word groups showing joint possession, only the last word is possessive in form.

EXAMPLES   sister-in-law**'s** shoes

Weber, Mendoza, and Stone**'s** law office

Joe and Clara**'s** song

> **NOTE** The possessive of an acronym is formed by adding an apostrophe and *s.*
>
> EXAMPLES   NBC**'s** latest sitcom
>
>   UNESCO**'s** new headquarters

Reference Note

For more about **compound nouns,** see page 4.

STYLE   **TIP**

Use a phrase beginning with *of* or *for* to avoid awkward possessive forms.

AWKWARD
the Society for the Preservation of Historic Homes's advertisement

BETTER
the advertisement **for** the Society for the Preservation of Historic Homes

When a possessive pronoun is part of a word group showing joint possession, each noun in the word group is also possessive.

EXAMPLES   Chen's, Ramona's, and **my** project

                 Juan's and **her** business

(6) Form the possessive of each noun in a word group showing individual possession of similar items.

EXAMPLES   Asimov's and Bradbury's stories

                 the doctor's and dentist's fees

(7) When used in the possessive form, words indicating time, such as *minute, hour, day, week, month,* and *year,* and words indicating amounts in cents or dollars require apostrophes.

EXAMPLES   a day's rest   four weeks' vacation

                 a dollar's worth   two cents' worth

Review C   **Forming Possessive Nouns and Pronouns**

Each of the following phrases expresses a possessive relationship. Revise each word group so that a possessive noun or pronoun expresses the same relationship.

EXAMPLES   1. promise of my sister-in-law

                 1. my sister-in-law's promise

                 2. bikes of Jane and Mia

                 2. Jane's and Mia's bikes

1. party of Juan and Geraldo
2. clothes of babies
3. singing of the birds
4. profits of ABC
5. pay of two weeks
6. restaurant of Charlie and Barney
7. worth of one dollar
8. coats of the gentlemen
9. jobs of my brothers-in-law
10. plans of the school board
11. victory of the players
12. languages of Spain and France
13. delay of six months
14. testimonies of the clerk and the customer
15. streets of West Baden
16. name of it
17. flooding of the Nile River
18. hope of everyone else
19. opinions of him
20. route of our mail carrier

Contractions

14t. Use an apostrophe to show where letters, numerals, or words have been omitted in a contraction.

A *contraction* is a shortened form of a word, word group, or numeral in which an apostrophe takes the place of all the letters, words, or numerals that are omitted.

STYLE **TIP**

Many people consider contractions informal. Therefore, it is generally best to avoid using them in formal writing and speech.

EXAMPLES	I am . . . . **I'm**	they had . . . . . . **they'd**
	let us . . . . **let's**	where is . . . . . . **where's**
	of the clock . . **o'clock**	we are . . . . **we're**
	she would . . . . **she'd**	you will . . . . **you'll**
	1999 . . . . **'99**	Pat is . . . . **Pat's**

The word *not* can be shortened to *n't* and added to a verb, usually without any change in the spelling of the verb.

EXAMPLES	is not . . . . **isn't**	has not . . . . **hasn't**
	do not . . . . **don't**	should not . . . . **shouldn't**
	does not . . . . . **doesn't**	were not . . . . . . **weren't**
	would not . . . . **wouldn't**	could not . . . . . **couldn't**
EXCEPTIONS	will not . . . . **won't**	cannot . . . . **can't**

Do not confuse contractions with possessive pronouns.

Contractions	Possessive Pronouns
It's [It is] late. **It's** [It has] been an exciting week.	**Its** wing is broken.
Who's [Who is] in charge? **Who's** [Who has] been keeping score?	**Whose** ticket is this?
You're [You are] a good student.	**Your** shoe is untied.
They're [They are] in the library. **There's** [There is] no one at home.	**Their** house is for sale. Those dogs are **theirs**.

Exercise 7 **Using Possessive Forms and Contractions Correctly**

Each of the following sentences contains at least one possessive form or contraction that has been written incorrectly. Rewrite each incorrect word, adding or deleting apostrophes as needed.

EXAMPLE
1. Its easy to see that youve been practicing.

1. *It's, you've*

1. Their still in the gym going over they're acrobatics routine.
2. Larry asked the woman whose in charge, and she said that the branch library doesnt have any of Octavio Paz's works.
3. If shes not here by six oclock, whose going to make the introduction?
4. Theirs plenty of potato salad and lemonade over on they're picnic table.
5. It look's as though I shouldve checked the lid more carefully before I shook this bottle.
6. Who wouldnt have laughed at that silly kitten chasing it's own tail?
7. Adam's busy; he cant help us with the script.
8. Lets go over there and see whose playing the flute.
9. Wed have gladly given the kids a puppet show if youd asked.
10. His bar mitzvah was in 99; what year was your's?

Plurals

14u. Use an apostrophe and an *s* to form the plurals of lowercase letters, symbols, numerals, some uppercase letters, and some words referred to as words.

EXAMPLES   The word *tomorrow* has two **r's** but only one *m*.

The accountant added **$'s** and **%'s** to all of the figures in the columns on the annual report.

I have three **7's** in my telephone number.

After the happy couple said their ***I do's,*** everyone cheered.

Some writers add only an *s* to form the plurals of such items—except lowercase letters—when the plural forms will not cause misreading.

EXAMPLE   The U.S. economy expanded rapidly in the mid- and late-**1990s.**

| S T Y L E   T I P |

Use apostrophes consistently.

EXAMPLE
Several of her grades had improved from **B's** to **A's.** [Without the apostrophe, the plural of *A* would spell *As.* The apostrophe in the plural of *B* is unnecessary but is included for consistency.]

Review D — Proofreading for Errors in Possessives, Contractions, and Plurals

Correctly write each incorrect possessive, contraction, or plural in the following sentences.

EXAMPLE

   1. Lets try to find a modern puzzle maze that wont be too difficult for us to explore.

     1. *Let's; won't*

1. Your lucky if youve ever been through an old-fashioned hedge maze such as the one pictured below.
2. Its like a maze from an English castle; in fact, we cant help being reminded of the maze at Hampton Court Palace.
3. From above, some of the bushes look like *h*s, *t*s, and other letters.
4. Dont you wonder if these people will find they're way out by dusk or even ten o clock?
5. Ive read that mazes like this one became popular in Europe during the sixteenth and seventeenth centuries; however, my uncle said that hes read about mazes that were built two thousand years ago.
6. When a maze is architectural, *labyrinth*s the word to use for it.
7. Youll be surprised to know that the biggest labyrinth dates back over forty century's ago; the extreme complexity of this labyrinth protected the tomb of Amenehet III.
8. Indeed, other ancient labyrinths may have been defensive structures; after all, theirs no general in the world whose going to send an army single file through a tricky tangle of passageway's.

S T Y L E   ✎   T I P

To form the plural of an abbreviation that ends with a period, add 's.

EXAMPLES

  M.D.'s   B.A.'s

To form the plural of an abbreviation not followed by a period, add either 's or s.

EXAMPLES

  CD-ROM's   or   CD-ROMs
  POW's   or   POWs

MECHANICS

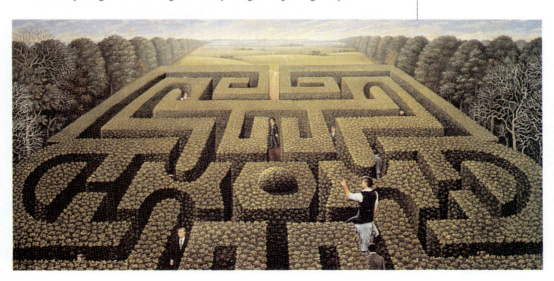

9. Cant you just imagine a cartoon of the confused soldiers with *?*s and *!*s over they're heads?
10. Today, the popularity of mazes drives sales of video game's on cartridges, disks, and CD-ROMs, where a maze can even have an upstairs and a downstairs, trapdoors, and all manner of deceptions.

Hyphens

14v. Use a hyphen to divide a word at the end of a line.

When dividing a word at the end of a line, remember the following rules:

- Do not divide a one-syllable word.

INCORRECT   The treaty that ended the war was sign-ed in Paris in 1783.

CORRECT   The treaty that ended the war was signed in Paris in 1783.

- Divide a word only between syllables.

INCORRECT   Shashona wrote a story about the enda-ngered gray wolf.

CORRECT   Shashona wrote a story about the endan-gered gray wolf.

- A word containing double consonants is usually divided between the double consonants.

INCORRECT   I couldn't believe that it was the beginn-ing of term.

CORRECT   I couldn't believe that it was the begin-ning of term.

- Divide an already hyphenated word at the hyphen.

INCORRECT   Among Elena's drawings were two self-por-traits.

CORRECT   Among Elena's drawings were two self-portraits.

- Do not divide a word so that one letter stands alone.

INCORRECT   Most of the buildings there are made of a-dobe.

CORRECT   Most of the buildings there are made of adobe.

HELP

Many dictionaries indicate how a word should be divided by breaking it into syllables. When you are not sure about how to divide a word, look up the word in a dictionary.

MECHANICS

- Divide words with prefixes or suffixes between the prefix and the root or between the root and the suffix.

INCORRECT   Did you know that Uncle Silas bought a very depen-dable car?

CORRECT   Did you know that Uncle Silas bought a very depend-able car?

Reference Note

For more about **adding prefixes and suffixes to words,** see page 364.

14w. Use a hyphen with compound numbers from *twenty-one* to *ninety-nine* and with fractions used as modifiers.

EXAMPLES   one hundred **fifty-five**

a **two-thirds** majority [Here, *two-thirds* is an adjective modifying *majority*.]

two thirds of them [Here, *two thirds* is not a modifier. *Thirds* is a noun modified by the adjective *two*.]

14x. Use a hyphen with the prefixes *ex–, self–, all–,* and *great–*; with the suffixes *–elect* and *–free*; and with all prefixes before a proper noun or proper adjective.

EXAMPLES

ex-mayor	**great-**uncle	**pre-**Waterloo
self-improvement	governor**-elect**	**mid-**Atlantic
all-star	sugar**-free**	**trans-**Siberian

14y. Hyphenate a compound adjective when it precedes the noun it modifies.

EXAMPLES

| a **well-designed** engine | an engine that is **well designed** |
| a **world-famous** skier | a skier who is **world famous** |

NOTE   Some compound adjectives are always hyphenated, whether they precede or follow the words they modify.

EXAMPLES

| an **up-to-date** look | a look that is **up-to-date** |
| a **well-informed** man | a man who is **well-informed** |

If you are unsure about whether a compound adjective is hyphenated, look up the word in a dictionary.

Do not use a hyphen if one of the modifiers before a noun is an adverb ending in *–ly*.

EXAMPLE   a **partly finished** research paper

STYLE   TIP

The prefix *half* often requires a hyphen, as in *half-life, half-moon,* and *half-truth*. However, sometimes *half* is used without a hyphen, either as a part of a single word (*halftone, halfway, halfback*) or as a separate word (*half shell, half pint, half note*). If you are not sure how to spell a word containing *half*, look up the word in a dictionary.

14z. Use a hyphen to prevent awkwardness or confusion.

EXAMPLES   de‑emphasize [The hyphen prevents the awkwardness of two identical vowels next to each other.]

anti‑inflammatory [The hyphen prevents the awkwardness of two identical vowels next to each other.]

re‑cover a chair [The hyphen prevents confusion with the word *recover.*]

a re‑creation of the event [The hyphen prevents confusion with the word *recreation.*]

Exercise 8 Writing Sentences Using Hyphens

Write ten sentences according to the following guidelines. In your sentences, use a variety of subjects and verbs.

EXAMPLE   1. Write a sentence in which you divide a word at the end of a line.

1. *My brother would love to have the toy frog in the catalog.*

1. Write a sentence containing a compound number.
2. Write a sentence containing a fraction used as an adjective.
3. Write a sentence containing a word with the prefix *ex–*.
4. Write a sentence containing a compound adjective that precedes the word it modifies.
5. Write a sentence in which you divide a word at the end of a line.
6. Write a sentence containing a word with the prefix *self–*.
7. Write a sentence containing a word with double consonants; at the end of a line, correctly divide that word.
8. Write a sentence containing a word with the suffix *–elect*.
9. Write a sentence containing a word with the prefix *all–*.
10. Write a sentence in which you divide an already hyphenated word at the end of a line.

Review E Using Apostrophes and Hyphens

Revise the following words or word groups by adding apostrophes and hyphens where needed. If a word or word group is already correct, write *C*.

EXAMPLE   1. post Reformation Europe

1. *post-Reformation Europe*

1. my sister in laws new truck

2. transAlaskan

3. Wheres the Shaker box you bought?

4. Youre from Peru, arent you?

5. one third of the class

6. Isnt soda bread Irish?

7. To whom do all of these *you*'s and *they*s refer?

8. one third finished with the project

9. There are three *a*s in *alphabetical*.

10. Its theirs, not ours.

11. antiindustrial sentiment

12. politics in the 1890's

13. dotted all of your *i*s

14. Didnt Anthony make your piñata?

15. my great grandmother

16. Its after five oclock.

17. part time job

18. Can you tell me, Denise, why no one answered the phone?

19. sugar free foods

20. Achilles heel

COMPUTER TIP

Some software programs can evaluate your writing for common errors in the use of punctuation marks. Such programs can help you proofread your writing.

MECHANICS

Review F **Proofreading a Paragraph for Correct Punctuation**

Most of the sentences in the following paragraph contain at least one error in the use of punctuation. Rewrite each incorrect sentence, adding and deleting punctuation as necessary. If a sentence is already correct, write *C.*

HELP

Some sentences in Review F have commas where other punctuation marks should be.

EXAMPLE [1] Can we be sure sports historians arent that Abner Doubleday invented baseball, that Princeton and Rutgers played the first football game, or that golf originated in China in the second century B.C.?

1. *Can we be sure (sports historians aren't) that Abner Doubleday invented baseball, that Princeton and Rutgers played the first football game, or that golf originated in China in the second century B.C.?*

[1] The origins of most sports are unknown try as we may, we cannot say exactly when or where or how such games as baseball, football, and golf were first played. [2] There is, however, one exception to this rule the game of basketball. [3] Historians of sports know precisely

where basketball began, they know precisely when it began, and perhaps the most interesting fact of all they know the name of the man who invented it Dr. James Naismith. [4] In the winter of 1891–1892, Naismith, who was then an instructor at the YMCA Training College now called Springfield College in Springfield, Massachusetts, had a problem on his hands. [5] The football season was over the baseball season had not yet begun. [6] His students wanted indoor exercise at a competitive sport however, no such sport existed. [7] Working with the materials at hand, Naismith decided to create a new indoor sport. [8] He fastened two peach basket's to the walls at opposite ends of a gymnasium and, using a soccer ball, devised the game that today we call basketball. [9] He started with eighteen available players, and the first rule he wrote read as follows There shall be nine players on each side. [10] Imagine eighteen players set loose on a modern basketball court!

Chapter Review

A. Using Semicolons and Colons Correctly

Rewrite each of the following sentences, adding semicolons and colons as necessary.

1. In the attic we found many interesting items an antique mirror, a World War II uniform, some silver bowls, and a chest full of letters.
2. Nicci gets up at six o'clock every weekday morning, consequently, she is never late for school.
3. On Thursday, the most hectic day of the week for me, my schedule includes band practice, 3 15 P.M. my part-time job, 5 00 P.M., and homework, 8 30 P.M.
4. Randy Newman is one of Hollywood's most successful film composers, he has composed the music for such films as *Toy Story, A Bug's Life,* and *James and the Giant Peach.*
5. In his 1961 presidential inaugural address, John Fitzgerald Kennedy delivered these famous words, "Ask not what your country can do for you—ask what you can do for your country."

┌**HELP**─

In Part A of the Chapter Review, you may need to replace a comma with a semicolon or colon in some sentences.

B. Using Underlining and Quotation Marks Correctly

Rewrite each of the following sentences, using underlining (italics) and quotation marks correctly. Change punctuation and capitalization as necessary.

6. One of the books we read this summer was William Golding's Lord of the Flies.
7. "Your essays about the space shuttle Discovery," said Ms. Buchanan, will be due in class on Monday, November 3".
8. "For next Monday," said Mr. Tillinghast, "read the chapter titled The Gilded Age."
9. According to the librarian, Gita has the latest issue of Scientific American.
10. "These written exercises, Catalina complained, "are hard to do, even when you've studied the material."

C. Using Apostrophes, Hyphens, Dashes, Brackets, Parentheses, and Ellipsis Points Correctly

Rewrite each of the following sentences, using apostrophes, hyphens, dashes, brackets, and parentheses correctly. Replace any italicized sections with ellipsis points. Change spelling as necessary.

11. Mr. Jones states, "They the joint chiefs of staff favor an increase in the defense budget."

12. Everybodys street clothes are in the locker room, a few minutes walk from here.

13. The critic said, "The meaning of the essay if indeed it had any meaning has been lost through the writer's lack of coherence."

14. It will be warmer in mid April, wont it?

15. Is this Gillian and Matthews house?

16. For his courageous leadership, Dr. Martin Luther King, Jr. 1929–1968, received the Nobel Peace Prize.

17. Whose in the office now?

18. The War Between the States (better known as the Civil War 1861–1865) was one of the defining periods of American history.

19. The ex senator is a well respected commentator on foreign policy.

20. Since the book was too boldly new and strange to win the attention of reviewers or readers *who had fixed ideas about poetry*, it's publication went nearly unnoticed.

D. Proofreading a Dialogue for Correct Punctuation

The following dialogue contains errors in the use of semicolons, colons, dashes, parentheses, italics (underlining), quotation marks, apostrophes, and hyphens. Rewrite the dialogue, correcting the errors, changing capitalization where necessary, and dividing it into paragraphs where appropriate.

[21] What in the world please dont think me too uninformed is a Renaissance festival"? Leon asked. [22] "Its a fair that celebrates Europes Renaissance, which lasted from about A.D. 1300 to around A.D. 1600," Janice said. [23] "Well, I'm ready to go, I know what to expect because I've seen the movies Camelot and The Princess Bride," Leon said. [24] "Even so, youll be amazed Janice said, because youll see people dressed up as: kings and queens, jesters, peasants, and knights. [25] "I suppose Id better mind my ps and qs with knights around"!

MECHANICS

Leon exclaimed. **[26]** "Oh, all the fierce looking knights actually are friendly," Janice said. **[27]** "There are many other sights to see jousts, mazes, elephants and camels, games of strength, music, and all kinds of crafts". **[28]** Leon asked, "isnt there any Renaissance food? **[29]** "Plenty!" Janice said. "My favorites are: bagels, which are sold from traveling carts, soup served in bowls made out of bread, which is freshly baked, and fruit fritters." **[30]** "I've been to several Renaissance fairs," Janice added. Including ones in Texas and Missouri, and I think theyre all great."

Writing Application
Using Contractions in Informal Dialogue

Using Contractions Correctly   You have decided to write and produce a short play and have already drafted a scene-by-scene outline of the play. In one scene, the two main characters have a heated discussion about something that's important to them. Write the dialogue for your scene. Use contractions to make the characters' speech sound natural and realistic.

Prewriting   First, brainstorm some ideas for your main characters. Once you decide who your characters are, think about the sort of discussion they might have. Decide how the characters will resolve their argument at the end of the scene.

Writing   Follow the form for presenting dialogue in a play. In your first draft, concentrate on getting down the basic content of your characters' conversation. You can polish the dialogue later as you evaluate and revise. Be sure that your dialogue focuses on a specific topic or issue and that you maintain a consistent tone throughout.

Revising   To help you evaluate the dialogue, ask two friends to read the parts aloud. As you listen, ask yourself these questions: Does each line of dialogue sound natural? Does the dialogue convey the proper tone? Do the characters resolve their argument in a realistic way? Use contractions to help your dialogue sound like an actual discussion between two people.

Publishing   Proofread your dialogue carefully for correct punctuation and paragraph breaks. You may want to produce your scene for the class. Cast two volunteer actors for the roles, and work with them to get the dialogue just right.

Reference Note

For more about the differences between **formal and informal English,** see page 241.

MECHANICS

Spelling
Improving Your Spelling

Diagnostic Preview

A. Proofreading Sentences for Spelling Errors

Identify and correct each misspelled word in the following sentences.

EXAMPLE   1. A braceing wind blasted down through the vallies.

1. *braceing—bracing, vallies—valleys*

1. Six steaming loafs of bread sat on the counter in readyness for the family reunion.
2. Where did the superstition about cats' having nine lifes originate?
3. Arctic foxs romped in the snowdrifts in gloryous delight.
4. I must have counted at least three thousand sheeps before I finaly fell asleep.
5. No, they're not argueing; they enjoy shouting about foriegn policy.
6. Study these suffixs closely; you can use them to decode words.
7. It's not a new car, but it's perfectly servicable and the monthly payments are managable.
8. Let's rexamine your data on sea gull's.
9. You can judge the ripeness of a melon by its smell and by taping it and listening for a hollow sound.
10. With our senses, we can percieve only a small part of the world.

B. Proofreading Sentences for Words Often Confused

Proofread the following paragraphs, and replace each incorrectly used word. If a sentence is already correct, write *C*.

EXAMPLE   **[1]** In speaking or writing, few things in language are more satisfying then discovering and using just the right word—for example, *copacetic*.

    1. *than*

[11] A friend of yours tells you about a peace of music by saying, "Man, it was copacetic." **[12]** Right away, you know your friend is paying the music a complement, because *copacetic* sounds to nice to be critical. **[13]** To state merely, as dictionaries do, that *copacetic* means "excellent" or "first class" would be selling the word short, because it connotes much more than simple superiority.

[14] It is not a strait word; it's smooth and curved; it doesn't take the shortest rout. **[15]** Like the ingenuous jazz musicians who used it in the late nineteenth century, it enjoys the scenery, and it does so with style and originality. **[16]** Some scholars say the word began in Harlem; others say it was borne in France. **[17]** Still others claim that while *copacetic* is Yiddish in derivation, it's Southern in accent.

[18] In short, etymologists are all together stumped; consequently, the origin of *copacetic* is formerly listed as unknown. **[19]** For now, we don't know weather this adjective is French, Italian, Hebrew, or an invention of African Americans. **[20]** Therefore, its origin will have to stay a personnel opinion, but one thing's for sure—*copacetic* is an American English word.

Good Spelling Habits

Using the following techniques will improve your spelling.

1. Pronounce words carefully.

EXAMPLES   ath•lete [not *ath•e•lete*]

           ac•ci•den•tal•ly [not *ac•ci•dent•ly*]

           can•di•date [not *can•i•date*]

           mis•chie•vous [not *mis•chie•ve•ous*]

┌HELP─

If you are not sure how to pronounce a word, look in a dictionary. In the dictionary, you will usually find the pronunciation given in parentheses after the word. The information in parentheses generally shows the sounds used, the syllable breaks, and any accented syllables. A guide to the pronunciation symbols is usually found at the front of the dictionary.

2. Spell by syllables. A *syllable* is a word part that is pronounced as one uninterrupted sound.

EXAMPLES   per•ma•nent [three syllables]

               op•ti•mis•tic [four syllables]

               oc•ca•sion•al•ly [five syllables]

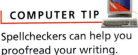

COMPUTER TIP

Spellcheckers can help you proofread your writing. Even the best spellcheckers are not foolproof, however. Some accept British spellings, obsolete words, and archaic spellings. Most accept words that are spelled correctly but are used incorrectly (such as *affect* for *effect*). Always double-check your writing to make sure that your spelling is error-free.

3. Use a dictionary. By using a dictionary, you will become familiar with the correct pronunciations and divisions of words. In fact, using a dictionary to check the spelling of one word may help you spell other words. For example, checking the spelling of *democracy* may help you spell other words ending in *–cracy*, such as *theocracy, autocracy,* and *aristocracy.*

4. Proofread for careless spelling errors. Always re-read what you have written so that you can eliminate careless spelling errors, such as typographical errors (*thier* for *their*), missing letters (*familar* for *familiar*), and the misuse of similar-sounding words (*than* for *then*).

5. Keep a spelling notebook. Divide each page into four columns.

COLUMN 1   Write correctly any word you find troublesome.

COLUMN 2   Write the word again, dividing it into syllables and marking the stressed syllable(s). (You will probably need to use a dictionary.)

COLUMN 3   Write the word again, circling the part(s) that cause you trouble.

COLUMN 4   Jot down any comments or mnemonics that will help you remember the correct spelling.

Here is an example of how you might make entries for two words that are often misspelled.

Correct Spelling	Syllables and Accents	Trouble Spot	Comments
probably	prob´•a•bly	prob(ab)ly	pronounce clearly
desirable	de•sir´•a•ble	desi(ra)ble	Study Rule 15 f.

MECHANICS

Exercise 1 — Dividing Words into Syllables

Without looking up the words in a dictionary, write the syllables of each of the following words, using hyphens between the syllables. Be sure that the division of each word includes all of the letters of the word. When you have finished, use a dictionary that shows syllable breaks to check your work.

EXAMPLE   1. accommodate

1. *ac-com-mo-date*

1. adversary
2. alias
3. barbarous
4. chimney
5. costume
6. deficit
7. genuine
8. incidentally
9. procrastinate
10. library

HELP

Rules 15a and 15b apply only when the *i* and the *e* are part of the same syllable.

EXAMPLES
de • i • ty
sci • ence

Spelling Rules

ie and *ei*

15a. **Write *ie* when the sound is long *e*, except after *c*.**

EXAMPLES   bel**ie**ve   f**ie**ld   n**ie**ce   conc**ei**t   c**ei**ling

EXCEPTIONS   **ei**ther   l**ei**sure   n**ei**ther   s**ei**ze   prot**ei**n

15b. **Write *ei* when the sound is not long *e*.**

EXAMPLES   forf**ei**t   fr**ei**ght   **ei**ght   n**ei**ghbor   w**ei**gh

EXCEPTIONS   anc**ie**nt   v**ie**w   fr**ie**nd   misch**ie**f   consc**ie**nce

Oral Practice — Spelling *ie* and *ei* Words

Correctly spell each of the following words aloud, supplying *ie* or *ei*.

EXAMPLE   1. retr . . . ve

1. *retrieve*

1. gr . . . f
2. th . . . r
3. v . . . l
4. h . . . r
5. bel . . . f
6. counterf . . . t
7. dec . . . ve
8. ch . . . ftain
9. perc . . . ve
10. rec . . . pt
11. p . . . rce
12. w . . . ld
13. th . . . f
14. sl . . . gh
15. bes . . . ge
16. shr . . . k
17. f . . . rce
18. . . . ght
19. cash . . . r
20. y . . . ld

MECHANICS

–cede, –ceed, and –sede

15c. The only English word ending in *–sede* **is** *supersede.* **The only English words ending in** *–ceed* **are** *exceed, proceed,* **and** *succeed.* **Most other words with this sound end in** *–cede.*

EXAMPLES   ac**cede**   con**cede**   inter**cede**

               pre**cede**   re**cede**   se**cede**

Adding Prefixes

A *prefix* is a letter or group of letters added to the beginning of a word or a root to create a new word.

EXAMPLES   il + legible = **il**legible   pre + historic = **pre**historic

               in + correct = **in**correct   un + certain = **un**certain

15d. When adding a prefix, do not change the spelling of the original word.

EXAMPLES   dis + satisfy = dis**satisfy**   im + mature = im**mature**

               mis + spell = mis**spell**   re + adjust = re**adjust**

Adding Suffixes

A *suffix* is a letter or group of letters added to the end of a word to create a new word.

EXAMPLES   help + less = help**less**   worry + ed = worri**ed**

               move + ment = move**ment**   hope + ful = hope**ful**

15e. When adding the suffix *–ness* **or** *–ly,* **do not change the spelling of the original word.**

EXAMPLES   open + ness = **open**ness   normal + ly = **normal**ly

               gentle + ness = **gentle**ness   final + ly = **final**ly

EXCEPTION   For most words ending in *y*, change the *y* to *i* before adding *–ness* or *–ly*.

               messy + ness = mess**iness**   merry + ly = merr**ily**

               heavy + ness = heav**iness**   ready + ly = read**ily**

─HELP─

One-syllable adjectives ending in *y* generally do not change the *y* to *i* before a suffix.

EXAMPLES

shy + ness = shy**ness**

sly + ly = sly**ly**

Exercise 2 **Spelling Words with Prefixes and Suffixes**

Spell each of the following words, adding the prefix or suffix given.

EXAMPLE **1.** in + active

1. *inactive*

1. mis + inform
2. habitual + ly
3. il + legal
4. dis + appear
5. stubborn + ness

6. crafty + ly
7. in + animate
8. im + movable
9. happy + ness
10. dis + similar

15f. **Drop the final silent *e* before adding a suffix that begins with a vowel.**

EXAMPLES create + ive = **creat**ive rate + ing = **rat**ing

achieve + able = **achiev**able simple + er = **simpl**er

EXCEPTIONS **1.** Keep the final silent *e* in most words ending in *ce* or *ge* before a suffix that begins with *a* or *o: peac**eable,** courag**eous.** Sometimes the *e* becomes *i,* as in *spacious* and *gracious.*

2. To avoid confusion with other words, keep the final silent *e* in some words: *dy**e**ing, sing**e**ing* (to prevent confusion with *dying* and *singing).*

3. mile + age = mileage

15g. **Keep the final silent *e* before adding a suffix that begins with a consonant.**

EXAMPLES fate + ful = fate**ful** time + ly = tim**ely**

care + less = care**less** place + ment = plac**ement**

EXCEPTIONS awe + ful = aw**ful** true + ly = tru**ly**

argue + ment = argu**ment** nine + th = nin**th**

15h. **For words ending in *y* preceded by a consonant, change the *y* to *i* before any suffix that does not begin with *i*.**

EXAMPLES sunny + est = sunn**iest**

accompany + ment = accompan**iment**

modify + ing = modif**ying**

┌─ **HELP** ─
When adding *–ing* to words that end in *ie,* drop the *e* and change the *i* to *y.*

EXAMPLES
die + ing = d**ying**
lie + ing = l**ying**
tie + ing = t**ying**

┌─ **HELP** ─
Some words can be spelled with or without the silent *e* before a suffix.

EXAMPLES
judg**ment** or judg**ement**

acknowledg**ment** or acknowledg**ement**

MECHANICS

15i. For words ending in *y* preceded by a vowel, keep the *y* when adding a suffix.

EXAMPLES	gray + est = gra**yest**	obey + ing = obe**ying**
	play + ed = pla**yed**	enjoy + ment = enjo**yment**

EXCEPTIONS day—da**ily**   lay—la**id**   pay—pa**id**   say—sa**id**

Exercise 3 Spelling Words with Suffixes

Spell each of the following words, adding the suffix given.

EXAMPLE **1.** delay + ed

1. delayed

1. employ + ment
2. thrifty + ness
3. beauty + fy
4. abate + ment
5. sure + ly
6. notice + able
7. share + ing
8. glide + ed
9. loose + est
10. tie + ing

15j. Double the final consonant before a suffix that begins with a vowel if the word both (1) has only one syllable or has the accent on the last syllable and (2) ends in a single consonant preceded by a single vowel.

EXAMPLES   win + er = wi**nner**

occur + ence = occu**rrence**

snap + ing = sna**pping**

refer + ed = refe**rred**

Do not double the final consonant unless the word satisfies both of the conditions.

EXAMPLES   prevent + ing = preven**ting** [*Prevent* has the accent on the last syllable but does not end in a single consonant preceded by a single vowel.]

falcon + er = falco**ner** [*Falcon* ends in a single consonant preceded by a single vowel but does not have the accent on the last syllable.]

refer + ence = refe**rence** [*Refer* satisfies both conditions, but the addition of a suffix causes a shift in the accent.]

┌HELP─

The final consonant of some words may or may not be doubled. Either spelling is acceptable.

EXAMPLES
cancel + ed = cance**led** or cance**lled**

travel + er = trave**ler** or trave**ller**

If you are not sure whether to double a final consonant, look up the word in a dictionary.

MECHANICS

Review A **Spelling Words with Suffixes**

Spell each of the following words, adding the suffix given.

EXAMPLE   **1.** exact + ly

         1. exactly

1. plan + ed	**8.** joy + ful	**15.** sudden + ness
2. stop + er	**9.** argue + ment	**16.** satisfy + ed
3. friendly + er	**10.** prepare + ed	**17.** day + ly
4. achieve + ment	**11.** sly + ly	**18.** prefer + ence
5. propel + er	**12.** trace + able	**19.** gentle + ly
6. seize + ure	**13.** wed + ing	**20.** steady + ing
7. definite + ly	**14.** happy + ly	

Review B **Proofreading a Paragraph for Spelling Errors**

Proofread the following paragraph, and correct each misspelled word.

EXAMPLE   **[1]** The sceintist Granville T. Woods was quite an inventor.

        1. sceintist—scientist

[1] After leaving school at the age of ten, Woods worked on the railroads in Missouri. [2] However, his love of electrical and mechanical devices led him to study engineering and later to open a factory where his managment skills and knowledge served him well. [3] Later, Woods succeded in devising a telegraph that allowed stationmasters to communicate with engineers on moving trains. [4] With this device, speeding trains could be notifyed of any problems along the track, and train engineers could quickly alert stations to dangerous situations. [5] His successes permited Woods to relocate to New York City. [6] There he learned that the method the-aters used for diming lights was responsible for many fires. [7] Woods revaluated the design and devised a new system. [8] This new lighting system operated safly and was, at the same time, 40 percent more efficient than the old one. [9] Not surprisingly, com-panies like American Bell Telephone and General Electric payed generous sums for Woods's inven-tions. [10] In all, Woods recieved more than 150 patents for his inventions, and many of those inven-tions, such as the electrified rail for New York City's subway, are still in use.

**MEETING THE
CHALLENGE**

One way to master spelling
is to understand how pre-
fixes, roots, and suffixes fit
together to make words.
For the younger students at
your school, design a game
that will help them master
this skill. For instance, you
could cut up index cards,
label them with prefixes,
roots, and suffixes, and
turn them facedown on a
table for a game of
Concentration. Students
would have to match parts
of the word. To get points,
students should also spell
the word correctly, making
any necessary changes.

┌HELP─

If you are not
sure how to spell the plural
of a word ending in *f* or *fe*,
look in a dictionary.

Forming the Plurals of Nouns

15k. Remembering the following rules will help you spell the
plural forms of nouns.

(1) For most nouns, add *s*.

SINGULAR	dancer	beagle	ship	lake	parasol	Morrison
PLURAL	dancer**s**	beagle**s**	ship**s**	lake**s**	parasol**s**	Morrison**s**

(2) For nouns ending in *s, x, z, ch,* or *sh*, add *es*.

SINGULAR	dress	fox	waltz	march	brush	Katz
PLURAL	dress**es**	fox**es**	waltz**es**	march**es**	brush**es**	Katz**es**

NOTE Some one-syllable words ending in *z* double the final consonant
when forming plurals.

EXAMPLES quiz—qui**zz**es   fez—fe**zz**es

(3) For nouns ending in *y* preceded by a vowel, add *s*.

SINGULAR	essay	journey	Friday	decoy	tray	Bailey
PLURAL	essay**s**	journey**s**	Friday**s**	decoy**s**	tray**s**	Bailey**s**

**(4) For nouns ending in *y* preceded by a consonant, change the
y to *i* and add *es*.**

SINGULAR	sky	folly	comedy	trophy	cavity	theory
PLURAL	sk**ies**	foll**ies**	comed**ies**	troph**ies**	cavit**ies**	theor**ies**

EXCEPTION For proper nouns, simply add *s*.

Brodsky—Brodsky**s**   Gregory—Gregory**s**

**(5) For some nouns ending in *f* or *fe*, add *s*. For others, change the
f or *fe* to *v* and add *es*.**

SINGULAR	gulf	roof	safe	leaf	shelf	knife
PLURAL	gulf**s**	roof**s**	safe**s**	lea**ves**	shel**ves**	kni**ves**

(6) For nouns ending in *o* preceded by a vowel, add *s*.

SINGULAR	studio	radio	cameo	video	igloo	Antonio
PLURAL	studio**s**	radio**s**	cameo**s**	video**s**	igloo**s**	Antonio**s**

(7) For nouns ending in *o* preceded by a consonant, add *es*.

SINGULAR	torpedo	tomato	hero	veto	potato
PLURAL	torpedo**es**	tomato**es**	hero**es**	veto**es**	potato**es**

For proper nouns ending in *o* preceded by a consonant and for some common nouns, especially those referring to music, add only *s*.

SINGULAR	Alvarado	taco	photo	piano	solo
PLURAL	Alvarado**s**	taco**s**	photo**s**	piano**s**	solo**s**

NOTE For some nouns ending in *o* preceded by a consonant, you may add either *s* or *es*.

SINGULAR	motto	tornado	cargo	lasso	banjo
PLURAL	motto**s**	tornado**s**	cargo**s**	lasso**s**	banjo**s**
	or	*or*	*or*	*or*	*or*
	motto**es**	tornado**es**	cargo**es**	lasso**es**	banjo**es**

(8) The plurals of a few nouns are formed in irregular ways.

SINGULAR	tooth	goose	woman	mouse	ox	child
PLURAL	t**ee**th	g**ee**se	wom**e**n	m**ice**	ox**en**	child**ren**

(9) For a few nouns, the singular and the plural forms are the same.

SINGULAR AND PLURAL	sheep	deer	Chinese
	moose	species	Japanese

(10) For most compound nouns, form the plural of only the last word of the compound.

SINGULAR	notebook	blueprint	disc jockey	two-year-old
PLURAL	notebook**s**	blueprint**s**	disc jockey**s**	two-year-old**s**

(11) For compound nouns in which one of the words is modified by the other word or words, form the plural of the noun modified.

SINGULAR	brother-in-law	passerby	rock garden
PLURAL	brother**s**-in-law	passer**s**by	rock garden**s**

NOTE Some compound nouns have two acceptable plural forms.

SINGULAR	attorney general	court-martial	notary public
PLURAL	attorney general**s**	court-martial**s**	notary public**s**
	or	*or*	*or*
	attorney**s** general	court**s**-martial	notar**ies** public

HELP

If you are ever in doubt about the plural form of a noun ending in *o* preceded by a consonant, check the spelling in a dictionary.

STYLE **TIP**

When it refers to a computer device, the word *mouse* can be made plural in either of two ways—*mouses* or *mice*. Someday, one of these forms may be the preferred style. For now, either is correct.

MECHANICS

HELP

Check an up-to-date dictionary whenever you are in doubt about the plural form of a compound noun.

(12) For some nouns borrowed from other languages, the plural is formed as in the original languages.

SINGULAR	alumnus [male]	alumna [female]	phenomenon
PLURAL	alumni [male]	alumnae [female]	phenomena

A few nouns borrowed from other languages have two plural forms. For each of the following nouns, the plural form preferred in English is given first.

SINGULAR	index	appendix	formula	cherub	cactus
PLURAL	index**es**	appendix**es**	formula**s**	cherub**s**	cactus**es**
	or	*or*	*or*	*or*	*or*
	ind**ices**	append**ices**	formul**ae**	cherub**im**	cact**i**

(13) To form the plurals of numerals, most uppercase letters, symbols, and words used as words, add either an *s* or both an apostrophe and an *s*.

SINGULAR	*8*	1760	*Q*	*&*	*and*
PLURAL	*8*s	1760s	*Q*s	*&*s	*and*s
	or	*or*	*or*	*or*	*or*
	8's	1760's	*Q*'s	*&*'s	*and*'s

To prevent confusion, add both an apostrophe and an *s* to form the plurals of all lowercase letters, certain uppercase letters, and some words used as words.

EXAMPLES   The word *Mississippi* contains four *s*'s and four *i*'s. [Without an apostrophe, the plural of *s* would look awkward, and the plural of *i* could be confused with *is*.]

Sebastian usually makes straight A's. [Without an apostrophe, the plural of *A* could be confused with *As*.]

Because I mistakenly thought Evelyn Waugh was a woman, I used *her*'s instead of *his*'s in my paragraph. [Without an apostrophe, the plural of *her* would look like the possessive pronoun *hers* and the plural of *his* would look like the word *hiss*.]

NOTE   To form the plural of an abbreviation that includes periods, add both an apostrophe and an *s*. To form the plural of an abbreviation that does not include periods, add an apostrophe and an *s*, or add only an *s*.

EXAMPLES   Ph.D.—Ph.D.'s   CD—CD's *or* CDs

Spelling the Plural Forms of Nouns

Spell the plural form of each of the following nouns.

EXAMPLE   **1.** shelf

       1. shelves

1. elk	**8.** box	**15.** Murphy
2. *o*	**9.** half	**16.** gulf
3. turkey	**10.** echo	**17.** penny
4. niece	**11.** soprano	**18.** father-in-law
5. politics	**12.** life	**19.** merry-go-round
6. valley	**13.** phenomenon	**20.** 1700
7. try	**14.** bunch	

Review C **Proofreading for Spelling Errors**

Correct each misspelled word in the following sentences.

EXAMPLES   **1.** After we renter the program, the cursor vanishs.

       1. reenter, vanishes

      2. David displays his trophys on a shelf in his room.

       2. trophies

1. Many varietys of fish thrive near continental shelfs.

2. Be more careful; your *a*s look like *o*s.

3. At center stage, two identical black grand pianoes stood facing each other like dinosaures.

4. What a horrific three-year struggle Hernando De Soto and his mans must have had as they made thier way through swamps and mosquitos and past alligatores and rattlesnakes.

5. Gracefuly, the mountain goats leap from rock to rock.

6. Not everyone succedes in mastering the art of *chanoyu*, the Japanese tea ceremony.

7. Walter E. Massey, Ph.D., a physicist, did much to bring the sceinces to both private industryies and schools.

8. These bootes are woven with a special material that keeps your foots warm.

9. Three sharp buzzs startled the workers who were eating their lunchs in the lounge.

10. Each of the runner-ups uneasyly shifted from one foot to the other as she awaited the announcment.

HELP—

No proper nouns or foreign words in Review C are misspelled.

MECHANICS

─HELP─

Generally, you should not spell out some numbers and use numerals for others in the same context. Be consistent by using numerals to express all of the numbers.

INCONSISTENT
Shakespeare wrote thirty-seven plays and 154 sonnets.

CONSISTENT
Shakespeare wrote **37** plays and **154** sonnets.

However, to distinguish between numbers that appear beside each other but that count different things, spell out one number, and use numerals for the other.

EXAMPLE
I need to buy **ten 34**-cent stamps.

Writing Numbers

15l. Spell out a *cardinal number*—a number that shows how many—if it can be expressed in one or two words. Otherwise, use numerals.

EXAMPLES

seven juniors	**203** juniors
fifty-one votes	**421** votes
one thousand miles	**1,242** miles

15m. Spell out a number that begins a sentence.

EXAMPLES   **Eighty-eight** senators voted in favor of the bill.

                    Three hundred thirty-two wreaths were sold.

If the number appears awkward when spelled out, revise the sentence so that it does not begin with the number.

AWKWARD   Two thousand five hundred sixty-four pounds is the combined weight of those sumo wrestlers.

IMPROVED   The combined weight of those sumo wrestlers is **2,564** pounds.

15n. Spell out *ordinal numbers*—numbers that express order.

EXAMPLES   Thurgood Marshall was the **first** [not *1st*] African American to serve on the U.S. Supreme Court.

                    The Rio Grande is the **twenty-second** [not *22nd*] longest river in the world.

15o. Use numerals to express numbers in conventional situations.

Conventional situations include

- identification numbers

EXAMPLES

Chapter **26**	pages **41–54**
Interstate **20**	lines **10–14**
Act **5**	Channel **8**

- measurements/statistics

EXAMPLES

98.6 degrees	**42** years old
14.3 ounces	**4 1/2** feet
8 percent	ratio of **5** to **1**

┌STYLE   TIP┐

In sentences, spell out the names of units of measurement (such as *ounces* and *feet*) whether they stand alone or follow numerals or spelled-out numbers. In charts and tables, however, you may use the abbreviations for units of measurement (such as *oz* and *ft*) when they follow numerals.

- addresses

EXAMPLE   **512** Willow Drive
Arrowhead, DE **34322-0422**

- dates

EXAMPLES   July **7, 1999**   **44** B.C.   A.D. **145**

- times of day

EXAMPLES   **6:20** P.M.   **8:00** A.M.

NOTE   Spell out a number used with *o'clock*.

EXAMPLE   **nine** o'clock

Exercise 5   **Proofreading for Spelling Errors**

Proofread the following sentences, and correct each misspelled or incorrectly written numerical expression.

EXAMPLE   1.   50 dollars for a pair of socks—let's get out of here!
          1.   *50—Fifty*

1. Not all Viking funerals involved burning a ship; a 30-foot vessel replete with thirty-two shields has been found buried in Norway.
2. Take State Road Seventeen straight down to Arcadia, and you'll be there by three P.M.
3. Pearls are weighed by grains, with 128,000 grains (that's about fourteen pounds) belonging to the heaviest pearl, which happened to be produced by an abalone.
4. I am not sure, but I think that Sergio and I are the 19th and 20th players to register.
5. The honor of being the 1st African American novelist belongs to William Wells Brown, whose novel *Clotel* was published in 1853.
6. Mom, for the third time in 2 days, Channel thirty-eight isn't coming in again.
7. On the Fahrenheit scale, two hundred twelve degrees is the boiling point of water; this temperature equals one hundred degrees on the Celsius scale.
8. On page twelve, you'll find a map of what the Bering Land Bridge might have looked like at that time.
9. Meet us at 10 o'clock Saturday morning at 459 Keeshond Drive.
10. 1 was delivered yesterday; the other 3 should be here tomorrow.

STYLE TIP

Do not use *A.M.* or *P.M.* with a spelled-out number or as a substitute for the word *morning, afternoon,* or *evening.*

EXAMPLES
Soccer practice begins at **4:00 P.M.**

Come home at **four o'clock in the afternoon.**

We'll go fishing early in the **morning.**

Reference Note

For information about **hyphenating numbers,** see page 353.

STYLE TIP

For large round numbers, you may use words or a combination of words and numerals.

EXAMPLES
13,700,000 people *or*
13.7 million people

MECHANICS

Review D Proofreading a Paragraph for Spelling Errors

Proofread the following paragraph, and correct each misspelled word or incorrectly written numerical expression.

EXAMPLE **[1]** What is the 1st thing that comes to mind when you hear the name Hermann Rorschach?

1. 1st—first

[1] Does this inkblot remind you of monkies? [2] Maybe you see faces and bodys of several people and animals, some faceing toward you and others facing in different directions. [3] Then again, maybe four geese chasing a dozen mice down Interstate Four is the image that comes to your mind as you gaze at the shapes in this inkblot. [4] To psychiatrists and psychologists who have taken special class's, the pictures that you imagine are really images of your own mind. [5] 1 of ten standard inkblots, this design is part of a special psychological test devised by Hermann Rorschach. [6] Although Rorschach was not the 1st to study inkblots and the imagination, his inkblots are one of the most famous methods of gaining insights into people's minds. [7] As you might suspect, a group of five-years-olds will see very different images in these inkblots than a group of adults will. [8] By having a person describe what he or she saw in each inkblot, Rorschach was able to infer a great deal about that person's fears, beliefes, desires, and hopes. [9] For example, what does it mean if you see seven tacos playing banjos made of white potatos, waltzing with two walruses on loaves of bread? [10] Maybe you're hungry, or maybe you feel like danceing and it's time to put on your tap shoe's.

Words Often Confused

You can prevent many spelling errors by learning the difference between the words grouped together in this section. Some of them are confusing because they are *homonyms*—that is, they are pronounced alike. Others are confusing because they are spelled the same or nearly the same.

Reference Note

If there is a word you cannot find in the list of words often confused, refer to the **Glossary of Usage** in Chapter 11, or look up the word in a dictionary.

all ready	[adjective] *all prepared* The players were *all ready* for the game.
already	[adverb] *previously* Jenna has *already* studied that chapter.
all right	[adjective] *satisfactory;* [adverb] *satisfactorily* The text was difficult, but Sam's translation was *all right.* I think I did *all right* on the quiz. [Although the spelling *alright* appears in some dictionaries, it has not become standard usage.]
all together	[adjective] *in the same place;* [adverb] *at the same time* My family will be *all together* for Thanksgiving. Please sing *all together* now.
altogether	[adverb] *entirely* Ms. Shapiro is *altogether* in favor of having a referendum.
altar	[noun] *a table or stand at which religious rites are performed* This is the *altar* used in the Communion service.
alter	[verb] *to change* Do not *alter* your plans on my account.
ascent	[noun] *a rise; a climb* The climbers' *ascent* was a slow one.
assent	[verb] *to agree;* [noun] *consent* Will they *assent* to our proposal? Our last proposal won their *assent.*
born	[verb form] *given life* Ynes Mexia was *born* in Washington, D.C.
borne	[verb form] *carried; endured* They have *borne* their troubles better than we thought they would.

(continued)

MECHANICS

(continued)

brake	[verb] *to stop or slow down;* [noun] *a device for stopping or slowing down* He *braked* and swerved to avoid hitting the child. An automobile *brake* will overheat if used too often.
break	[verb] *to cause to come apart; to shatter;* [noun] *a fracture* If you're not careful, you'll *break* the mirror. The *break* in the bone will heal in six weeks.
capital	[noun] *a city that is the seat of government of a country or state; money or property;* [adjective] *punishable by death; an uppercase letter; important, serious* Manila is the *capital* of the Philippines. The company has *capital* of $100,000. *Capital* punishment was the subject of the debate. A proper noun begins with a *capital* letter. That is an issue of *capital* concern.
capitol	[noun] *building in which a legislature meets* [capitalized when it refers to the building where the U.S. Congress meets] The *capitol* in Austin is a tourist attraction. Meet us in front of the *Capitol* in Washington, D.C.
clothes	[noun] *apparel* I'd like to buy some summer *clothes*.
cloths	[noun] *pieces of fabric* Please use these *cloths* to clean the car.

—HELP—

To remember the spelling of *capitol,* use this sentence: The capit**o**l has a d**o**me.

MECHANICS

Exercise 6 **Distinguishing Between Words Often Confused**

From the choices in parentheses, select the correct word or words for each of the following sentences.

EXAMPLE   1. My sister Lela was (*born, borne*) on March 5, 1985.

     1. born

1. Your arguments are not (*all together, altogether*) convincing.
2. We have finished packing and are (*all ready, already*) to go.
3. Saying nothing, the major gave a nod of (*ascent, assent*).
4. At night, Tokyo, the (*capital, capitol*) of Japan, is filled with vivid neon lights advertising all sorts of shops, clubs, and products.

5. The little boy was scared but otherwise (*all right, alright*).
6. Slow down! Please keep your foot on the (*brake, break*).
7. The expenditures will be (*born, borne*) by the taxpayers.
8. Seminole jackets are made from long, narrow strips of different-colored (*cloths, clothes*) carefully sewn together to make one garment.
9. The new dam will (*altar, alter*) the course of the river.
10. The governor said the roof of the (*capital, capitol*) needs repair.

coarse	[adjective] *rough, crude* The driveway was covered with *coarse* sand. His *coarse* language and manners prevented him from getting the job.
course	[noun] *path of action, passage, or way; study or group of studies; part of a meal* [also used with *of* to mean *naturally* or *certainly*] What *course* do you think I should follow? The *course* in world history lasts a full year. My favorite main *course* is bolichi. Of *course*, you may go with us.
complement	[noun] *something that makes whole or complete;* [verb] *to make whole or complete* The diagram shows that the angle *WXY* is the *complement* of the angle *YXZ*. A good shortstop would *complement* the team.
compliment	[noun] *praise; respect;* [verb] *to express praise or respect* The performer was pleased and flattered by the critic's *compliments*. Did the critics *compliment* all of the other performers, too?
consul	[noun] *a person appointed by a government to serve its citizens in a foreign country* The Israeli *consul* held a press conference to pledge his support for the peace talks.
council	[noun] *a group assembled for conferences or legislation* The student *council* meets this afternoon.
counsel	[noun] *advice;* [verb] *to advise* Shandra sought *counsel* from Mr. Nakai. Mr. Nakai *counseled* her to apply for the scholarship.

(continued)

—HELP—

To remember the spelling of *complement,* keep in mind that a complement completes.

MECHANICS

(continued)

councilor	[noun] *a member of a council* The city *councilors* met together for several hours but could not agree.
counselor	[noun] *one who gives advice* Shandra's guidance *counselor* helped her complete the application.
desert	[noun, pronounced des'•ert] *a dry region* Irrigation has brought new life to the *desert*.
desert	[verb, pronounced de•sert'] *to leave or abandon* A good soldier never *deserts* his or her post.
dessert	[noun, pronounced des•sert'] *a sweet, final course of a meal* My favorite *dessert* is frozen yogurt with strawberries on top.
formally	[adverb] *in a strict or dignified manner* Mayor Pérez will *formally* open the new recreation center on Wednesday.
formerly	[adverb] *previously* Mrs. Ling was *formerly* the head of the math department at Leland High School.
ingenious	[adjective] *clever, resourceful, skillful* Carla has an *ingenious* plan to earn some money this summer.
ingenuous	[adjective] *innocent, trusting, frank* Ian is as *ingenuous* as a five-year-old child.
its	[possessive form of the pronoun *it*] *belonging to it* Our city must increase *its* water supply.
it's	[contraction of *it is* or *it has*] *It's* almost time for the bell to ring. *It's* been nice talking to you.
later	[adjective] *more late;* [adverb] *at a subsequent time* I wasn't on time, but you were even *later*. I'll see you *later*.
latter	[adjective] *the second of two* (as opposed to *former*) Dr. Edwards can see you in the morning or the afternoon, but the *latter* time is more convenient for her.

MECHANICS

lead	[verb, pronounced "leed"] *to go first; to guide*
	Who will *lead* the discussion group?
led	[verb, past tense of *lead*]
	Elaine *led* the band onto the field.
lead	[noun, pronounced "led"] *a heavy metal; graphite in a pencil*
	The mechanic used small weights made of *lead* to balance the wheel.
	My pencil *lead* broke during the test.

Exercise 7 **Distinguishing Between Words Often Confused**

For each of the following sentences, select the correct word from the pair in parentheses.

EXAMPLE
1. Are you taking a (*coarse, course*) in computer programming?

1. *course*

1. Court is (*formally, formerly*) opened with a bailiff's cry of "Oyez, Oyez!"
2. When her painting was displayed in the museum, the artist received many (*complements, compliments*).
3. After dinner, my new stepfather sometimes says, "What's next—(*desert, dessert*) or (*desert, dessert*) the table?"
4. The development of synthetic fibers must have required an (*ingenious, ingenuous*) mind.
5. I enjoy both chicken and fish but prefer the (*later, latter*).
6. One of the guidance (*councilors, counselors*) (*lead, led*) me to information on a new (*coarse, course*) of study.
7. Do you find the texture rather (*coarse, course*)?
8. Ebenezer D. Basset, the first African American diplomat, was appointed minister to Haiti by President Grant; Basset later served as Haiti's (*consul, council*) general.

I'M SORRY, DID I SAY "DESERT"? I MEANT "DESSERT" TRAY.

9. Do you know the song "(*Its, It's*) Later Than You Think"?

10. The stark simplicity of the sand painting forms a perfect (*complement, compliment*) to its complex spiritual meaning.

loose	[adjective, rhymes with *noose*] *not firmly fastened; not tight* The front wheel on your bike is *loose*. Clothes with a *loose* fit are stylish now.
lose	[verb, rhymes with *shoes*] *to suffer loss* The trees will *lose* their leaves soon.
miner	[noun] *a worker in a mine* American *miners* lead the world in the production of coal.
minor	[noun] *a person under legal age;* [adjective] *of small importance* (as opposed to *major*) A *minor* is not permitted to sign the form. Let's not list any of the *minor* objections to the plan.
moral	[adjective] *good, virtuous;* [noun] *a lesson of conduct derived from a story or event* Good conduct is based upon *moral* principles. The *moral* of this old folk tale is "Be true to yourself."
morale	[noun] *spirit; mental condition* Teamwork is impossible without good *morale*.
passed	[verb, past tense of *pass*] *went by* The deadline for applications *passed* already.
past	[adjective] *ended;* [noun] *time gone by;* [preposition] *farther than, beyond* This *past* week has been a nightmare. History is the study of the *past*. We walked *past* the bookstore.
peace	[noun] *calmness* (as opposed to *strife* or *war*) Disarmament is an important step toward *peace*.
piece	[noun] *a part of something;* [verb] *to assemble slowly* Four *pieces* of the puzzle are missing. The detective *pieced* the clues together.

TIPS & TRICKS

To remember the spelling of *piece,* use this sentence: I'd like a **pie**ce of **pie**.

personal	[adjective] *individual; private*
	My *personal* opinion has nothing to do with the case.
	Do you truly feel that details of the candidates' *personal* lives should be made public?
personnel	[noun] *a group of people employed in the same work or service*
	Most companies prefer to recruit executive *personnel* from among college graduates.
plain	[adjective] *not fancy, undecorated; clear;* [noun] *a large area of flat land*
	The new uniforms are *plain*, but quite attractive.
	Does my explanation make things *plain* to you?
	Many Western movies are set in the Great *Plains*.
plane	[noun] *a flat surface; a woodworking tool; an airplane*
	Some problems in physics deal with the mechanical advantage of an inclined *plane*.
	Use this *plane* to make the wood smooth.
	We watched the *plane* circle for its landing.
principal	[noun] *the head of a school;* [adjective] *main, most important*
	The *principal* will address the entire student body.
	Florida and California are our *principal* citrus-growing states.
principle	[noun] *a rule of conduct; a fact or a general truth*
	The *principle* of the Golden Rule is found in many religions.
	The author was trying to convey a *principle*.
quiet	[adjective] *still, silent*
	The library is usually a *quiet* place to study.
quite	[adverb] *completely; rather; very*
	Are you *quite* finished?
	We are *quite* proud of Angel's achievements.
rout	[noun] *a disorderly flight;* [verb] *to put to flight; to defeat overwhelmingly*
	What began as an orderly retreat ended as a *rout*.
	The coach predicts that his Bears will *rout* the Wildcats in the playoffs.
route	[noun] *a road; a way to go*
	This highway is the shortest *route*.

TIPS & TRICKS

To remember the spelling of *principal*, use this sentence: The princi**pal** is your **pal.**

MECHANICS

For each of the following sentences, select the correct word from the pair in parentheses.

EXAMPLE
1. Have you met Ms. Cordero, our new (*principal, principle*)?
   1. *principal*

1. The (*principal, principle*) duty of Surgeon General Antonia Novello was to safeguard the health of Americans.
2. In the recent (*passed, past*), automated methods of extracting ore have put thousands of (*miners, minors*) out of work.
3. Coral has a sign on her desk in the library: "(*Quiet, Quite*) please. Genius at work."
4. When Kurt's (*plain, plane*) failed to return, the (*moral, morale*) of his squadron sank to zero.
5. The accident that completely demolished the car was caused by a (*loose, lose*) cotter pin worth ten cents.
6. Follow the marked (*rout, route*), or you will surely (*loose, lose*) your way.
7. The (*principal, principle*) that underlies that company's choice of (*personal, personnel*) is "An educated person is usually willing to learn more."
8. The columnist described the game as a (*rout, route*) for our team.
9. To prevent infection, always apply first aid to (*miner, minor*) cuts.
10. For his contributions toward ending the first Arab-Israeli war, Dr. Ralph J. Bunche received the Nobel Prize for (*piece, peace*) in 1950.

MECHANICS

TIPS & TRICKS

To remember the spelling of *stationery*, use this sentence: You write a lett**er** on station**er**y.

stationary	[adjective] *in a fixed position* The new state power plant contains large *stationary* engines.
stationery	[noun] *writing paper* I save my best *stationery* for important letters.
straight	[adjective] *not crooked or curved; direct* Draw a *straight* line that connects points A and B.
strait	[noun] *channel connecting two large bodies of water;* [noun, usually plural] *difficulty; distress* The *Strait* of Gibraltar links the Atlantic Ocean and the Mediterranean Sea. His family helps him when he is in bad *straits*.

than	[conjunction, used for comparisons] Loretta is taller *than* I am.
then	[adverb] *at that time; next* We lived on Garden Street until last year; *then* we moved to our new house.
their	[possessive form of the pronoun *they*] *belonging* *to them* The singers are practicing *their* parts.
there	[adverb] *at that place;* [also an expletive, used to begin a sentence] The chorus director will be *there* soon. *There* will be two performances of the concert.
they're	[contraction of *they are*] *They're* presenting the concert next weekend.
theirs	[possessive form of the pronoun *they*] *something* *belonging to them* The fence separates our property from *theirs*.
there's	[contraction of *there is* or *there has*] *There's* one other way to solve the problem. *There's* been a change in the softball team's starting lineup.
to	[preposition; sign of the infinitive form of a verb] Let's go *to* the movies. After the rain, the birds began *to* sing.
too	[adverb] *more than enough; also* Is it *too* far to walk? You, *too,* are invited to the sports banquet.
two	[adjective] *one plus one;* [noun] *the number* *between one and three; a pair* They serve *two* flavors: vanilla and chocolate. *Two* of my favorite writers are Nadine Gordimer and Ntozake Shange.
waist	[noun] *the midsection of the body* These slacks are too tight at the *waist.*
waste	[noun] *useless spending; unused or useless material;* [verb] *to use foolishly* The movie last night was simply a *waste* of two hours of my time. Don't *waste* your money on movies like that.

(continued)

weather	[noun] *atmospheric conditions* We had good *weather* for the picnic.
whether	[conjunction indicating an alternative or doubt] I don't know *whether* Denzel will help us.
who's	[contraction of *who is* or *who has*] *Who's* [Who is] going to take the dog to the vet's office? *Who's* [Who has] been tutoring you?
whose	[possessive form of *who*] *belonging to whom* *Whose* earrings are these?
your	[possessive form of the pronoun *you*] *belonging to you* Is *your* sister still in college?
you're	[contraction of *you are*] If *you're* not busy, let's discuss the assignment.

Exercise 9 · Distinguishing Between Words Often Confused

For each of the following sentences, select the correct word or words from the choices given in parentheses.

EXAMPLE   **1.** (*Who's, Whose*) golf clubs are these?

　　　　　　 1. *Whose*

1. (*Their, There*) Great Dane is even taller and heavier (*than, then*) (*your, you're*) Irish wolfhound.

2. Since the roof of the stadium is not (*stationary, stationery*), we can put it up or take it down as needed.

3. If the (*weather, whether*) isn't (*to, too, two*) awful, we will go (*to, too, two*) the game.

4. The women over (*there, their, they're*) are wearing *rebozos*, versatile shawls worn over the head, around the shoulders, or about the (*waist, waste*).

5. (*Who's, Whose*) planning to write a term paper about Ida Tarbell?

6. That is not (*your, you're*) car; (*who's, whose*) is it—(*there's, theirs*)?

7. I wonder how many tons of food are (*waisted, wasted*) every year in the United States.

8. What did (*your, you're*) family say when you told them about the scholarship (*your, you're*) going to get?

9. What styles of (*stationary, stationery*) did you order for the class pen-pal project?

10. Deep in the jungles of Cambodia lies a maze of (*straight, strait*) roads and canals that were part of the ancient Khmer capital of Angkor Thom.

Proofread the following paragraphs, and correct each misspelled or misused word. If a sentence is already correct, write *C*.

EXAMPLE [1] On my trip to Peru, I learned a great deal about the anceint Nazca people.

    1. *anceint—ancient*

[1] Last winter, as we flew over the Nazca Plains of Peru, I took photographs of the eighteen famous images that have puzzled archaeologists for years. [2] Excitement rippled through the aircraft as the dessert seemed to come alive with mysterious images like this one. [3] Although the group of figures covers two hundred square miles, each figure is made only of lose mounds of rocks and pebbles. [4] The dry whether in the region has preserved these fragile images for more than fifteen hundred years.

[5] Because many of the designs cannot be perceived from the ground, some people believe that the Nazca had aircraft, perhaps balloons or huge kites, capable of an assent to a thousand feet or more. [6] To test this hypothesis, one group of investigators actually

Nazca Plains

HELP

No proper nouns or proper adjectives in Review E are misspelled.

MECHANICS

constructed a crude hot-air balloon made of course vegetable fiber. [7] A violent gust threw the balloon and it's passengers to the ground before a strong wind carried them some three miles away.

[8] One of the more astounding theories about the designs is that the strait lines were landing strips for spaceships. [9] Other theorists wonder whether the flight routs of the birds represented by some of the patterns helped warn the Nazca of cold winds and rain. [10] Maria Reiche, an astronomer and mathematician who has studied the area, believes that the lines form an ingenuous calendar. [11] However, a computer analysis of lunar and solar patterns has lead other astronomers to doubt this theory.

[12] As our plane landed, we tourists were already for a closer look at these weird figures. [13] Early the next day, we met our tour guide in front of the hotel and boarded a small bus; than we headed for the Nazca lines.

[14] Our guide told us that parts of the fragile figures have all ready been ruined by car and foot traffic. [15] Following the consul of Maria Reiche, the Peruvian government no longer allows tourists to walk or drive over the area. [16] Consequently, we could view the figures only from an observation tower that had been built close too them. [17] Nevertheless, we were quiet impressed by the amount of planning and work that must have been required to create these fascinating lines.

[18] When our guide signaled us back to the bus, I picked up a stone and, for a moment, wondered whether I held a peace of history in my hand; then I carefully placed the stone back where I had found it. [19] Latter, I sat in my hotel room and thought about the Nazca and the unusual images they had made. [20] Who, I wondered, were these ancient people who's achievements continue to baffle modern science?

Chapter Review

A. Recognizing Misspelled Words

Correctly write the word in each group that is spelled incorrectly.

1. modifying, trodden, recieve
2. studios, disimilar, craftily
3. emptiness, handkerchiefs, desireable
4. journies, runners-up, freight
5. formaly, relief, illegible
6. surely, propeller, excede
7. alumna, iciness, managable
8. secede, indices, infered
9. precede, dareing, unforgettable
10. nineth, loneliness, adorable
11. gently, merryment, referral
12. kindlyness, adjustment, carefully
13. frayed, winning, dissappear
14. conceed, conceited, considered
15. rueful, augmented, earlyest

B. Proofreading a Paragraph for Spelling Errors

Correctly write each misspelled or incorrectly used word or numeral in the following paragraph.

[16] 150 people attended the program on San Francisco, and I'm sure no one was disappointed. [17] We learned many facts about the "City by the Bay" and discovered that it is an enchantting place. [18] In the 1st part of the program, the speaker showed slides of various landmarks, including the Golden Gate Bridge, Telegraph Hill, and The Palace of Fine Arts. [19] The size of Golden Gate Park surprised me; it covers more than 1,000 acres! [20] We also saw many photoes of the city's famous cable cars and of Lombard Street. [21] I could understand why Lombard Street is called the Crookeddest Street in the World! [22] Everyone enjoied seeing pictures of San Francisco's colorful Chinatown, as well. [23] Finally, the speaker told us about Union Square, a famous shopping area, and said that shoppers would not be

disatisfied there. [24] I would like time to explore the city's sights and sounds at my liesure. [25] Because of the presentation, my previous travel desires have been superceded by a longing to go to San Francisco.

C. Forming the Plural Forms of Words

Write the correct plural form of each of the following words.

26. 1980
27. species
28. phenomenon
29. two-year-old
30. dictionary
31. Getty
32. president-elect
33. lynx
34. calf
35. Coronado
36. boxer
37. array
38. zero
39. goose
40. house

D. Distinguishing Between Words Often Confused

In each of the following sentences, write the correct word of the pair in parentheses.

41. The ancient Egyptians developed an (*ingenuous, ingenious*) method of irrigating crops.
42. "I have trouble remembering whether Abraham Lincoln was (*borne, born*) in Illinois or in Kentucky," William said.
43. "Both states are important in Lincoln's life, but he was born in the (*later, latter*) state," Mr. Gallegos said.
44. Many places are named for famous explorers, such as the (*Straight, Strait*) of Magellan, named after Ferdinand Magellan.
45. That ornate (*altar, alter*) was made by a Bavarian woodcarver.
46. Let's ask the team members if (*they're, their*) willing to participate in the highway cleanup project.
47. Congress must give its (*ascent, assent*) before a bill can become a law.
48. Which (*rout, route*) to the stadium has fewer traffic lights?
49. The trail to the ruins is longer (*than, then*) it looks.
50. "I don't buy much (*stationary, stationery*) now that I use e-mail," Mandy said.

Writing Application

Using Correct Spelling in a Paragraph

Words Often Confused   Write a paragraph about your favorite CD or television show. Be sure to use correctly at least five of the words that are listed in this chapter as Words Often Confused.

Prewriting   Pick a favorite CD or television show and make a list of the reasons you prefer it over other music or shows. If you decide to write about a television show, for example, you may want to compare it to a similar television show.

Writing   As you write your first draft, be sure to include information about the CD or television show, such as who wrote the music or the show, who directed or produced it, or who performed the music or acted on the program. Remember to use a dictionary to help with correct spelling.

Revising   As you read your draft, make sure you have used enough details to support your reasons. Check the organization of your comparisons. Are they in a clear and logical order?

Publishing   Check your paragraph for spelling mistakes. Use a computer spellchecker, if one is available, but remember that spellcheckers will not recognize a misused word (for example, *principle* for *principal*), as opposed to a misspelled word. Also, pay attention to the spelling of foreign words, and consult a dictionary if you have any doubt. Exchange your report with a partner, and check each other's spelling. Read your report aloud to the class and compare each other's favorite CDs and television shows.

300 Spelling Words

The following list contains three hundred commonly misspelled words. To master any words that give you difficulty, follow the procedure given at the beginning of this chapter.

MECHANICS

accidentally
accommodate
accurate
acknowledgment *or*
    acknowledgement
acquaintance
across
aerial
aisle
all right
always
amateur
analyze
announce
anonymous
apologize
appearance
appreciate
approaching
appropriate
approval
arctic
argument
arrangement
assassinate
association
athletics
atomic
attach
attention
attitude
auxiliary
awful
awkward

bachelor
background

banana
bargain
beggar
beginning
believe
benefited
bicycle
biscuit
bookkeeper
bracelet
breathe
bruise
bulletin
bureau
business

calendar
campaign
candidate
catastrophe
cellophane
cemetery
ceremony
challenge
chaperon *or*
    chaperone
classroom
college
colonel
colossal
column
commission
committee
comparatively
compel
competition
completely

complexion
concentrate
conscience
conscientious
contemptible
convenience
copies
cordially
corps
correspondence
corroborate
courageous
courteous
criticism
criticize
cylinder

decide
decision
defense
definitely
dependent
descendant
descent
description
desirable
develop
dictionary
different
dining
dinosaur
disappear
disappoint
discipline
discuss
disease
dissatisfied

divided
doesn't

economical
efficient
eighth
elementary
eligible
embarrass
emphasize
endeavor
environment
equipment
especially
etiquette
exaggerate
excellent
excitement
exercise
exhausted
existence
expense
experienced
extraordinary

familiar
fascinating
fatigue
February
feminine
fiery
financial
foreign
forfeit
fourth
fragile

generally

genius
government
governor
grammar
grateful
guarantee
guard
gymnasium

handkerchief
happened
harass
haven't
height
heroes
hindrance
hoping
horizon
hospital
humorous

imitation
immediately
incident
inconvenience
indispensable
inevitable
influence
initial
interpreted
interrupted
irrelevant
irresistible

jewelry

laboratory
leisure
license
lightning
likelihood
literacy
loneliness
losing

luxurious

maintenance
maneuver
marriage
matinee *or*
    matinée
meant
medicine
medieval
mentioned
microphone
minimum
mischievous
missile
misspelled
movable *or*
    moveable
municipal

necessary
neighbors
nickel
ninety
ninth
nonsense
noticeable
nuclear
nuisance

occasionally
occur
occurred
omitted
opinion
opportunity
optimistic

pamphlet
parallel
parliament
particularly
pastime
permanent

permissible
perseverance
personally
personnel
perspiration
persuade
playwright
pleasant
pneumonia
possess
possibility
potato
practice
preference
prejudice
privilege
probably
procedure
professor
pronunciation
propaganda
propeller
prophecy
psychology
pursue

questionnaire

realize
receive
recognize
recommend
referral
rehearse
reign
relief
repetition
representative
restaurant
rhythm

satisfactorily
schedule
scissors

seize
semester
separate
sergeant
shiny
siege
similar
sincerely
souvenir
straight
strategy
subtle
successful
sufficient
suppress
surprised
suspension
syllable
sympathy
synonym

tariff
television
temperament
temperature
thoroughly
tomorrow
tournament
traffic
tragedy
transferred
twelfth
tyranny

undoubtedly
unforgettable
unfortunately
unnecessary

vacuum
valuable
villain

weird

16 | Correcting Common Errors

Key Language Skills Review

This chapter reviews key skills and concepts that pose special problems for writers.

- **Sentence Fragments and Run-on Sentences**
- **Subject-Verb and Pronoun-Antecedent Agreement**
- **Clear Pronoun Reference**
- **Verb Forms**
- **Comparison of Modifiers**
- **Misplaced and Dangling Modifiers**
- **Standard Usage**
- **Capitalization**
- **Punctuation—End Marks, Commas, Semicolons, Colons, Quotation Marks, and Apostrophes**
- **Spelling**

Most of the exercises in this chapter follow the same format as the exercises found throughout the grammar, usage, and mechanics sections of this book. You will notice, however, that two sets of review exercises are presented in standardized test formats. These exercises are designed to provide you with practice not only in solving usage and mechanics problems but also in dealing with such problems on standardized tests.

HELP

Remember that all of the exercises in Chapter 16 are testing your knowledge of the rules of **standard, formal English.** These are the rules you should follow in your schoolwork.

Reference Note

For information on **standard** and **nonstandard English** and **formal** and **informal English,** see page 241.

Exercise 1 Identifying and Revising Sentence Fragments

Decide which of the following word groups are sentences and which are sentence fragments. If an item contains a sentence fragment, revise the fragment to make it a complete sentence. If it contains a complete sentence, write *C*.

EXAMPLE   **1.** While she was preparing the score for the video.

1. *While she was preparing the score for the video, they shot the scenes.*

1. Consider this.
2. Such as monarchies, aristocracies, oligarchies, and democracies.
3. The first to exploit the assembly line's potential for profit.
4. However, this boy who stammered became one of the great actors of our time—James Earl Jones.
5. Twisting thousands of strips of crepe paper into flowers.
6. In an antique tin box inside a trunk buried under a dozen boxes.
7. To attend the display of archaeological artifacts at the museum.
8. He, not I, would carry the project to its completion.
9. Subsequently, produced some of the finest ceramic pieces ever created in North America.
10. Eventually finished the house and made plans for a deck.

Exercise 2 Identifying and Revising Run-on Sentences

Most of the following items are run-on sentences. Revise each run-on sentence to make at least one complete sentence. Add or delete words wherever necessary. Be sure to check your revised version for correct capitalization and punctuation. If a sentence is already correct, write *C*.

EXAMPLE   **1.** Time travel may be theoretically possible it does pose some practical difficulties.

1. *Time travel may be theoretically possible; however, it does pose some practical difficulties.*

or

Although time travel may be theoretically possible, it does pose some practical difficulties.

1. Fortunately, the program will run under your operating system, you will need a software patch first.

Reference Note

For information on **sentence fragments,** see pages 31 and 446.

HELP

Although the example in Exercise 2 shows two possible revisions, you need to give only one for each item.

Reference Note

For information on **run-on sentences,** see page 451.

COMMON ERRORS

2. Those small bumps on the elevator's control panel are Braille letters, after all, people who are visually impaired need to use the elevators, too.

3. For two years, Ron had been working on the old jalopy, now it was finally ready for a test drive.

4. Even simple household repairs can be expensive publishers do a brisk business in do-it-yourself books.

5. Squirrels played tag among the branches, we watched from our upstairs window.

6. You should have some fun with math look at factoring as play.

7. We were unfamiliar with the customs of our neighbors from India, so they explained some of their traditions to us.

8. These birds above us, however, are on their way to Mexico spring will bring them back again.

9. Low-flying planes over Bristol Bay frightened the walruses the Marine Mammal Protection Act now forbids such flights.

10. Finding my little sister's runaway lizard in the house is easy capturing him is the hard part.

Exercise 3   **Revising Sentence Fragments and Run-on Sentences**

Reference Note

For information on **sentence fragments,** see pages 31 and 446. For information about **run-on sentences,** see page 451.

Each of the following items contains a sentence fragment or a run-on sentence. Revise each item to correct the sentence fragment or run-on sentence. Be sure to check your revisions for correct capitalization and punctuation.

EXAMPLE   1. Musicians, clowns, mimes, and a juggler entertained the crowd at the carnival. Which began on my birthday.

      1. *Musicians, clowns, mimes, and a juggler entertained the crowd at the carnival, which began on my birthday.*

1. To protect the seedlings from the damaging effects of the summer sun. We shaded the young plants in a makeshift greenhouse.

2. Many prospectors were deceived by the glittering mineral pyrite. Which became known as fool's gold.

3. Next door, a new building was under construction consequently, trucks and construction materials covered much of the parking lot.

4. The children sat on the floor. And laughed at the kittens playing with a ball of yarn that had tumbled down from Mother's lap.

5. After he worked on my computer. The technician assured me that it would work more efficiently.
6. The Chippewa mastered the art of harvesting birch bark, properly stripped trees do not die.
7. Sara gave her updated photography portfolio to Mrs. Strunz. Her photojournalism professor.
8. The baseball coach said he thought I would make the team next year he intends to train some students over the summer.
9. As in agricultural communities everywhere. The cycle of the seasons governs much of life in rural Africa.
10. Uncle Joseph's favorite class in high school was creative writing, no wonder he's chosen writing as his profession!

Exercise 4 **Revising Sentence Fragments and Run-on Sentences**

The following paragraphs contain sentence fragments and run-on sentences. Revise the sentence fragments and run-on sentences, changing the punctuation and capitalization as necessary to make each sentence clear and complete.

EXAMPLE   [1] Pablo Picasso was born in Spain in 1881, he moved to France in 1904.

    1. *Pablo Picasso was born in Spain in 1881. He moved to France in 1904.*

[1] Generally recognized as one of the greatest painters of the twentieth century. [2] Picasso stands among the masters of art, his work reveals the full range of human emotion. [3] From the calm restraint of his line drawings to the harsh drama of *Guernica.* [4] Picasso's work encompasses many of the artistic trends of the century he is perhaps best known for his abstract, neoclassical, and cubist works.

[5] Always moving ahead, never settling on any one style. [6] Picasso created in various mediums, not just paint, these include ceramics, sculpture, and engraving, he also developed a new collage technique with Georges Braque. [7] Whose fame partly rests on the famous collages that emerged from this period.

[8] Reflecting the confusion and fragmentation of life in the modern world. [9] Picasso's cubist works offer viewers multiple viewpoints on people and objects, indeed, these works cannot be fully appreciated from only one perspective. [10] Picasso teaches us to "see," he challenges us to look at the world from many vantage points.

Reference Note

For information on **sentence fragments,** see pages 31 and 446. For information on **run-on sentences,** see page 451.

COMMON ERRORS

Reference Note

For information on **subject-verb agreement,** see page 96.

For each of the following sentences, choose the correct form of the verb in parentheses.

EXAMPLE
1. Two thousand years (*is, are*) a long time for a tool to resist improvement, yet the blacksmith's anvil has retained the same general shape all that time.

1. *is*

1. Since ancient times, blacksmiths (*has, have*) provided a valuable service to people all over the world.
2. In the past, all necessary nails, pliers, and shears (*was, were*) made by blacksmiths.
3. By the mid-1800s, U.S. factories (*was, were*) producing such items; hence, blacksmiths made their livings more by servicing than by producing these and other items made of iron.
4. Nevertheless, blacksmiths throughout the country (*has, have*) continued to produce many types of ironwork.
5. Travelers in the South often (*notice, notices*) the elegant ironwork decorating architecture there.
6. In South Carolina many of the homes and historical buildings (*feature, features*) the work of several generations of African American blacksmiths.
7. Similarly, New Orleans (*is, are*) filled with impressive grillwork.
8. Today, one of the best-known smiths is Philip Simmons, who (*has, have*) been named a National Heritage Fellow.
9. The animal shapes in his ironwork (*is, are*) a prominent feature.
10. The news of Simmons's selection by the National Endowment for the Arts (*was, were*) welcomed by those who knew his work.

Exercise 6 **Proofreading for Subject-Verb Agreement**

Most of the following sentences contain an error in subject-verb agreement. Identify each incorrect verb, and write the correct form. If a sentence is already correct, write *C.*

EXAMPLE
1. Anyone who eats in the presence of others are well-advised to learn the local etiquette.

1. *are—is*

1. Most of the following dining guidelines is simply common courtesy in our country.

Reference Note

For information on **subject-verb agreement,** see page 96.

COMMON ERRORS

2. A thoughtful host always try to seat guests with similar interests near one another.

3. After sitting down, guests places their napkins on their laps to protect their clothing.

4. During the meal both men and women avoids placing their elbows on the table.

5. They eat bread in a polite manner, breaking off bite-sized pieces one at a time.

6. Neither a gentleman nor a lady drink from his or her bowl or saucer.

7. Generally speaking, the rules of proper etiquette dictates that only someone expecting an urgent call should wear a pager at a party.

8. Aren't the ringing of mobile phones also likely to disturb the people at the table?

9. A woman who put on makeup at the dinner table is not following proper etiquette.

10. Following rules of dining etiquette are one way to show respect for others.

Exercise 7 Proofreading for Subject-Verb Agreement

Most of the following sentences contain an error in subject-verb agreement. Identify each incorrect verb, and write the correct form. If a sentence is already correct, write *C*.

Reference Note

For information on **subject-verb agreement,** see page 96.

EXAMPLE   1. Genetics have become an active area of medical research.

        1. *have—has*

1. Solutions to any problem is usually the result of serious reflection and action.

2. Many a child around here imagine the lives of the Pueblos of long ago.

3. Don't she know the address of the new florist?

4. There before them stand the awesome sight of Angel Falls.

5. Have the news been on yet, Alexandra?

6. Either Mrs. Jordan or the Wright twins visits the nursing home on the weekend.

7. *Green Mansions* is the only movie on tonight.

8. Here's the answers to that crossword puzzle.

9. That's right—the band playing the best salsa tunes receive a recording contract!

10. Are Jackson's Sporting Goods still having that sale on backpacks?

COMMON ERRORS

Reference Note

For information on **pronoun-antecedent agreement,** see page 111.

Exercise 8 **Supplying Pronouns That Agree with Their Antecedents**

Complete each of the following sentences by supplying at least one pronoun that agrees with its antecedent. Use standard, formal English.

EXAMPLE   1. Everyone in the class will do _____ part to make the play a success.

      1. *his or her*

1. Cindy has the best plan for the castle, so _____ will supervise the construction of the set.
2. Melissa or Elena has offered _____ time on Tuesday afternoon to call several companies about donating the cardboard.
3. If Kyle and Larry can borrow a van, _____ will bring the cardboard to school.
4. Both of the twins are artists, so _____ will draw architectural details.
5. One of the boys will bring _____ keyboard and play the background music.
6. Each of my sisters has volunteered to bring _____ video equipment to tape the play.
7. Several members of the industrial arts class will contribute _____ time to build a castle on the stage.
8. Mr. Faust is a tailor, and _____ has offered to let us use his sewing machines to create costumes.
9. If someone doesn't have an assignment, _____ will need to see me.
10. Anybody who can supply paint should talk to _____ team leader.

Reference Note

For information on **pronoun-antecedent agreement,** see page 111.

Exercise 9 **Proofreading for Pronoun-Antecedent Agreement**

Most of the following sentences contain an error in pronoun-antecedent agreement. Identify each incorrect pronoun, and supply the correct pronoun form. If the sentence is already correct, write *C*.

EXAMPLE   1. Do you know the tale of William Tell and their crossbow?

      1. *their—his*

1. The bow, together with the arrows it shoots, has made their mark on history.
2. People in Asia and Europe used the bow, just as people in Africa and the Americas used them.
3. Many American Indians armed themselves with bows and arrows to obtain food and to defend themselves.

4. The reputations of the conquerors Genghis Khan and Attila the Hun were based largely on his troops' skill with bows.

5. European history is full of stories about famous archers and his or her exploits, including tales of Robin Hood.

6. Of Robin Hood's men, was Friar Tuck or Little John more famous for their skill with a bow?

7. Today, archery is practiced around the world, and an archer can choose their bow from among many styles.

8. In Japan the art of archery attracts students who consider it a form of meditation.

9. One of the twentieth century's greatest female archers was Janina Spychajowa-Kurkowska from Poland; in the 1930s and 1940s, they won seven world titles.

10. If anyone has an interest in this sport, they should contact local schools that offer archery classes.

Exercise 10 Proofreading for Subject-Verb and Pronoun-Antecedent Agreement

Most of the following sentences contain at least one error in subject-verb agreement or pronoun-antecedent agreement. Identify and correct each error. If a sentence is already correct, write *C*.

EXAMPLE   [1] A goldsmith in the Ashanti Empire has a long and distinguished history behind them.

        1. *them—him*

[1] The Ashanti King Otumfuo Opoku Ware II has adorned himself with weighty golden ornaments for a celebration of its twenty-fifth year on the throne. [2] So important is this event that they have lasted a whole year. [3] Several men, perhaps bodyguards, look warily around; the sword bearers and they wear wondrous golden caps on their heads. [4] The king's advisors and ministers conducts himself with great solemnity. [5] One wealthy young woman has actually dusted their face with gold. [6] Her spouse and she will pass on the gold to their children. [7] Wives or princesses who are of the royal bloodline have merely borrowed her finery from the royal treasury. [8] Wearing lively *kente* cloth, some of the women dance; each of them can explain the meaning of every move she makes. [9] One woman draw particular attention; friends smile and admire the dancers and her. [10] None of the onlookers remains unimpressed by the festivities, and all of them will forever keep this moment in his or her memories.

Reference Note

For information on **subject-verb agreement**, see page 96. For information on **pronoun-antecedent agreement**, see page 111.

COMMON ERRORS

Reference Note

For information on **subject-verb agreement,** see page 96. For information on **pronoun-antecedent agreement,** see page 111.

Exercise 11 Proofreading for Subject-Verb Agreement and Pronoun-Antecedent Agreement

Rewrite each of the following sentences to correct any errors in subject-verb agreement and pronoun-antecedent agreement.

EXAMPLE   [1] Our club at school help elementary students.

1. Our club at school helps elementary students.

[1] Each Friday afternoon, we and our sponsor goes to Alcott Elementary, where we tutor younger students. [2] Either Mrs. de Salvo or Mr. Newman drive her or his van on the ride over. [3] The fifth-graders usually meets us high school students in the library. [4] All of the younger students enjoy seeing his or her tutors, and of course we look forward to seeing them. [5] Mathematics, especially fractions, are a problem for some of the students. [6] Karen or Elena usually teach that subject. [7] Mike is probably the most popular tutor; not one of the other tutors gets along better with the ten-year-olds than he does. [8] English is easy for me, so I usually takes the language arts students. [9] During the week, Mike and Elena often prepare a special activity, such as making mobiles or playing games, for his or her students. [10] Somebody in the group usually bring a snack for our break, and, to tell the truth, the break is the part we all like most—just talking, snacking, and laughing together.

Exercise 12 Selecting Correct Forms of Pronouns

Reference Note

For information on **using pronouns correctly,** see Chapter 6.

Choose the correct form of the pronoun in parentheses in each of the following sentences. Use standard, formal English.

EXAMPLE   1. Do you know (*who, whom*) your lab partner in chemistry class is?

1. *who*

1. The runoff election will be between Barbara and (*she, her*).
2. When ducklings hatch, they will follow (*whoever, whomever*) they see first.
3. By the time we arrived, the only ones left at the party were Joe, Stephen, and (*he, him*).
4. Please ask Nicole and (*she, her*) about the entrance fee.
5. Red Cloud, (*who, whom*) died in 1909, was a principal chief of the Oglala Sioux.
6. This new exercise program has been designed for people like (*me, myself*).

7. I never dreamed that the winner would be (*I, me*).

8. The museum director arranged a private tour for (*we, us*) art history students.

9. Samuel Clemens, (*who, whom*) readers know as Mark Twain, wrote works that from time to time become subjects of controversy.

10. Did Jason and (*you, yourself*) do all the computer programming for the project?

Reference Note

For information on **using pronouns correctly,** see Chapter 6.

Exercise 13 **Proofreading for Correct Pronoun Usage**

Most of the following sentences contain an error in pronoun usage. Identify and correct each error, using the rules of standard, formal English. If a sentence is already correct, write *C*.

EXAMPLE　1. Sean still corresponds with his former teachers, Mr. Finn and she.

　　　　　1. *she—her*

1. Even for native Spanish speakers like myself, translations are not always easy.

2. Actually, this is something that I'm doing for me.

3. I believe that Christy earned as much money as her.

4. No, him practicing the scales never bothers me.

5. Why don't we give Rhonda and they a going-away party?

6. Nobody, at least nobody I know, is more talented than him.

7. Who would have guessed that this year's candidates would be us two?

8. The oldest siblings in the family, Ted and me, usually help take care of the younger kids.

9. Surely you are familiar with the Marsalis family, many of whom are well known for their musical abilities.

10. Him making kites from scratch inspired Althea to do the same.

Exercise 14 **Revising Sentences by Correcting Faulty Pronoun References**

Most of the following sentences contain ambiguous, general, weak, or indefinite pronoun references. Revise each sentence that contains a faulty pronoun reference. If a sentence is already correct, write *C*.

EXAMPLE　1. Over the door, it read "No Admittance."

　　　　　1. *Over the door, a sign read "No Admittance."*

1. When foods are high in calories but low in nutrients, this leads to their being called junk foods.

2. When the limousine passed the bus, it swerved sharply to the right.

COMMON ERRORS

┌─HELP─

Although sentences in Exercise 14 can be corrected in more than one way, you need to give only one revision for each item.

Reference Note

For information on **clear pronoun reference,** see Chapter 7.

3. The fans began leaving the bleachers and heading toward their cars when it started raining harder.
4. In reports to the United Nations, they concentrated on regions that had suffered drought.
5. Karen talked to Eileen about her plans for college.
6. Bill enjoys shopping in secondhand clothing stores, where he often finds very nice ones.
7. Several inexperienced hikers were late returning to the trailhead, which worried the rangers.
8. On the notice, it does not give a specific time and place for the meeting.
9. The traffic on Highway 183 was brought to a crawl by the road construction; this is expected to continue until next fall.
10. Officials told members of the council that they did not need to attend the conference.

HELP

Although sentences in Exercise 15 can be corrected in more than one way, you need to give only one revision for each item.

Reference Note

For information on **clear pronoun reference,** see Chapter 7.

Exercise 15 **Revising Sentences by Correcting Faulty Pronoun References**

Most of the following sentences contain ambiguous, general, weak, or indefinite pronoun references. Revise each sentence that contains a faulty pronoun reference. If a sentence is already correct, write *C*.

EXAMPLE
1. Sergeant Wu taught Lisa fingerprinting techniques, and she will demonstrate them to our class.

1. *Sergeant Wu taught Lisa fingerprinting techniques, and Lisa will demonstrate them to our class.*

or

Sergeant Wu taught Lisa fingerprinting techniques and will demonstrate them to our class.

1. No two people ever have exactly the same fingerprints, which Sir Francis Galton discovered.
2. For instance, Marcie's fingerprints are different even from those of her identical twin.
3. Also, even as a person ages, they say all ten fingerprints will stay the same.
4. Sir Edward Henry, who later became the commissioner of Scotland Yard, analyzed the characteristics of fingerprints, and it has helped police the world over.
5. He noticed patterns such as arches and loops, which is how he created a system for filing and classifying fingerprints.

6. Although fingerprinting is common today, it has helped police solve crimes for only about a hundred years.

7. Today, police use fingerprints left at crime scenes to identify suspects—and they are not always easy to find.

8. In many detective stories, they tell of the clever techniques that criminals devise to avoid leaving fingerprints.

9. Mario asked Mr. Lincoln about a field trip to the police station; he said the whole class would enjoy it.

10. Mario's dad, who is on the police force, told us about fingerprints, and it was quite interesting.

Exercise 16 Using the Past and Past Participle Forms of Irregular Verbs

Give the correct form (past or past participle) of the irregular verb in parentheses in each of the following sentences.

EXAMPLE   1. Could a huge island like Atlantis have (*sink*) without a trace?

1. *sunk*

1. The mongoose (*strike*) the cobra.
2. A sudden gust had (*take*) the kite into the trees.
3. Resolutely, General MacArthur (*swear*) that he would return to the Philippines.
4. What an interesting essay you have (*write*)!
5. Dress gloves are rarely (*wear*) nowadays, even on formal occasions.
6. Holding her breath, Lawanda (*swim*) the entire length of the pool.
7. The tornado (*tear*) the roof off the shed.
8. Oh, yes, they have (*speak*) of you often.
9. Hey! These new jeans have (*shrink*)!
10. Because Prometheus had (*steal*) fire from the gods, he was savagely punished.

Exercise 17 Proofreading Sentences for the Correct Use of Irregular Verbs

Most of the following sentences contain an error in the use of irregular verbs. If a verb is incorrect, supply the correct form. If a sentence is already correct, write *C*.

EXAMPLE   1. The developers of Starbright World have maked a computer game especially for hospitalized children.

1. *made*

Reference Note

For information on **using irregular verbs correctly,** see page 164.

Reference Note

For information on **using irregular verbs correctly,** see page 164.

COMMON ERRORS

1. Starbright World, a sophisticated computer playground, has gave children who are in the hospital a chance to play together in a computerized wonderland.
2. The Starbright team has strove to create sophisticated input devices that can be operated by tiny movements—even by breaths of air.
3. Once inside the program, a child chooses a character and then controls that character's actions and interactions with others in the Starbright World.
4. As the Starbright project has progressed, it has growed.
5. Multiple virtual worlds becomed part of the plans.
6. Soon several major companies seen the potential of the project and made significant contributions.
7. In fact, some of the most imaginative people in the country, including Steven Spielberg, finded the project irresistible.
8. At one presentation, Spielberg speaked of creating virtual toy stores and team sports.
9. He also redesigned some of the carts that house the computers and made the carts look like fanciful toys.
10. By 1995, some children's hospitals had began testing the Starbright network.

Exercise 18 Proofreading Sentences for Correct Verb Forms

Give the correct form for each incorrect verb in the following sentences. If a sentence is already correct, write *C*.

EXAMPLE   1. Has anyone wrote a book about Africa's traditional fabrics?
            1. *written*

1. Clothing with traditional African colors and patterns has growed quite popular in the United States.
2. Have you ever buyed any garments made of raffia or cut-pile cloth?
3. For another type of African cloth, bark is cutted from trees and then soaked in water or steamed.
4. Later, the bark is beaten with a mallet.
5. Gradually, after the bark has been striked many times, the softened fibers mat together and become pliable material.
6. This material is knowed as bark cloth.

Reference Note

For information on **using verbs correctly,** see Chapter 8.

7. Other cloth is made on a loom, sometimes from thread that has been spun by hand.
8. After cloth has laid in dye baths for a time, it is removed and washed.
9. Many an African woman has holded her baby in a sling made from traditional African cloth.
10. Quite a few women in the United States have adopted this practice, and today, many babies in this country have rode in these slings.

Exercise 19 Proofreading a Paragraph for Consistent Verb Tenses

Decide whether the following paragraph should be written in present or past tense. Then, change the verbs to correct any unnecessary shifts in tense.

EXAMPLE   **[1]** Because it is a beautiful day, I wanted to be outside.

    1. *Because it is a beautiful day, I want to be outside.*

                                        or

        Because it was a beautiful day, I wanted to be outside.

[1] I am hanging laundry out to dry. [2] Our playful new puppy ran around in circles under the clothesline. [3] Too busy for games, I just ignored him and continue my work. [4] However, he won't take no for an answer and jumped up and bit the corner of a clean, white sheet. [5] Of course, I tell him to stop, but he has his mind made up. [6] He growls, shakes his shaggy head, and tears the sheet from the line. [7] Gleefully, he dragged the sheet through the yard. [8] He is really enjoying himself and evidently thinks that I am, too! [9] Angry, I chase him but accidentally step on the sheet and fall into the tangle of wet fabric. [10] Ecstatic, the puppy jumps on my stomach and licked my face.

Exercise 20 Proofreading Sentences for Correct Verb Tenses

Each of the following sentences contains an error in the use of tenses. Revise each sentence, using the correct verb form.

EXAMPLE   **1.** As technology changes, our pace of life has changed.

    1. *As technology has changed, our pace of life has changed.*

                                        or

        As technology changes, our pace of life changes.

╔HELP╗
Although the example in Exercise 19 gives two revisions, you need to give only one for each item.

Reference Note
For information on **verb tense,** see page 182.

╔HELP╗
Although the example in Exercise 20 gives two revisions, you need to give only one for each item.

Reference Note
For information on **using verb tenses correctly,** see page 182.

COMMON ERRORS

1. Did you restart the computer after you change the start-up file?
2. Although the Nakayamas left before noon, they didn't arrive until very late at night.
3. Carlos finished the book before Marcel started reading it.
4. Everyone applauded as the floats pass by.
5. If you would have done what I asked you to do, we would not have been in all that trouble.
6. We always remembered to wash the vegetables carefully before we cook them.
7. The House of Representatives is going to study the bill before the representatives are voting on it.
8. By the time I take the test tomorrow, I will surely memorize every date that appears in Chapter 13.
9. We would have made reservations if they would have told us about the convention.
10. Although his new car goes more than one hundred miles an hour, Mr. Reynolds never exceeded the speed limit.

Exercise 21 Proofreading Sentences for Correct Comparison

Most of the following sentences contain an error in comparison of modifiers. Revise each sentence that contains an error. If a sentence is already correct, write *C*.

EXAMPLE
1. Of all the cars on the market, which one runs more economically?

1. *Of all the cars on the market, which one runs most economically?*

1. My best friend sings better than anybody I know.
2. Which was more hard for you to learn, tennis or racquetball?
3. Too late, we discovered that we should have tied the boat most securely than we did.
4. Exercise sometimes makes an injury worse.
5. That dog can bark louder than any dog I've ever heard!
6. Please identify the modern city that is most closest to the site of the ancient city Pompeii.
7. Of all the varieties of trees that were damaged last winter, the orange trees were hurt worse.
8. Keisha and Tommie have promised that this year's prom will be the elegantest ever.
9. Of the two possibilities, Pat's is the best solution to the problem.

Reference Note

For information about **using comparative and superlative forms correctly,** see page 219. For information on **comparison within a group,** see page 220.

COMMON ERRORS

10. At that moment, the mountain climbers seemed to be the least fearfulest people on earth.

Exercise 22 **Proofreading Sentences for Correct Use of Modifiers**

Revise the following sentences by correcting errors in the use of modifiers.

EXAMPLE   **1.** Which do you like best to sleep under, a blanket or a quilt?

   1. Which do you like better to sleep under, a blanket or a quilt?

Reference Note

For information on **using modifiers correctly,** see Chapter 9.

1. On a cold night in January, you may find yourself searching for a more warmer blanket.

2. For many people an old quilt may be the better cover of any in the house.

3. To a quilter a seemingly worthless scrap of cotton may be worth more than any piece of cloth.

4. In fact, many quilts are made out of the inexpensivest materials that a person has at hand, such as strips of cloth salvaged from a family's old clothes.

5. These quilts are often more valuable than ordinary covers, for they may help recall the quilter's most fond memories.

6. The stitches in a quilt may be arranged as precise as the rows in an accountant's ledger.

7. The hand stitching of bygone days is sometimes replaced by efficienter machine-made stitches now.

8. With computer programs, designing quilts is now even more easier.

9. Some of the most beautifulest quilts hang in museums.

10. Harriet Powers sewed good, and one of her pictorial quilts hangs in the Smithsonian.

Exercise 23 **Proofreading for the Correct Use of Modifiers**

Most of the sentences in the following paragraph contain an error in the use of modifiers. Correct each error. If a sentence is already correct, write *C*.

EXAMPLE   **[1]** Few places in the world are more beautifuler than Cuba.

   1. more beautiful

Reference Note

For information on **using modifiers correctly,** see Chapter 9.

[1] Perhaps no Cuban has had as rich and varied a career as the Cuban writer José Martí. [2] Martí is most famous for his revolutionary politics than for his writing. [3] However, it is his writing that gives more deeper dimension to the man. [4] Without it, he would be just another revolutionary. [5] Martí took the formal style of a sermon, added the more angrier, colorful phrases of the street, and arrived at a persuasive appeal strong enough to spark a revolution. [6] Although that kind of prose power might be enough for anybody, it was not enough for Martí. [7] Worldly and well traveled, Martí knew that life itself is more important than politics. [8] Heart and soul matter, too, so he wrote stories for children as well as poetry that is more directer than flowery, romantic verse. [9] Martí was both a writer and revolutionary; his range was wider than almost any other person. [10] No one can say which life is better—that of a poet, a revolutionary, or a sociopolitical analyst; Martí was all of these.

Exercise 24 Proofreading Sentences for Misplaced Modifiers

The following sentences each contain an error in the placement of modifiers. Revise each sentence so that its meaning is clear and correct.

Reference Note

For information on **misplaced modifiers,** see page 230.

EXAMPLE   1. He dreamed of competing in the Olympics in the barn.

           1. *In the barn, he dreamed of competing in the Olympics.*

1. The snow was piled in deep drifts on the mountainside that had fallen in the night.
2. The community recreation center only will admit people with valid memberships.
3. The airline clerk told me that my flight would be boarding at 2:00 P.M. on the telephone.
4. The meteor shower was the most spectacular one I had ever seen that occurred last night.
5. After bucking off every rider, the ranch hands wearily sat on the fence as the mustang grazed peacefully.
6. The largest branch of the grapefruit tree touched the ground, which was heavy with fruit.
7. The general reported that three thousand troops were awaiting supplies during the briefing.
8. Only break glass in case of fire.
9. The firefighters quickly rescued the little boys with the tall ladder.
10. The scouts found several plants and vines in the woods that are poisonous.

Correcting Dangling Modifiers in Sentences

Most of the following sentences contain a dangling modifier. Revise each incorrect sentence so that its meaning is clear and correct. If a sentence is already correct, write *C*.

EXAMPLE   1. To play better, more practice is necessary.

1. *To play better, you need to practice more.*

1. Having studied all weekend, the test was easy.
2. While standing in the moonlight, hundreds of fireflies appeared.
3. After watching the eclipse for a while, its novelty waned.
4. When making arrangements for the play, access for people using wheelchairs should not be forgotten.
5. Traveling to stars light-years away, new life forms might be found.
6. After loading the lumber onto the flatbed, the truck drove away.
7. While replacing the battery in the smoke detector, the alarm went off.
8. To manage your finances, a budget will definitely be needed.
9. Dressed as if they were going to a fancy restaurant, the family sat down at their own dining table.
10. Having already seen the movie that was playing, a game of chess seemed more inviting.

Reference Note

For information about **dangling modifiers,** see page 232.

Exercise 26 **Identifying Correct Usage**

Choose the correct word or words in parentheses in each of the following sentences.

EXAMPLE   1. Wow! You're playing (*good, well*) today.

1. *well*

1. Ask for directions from (*those, them*) people over there, Dad.
2. (*Lay, Lie*) down and rest for a while, Samantha.
3. She (*done, did*) the first part, and then she got a phone call and left.
4. (*Let, Leave*) him have a turn at bat, Orson.
5. Is the home team playing very (*bad, badly*)?
6. Well, the joke was based on an (*illusion, allusion*) to *Don Quixote*.
7. Use a comma with (*these types, this type*) of expression.
8. You (*ought, had ought*) to give yourself a chance to like sushi.
9. Will similes, metaphors, (*etc., and etc.*) be covered on the test?
10. Yes, sir, (*this, this here*) old guitar was once played by the legendary Muddy Waters.

Reference Note

For information on **common usage errors,** see Chapter 11.

COMMON ERRORS

Reference Note

For information on **common usage errors,** see Chapter 11.

Exercise 27 Correcting Errors in Usage

Most of the following sentences contain an error in usage. Revise each sentence that contains an error. If a sentence is already correct, write *C*.

EXAMPLE   1. These noodles taste well with this sauce.

                1. *These noodles taste good with this sauce.*

1. One of Japan's most popular dining attractions is the *yatai,* a type of small food shop that can be found almost everywheres in Japanese cities.
2. On the way home from work, many Japanese they stop to get a bite to eat at one of these street stalls.
3. These type of stalls is equipped with a kitchen and is movable.
4. A large amount of these stalls appear on back or side streets after sunset.
5. Being as people are tired and hungry after a day's work, they appreciate the convenience of these stalls.
6. Choosing among braised chicken, stewed vegetables, and one of the other main dishes is often difficult.
7. One reason people stop at the *yatai* is because they enjoy the companionship of new and old acquaintances.
8. Sitting besides strangers from all walks of life can be fun.
9. No doubt, Japanese who emigrate to the United States miss the food, atmosphere, and camaraderie at the *yatai.*
10. Although fast-food restaurants in the United States are places where people can gather, customers usually visit them primarily for convenience rather then for companionship.

Reference Note

For information on **common usage errors,** see Chapter 11.

Exercise 28 Correcting Errors in Usage

Each of the following sentences contains an error in usage. Revise each sentence.

EXAMPLE   1. I'm going to join the navy, like my father did.

                1. *I'm going to join the navy, as my father did.*

1. Do you want to try one of these free samples that I got off of the man at the bakery counter?
2. Neither the museum or the art school has information on him.
3. Oh, no! I must of locked the keys in the car again.
4. This answer don't make sense to me, Mr. Washington.
5. The reason for the delay is because severe thunderstorms have grounded all flights.

6. The baseball that busted the living room window had Patrick's name on it.

7. Where will the party be at tonight?

8. Did you read where a faster computer chip has been created?

9. The engine sounded like it had been filled with gravel, not gasoline.

10. A warm boot is when a computer is restarted by keyboard strokes.

Exercise 29 **Correcting Double Negatives and Other Errors in Usage**

Eliminate the double negatives and other errors in usage in the following sentences.

EXAMPLES   **1.** The musicians couldn't hardly wait for the concert to begin.

     1. The musicians could hardly wait for the concert to begin.

   2. Our lunch break was so short that we didn't scarcely have time to eat.

     2. Our lunch break was so short that we scarcely had time to eat.

1. What affect does the gravitational pull of the moon have on the tides of the Atlantic Ocean?

2. They said that they didn't know nothing about the school dance on Friday night.

3. The concert hall was so crowded that the management wouldn't let no one else in.

4. I read where this movie theater no longer accepts discount passes for new releases.

5. Arturo and Jason should of realized that their voices would echo loudly in that deep, narrow canyon.

6. Isn't nobody going to help me bring in the groceries?

7. In the early nineteenth century, Robert Owen tried to create an utopia—an ideal or perfect place—in New Harmony, Indiana.

8. His fingers moved so fast that I couldn't hardly see all the chords he played.

9. Less species of fish live in the Arctic and Antarctic Oceans than in other, warmer oceans.

10. Don't you wash no dog in my clean bathtub!

HELP

Although some of the sentences in Exercise 29 can be corrected in more than one way, you need to give only one revision for each item.

Reference Note

For information on **common usage errors,** see Chapter 11.

COMMON ERRORS

Grammar and Usage Test: Section 1

DIRECTIONS   Read the paragraph below. For each numbered blank, select the word or word group that best completes the sentence. Indicate your response by shading in the appropriate oval on your answer sheet.

EXAMPLE   Until the early twentieth century, the nations of the world __(1)__ no strategy for collectively solving international problems.

        1. (**A**) they had
            (**B**) didn't have
            (**C**) have
            (**D**) had
            (**E**) having

ANSWER   1.

    With the horrors of World War I fresh in their minds, representatives from around the world __(1)__ in Geneva, Switzerland, to find a peaceful way to solve __(2)__ disputes. The solution that they reached __(3)__ to form an international organization. Established in 1920, the League of Nations __(4)__ to mediate conflicts. However, the League __(5)__ power to make countries comply with __(6)__ decisions. Moreover, the refusal of the United States to join __(7)__ weakened what little authority the League did have. Ironically, it was U.S. President Woodrow Wilson __(8)__ had first suggested forming the League. __(9)__ the League was so weak, it could do nothing in the 1930s to stop Japan, Italy, and Germany's mounting aggression, which led to the outbreak of World War II. In 1946, the League of Nations __(10)__ apart, and the United Nations took its place.

---

1. (**A**) was meeting
   (**B**) meeted
   (**C**) meets
   (**D**) met
   (**E**) would have met

2. (**A**) them
   (**B**) his or her
   (**C**) their
   (**D**) they're
   (**E**) these kind of

3. (**A**) it was
   (**B**) has been
   (**C**) were
   (**D**) being
   (**E**) was

4. (**A**) were formed
   (**B**) was formed
   (**C**) was forming
   (**D**) forming
   (**E**) forms

5. (A) had no
   (B) didn't have no
   (C) scarcely had no
   (D) had barely no
   (E) never had no

6. (A) it's
   (B) its
   (C) their
   (D) his or her
   (E) them

7. (A) greater
   (B) more greater
   (C) more greatly
   (D) greatly
   (E) greatlier

8. (A) whom
   (B) which
   (C) whose
   (D) whoever
   (E) who

9. (A) Being as
   (B) Although
   (C) Because
   (D) Being that
   (E) Until

10. (A) broke
    (B) breaked
    (C) broken
    (D) break
    (E) busted

Grammar and Usage Test: Section 2

DIRECTIONS Using the rules of standard written English, choose the answer that most clearly expresses the meaning of the underlined portion of each of the following sentences. If the sentence is best written as is, choose A. Indicate your response by shading in the appropriate oval on your answer sheet.

EXAMPLE   1. Romare Bearden gained artistic fame for his collages his works are made of pieces of paper that have been cut or torn.

   (A) collages his works are made of pieces of paper that have been cut or torn
   (B) collages, his works are made of pieces of paper that have been cut or torn
   (C) collages, which are made of pieces of paper that have been cut or torn
   (D) collages, his works being made of pieces of paper that have been cut or torn
   (E) collages, collages are made of pieces of paper that have been cut or torn

ANSWER   1.   A   B   C   D   E

1. <u>Raiding the garden, Dad hollered at the raccoon.</u>
   (A) Raiding the garden, Dad hollered at the raccoon.
   (B) While raiding the garden, Dad hollered at the raccoon.
   (C) Dad, raiding the garden, hollered at the raccoon.
   (D) Dad hollered at the raccoon while he was raiding the garden.
   (E) Dad hollered at the raccoon raiding the garden.

2. <u>In this article it says</u> that Sir Arthur Conan Doyle was a doctor.
   (A) In this article it says
   (B) This article says
   (C) This article it says
   (D) In this article says
   (E) In this article they say

3. <u>That violinist Midori, whom audiences all over the world admire.</u>
   (A) That violinist Midori, whom audiences all over the world admire.
   (B) That violinist is Midori, who audiences all over the world admire.
   (C) That violinist is Midori, audiences all over the world admire her.
   (D) That violinist is Midori, whom audiences all over the world admire.
   (E) That violinist Midori, admired by audiences all over the world.

4. The Chinese poet T'ao Ch'ien liked to work in his <u>garden, Li Po preferred to travel.</u>
   (A) garden, Li Po preferred to travel
   (B) garden; Li Po preferred to travel
   (C) garden Li Po preferred to travel
   (D) garden, so Li Po preferred to travel
   (E) garden; moreover, Li Po preferred to travel

5. After she had a nightmare about a scientist's monstrous experiment, Mary Shelley <u>writes her novel *Frankenstein*.</u>
   (A) writes her novel *Frankenstein*
   (B) writing her novel *Frankenstein*
   (C) had written her novel *Frankenstein*
   (D) she wrote her novel *Frankenstein*
   (E) wrote her novel *Frankenstein*

6. E. G. Valens's book *The Other Side of the Mountain,* which tells the story of Jill Kinmont's remarkable life.

   (A) E. G. Valens's book *The Other Side of the Mountain,* which tells the story of Jill Kinmont's remarkable life.

   (B) E. G. Valens's book *The Other Side of the Mountain* tells the story of Jill Kinmont's remarkable life.

   (C) The remarkable E. G. Valens wrote the book *The Other Side of the Mountain,* it tells the story of Jill Kinmont's life.

   (D) E. G. Valens's book *The Other Side of the Mountain* telling the story of Jill Kinmont's remarkable life.

   (E) E. G. Valens wrote the book *The Other Side of the Mountain* it tells the story of Jill Kinmont's remarkable life.

7. Soon after the Worthingtons had moved to the neighborhood, the Smiths invited them to a barbecue.

   (A) Soon after the Worthingtons had moved to the neighborhood, the Smiths invited them to a barbecue.

   (B) The Smiths invited the Worthingtons to a barbecue soon after they had moved to the neighborhood.

   (C) Soon after they had moved to the neighborhood, the Smiths invited the Worthingtons to a barbecue.

   (D) Having just moved to the neighborhood, the Smiths invited the Worthingtons to a barbecue.

   (E) Soon after the Smiths had moved to the neighborhood, the Worthingtons invited them to a barbecue.

8. Many woodcarvers in Mexico's Oaxaca Valley make colorful figures, they sell them to visitors from all over the world.

   (A) Many woodcarvers in Mexico's Oaxaca Valley make colorful figures, they sell them to visitors from all over the world.

   (B) Many woodcarvers in Mexico's Oaxaca Valley, who make colorful figures, they sell them to visitors from all over the world.

   (C) Many woodcarvers in Mexico's Oaxaca Valley make colorful figures, and they are sold to visitors from all over the world.

   (D) Many woodcarvers in Mexico's Oaxaca Valley make colorful figures and sell them to visitors from all over the world.

   (E) Many woodcarvers in Mexico's Oaxaca Valley made colorful figures that they will sell to visitors from all over the world.

9. While excavating the ruins, pieces of jewelry made of lapis lazuli were discovered by the archaeologists.

    (A) While excavating the ruins, pieces of jewelry made of lapis lazuli were discovered by the archaeologists.

    (B) While excavating the ruins, pieces of jewelry were discovered by the archaeologists, made of lapis lazuli.

    (C) The archaeologists discovered pieces of jewelry made of lapis lazuli excavating the ruins.

    (D) The archaeologists discovered pieces of jewelry while excavating the ruins made of lapis lazuli.

    (E) While excavating the ruins, the archaeologists discovered pieces of jewelry made of lapis lazuli.

10. While studying bristlecone pines, their great age was discovered.

    (A) While studying bristlecone pines, their great age was discovered.

    (B) While scientists were studying bristlecone pines, their great age was discovered.

    (C) While studying bristlecone pines, scientists discovered these trees' great age.

    (D) While studying bristlecone pines, scientists discovered their great age.

    (E) While studying bristlecone pines, their great age were discovered.

WORD FOR WORD reprinted by permission of Associated Press.

Exercise 30 Proofreading for Correct Capitalization

Most of the sentences in the following paragraph contain at least one error in capitalization. Correct each error. If a sentence is already correct, write *C*.

Reference Note

For information on **capitalization rules,** see Chapter 12.

EXAMPLE
1. Whether it's just a bend in the Road or New York city, almost everyone loves his or her hometown.

1. *road, City*

[1] However, many of us at Marshall high school don't want to spend our whole lives sitting in a red vinyl booth at Angie's restaurant, sipping an iced tea after services at Trinity church. [2] In the old days, some students used to go to europe after they graduated; doing so was a tradition. [3] Of course, not everybody wants to go that far; but some of our class do have dreams that take us all around the Earth. [4] bob and Alma would love to see Ireland, where their Grandmother agnes was born. [5] Jomo, dr. Henry's son, actually wants to make Kenya his home after he finishes up at river city junior college. [6] As for me, i want to see the East—the far East, that is—the one with the great wall of China, Chinese new year, the Yellow river, and those little oranges. [7] If the *orient-express* is still rolling down the tracks, maybe I'll just keep going east until I reach the west again. [8] On the way, I'll be sure to sail the Mediterranean sea, check out the temple of apollo, visit the land of the talmud, stand beside the Eiffel tower, and, in general, make sure that *National Geographic Explorer* has its facts straight. [9] Hey! Maybe I'll even write up my adventures and call them "the Grand Tour In The Twenty-First Century." [10] Imagine that—me published in *National Geographic*!

Exercise 31 Correcting Errors in Capitalization

Correct any error in capitalization in each of the following items. If an item is already correct, write *C*.

Reference Note

For information on **capitalization rules,** see Chapter 12.

EXAMPLES
1. "Secret World Of A Pond"

1. *"Secret World of a Pond"*

2. a hindu tradition

2. *a Hindu tradition*

1. the Restaurants of New York city
2. polynesian music
3. my Cousin's shoe store
4. in san francisco
5. ms. julia child

6. Russian dressing on my salad
7. dates and figs from israel
8. salmon from the pacific area
9. the fair at central park
10. home economics II
11. the board of health
12. the snack bar in the Regal hotel
13. celebrating kwanzaa
14. a cup of Lipton® Tea
15. during the dark ages
16. brought to spain by Columbus
17. astronauts aboard the *Discovery*
18. the summer issue of *Native peoples* magazine
19. stop the presses, alice!
20. a cherokee name
21. a baptist minister
22. *The big Book Of Tell me Why*
23. Enlighten us, o Athena!
24. named for the god jupiter
25. the house of representatives

Exercise 32 Correcting Sentences by Adding Commas

Reference Note

For information on **using commas,** see page 301.

Rewrite each of the following sentences, inserting commas where they are needed.

EXAMPLE 1. Paul why don't you come over tonight and see our new computer?

1. *Paul, why don't you come over tonight and see our new computer?*

1. Saturday August 5 2000 was a big day for everyone in our family.
2. When we first got the computer no one in the family knew much about how to use it.
3. Mom read the directions for setting up the hardware and I hooked up the monitor keyboard and speakers.
4. When we turned on the computer we hadn't realized that the volume was turned up very high.
5. Naturally we all jumped when the computer blasted out a musical welcome.
6. My youngest brother Derek who has played with computers since he was in nursery school knew just what to do.

COMMON ERRORS

7. With hardly a moment of hesitation he reached out and turned down the volume and then pushed a button.
8. The CD drawer slid out in one smooth sudden motion.
9. He picked up a shiny silver disc that had a program about dinosaurs popped it in and pressed the button again.
10. After reading the directions for a few minutes Dad typed in a short command, pressed a key, and entered a virtual prehistoric world.

Exercise 33 Correcting Sentences by Adding Periods, Question Marks, Exclamation Points, and Commas

Rewrite the following sentences, adding periods, question marks, exclamation points, and commas as needed. If a sentence is already correct, write *C*.

EXAMPLE
1. Mr Cross please fax this to headquarters immediately
1. *Mr. Cross, please fax this to headquarters immediately.*

or

Mr. Cross, please fax this to headquarters immediately!

1. Mike Joe and I will meet at 8:00 P.M. at the corner of Elk St. and Fifth Ave
2. "Don't you dare" I yelled to my sister when she turned on the water picked up the garden hose and pointed it at me.
3. Doesn't your oldest sister Susan go to that junior college Tim
4. On the wall were three large glossy photographs—one of Secretary of State Colin Powell one of President John F Kennedy and one of Dr. Martin Luther King Jr
5. Oh what a beautiful sunset this is
6. No person who has purchased a ticket will be excluded from the school carnival.
7. In the fall of last year archaeologists I believe found a site that dates back to 200 B C
8. For example many of the pesticides that are used in agriculture can eventually filter into our water supply.
9. I wondered moreover whether the shipment would even arrive by July 10 2002.
10. Remember to ask Dr Franklin about whether you should exercise your knee

HELP

Although the example in Exercise 33 gives two possible revisions, you need to give only one for each sentence.

Reference Note

For information on **using commas,** see page 301. For information on **using end marks,** see page 294.

┌HELP┐

Some sentences
in Exercise 34 have a
comma where a semicolon
or a colon should be.

Reference Note

For information on **using
semicolons and colons,**
see pages 322 and 324.

Exercise 34 Proofreading Sentences for the Correct Use of Semicolons and Colons

Rewrite the following sentences, adding or deleting semicolons and colons as needed.

EXAMPLE   1. Only fragments of these ancient scrolls exist, however, scholars are attempting to piece the text together.

1. *Only fragments of these ancient scrolls exist; however, scholars are attempting to piece the text together.*

1. The President did not veto the bill, in other words, he allowed it to become law.
2. There are many possible titles for your paper for example, you could use "Legacy of Laughter The Stories of Toni Cade Bambara."
3. By 8 00 at night, a dense fog had obscured our view only the lights of the house next door were visible.
4. The vase was filled with flowers daisies, irises, daffodils, and tulips.
5. The following materials are necessary to assemble the cart, a screw-driver, eighteen half-inch screws, and eighteen nuts.
6. My uncle loves to fish, in fact, he goes fishing every weekend.
7. Her choice was clear, Find a way out of the jungle or die.
8. We set out with: a compass, a canteen of water, a blanket, and a tattered copy of Psalm 23 1–6.
9. The film will be shown three times: Sunday, March 15, Friday, April 3, and Saturday, April 25.
10. Her mother was, I think, originally from Veracruz, Mexico but she has lived in Sacramento, California, for more than thirty years.

Reference Note

For information about
punctuating dialogue,
see page 336.

Exercise 35 Proofreading a Dialogue for Correct Punctuation

Rewrite the following dialogue, correcting any errors in the use of quotation marks and other marks of punctuation. Also, correct any errors in the use of capitalization, and begin a new paragraph each time the speaker changes.

EXAMPLE   [1] I have two very important papers due next week! Eric sighed. "Have you started on them yet? Rita asked.

1.   *"I have two very important papers due next week,"
        Eric sighed.
        "Have you started on them yet?" Rita asked.*

[1] "Well, I've decided," Eric answered, "On a topic for one, and I've done research for another one."

[2] "You do have a lot of work to do! Rita exclaimed. I guess you won't be going out this weekend."

[3] How are you doing on your papers? Eric asked. Rita answered "I still have to edit, print, and proofread one." The other is almost done, too."

[4] "How do you manage to get it all done"? Eric asked.

[5] "Every time I get a big assignment, I make a list of all the things I'll need to do. Then I estimate how long each step will take me." she replied.

[6] Eric said, shaking his head, "that sounds like extra work to me."

[7] "Well, it keeps me on schedule and helps me avoid having to rush through the writing process.

[8] Hmm, I see what you mean," Eric mused. "I guess it's too late for me to get organized now." "Rita replied, I don't think so."

[9] "It's not too late. Never say "never"." Just take the time you have left, and figure out what needs to be done each day.

[10] "Okay, I think I'll give your plan a try in study hall. Eric said.

Exercise 36 Proofreading a Dialogue for Correct Punctuation

Rewrite the following dialogue, correcting any errors in the use of quotation marks and other marks of punctuation. Also, correct any errors in the use of capitalization, and begin a new paragraph each time the speaker changes.

Reference Note

For information about **punctuating dialogue,** see page 336.

EXAMPLE **[1]** I understand that you began flying in the 1930s, Colonel Scott, the interviewer stated. "Yes, that's right, Scott agreed.

1.   *"I understand that you began flying in the 1930s, Colonel Scott," the interviewer stated. "Yes, that's right," Scott agreed.*

[1] In those days, flying was the hottest thing around. Being a pilot then was better than being a rock star today, for me, anyway. All I ever wanted to do was fly. I used to hang around the field doing odd jobs, hoping to get some flight time in.

[2] Was that how you met Jackie Cochran? Were you working for her?" the interviewer questioned.

[3] "I was just a kid. I ran a few errands for her. Later, we became good friends in Europe. We'd be "socked in" and get to talking."

[4] Excuse me, but what's "socked in?"

[5] "When bad weather grounds a plane, the pilots are "socked in". Lots of times I'd see her when she ferried a plane. You know, Jackie was the one who really got the WASPs going." "The Women Airforce Service Pilots"? the interviewer interrupted.

[6] "That's right. Jackie liked being first. She was a competitor from the word go. Jackie didn't really have much of a childhood," Scott mused. "Maybe she took all that kid's excitement and funneled it into flying. I don't know."

"I do know that she grew up in a foster home. She was working in a cotton mill when she was nine or so. She quit school—such things weren't unusual in those days".

[7] "How old was she when she got her pilot's license"? "Around twenty. She wasn't much more than that when she set her sights on that Bendix Transcontinental Air Race and wouldn't let up. I was with her when she took off in '38".

[8] "That was the year she won, wasn't it", the interviewer continued.

[9] "Sure was. Nobody could beat her—and, believe me, there were some very good pilots around. Whether it was altitude, speed, or endurance records, it didn't matter. She won them all.

[10] 'Thank you, Colonel, for sharing your memories of Jacqueline Cochran, a member of the National Aviation Hall of Fame.'

Exercise 37 Using Apostrophes Correctly

Most of the following items contain at least one error in the use of apostrophes. Correct each error. If an item is already correct, write *C*.

EXAMPLE   **1.** Its easy.

1. It's easy.

1. The rest is her's.
2. Lets dance!
3. Kim wont be late.
4. We were reading Jo's essay.
5. Im not finished.
6. Is this your's?
7. nobodys fool
8. my sister's-in-law house
9. six day's time
10. P. J. and Tims treehouse
11. two o clock
12. Follow it's trail.
13. mens' clothing

14. Youll be fine.
15. Were home!
16. too many *and*s
17. Who's keys' are these?
18. Theres the girls' team.
19. You're right.
20. cat and dogs' ears
21. somebodys' wallet
22. Theyre here!
23. Jon made three As.
24. Ada hasnt sneezed.
25. Wasn't 99 a great year?

┌H E L P┐
You may need to change the spellings of some words in Exercise 37.

Reference Note
For information about **apostrophes,** see page 345.

COMMON ERRORS

Reference Note

For information about **punctuation,** see Chapters 13 and 14.

Exercise 38 Proofreading Sentences for Correct Punctuation

Rewrite the following sentences, adding, deleting, or changing punctuation as necessary.

EXAMPLE
  1. Langston Hughes, 1902–1967, was one of many poets and artists to gain fame during the Harlem Renaissance.

  1. *Langston Hughes (1902–1967) was one of many poets and artists to gain fame during the Harlem Renaissance.*

1. Oh, I dont mind", Hazel replied.
2. The dog on the fire engine was the firefighters' traditional mascot the Dalmatian.
3. Roseannes presentation required twenty seven visuals.
4. Engraved inside the ring was the Latin expression imo pectore which means "from the bottom of the heart.
5. Mr Hilliard your team will include these players, Barbara, Trang, Kyle, and Tracy.
6. The hugely-successful strategy was worth the time we took.
7. Carrie won the election with a three fourths majority.
8. Ms. Levine [Kathy's mother] will speak to our class on career choices in medicine.
9. The hull of the sleek new space shuttle Atlantis gleamed as the spacecraft glided into orbit.
10. We've studied skeletal structure, we'll study circulation next week.

Reference Note

For information about **spelling rules,** see Chapter 15.

Exercise 39 Proofreading Sentences for Spelling Errors

Correct each misspelled word in the following sentences.

EXAMPLE
  1. Why do truck's have to pull over along highways to be wieghed?

  1. *trucks, weighed*

1. Slowly, the waters receeded, and we carefuly made our way across the creek.
2. The puppy was so adoreable that we didn't mind doing the extra dayly chores that caring for it requireed.
3. Forty-two students have applied for the scholarship and have recieved replies from the scholarship committee.
4. As soon as our nieghbor's lawn mower stoped, I napped for a few minutes.

COMMON ERRORS

5. We could see geeses, deer, and other wildlife on the shore of the lake.

6. The knife's blade was dull, so I checked the drawers and shelfs, but I couldn't find anything to open the box except a few more dull table knifes.

7. The O'Grady twins always seem to be up to mischeif and keep the O'Gradies wondering what the next disaster will be.

8. Both of my brother-in-laws prefered raising sheeps to raising chickens.

9. On September seventh at 4:00 P.M., the temperature exceded ninety-five degrees.

10. Dozens of monkies chattered among the branchs of the trees.

┌HELP┐
No proper nouns are misspelled or misused in Exercise 40.

Reference Note
For information about **spelling rules,** see Chapter 15. For information about **words often confused,** see page 375.

Exercise 40 Proofreading for Spelling Errors and Words Often Confused

Correct each misspelled or incorrect word in the following sentences.

EXAMPLES [1] The capitol of Pennsylvania, the 5th most populous state, is Harrisburg.

1. *capital, fifth*

[2] While Pennsylvania is often thought of for its manufactureing and industry, another area of commerce is also interesting.

2. *manufacturing*

[1] Pennsylvania's history and it's economy intersect in the feild of communication. [2] In 1719, the *American Weekly Mercury* became the 1st newspaper in the colony; a few years latter, another paper destined to make history, the *Pennsylvania Gazette,* became the property of Ben Franklin. [3] A strong tradition of communication is the heritage of the Keystone State, and in 1920, Pittsburgh renewed Pennsylvania's heritage and claimed quiet a prize when it became the site of the first commercialy operated radio station in the whole world.

[4] Today, of coarse, radio and newspapers have been joined by television stations, but the principle economic activity is manufacturing. [5] Farms also play an economic role; although livestock, such as cattle, contributes the most income, agricultureal crops, such as peaches and tomatos, are also important to the economy. [6] Interestingly enough, for some time the countys of Delaware and Chester have lead the nation in the production of mushrooms.

COMMON ERRORS

[7] Although forestry once thrived their, the state is now expereincing a drop in lumber production. [8] Unfortunatly, overcuting forests in the 1800s is still having an effect.

[9] From Valley Forge too Gettysburg, the cities of Pennsylvania offer a veiw straight into American history. [10] However, as spectacular as this state's history is, for many people nothing could be more glorious then the sight of Pennsylvania's colorful fall leafs.

Exercise 41 Distinguishing Between Words Often Confused

Choose the correct word or word group from each pair in parentheses in the following sentences.

EXAMPLES 1. Soldiers who decided to (*desert, dessert*) had to cross the hot and endless sands of the (*desert, dessert*).
1. *desert, desert*

2. We could see the dome of the (*capital, capitol*) during our trip to the nation's (*capital, capitol*).
2. *capitol, capital*

1. Three sky divers jumped out of the (*plain, plane*).
2. (*Who's, Whose*) going to decide (*who's, whose*) plan for the party is the best one?
3. From the edge of the cliff, (*it's, its*) difficult to see the eagle in (*it's, its*) nest.
4. What (*led, lead*) to the discovery of the poisonous nature of (*led, lead*)?
5. The kindergartners grew (*quite, quiet*) as the teacher began to read the story.
6. (*There, Their, They're*) is the new lantern that (*there, their, they're*) taking with them.
7. (*You're, Your*) going to have to make up (*you're, your*) mind sooner or later.
8. Mike said that he would go to the movies rather (*then, than*) to the skating rink.
9. This math question is (*altogether, all together*) too easy to put on the final exam.
10. If the chickens get (*lose, loose*) again, we will almost certainly (*lose, loose*) a few.

Reference Note

For information on **words often confused,** see page 375.

COMMON ERRORS

Exercise 42 Proofreading for Mechanics

Correct any errors in mechanics in each of the following items.

EXAMPLE   **[1]** 933 West Forty fifth St

       1. *933 West Forty-fifth St.*

[1] New York, NY, 10023
February 3, 2001

[2] Ms Annelise Wilson
Widgets and Gadgets, Inc.
87 Beaumont Ave.
New York, NY 10027

[3] Dear Ms. Wilson,

[4] Thank you for coming to speak to our local chapter of the young entrepreneurs club.

[5] My fellow club members and I hope that you enjoyed the reception as much as we enjoyed hearing you're advice. **[6]** Your word's were a great help to those of us who hope to have careers in business. **[7]** Thank you for giving us students a chance, to learn about many of the challenges of starting a business.

[8] Please except the enclosed certificate as a small token of our appreciation. **[9]** We look forward to seeing you at the upcoming convention at the Seacrest hotel.

[10] Sincerely:

Rodney Alvarez

Rodney Alvarez
President,
Young Entrepreneurs
Club

Enclosure

Mechanics Test: Section 1

DIRECTIONS   For each of the following sentences, choose the answer that shows the correct capitalization, punctuation, and spelling of the underlined part. If there is no error, choose answer E (*Correct as is*). Indicate your response by shading in the appropriate oval on your answer sheet.

EXAMPLE   1. It <u>would, of coarse, be</u> wise to bring a flashlight for exploring the caves.

   (A) would of coarse be
   (B) would, of course be
   (C) would of course, be
   (D) would, of course, be
   (E) Correct as is

ANSWER   1.

1. "Have you seen Spielberg's latest <u>movie," asked Tasha.</u>
   (A) movie"? asked Tasha.
   (B) movie? asked Tasha.
   (C) movie,"? asked Tasha.
   (D) movie?" asked Tasha.
   (E) Correct as is

2. On the corner, musicians from <u>the Salvation army</u> were playing Christmas carols.
   (A) the salvation army
   (B) the Salvation army,
   (C) the Salvation Army
   (D) the salvation Army
   (E) Correct as is

3. These engine parts are manufactured in <u>Detroit Mi.</u>
   (A) Detroit, MI.
   (B) Detroit MI.
   (C) Detroit Michigan
   (D) Detroit, Michigan.
   (E) Correct as is

4. Did you know that both of my <u>brother-in-laws repair their</u> own cars?

    (A) brothers-in-laws repair thier

    (B) brother-in-law's repair their

    (C) brothers-in-law repair their

    (D) brothers-in-law repair they're

    (E) Correct as is

5. Gerry announced that the refreshment committee still <u>needs cups, plates, and napkins.</u>

    (A) needs: cups, plates, and napkins.

    (B) needs cups plates and napkins.

    (C) needs—cups, plates, and napkins.

    (D) needs, cups, plates, and napkins.

    (E) Correct as is

6. Did you <u>say "That</u> Michelangelo began painting the ceiling of the Sistine Chapel in 1508?

    (A) say that

    (B) say, "that

    (C) say that,

    (D) say, "That

    (E) Correct as is

7. The green ice chest in the back of the truck is <u>their's; the</u> red one is mine.

    (A) there's; the

    (B) theirs; the

    (C) thiers; the

    (D) theirs; The

    (E) Correct as is

8. The names of the <u>students, who made the honor roll, are</u> posted on that bulletin board.

    (A) students who made the honor roll, are

    (B) students who made the honor roll are

    (C) students (who made the honor roll) are

    (D) students, who made the honor roll are

    (E) Correct as is

9. I haven't read _Hamlet_ yet, consequently, I don't understand Ms. Klein's references to Ophelia.

   (A) _Hamlet_ yet; consequently, I
   (B) _Hamlet_ yet consequently, I
   (C) _Hamlet_ yet consequently I
   (D) _Hamlet_ yet; consequently I
   (E) Correct as is

10. On my cousins' farm in Texas, the peach trees are covered with blossoms each spring.

    (A) cousins farm in Texas,
    (B) cousins farm in Texas
    (C) cousins' farm in texas
    (D) cousins' farm in texas,
    (E) Correct as is

COMMON ERRORS

Mechanics Test: Section 2

DIRECTIONS Each numbered item below contains an underlined group of words. Choose the answer that shows the correct capitalization, punctuation, and spelling of the underlined part. If there is no error, choose answer E (*Correct as is*). Indicate your response by shading in the appropriate oval on your answer sheet.

EXAMPLE   [1] <u>41, Maple Ridge Road</u>

     1. (A) Forty one, Maple Ridge Road

       (B) Forty One Maple Ridge Road

       (C) 41, Maple ridge road

       (D) 41 Maple Ridge Road

       (E) Correct as is

ANSWER   1.

---

[1] <u>October 17, 2001</u>

[2] <u>Dr Maria H. Ramirez</u>
Grove Health Center

[3] 2104 <u>Fifty-Third</u> Street, #14
Des Moines, IA 50318

[4] <u>Dear Dr. Ramirez,</u>

Thank you for agreeing to speak to our [5] <u>high school's Brainstormers' club</u>. We have reserved the auditorium for the afternoon of [6] <u>Thursday, November, 9</u>. As you requested, I will introduce you at [7] <u>300 P.M.</u> Our vice president, Julie Jackson, will meet you at the school's front office fifteen minutes beforehand. Please let me know [8] <u>weather we need to alter</u> these arrangements. [9] <u>37 students</u> have [10] <u>already signed up for you're</u> talk! We all look forward to seeing you soon.

Yours truly,

George Karras

George Karras
President, Brainstormers' Club

1. (A) October, 17, 2001
   (B) October 17 2001
   (C) October 17th, 2001
   (D) Oct 17, 2001
   (E) Correct as is

2. (A) Dr. Maria H Ramirez
   (B) Dr Maria H Ramirez,
   (C) Dr Maria H. Ramirez
   (D) Dr. Maria H. Ramirez
   (E) Correct as is

3. (A) Fifty-third
   (B) Fiftythird
   (C) Fifty Third
   (D) fifty third
   (E) Correct as is

4. (A) Dear Dr. Ramirez:
   (B) Dear Dr Ramirez:
   (C) Dear Dr Ramirez,
   (D) Dr Ramirez:
   (E) Correct as is

5. (A) high schools
       Brainstormers' club
   (B) High School's
       brainstormers' Club
   (C) high school's
       Brainstormers' Club
   (D) High schools
       Brainstormers' club
   (E) Correct as is

6. (A) Thursday November 9
   (B) Thursday, November 9th
   (C) Thursday, Nov. 9th
   (D) Thursday, November 9
   (E) Correct as is

7. (A) 3:00 o'clock P.M.
   (B) 3:00 P.M.
   (C) 3 oclock P.M.
   (D) three P.M.
   (E) Correct as is

8. (A) weather we need too alter
   (B) whether we need to alter
   (C) weather we need to altar
   (D) whether we need to altar
   (E) Correct as is

9. (A) Thirty-seven students
   (B) 37 Students
   (C) Thirty seven students
   (D) Thirty-seven student's
   (E) Correct as is

10. (A) all ready signed up
        for you're
    (B) already signed up
        for youre
    (C) allready signed up
        for your
    (D) already signed up
        for your
    (E) Correct as is

Sentences

go.hrw .com **GO TO:** go.hrw.com

Writing Clear Sentences

Diagnostic Preview

A. Using Coordination and Subordination

Revise each of the following pairs of sentences by using coordination or subordination. You may have to add or delete words and change the word order to make the relationship between the ideas clear.

EXAMPLE 1. We could not see the screen clearly. We moved to different seats in the theater.

1. *We moved to different seats in the theater because we could not see the screen clearly.*

1. Walter didn't make the team this year. He still practices every day.
2. The new books arrived. The librarian shelved them in a special area.
3. Ms. Garza is now teaching at another high school. She was my homeroom teacher last year.
4. Rita was late getting to the airport. She still made her flight.
5. Chris was packing the bags. Michelle called a taxi.
6. My friend Ralph recently moved to Chicago. I have known him since the second grade.
7. The magazine article about the governor appeared yesterday. It was written by a well-known investigative reporter.
8. Almost no rain fell last spring. All the corn is stunted.

9. Have you read the installation instructions? They were in the software package.
10. I looked for Amy at the festival. I did not find her.

B. Revising Sentences by Using Parallel Structures

Revise the following sentences by correcting unparallel sentence structures. You may need to delete, add, or move some words to bring the ideas into balance.

EXAMPLE   1. When I go home after school, I not only have to do my homework, but also my chores have to be done.

         1. *When I go home after school, I have to do not only my homework but also my chores.*

11. For centuries, human beings dreamed of reaching the moon, exploring the planets, and space travel.
12. To outline a research paper is as crucial as writing the paper.
13. Jack's list of errands included taking the books back to the library and to get a haircut.
14. The jeweler carefully and with precision placed the enormous ruby into the setting.
15. My parents say that I should appreciate my English teacher's patience, persistence, and how she is always courteous.

C. Identifying Sentences, Sentence Fragments, and Run-on Sentences

Identify each of the following word groups as a *sentence*, a *sentence fragment*, or a *run-on sentence*. Then, if a word group is a fragment, revise the word group to make it a complete sentence. If a word group is a run-on, revise it to make one or more complete sentences.

EXAMPLE   1. At two o'clock the weather was clear and cloudless, within a few minutes, a fierce wind arose, and ominous black clouds darkened the sky.

         1. *run-on—At two o'clock the weather was clear and cloudless, but within a few minutes, a fierce wind arose, and ominous black clouds darkened the sky.*

16. The rain poured down in sheets; water filled the gutters and ran across the streets and sidewalks.
17. Lightning crashed and thunder boomed, the lights flickered.

18. Jerry looked for batteries for the flashlight his sister found some in a kitchen drawer.
19. Sitting at the window and watching the storm.
20. The noise of the storm grew louder, the howling wind rattled the windows.
21. While Jerry and his family waited for the storm to pass.
22. A small battery-powered radio kept them informed about the weather, providing updates every ten minutes.
23. A tornado touching down in another part of the county.
24. They played cards by the light of the flashlight, finally, Jerry fell asleep with his head on the table.
25. The next morning, the sky was a clear, brilliant blue, a few broken branches and the soggy ground were the only reminders of the storm.

Ways to Achieve Clarity

Have you ever adjusted a camera lens to bring an image into focus? Just as you can sharpen the focus of a camera to take a better picture, you can sharpen the focus of your writing to express your meaning more clearly. One of the best ways to achieve clarity is to write sentences that reveal the appropriate relationships between ideas. Usually, you reveal these relationships by adapting the structure of your sentences.

Coordinating Ideas

Equally important ideas in a sentence are called *coordinate* ideas. To show that ideas are coordinate, you can join them with a coordinating conjunction (*and, but, for, nor, or, so, yet*) or another connective. The connective tells your reader how the ideas are related; for example, *and* links equal and similar ideas, while *but* links equal and contrasting ideas.

In each of the following sentences, notice how the writer uses a coordinating conjunction to join two complete thoughts, or *independent clauses.* When you use coordination to link two independent clauses, the result is a *compound sentence.*

EXAMPLES A colony of weaverbirds lived in a tree near his house, **and** he spent time watching them build and maintain their baglike nests.

Richard Preston, *The Hot Zone*

It is thrilling to be in touch with the world at all times**, but** it's also draining.

David Shenk, *Data Smog*

You can also form a compound sentence with a semicolon and a conjunctive adverb, or just a semicolon.

EXAMPLE   But that L-shaped rip on the left sleeve got bigger**;** bits of stuffing coughed out from its wound after a hard day of play.

Gary Soto, "The Jacket"

NOTE   When you join two independent clauses with a coordinating conjunction, you usually put a comma before the conjunction.

We walked along the shore for a while**,** and then we dove into the ice-cold water.

However, a comma is not necessary if the clauses are very short and clear.

Shawna swam and I sunbathed.

Reference Note

For more about using commas with **coordinating conjunctions,** see page 303.

Sometimes you may have several equal, related ideas within a single independent clause. In addition to linking coordinate independent clauses, you can also use coordinating conjunctions to link coordinate words and phrases in a sentence.

Reference Note

For more about **combining sentences by coordinating ideas,** see page 467.

EXAMPLES   **Software piracy and component theft** alone are estimated to cost over $24 billion worldwide. [compound subject]

Mark Stuart Gill, "Cybercops Take a Byte Out of Computer Crime," *Smithsonian*

Few people **knew or cared** about the dangers of such a policy. [compound predicate]

Malcolm E. Weiss, *Toxic Waste*

Anyone who had passed the day with **him and his dog** refused to share a bench with them again. [compound object of a preposition]

Kurt Vonnegut, "Tom Edison's Shaggy Dog"

Lifting her skirt, leveling her cane fiercely before her, like a festival figure in some parade, she began to march across. [coordinate verbal phrases]

Eudora Welty, "A Worn Path"

SENTENCES

COMPUTER TIP

Use your computer's Cut and Paste functions to move clauses within sentences.

Subordinating Ideas

Pennies, nickels, dimes—they are all units of money, but they are certainly not equal in value. Just as some coins have greater value than others, some of your ideas in writing are more important than others. However, the importance of an idea is not always as obvious as the worth of a coin. To make the main ideas stand out in your writing, you need to downplay, or **subordinate,** the less important ones.

You can subordinate an idea in a sentence by putting the idea in a subordinate clause. The subordinate clause elaborates on the thought expressed in the independent clause.

EXAMPLES   Maria, **who likes disaster movies,** saw the movie *Titanic* three times.

Titanic is a good example of the way historical events can be brought to life **because the story focuses on the relationships between people on the ship.**

Adverb Clauses

An **adverb clause** modifies a verb, an adjective, or an adverb in a sentence. You introduce an adverb clause with a subordinating conjunction (*although, after, because, if, since, when, whenever, where, while*).

EXAMPLES   **Although symbolic puns are relatively rare in dreams,** they do occasionally show up in surprising ways.

Keith Harary, "Language of the Night," *Omni*

This confession he spoke harshly **because its unexpectedness shook him.**

Bernard Malamud, "The Magic Barrel"

The controversy began simmering more than a year ago, **when Louis Sullivan, then Secretary of Health and Human Services, proposed a $400 million federal research program on violence.**

Anastasia Toufexis, "Seeking the Roots of Violence," *Time*

If there'd been any farther west to go, he'd have gone.

John Steinbeck, *The Red Pony*

The subordinating conjunction you use is important. It shows your reader the relationship between the ideas in the adverb clause and the independent clause. This chart lists the subordinating conjunctions you can use to express the following relationships of *time or place*, *cause or reason*, *purpose or result*, or *condition*.

Subordinating Conjunctions			
Time or Place	after as before since	until when whenever	where wherever while
Cause or Reason	as because	since	whereas
Purpose or Result	in order that	that	so that
Condition	although even though	if provided that	unless while

STYLE   TIP

As you can see from the examples given, an adverb clause can make sense at either the beginning or the end of a sentence. Try a clause in both positions to see which sounds better to you. When you place an adverb clause at the beginning of a sentence, remember to separate it from the independent clause with a comma. Otherwise, you may confuse your reader.

EXAMPLE
The soils of boreal forests have high acid counts **because of the buildup of acidic tree needles.**
or
Because of the buildup of acidic tree needles, the soils of boreal forests have high acid counts.

Exercise 1 Selecting Appropriate Coordinating and Subordinating Conjunctions

For each of the following sentences, choose an appropriate coordinating or subordinating conjunction to fill in the blank. The hint in parentheses tells you what kind of relationship the conjunction should express.

EXAMPLE   1. For our family vacation, we decided to do something outdoors _____ we could get away from the noise and hustle of the city. (purpose or result)

1. *For our family vacation, we decided to do something outdoors so that we could get away from the noise and hustle of the city.*

1. It is called a lake, _____ Moraine is really a three-acre pond located beneath a high, majestic ridge on Grapetree Mountain. (condition)
2. _____ we visited Lake Moraine, we heard wild geese and saw beavers building dams. (time)
3. We sat by the tent one summer evening _____ a snowshoe hare crept from behind the pine trees to eat lettuce from our hands. (time)

Scientist taking water sample.

4. Lake Moraine, a wonderful, peaceful place, is now threatened _____ acid rains are destroying the brook trout that swim in its waters. (cause or reason)

5. _____ acid pollutants from factory fumes enter the atmosphere, they fall to the earth in rain and snow. (time)

6. High-altitude ponds such as Lake Moraine get a heavy dose of acid rains _____ the mountains trap moisture-bearing air masses. (cause or reason)

7. _____ the acid pollutants end up in the mountain ponds, fish, especially trout, suffer and die in great numbers. (time)

8. Many remote trout ponds are encased in granite _____ little soil or organic matter exists to trap or buffer the acid rain. (purpose or result)

9. _____ it is possible to develop acid-tolerant strains of trout, such a program of selective breeding will likely take many years. (condition)

10. More and more isolated ponds like Lake Moraine will become trout graveyards _____ we don't find a way to combat the effects of acid rain. (condition)

Adjective Clauses

An *adjective clause* modifies a noun or pronoun and usually begins with *who, whom, whose, which, that,* or *where.*

EXAMPLES   I was camped near a creek **that emptied into the bay.**

Timothy Treadwell and Jewel Palovak,
Among Grizzlies

Chicago seemed an unreal city **whose mythical houses were built of slabs of black coal wreathed in palls of gray smoke,** houses **whose foundations were sinking slowly into the dank prairie.**

Richard Wright, *American Hunger*

Before you use an adjective clause in a sentence, you need to decide which idea you want to emphasize and which you want to subordinate, or downplay. For example, suppose you want to combine these two ideas in one sentence:

> Advertising became big business in the 1920s. It fueled the demand for cars and other consumer goods.

If you want to emphasize that advertising became big business in the 1920s, put the information in the second sentence into an adjective clause.

> Advertising, **which fueled the demand for cars and other consumer goods,** became big business in the 1920s.

However, if you want to emphasize that advertising fueled consumers' demand for goods, put that information in an independent clause and the other information in an adjective clause.

> Advertising, **which became big business in the 1920s,** fueled the demand for cars and other consumer goods.

NOTE When using an adjective clause to transform two sentences into one, you may need to change the **word order** of the adjective clause to make the new sentence work. For clarity, be sure that you place the adjective clause next to the word it modifies.

STYLE TIP

Note that adjective clauses may be embedded within an independent clause or sentence.

Reference Note

For more about **combining sentences by subordinating ideas,** see page 469.

Exercise 2 **Subordinating Ideas by Using Adjective Clauses**

Change the emphasis in each of the following sentences. Emphasize the idea that is now in the subordinate clause, and subordinate the idea that is now in the independent clause. You may have to delete some words, change the word order, or use a different word to begin the new subordinate clause. Which version of the sentence sounds better to you? Why?

EXAMPLE 1. N. Scott Momaday, who is an accomplished painter, writes novels and poetry.

   1. *N. Scott Momaday, who writes novels and poetry, is an accomplished painter.*

1. N. Scott Momaday, who writes eloquently about American Indian culture, won a Pulitzer Prize for the novel *House Made of Dawn*.

2. *House Made of Dawn,* which was published in 1968, focuses on an American Indian man's struggle to reconcile traditional tribal values with modern-day American life.
3. This novel, which was Momaday's first, is his best-known work.
4. Momaday, who is half Kiowa, grew up in New Mexico and Oklahoma.
5. Momaday spent his boyhood on several different reservations, where he acquired extensive knowledge of American Indian history and culture.
6. Momaday, who doesn't speak Kiowa, was given the name of Rock-Tree-Boy when he was still an infant.
7. Momaday's second novel, which was finished twenty years after his first was published, focuses on the myth behind his Indian name.
8. Momaday's book *The Way to Rainy Mountain,* which gives a perceptive account of American Indian life, focuses on the history and culture of the Kiowas.
9. Momaday, who has also published two collections of poems, considers himself primarily a poet.
10. Momaday, who believes his cultural heritage is important to his work, is proud of his American Indian roots.

Correcting Faulty Coordination

Before you join ideas with a coordinating conjunction, it is important to make sure the ideas are of equal importance. Otherwise you may end up with *faulty coordination,* unequal ideas presented as if they were coordinate. Faulty coordination blurs the focus of your writing because it does not show the relationships between ideas. You can correct faulty coordination by putting the less-important ideas into phrases or subordinate clauses.

FAULTY   Norway's coastal waters are influenced by the warm Atlantic Ocean currents and the westerly winds, and the coastal waters stay ice-free, and they are ice-free all year.

REVISED   **Because Norway's coastal waters are influenced by the warm Atlantic Ocean currents and westerly winds,** they stay ice-free **all year.**

or

Norway's coastal waters, **which are influenced by the warm Atlantic Ocean currents and the westerly winds,** stay ice-free **all year.**

Using Parallel Structure

Like a comfortable bicycle ride, writing should have smooth movement; it shouldn't be a bumpy journey over mental potholes and gravel. You can make your writing smoother and clearer by checking your sentences for **parallel structure.**

You create parallel structure in a sentence by using the same grammatical form to express equal, or parallel, ideas. For example, you pair a noun with a noun, a phrase with a phrase, a clause with a clause, and an infinitive with an infinitive.

Use parallel structure when you link coordinate ideas.

NOT PARALLEL	Mrs. Silva prefers exercising and to paint. [gerund paired with infinitive]
PARALLEL	Mrs. Silva prefers **to exercise** and **to paint.** [infinitive paired with infinitive]

NOT PARALLEL	Our computer club promises that we will visit a college and a banquet. [noun clause paired with a noun]
PARALLEL	Our computer club promises **that we will visit a college** and **that we will have a banquet.** [noun clause paired with noun clause]

Use parallel structure when you compare or contrast ideas.

NOT PARALLEL	To think logically is as important as calculating accurately. [infinitive compared with a gerund]
PARALLEL	**Thinking** logically is as important as **calculating** accurately. [gerund compared with a gerund]

NOT PARALLEL	Einstein liked doing mathematical research more than to supervise a large laboratory. [gerund phrase contrasted with an infinitive phrase]
PARALLEL	Einstein liked **doing mathematical research** more than **supervising a large laboratory.** [gerund phrase contrasted with a gerund phrase]

Use parallel structure when you link ideas with the conjunctions *both . . . and, either . . . or, neither . . . nor,* or *not only . . . but also.* These pairs are called **correlative conjunctions.**

NOT PARALLEL	In a Puritan village of 1680, a girl had to help her mother not only as a maker of household remedies, such as palsy drops and pokeberry plaster, but also in cooking.
PARALLEL	In a Puritan village of 1680, a girl had to help her mother not only **as a maker of household remedies,** such as palsy drops and pokeberry plaster, but also **as a cook.**

S T Y L E   T I P

Parallel structure can add more than clarity to language—it can also add rhythm and emphasis. One good way to tell if your use of parallelism provides the emphasis you intend is to read the sentence aloud. Do you *hear* the similarities between the parallel ideas?

When you use correlative conjunctions, be sure the conjunctions are followed by parallel terms. Otherwise the relationship between the ideas will not be clear.

UNCLEAR	The tornado not only destroyed the shed behind the store but also the water tower across the street.
CLEAR	The tornado destroyed **not only** the shed behind the store **but also** the water tower across the street.
UNCLEAR	The person who both finishes first and who finds everything on the list will win the scavenger hunt.
CLEAR	The person who **both** finishes first **and** finds everything on the list will win the scavenger hunt.

Exercise 3 **Revising Sentences by Using Parallel Structure**

Some of the following sentences are out of balance. Bring balance to them by putting the ideas in parallel form. You may need to delete, add, or move some words. If a sentence is already correct, write *C*.

EXAMPLE
1. Tara says that watching sports is popular, engaging, and provides fun.

1. *Tara says that watching sports is popular, engaging, and fun.*

1. Sports fans may disagree about whether going to baseball games or to watch football is more fun, but few people can ignore the importance of sports in America.
2. Sports has always been a topic for friendly and not-so-friendly arguments.
3. Some sports fans argue endlessly and with anger about whether football or baseball is truly the American pastime.
4. Baseball backers may insist that baseball is the more important game because it requires skill, dexterity, and to be fast.
5. On the other hand, football fans may praise a quarterback's speed, skill, and how agile he is.
6. I myself prefer basketball because of its swiftness, unpredictability, and how stunning the moves are.
7. It's also a sport in which women are catching up to men in terms of respect, popularity, and being famous.
8. In basketball, moving quickly is as important as to aim accurately.
9. This weekend my family is going to see a basketball game and a restaurant.

10. Watching sports and to argue over the best one has become one of our favorite pastimes.

Review A **Revising Paragraphs for Clarity**

Faulty coordination and faulty parallelism make the following paragraphs confusing. Using the methods you have learned in this chapter, revise each faulty sentence to make it clear and smooth. You may need to add, delete, or rearrange some words in the sentences. Remember to check the placement of correlative conjunctions.

EXAMPLE   I love Amy Tan's writing because of her believable
           characters and how she uses humor.

           I love Amy Tan's writing because of her believable
           characters and her humor.

Amy Tan is a Chinese American writer, and she writes skillfully about the lives of second-generation Chinese Americans. In her first two novels, The Joy Luck Club and The Kitchen God's Wife, she portrays family relationships both with humor and insightfully. These novels were praised by critics, and they deal with the difficulties mothers and daughters have in truly understanding one another.

In her third novel, The Hundred Secret Senses, Tan shifts to the relationship between sisters. The younger sister is embarrassed and has resentment of her older sister until the two travel to China together.

Tan seems like a natural-born storyteller, but she did not always plan to write fiction. In fact, her parents hoped she would become a neurosurgeon. Tan was working as a freelance business writer, and she decided to try her hand at writing short stories. She joined a writing workshop and submitted her first story. She was revising it, and the story grew, changed, and eventually to become the basis for her first novel. Once The Joy Luck Club was published, Tan became an instant celebrity. With her third novel, The Hundred Secret Senses, Tan has proven that she has an important subject and her talent is lasting.

Obstacles to Clarity

In the first part of this chapter, you had some practice at putting your ideas in proper relationship to one another. The next important step toward clarity is to check your sentences for completeness. As you revise, you need to be on the alert for two obstacles to clarity: *sentence fragments* and *run-on sentences*.

Sentence Fragments

A sentence should express a complete thought. If you capitalize and punctuate a part of a sentence as if it were a complete sentence, you create a **sentence fragment.**

FRAGMENT	Has large horns shaped like corkscrews. [The subject is missing. *What* has large horns shaped like corkscrews?]
SENTENCE	**A male kudu** has large horns shaped like corkscrews.
FRAGMENT	The kudu, a type of antelope, in Africa. [The verb is missing.]
SENTENCE	The kudu, a type of antelope, **lives** in Africa.
FRAGMENT	The kudu, a type of antelope, found in Africa. [The helping verb is missing.]
SENTENCE	The kudu, a type of antelope, **is** found in Africa.
FRAGMENT	While the kudu stands five feet high at the shoulder. [This has a subject and a verb, but it doesn't express a complete thought.]
SENTENCE	While the kudu stands five feet high at the shoulder, **with its long horns its total height can reach past ten feet.**

The meaning of a fragment you have written may seem clear to you because you know the information you have left out. Try looking at what you have written as though the information is all new to you. Ask what else a reader might need to know.

NOTE Experienced writers sometimes use fragments deliberately for effect. For example, in the following excerpt, Leslie Norris uses fragments to imitate the sounds of natural speech. Notice that the meaning of the fragments is made clear by the sentences that come before and after the fragments.

> "This was an unusual goose," my uncle said. "Called at the back door every morning for its food, answered to its name. An intelligent creature. Eddie's sisters tied a blue silk ribbon around its neck and made a pet of it. It displayed more personality and understanding than you'd believe possible in a bird. Came Christmas, of course, and they couldn't kill it."
>
> Leslie Norris, "A Flight of Geese"

Fragments can be effective when they are used as a stylistic technique. You may want to experiment with using them in expressive and creative writing such as journals, poems, and short stories. You can also use fragments when an informal, shorthand style is appropriate—for example, in classified ads.

However, do not use fragments if they might interfere with your purpose or confuse your audience. For example, you would not use fragments in a research paper or a book report, since your readers expect formal, straightforward language in these types of informative writing.

Oral Practice Identifying and Revising Sentence Fragments

Read each of these word groups aloud, and decide which are sentences and which are fragments. If an item contains only complete sentences, say *correct*. If it contains a fragment, revise the fragment to make it a complete sentence.

EXAMPLE 1. Going to a good college nowadays.
1. *Going to a good college is important nowadays.*

1. Many great Americans had little or no formal education. Among these are political leaders, writers, artists, scientists, and business executives.
2. Eleanor Roosevelt had little formal education. Susan B. Anthony the equivalent of a high school education.

Susan B. Anthony

Obstacles to Clarity   **447**

Willa Cather

Reference Note

The **types of phrases** include **prepositional, verbal, absolute, and appositive.** For explanations of these types of phrases, see pages 54, 58, 59, and 68.

3. When Abraham Lincoln was a young man, he worked in a general store. And at the same time studied books on law.
4. Although Carl Sandburg left school when he was thirteen years old. He later went on to Lombard College after serving in the army during the Spanish-American War.
5. Andrew Carnegie, who gave away many millions to charity, started to work at the age of thirteen. He did not go to high school.
6. Gordon Parks, who had a high school education, the World Press Photo Award in 1988.
7. Booker T. Washington walked two hundred miles to attend school at Hampton Institute. Later founded Tuskegee Institute.
8. One of the great letter writers of all time, Abigail Adams, had little formal schooling.
9. Ben Franklin, who became a printer's apprentice when he was only twelve. He taught himself to become a proficient writer by studying and imitating essays in *The Spectator*.
10. On the other hand, many famous Americans had excellent educations. As a child, Willa Cather, for instance, was taught Greek and Latin by a Nebraska shopkeeper.

Phrase Fragments

One type of sentence fragment is a phrase fragment. A *phrase* is a group of related words that acts as a single part of speech and that does not contain a subject and a verb. Because a phrase does not express a complete thought, it cannot stand on its own as a sentence.

Often, you can correct a phrase fragment by attaching it to the sentence that comes before or after it.

FRAGMENT **During her long and productive life.** Nina Otero-Warren excelled as an educator, writer, and public official. [prepositional phrase]

SENTENCE During her long and productive life, Nina Otero-Warren excelled as an educator, writer, and public official.

FRAGMENT **Descended from a long line of political leaders.** Otero-Warren became active in politics soon after she graduated from college. [verbal phrase—participial]

SENTENCE Descended from a long line of political leaders, Otero-Warren became active in politics soon after she graduated from college.

FRAGMENT	She was one of the first Mexican American women. **To hold important public posts in New Mexico.** [verbal phrase—infinitive]
SENTENCE	She was one of the first Mexican American women to hold important public posts in New Mexico.

FRAGMENT	In 1917, she became superintendent of schools in Santa Fe County. **An unusual position for a woman at that time.** [appositive phrase]
SENTENCE	In 1917, she became superintendent of schools in Santa Fe County, an unusual position for a woman at that time.

FRAGMENT	**Her heritage being an important influence in her life.** Nina Otero-Warren wrote *Old Spain in Our Southwest,* a narrative account of the history and folklore of the Southwest. [absolute phrase]
SENTENCE	Her heritage being an important influence in her life, Nina Otero-Warren wrote *Old Spain in Our Southwest,* a narrative account of the history and folklore of the Southwest.

Subordinate Clause Fragments

A *clause* is a group of words that contains a subject and a verb. An *independent clause* expresses a complete thought and can stand alone as a sentence. However, a *subordinate clause* does not express a complete thought and cannot stand alone as a sentence. If you see a subordinate clause standing alone, it is another type of sentence fragment.

FRAGMENT	Felicia enjoyed watching the Comets' game. **Which was televised last Monday.**
CORRECT	Felicia enjoyed watching the Comets' game, which was televised last Monday.

FRAGMENT	Felicia hopes to play professionally. **When she graduates from college.**
CORRECT	Felicia hopes to play professionally when she graduates from college.

While checking over your work, you may find that two other constructions cause you trouble: items in a series and compound verbs.

FRAGMENT	We had terrible weather. **Heat, drought, and thunderstorms.** [items in a series]
CORRECT	We had terrible weather. **We had** heat, drought, and thunderstorms.

or

We had terrible weather: heat, drought, and thunderstorms.

Reference Note

If you have any questions about the **difference between independent clauses and subordinate clauses,** see pages 76 and 77.

FRAGMENT	Tinesha tried to jog. **But could not tolerate the heat.**
	[compound verb]
CORRECT	Tinesha tried to jog, **but she could** not tolerate the heat.

Nat Love

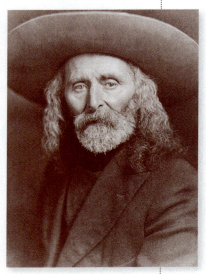

Andrew García

Exercise 4 Revising to Eliminate Fragments

Some of the following items are sets of complete sentences, while others contain fragments. If an item has only complete sentences, write *C*. If it contains a fragment, revise it to include the fragment in a complete sentence.

EXAMPLE **1.** Learning about Nat Love, who was famous in the Old West.

     1. We are learning about Nat Love, who was famous in the Old West.

1. Nat Love, who was born a slave in Tennessee, became a cowboy. When he was just fifteen years old.

2. Love being an expert horseman. He traveled throughout the West. Driving cattle on the open range.

3. After taking first prize in a riding, roping, and shooting contest in Deadwood, South Dakota, became known as "Deadwood Dick."

4. In 1907, Love published his autobiography, *The Life and Adventures of Nat Love, Better Known in Cattle Country as Deadwood Dick.*

5. The book both true stories and tall tales about Love and other famous characters of the Old West. Because Love did have many real-life adventures, it's difficult to tell which stories are fact and which are fiction.

6. Another figure of the Old West. Andrew García, tells of similar exploits in his autobiography *Tough Trip Through Paradise.*

7. García describes some of the tough characters he met when he traveled with an outlaw band. One of the most notorious characters was the horse thief George Reynolds, better known as "Big Nose George."

8. Like many of the outlaws García knew. Reynolds died a violent death.

9. Although tempted to become an outlaw himself. García eventually settled down. And began writing his exciting account of his life.

10. García not living to see his memoirs published. The manuscripts, which he had packed away in dynamite boxes. Were discovered years after his death.

Run-on Sentences

When you are writing a draft, you may like to race full-speed ahead to get your thoughts down on paper. When you revise, however, it is important to know when to put on the brakes. Each complete thought should come to a full stop or be linked correctly to the next thought. If you run together two sentences as if they were a single thought, you create a **run-on sentence.**

There are two kinds of run-on sentences. A **fused sentence** has no punctuation at all between the two complete thoughts. A **comma splice** has just a comma between them.

FUSED Lightning speeds to our eyes at 186,000 miles per second thunder creeps to our ears at 1,087 feet per second.

COMMA We cannot hear and see the event at the same time, we
SPLICE sense it twice in different ways.

There are many different ways to correct a run-on sentence. Depending on the relationship you want to show between the two ideas, one method may be better than another.

1. You can make two sentences.

Lightning speeds to our eyes at 186,000 miles per second**.** **T**hunder creeps to our ears at 1,087 feet per second.

2. You can use a comma and a coordinating conjunction.

Lightning speeds to our eyes at 186,000 miles per second**, but** thunder creeps to our ears at 1,087 feet per second.

3. You can change one of the independent clauses to a subordinate clause.

While lightning speeds to our eyes at 186,000 miles per second, thunder creeps to our ears at 1,087 feet per second.

4. You can use a semicolon.

Lightning speeds to our eyes at 186,000 miles per second**;** thunder creeps to our ears at 1,087 feet per second.

5. You can use a semicolon and a conjunctive adverb.

Lightning speeds to our eyes at 186,000 miles per second**;** **however,** thunder creeps to our ears at 1,087 feet per second.

NOTE You have probably noticed that well-known writers sometimes use run-on sentences in their works. You might wonder: If an expert writer uses run-ons, why can't I use them, too?

You *can* use run-ons occasionally in short stories, journal entries, and other kinds of expressive and creative writing. Run-ons can be especially effective in *stream of consciousness* writing, a style that imitates the natural flow of a character's thoughts, feelings, and perceptions. What is the effect of the run-on sentence below?

> The blue light from Cornelia's lampshade drew into a tiny point at the center of her brain, it flickered and winked like an eye, quietly it fluttered and dwindled.
>
> Katherine Anne Porter, "The Jilting of Granny Weatherall"

Always check your writing for unintentional run-ons. If you use run-ons for effect, make sure that your meaning will be clear to your reader.

Exercise 5 Revising Run-on Sentences

The following items are confusing because they are run-on sentences. Revise each run-on by using the method given in parentheses. (The examples on page 451 will help you.) If you have to choose a connecting word or subordinate an idea, make sure your revised version shows the appropriate relationship between the ideas.

EXAMPLE 1. In my English class I am reading about the Victorian era many of our literature book's short stories were written during that time. (two sentences)

1. *In my English class I am reading about the Victorian era. Many of our literature book's short stories were written during that time.*

1. The Victorians were very concerned with etiquette they had strict rules regarding proper behavior. (semicolon)
2. On the night a Victorian girl was presented to society, she was allowed to dance her partner for the first dance would be carefully selected by her mother. (comma and coordinating conjunction)
3. Married couples could dance only once together at a party they had to follow the rules of etiquette as well. (two sentences)
4. Public behavior was not the only aspect of society controlled by etiquette it governed even letter writing. (subordinate clause)

5. The paper a letter was written upon had to be thick colored inks were not supposed to be used. (comma and coordinating conjunction)

6. The Victorian era was a time of extreme delicacy and tact in language, direct references to the body were considered offensive in polite society. (two sentences)

7. The word *limb* had to be used instead of *leg* or *arm* even a reference to the "leg" of a chair was considered impolite. (semicolon)

8. In reference to poultry, the thigh was called the second joint the leg was called the first joint or the drumstick. (comma and coordinating conjunction)

9. Delicate language was carried to an even greater extreme by some people, they referred to a bull as a "gentleman cow." (subordinate clause)

10. This kind of euphemistic language seems funny to us now, even today we use indirect language to replace words and phrases that might be considered offensive. (semicolon, conjunctive adverb, and comma)

Review B **Revising Paragraphs to Eliminate Fragments and Run-on Sentences**

Revise the following paragraphs to eliminate the fragments and run-ons. Add or delete words wherever necessary. Be sure to check your revised version for correct capitalization and punctuation.

EXAMPLE   Although few people want to take part in wars.

Although few people want to take part in wars, many like to read about wartime experiences.

War reports—both fact and fiction—have fascinated people since the first warriors and bards sat around campfires. Not all war literature is based on firsthand experience some comes out of imagination. One of America's most prominent war novelists, Stephen Crane, wrote about war before he ever saw a battle, Crane's short novel <u>The Red Badge of Courage</u> about a young soldier's reactions to fear during a major Civil War battle. Was written almost thirty years after the battle took place.

On the other hand, many of Ernest Hemingway's novels and stories were based on his own experiences during World War I before the United States entered the war Hemingway worked as an ambulance driver for the Italian army. His novel A Farewell to Arms. Which is often called the most important novel about World War I, follows the experiences of a young ambulance driver.

After World War II. Writer John Hersey introduced a journalistic technique to war fiction his book Hiroshima which describes the effect of the dropping of the A-bomb combines the literary techniques of fiction with the factual style of journalism. The Vietnam era produced several notable works of nonfiction. Including Ron Kovic's Born on the Fourth of July. A Vietnam veteran. Kovic describes how his feelings about war changed after he lost the use of his legs.

World War II soldiers in the field

Recently, even historical books have been influenced by fictional and autobiographical accounts of war. Citizen Soldiers, a history of World War II. Recounts the experiences of ordinary soldiers in the field instead of focusing on the personalities of the generals or on battle strategies. Stephen E. Ambrose, the author of Citizen Soldiers, is able to provide gut-wrenching details usually found only in novels or memoirs, he gathered much of his material from the oral history accounts of soldiers who fought in the trenches.

Memoirs of war also include diaries. Though not always the personal writing of soldiers. Mary Chesnut, wife of Confederate general James Chesnut, kept a diary. How war affected the daily lives of people in the South. From ordinary people to generals and political figures, like Jefferson Davis, the president of the Confederacy. Her diary was first published as Diary from Dixie her words and observations used extensively in Ken Burns's documentary The Civil War.

Chapter Review

A. Revising Paragraphs for Clarity

Revise the following paragraphs to improve coordination and subordination of ideas and to correct faulty parallelism. You may need to add, delete, or rearrange words in the sentences.

Ruth Fulton Benedict was an important American anthropologist, and she lived from 1887 to 1948. Benedict's name may not be as familiar as Margaret Mead, her friend and fellow anthropologist, and Benedict's influence on cultural anthropology was profound. Benedict was most interested in the influence of culture on individual personality, so she argued that a culture's "personality" defined the individuals within it. Each culture's customs, practices, and what they believed, according to Benedict, determined whether the individual member would be considered a success or if the person was a misfit in the culture. Her book *Patterns of Culture* (1934) explained the idea of culture to the general American public, for it was a bestseller.

Benedict graduated from Vassar College in 1909, spent a short time as a social worker, and was teaching school. In 1914 she married a biochemistry professor, Stanley Benedict, and in 1919 she began taking courses again. First she took courses at Columbia University with John Dewey, and then at the New School for Social Research, and there her interest in anthropology began. In 1923, working with Franz Boas at Columbia University, she earned a doctorate. Her first book was published in 1931, and she had spent eleven years doing fieldwork with American Indians in California, the Southwest, and the Northwest.

Like her mentor Boas, Benedict became an expert on North American Indians, for the range of cultures she studied was wide. During World War II, she was an advisor to the Office of War Information, but she applied anthropological methods to modern cultures. Her final work for the OWI was a study of Japan, and out of that study came *The Chrysanthemum and the Sword: Patterns of Japanese Culture,* and it was published in 1946. *The Chrysanthemum and the Sword* also became a bestselling book, and is still in print. Benedict became a full professor at Columbia in 1948, she started a broad study of contemporary European and Asian cultures, she became ill after a trip to Europe, and she died in September of 1948.

B. Revising Paragraphs to Eliminate Fragments and Run-on Sentences.

Revise the following paragraphs to eliminate any sentence fragments and run-on sentences. You may need to add, delete, or rearrange words in the sentences.

The history of even the most ordinary, everyday objects can be fascinating. For example, the humble pencil—the kind of pencil everyone has been using since kindergarten. If asked to imagine the pencil, most Americans would probably picture a yellow stick with a little metal band holding in the eraser on one end, they would probably describe the part of the pencil that actually makes marks as a "lead."

Of course, pencil "leads" are not made from lead at all, lead was used for some early writing instruments. The core of a pencil often includes graphite, a dark, very soft mineral, the use of graphite for writing became widespread after a large deposit of the mineral was discovered. In England in 1564. The mineral so soft and brittle that it had to be enclosed in a holder. At first, the lengths of graphite were wrapped in string, later users inserted graphite into sticks that had been hollowed out by hand.

The first mass-produced pencils made in Germany in 1662 and were left unpainted to show off the quality of the wood, the first American pencils were made in 1812. Following the discovery of a large, high-quality graphite deposit in Siberia near the Chinese border. American manufacturers wanted a way to advertise their use of the superior Asian graphite. In the 1890s, they began to paint the pencils bright yellow. A color associated in China with royalty and respect. Even today, 75 percent of the pencils sold in the United States are yellow.

Pencil leads are actually made from a mixture of graphite and clay, manufacturers control the hardness of the lead by adjusting the proportions of the graphite and clay. Writing pencils designated by numbers from one (the softest) to four (the hardest). Soft pencils contain more graphite when they are pressed on paper, more graphite is deposited. Making a darker, heavier mark.

Combining Sentences

Diagnostic Preview

A. Combining Sentences by Inserting Words and Phrases

Combine the sentences in the following items by inserting words or phrases from one sentence into the other sentence.

EXAMPLE   **1.** This spring I will be acting in a play. It was written by my English teacher, Mrs. Benjamin.

          1. This spring I will be acting in a play written by my English teacher, Mrs. Benjamin.

1. My friend Joey performs at children's birthday parties. He is an amateur magician.

2. Her hair was flying in the wind. She handled the sailboat expertly.

3. Those old houses are no longer occupied. They are near the beach on the far side of the island.

4. Matt realized that he hadn't had enough sleep. He was stretching and yawning.

5. The assembly instructions were incomplete and confusing. They were supposed to have been simple.

6. He worked on the final project all weekend. He was determined to make a high grade in the class.

7. Stars twinkled in the inky night sky. The young campers finally fell asleep in their tents.
8. The baron's castle loomed over their heads. It was a fantastic concoction of towers, turrets, gables, and walls.
9. Many of the trees in this part of the park are hundreds of feet tall. They are ancient.
10. After the movie, meet us at the restaurant. The restaurant is on the corner across the street from the theater.

B. Combining Sentences by Coordinating Ideas

Combine the sentences in each of the following items by forming a compound subject, a compound predicate, or a compound sentence.

EXAMPLE   1. Martha is writing a mystery novel. Jack is helping her edit it.

1. *Martha is writing a mystery novel, and Jack is helping her edit it.*

11. Last Saturday, Annie mowed the lawn. Then she trimmed the hedges and raked up all the grass and trimmings.
12. Frank is planning a trip to Hawaii. His cousin Michael is planning the trip, too.
13. Did Curtis turn in his paper on time? Did Mr. Branch give him an extension on the deadline?
14. The yearbook staff will be accepting early-bird orders through next Tuesday. After that, the price of the yearbook will increase.
15. I looked everywhere for my jacket. I finally found it under the bed.

C. Combining Sentences by Subordinating Ideas

Combine the sentences in each of the following items by subordinating one of the sentences to the other.

EXAMPLE   1. Brock and Rei are working together on a presentation. The presentation will cover several techniques for improving writing style.

1. *Brock and Rei are working together on a presentation that will cover several techniques for improving writing style.*

16. The doctor explained the diagnostic tests to her patient. The patient would be having the tests the next week.
17. The house painters masked all the trim. Then they sprayed the paint on in about two hours.

18. Anybody can help at the car wash. He or she should sign up on the list in the hall.
19. Neil will play a different position next year. He told me that yesterday.
20. My cousins will be staying with us next summer. They are several years younger than I am.
21. Carolyn missed a whole week of school last month. She had the flu.
22. Rick woke up early so that he could be one of the first in line at the box office. He was still too late to get the best seats.
23. The snow in the mountains was deep. It came up to the bottom of the cabin's windowsills.
24. The child beamed a sweet, sticky smile at his mother. His face was covered with strawberry jam and peanut butter.
25. This is what you need to do now. You need to call her up and apologize for losing your temper.

Combining Sentences for Style

Revising is not just a matter of checking your writing for completeness and correctness. When you revise, you also look at your writing with an eye for style. It is important to notice how your sentences work together to shape each of your paragraphs. A short sentence may be fine by itself, but a long series of short sentences can make writing sound choppy and dull.

Read the following sentences. Does the writing style help hold your interest, or does it distract you from the meaning of the paragraph?

```
There is an object at hand. It resembles an
eggbeater. The eggbeater is fancy. It is squat
and top-heavy. It blends style with utility.
The style is Victorian, and the utility is
Industrial. It is an electric pen. The pen is
from Thomas Edison. He did not make it for a
while. He was 28 when he made it. He had been
granted patents. There were nearly 100 he had
been granted. He had spent most of his adult
life tinkering. He had been tinkering with
telegraphs.
```

The choppy sentences you just read are based on the following well-crafted sentences by journalist Bruce Watson. Notice how varying the length and structure of his sentences gives his paragraph a natural flow and rhythm.

> The object at hand resembles a fancy eggbeater. Squat and top-heavy, it blends Victorian style with Industrial Age utility. It is Thomas Edison's electric pen. By the time he got around to making it, Edison was 28. He had been granted nearly 100 patents and had spent most of his adult life tinkering with telegraphs.
>
> Bruce Watson, "A Wizard's Scribe," *Smithsonian*

Perhaps you have your own sentence style, one that is unique to your writing. No matter what your style, however, you can add rhythm and variety to your writing by balancing short sentences with longer, more detailed ones. Sentence combining helps you create this balance; it also helps make your sentences more precise by eliminating repeated words and ideas.

Combining Sentences by Inserting Words and Phrases

Often, you can combine related sentences by taking a key word or phrase from one sentence and inserting it into another sentence. The word or phrase adds detail to the other sentence, and repeated words are eliminated.

THREE SENTENCES	This barometer measures the pressure of the atmosphere. It uses a glass tube of mercury to do this. The barometer measures changes in pressure.
ONE SENTENCE	Using a glass tube of mercury, this barometer measures the changes in the pressure of the atmosphere.

or

With a glass tube of mercury, this barometer measures the changes in the pressure of the atmosphere.

Usually you will have some choice in where you insert a word or phrase. Just watch out for awkward-sounding combinations and ones that confuse the meaning of the original sentences. For example, avoid combinations like this one: *Changes in the pressure of the atmosphere,*

TIPS & TRICKS

When should you combine sentences for style? One good way to find out is to circle the first five words in each sentence in a paragraph. If the subject and verb are located within the circles in four consecutive sentences, combine two of the sentences using one of the techniques described in this chapter.

COMPUTER TIP

If you are using a computer, you can use a word-processing program's cut and paste commands to move words, phrases, paragraphs, or blocks of text within a document. If you change your mind, you can always move the text again.

with a glass tube of mercury, this barometer measures. Be sure to read your sentence and make sure it is clear and grammatically correct.

Single-Word Modifiers

Sometimes you can take a word from one sentence and insert it directly into another sentence as a modifier. Other times you will need to change the word into an adjective or adverb before you can insert it.

Using the Same Form	
ORIGINAL	Timing is essential for performing magic tricks. The magician's timing must be excellent.
COMBINED	**Excellent** timing is essential for performing magic tricks.
ORIGINAL	Magicians guard the secrets of their tricks. They guard them carefully.
COMBINED	Magicians **carefully** guard the secrets of their tricks.
Changing the Form	
ORIGINAL	The famous magician Harry Houdini performed impossible escapes. The escapes only seemed impossible.
COMBINED	The famous magician Harry Houdini performed **seemingly** impossible escapes.
ORIGINAL	He escaped from a sealed crate that had been lowered into a river. He had handcuffs on.
COMBINED	**Handcuffed,** he escaped from a sealed crate that had been lowered into a river.

Prepositional Phrases

You can usually take a prepositional phrase from one sentence and insert it into another without any change in form.

ORIGINAL	Our English class is reading "Everyday Use." It is by Alice Walker.
COMBINED	Our English class is reading "Everyday Use" **by Alice Walker.**

You can also combine sentences by changing part of a sentence into a prepositional phrase.

ORIGINAL	A female narrator tells the story. Her tone is conversational.
COMBINED	A female narrator tells the story **in a conversational tone.**

Exercise 1   Combining by Inserting Single-Word Modifiers and Prepositional Phrases

Combine each group of short, related sentences by inserting adjectives, adverbs, or prepositional phrases into the first sentence. You may need to change the forms of some words before you insert them. Add commas where they are necessary.

Reference Note

For more on **using commas with introductory prepositional phrases,** see page 309.

EXAMPLE
1. The Iroquois moved to the Northeast. They moved during the thirteenth century. They moved from the Mississippi region.

1. *During the thirteenth century, the Iroquois moved from the Mississippi region to the Northeast.*

1. The Iroquois formed a confederation. The confederation was powerful. The Iroquois formed the confederation in the Northeast region.
2. A central council of the confederation made decisions. The council made decisions unanimously.
3. Women nominated delegates. The women were from the confederation. They nominated delegates to the central council.
4. The Iroquois confederation subdued other groups of people. The groups of people were American Indians. The subduing of the groups was systematic.
5. The groups exchanged belts to ratify treaties. Their belts were of wampum. The treaties were important.
6. The Iroquois developed trade routes. The trade routes were extensive. The trade routes were along waterways and trails.
7. Hunting was an important activity. It was an annual activity in Iroquois society for the men. The hunt took place every fall.
8. The Iroquois also depended on farming. Their dependence on the farming done by the women was heavy.
9. Entire villages moved in search of soil. They were searching for soil that was richer. They needed the rich soil for farming.
10. The structure of Iroquoian life changed. The structure was complex. The change was considerable. The structure changed during the late seventeenth century.

Participial Phrases

A *participial phrase* contains a participle and any modifiers or complements related to the participle. The whole phrase acts as an adjective and, like other modifiers, adds concrete details to sentences.

Reference Note

For more on **participles and participial phrases,** see pages 58 and 59.

EXAMPLE   **Awakened by the uproar,** the group's guide, Simon Qamanariq, stumbled from his tent to find the bear between him and his *qamatiik,* the sledge **pulled by his snowmobile, where he kept his rifle.**

Paul Rauber, "On Top of the World," *Sierra*

Sometimes you can lift a participial phrase directly from one sentence and insert it into another sentence. Other times you will need to change a verb into a participle before you can insert the idea into another sentence.

ORIGINAL   Storm clouds revolve around a hurricane's calm center. The calm center is called the eye.

COMBINED   Storm clouds revolve around a hurricane's calm center, **called the eye.**

ORIGINAL   Hurricanes gather strength and size as they move over the water. They move westward initially.

COMBINED   **Initially moving westward,** hurricanes gather strength and size as they move over the water.

NOTE   Be sure to place a participial phrase close to the noun or pronoun you want it to modify. Otherwise, your sentence may end up with a meaning you did not intend.

MISPLACED   Broadcast by the National Hurricane Center, the town's residents listened to the forecast.

IMPROVED   The town's residents listened to the forecast **broadcast by the National Hurricane Center.**

Absolute Phrases

An *absolute phrase* consists of (1) a participle or a participial phrase, (2) a noun or a pronoun that the participle or participial phrase modifies, and (3) any other modifiers of that noun or pronoun. The entire word group is used as an adverb to modify the independent clause of a sentence. Absolute phrases are valuable tools for combining sentences. They bring in additional information and help to emphasize certain ideas.

EXAMPLE   **Excited sea gulls screeching in protest,** the men on horseback raced down the beach.

Exercise 2 Combining by Inserting Participial and Absolute Phrases

Combine each of the following sentence pairs. First, reduce one of the sentences to a participial or an absolute phrase, changing the form of the verb if necessary. Then, insert the phrase into the other sentence. Be sure to place a participial phrase next to the noun or pronoun it modifies.

EXAMPLE
1. Virtual reality is a simulated, three-dimensional environment. It is usually produced by a computer.

1. *Usually produced by a computer, virtual reality is a simulated, three-dimensional environment.*

1. Virtual reality systems can be used to train pilots, doctors, and engineers. These systems are seen most often in video games.
2. A head-mounted display is made of a headset with a screen for each eye. The display connects to a computer.
3. A tracking device senses the eye movements of the user. Tracking devices are usually built into the headset.
4. The computer creates an artificial world that seems real to the user. The images of the two screens are blended by the computer.
5. Some virtual reality systems include a small speaker for each ear. These systems use sound to enhance the illusion of the simulated world.
6. The virtual reality systems can't reproduce all the minute aspects of the real world. The virtual reality systems are limited in their technology.
7. A special glove is often used. The glove discerns the movements of a person's hand.
8. A motorized joystick is another virtual reality device. The joystick allows a person to sense the weight of a virtual object.
9. Some video games use a special vibrating controller. The special controller allows players to receive feedback from the games.
10. Virtual reality systems have come a long way since the start of research in the 1960s. Virtual reality systems are both teaching tools and great entertainment.

Appositive Phrases

Appositive phrases can also add detail to your sentences. An ***appositive phrase*** is made up of an appositive and its modifiers. (An appositive identifies or describes a noun or pronoun in a sentence.) Like a par-

┌HELP──

Note that an absolute phrase is not obviously connected to the rest of the sentence, and the noun in an absolute phrase is always different from the subject of the sentence.

EXAMPLE
The **horse** standing and blowing in its exhaustion, the **knight** dismounted to kneel before his king.

If the noun of the absolute phrase is missing, the result is a dangling participial phrase.

EXAMPLE
Standing and blowing in its exhaustion, the knight dismounted to kneel before his king. [dangling participial phrase]

ticipial phrase, an appositive phrase should be placed directly before or after the noun or pronoun it renames. It should be set off by a comma (or two commas if you place the phrase in the middle of the sentence).

EXAMPLE Tombaugh climbed up into the scaffolding of the sixteen-inch telescope, **a steel-and-glass affair that loomed up into the dark.**

Timothy Ferris, "Seeing in the Dark," *The New Yorker*

You can combine two sentences by placing one of the ideas in an appositive phrase.

TWO SENTENCES Arna Bontemps wrote for the magazine *Opportunity.* Arna Bontemps was a major figure in the Harlem Renaissance.

ONE SENTENCE Arna Bontemps, **a major figure in the Harlem Renaissance,** wrote for the magazine *Opportunity.*

or

A major figure in the Harlem Renaissance, Arna Bontemps wrote for the magazine *Opportunity.*

or

Arna Bontemps, **a writer for the magazine Opportunity,** was a major figure in the Harlem Renaissance.

Notice that the last combination emphasizes Bontemps's role in the Harlem Renaissance, while the first two combinations emphasize his work for *Opportunity*. In the last example, the ideas have been rearranged to change the emphasis, and the verb *wrote* has been changed to a noun, *writer,* to form the appositive.

Exercise 3 Combining by Inserting Appositive Phrases

Combine each pair of sentences by turning one of the sentences into an appositive phrase. You may see several ways to create the appositive; choose the combination that sounds best to you. Be sure to set off the appositive phrase with commas.

EXAMPLE 1. Calligraphy is an elegant form of handwriting. It requires a special pen or brush.

1. *Calligraphy, an elegant form of handwriting, requires a special pen or brush.*

1. Calligraphy has been used for over two thousand years to decorate books and paintings. It is an ancient art form.

2. Chinese calligraphy is done with a brush. Chinese calligraphy is the oldest form of calligraphy.

3. In the 600s, Japanese artists learned calligraphy from the Chinese. The Chinese were the first masters of the art.

4. Islamic artists developed Kufic writing. Kufic writing is one of the most graceful styles of calligraphy.

5. In Islamic countries, you can see sentences from the Koran inscribed in beautiful calligraphy on buildings. The Koran is the Islamic holy book.

6. A new type of writing was used for copying the Koran. This type of writing is the *nashki* script.

7. The *nashki* script was developed around A.D. 1000. It is still a very popular form of Arabic calligraphy.

8. Another type of calligraphy was developed in Turkey. This mannered script is called *divani*.

9. Turkish calligraphy has a cipher called the *tugra*. This cipher was a complicated and exquisite design.

10. From the sixteenth century, fine calligraphy has been collected in albums. Calligraphy is a greatly appreciated art.

Brush

Pen

Combining Sentences by Coordinating Ideas

Sometimes you will want to combine sentences that contain *coordinate,* or equally important, ideas. You can join coordinate words, phrases, or clauses with coordinating conjunctions (*and, but, for, nor, or, so,* and *yet*) or correlative conjunctions (*both . . . and, either . . . or, neither . . . nor*). The relationship of the ideas determines which connective works best. When they are joined in one sentence, the coordinate ideas form compound elements.

Reference Note

For more information on **coordination**, see page 436.

ORIGINAL	Juan will work in the concession stand. Kinesha will work in the concession stand.
COMBINED	**Both Juan and Kinesha** will work in the concession stand. [compound subject]

ORIGINAL	Mrs. Braxton could sponsor our class trip. Mrs. Braxton could recruit parents to help her.
COMBINED	Mrs. Braxton **could sponsor our class trip or recruit parents to help her.** [compound predicate]

ORIGINAL	The class officers wanted to schedule the trip for May. Mrs. Braxton had already chosen June.
COMBINED	The class officers wanted to schedule the trip for May, **but** Mrs. Braxton had already chosen June. [compound sentence]

You can also form a compound sentence by linking independent clauses with a semicolon or with a semicolon, a conjunctive adverb (*however, likewise, therefore*), and a comma.

EXAMPLES   You learn from every mistake**;** mistakes are therefore of great importance.

Tessa walked the new puppy, Asta**; meanwhile,** Sean fed the cats and set the table.

Exercise 4 Combining by Coordinating Ideas

Combine each of the following sets of sentences by forming a compound element. Be sure to choose a connective that expresses the correct relationship between the ideas. You may need to add punctuation, too.

EXAMPLE   1. Lucy Maud Montgomery was born in 1874. She died in April of 1942.

1. *Lucy Maud Montgomery was born in 1874 and died in April of 1942.*

1. L. M. Montgomery was born on Prince Edward Island. Many of her books were set there.
2. Montgomery had a difficult childhood. She would use her imagination as a means of escape.
3. She read famous authors such as Dickens and Longfellow. She realized that she wanted to be a writer.
4. A local paper published her work. Several other periodicals published her work.
5. Montgomery earned her teacher's certificate. She worked as a schoolteacher.
6. She started looking for another idea for a story. She decided to write her first book about a girl she named Anne.
7. Montgomery has written many different books. She is best known for her creation of the character Anne.
8. Anne is the main character in Montgomery's novel *Anne of Green Gables*. Anne is an orphan.
9. The novel was an immediate success. The novel made Montgomery a great deal of money.
10. Montgomery continued the story of Anne in seven more books. She also wrote many other novels.

Combining Sentences by Subordinating Ideas

If two sentences are unequal in importance, you can combine them by placing the less-important idea in a subordinate clause.

Reference Note

For more information on **subordinate clauses,** see page 77.

EXAMPLES   He had a habit of pausing to fix his gaze on part of the congregation as he read, and that Sunday he seemed to be talking to a small group of strangers **who sat in the front row.** [adjective clause]

Andrea Lee, "New African"

My luck ran out in mid-April **when a freak snowstorm moved in at midday and, in the next thirty hours, dumped eighteen inches of snow on the surrounding forest, the eagles' nest, and me.** [adverb clause]

Dr. Scott Nielsen, *A Season with Eagles*

What he had the most of was time. [noun clause]

Juan Sedillo, "Gentleman of Río en Medio"

Adjective Clauses

You can change a sentence into an adjective clause by replacing its subject with *who, whose, which,* or *that.* Then you can use the adjective clause to give information about a noun or pronoun in another sentence.

ORIGINAL   Aztec sculptures were used to decorate temples and other buildings. The sculptures were quite intricate.

REVISED   Aztec sculptures, **which were quite intricate,** were used to decorate temples and other buildings.

ORIGINAL   The Aztecs founded the city of Tenochtitlán. They prospered during the 1400s and early 1500s.

REVISED   The Aztecs, **who prospered during the 1400s and early 1500s,** founded the city of Tenochtitlán.

Be sure to put the idea you want to emphasize in the independent clause.

NOTE   How you punctuate an adjective clause depends on whether the clause is essential to the meaning of the sentence. If the clause is not essential, you need to set it off from the rest of the sentence with a comma or commas. If the clause is essential, no commas are necessary.

Reference Note

For more information on **punctuating adjective clauses,** see page 306.

NONESSENTIAL   The bicycle race, **which was sponsored by the student council,** will be the first activity on Saturday.

ESSENTIAL   Earl entered the race **that Tyrone won last year.**

SENTENCES

Adverb Clauses

An adverb clause modifies a verb, an adjective, or another adverb in the sentence to which it is attached. To make a sentence into an adverb clause, add a subordinating conjunction like *although, after, because, if, when, where,* or *while* at the beginning. The conjunction shows the relationship between the ideas in the adverb clause and the independent clause. It can show a relationship of time, place, cause or reason, purpose or result, or condition.

Reference Note

For more about **using adverb clauses to subordinate ideas,** see page 438.

ORIGINAL   The Spanish explorer Hernando Cortes landed on the coast of Mexico. He and his men marched to the capital of the Aztecs.

REVISED   **After the Spanish explorer Hernando Cortes landed on the coast of Mexico,** he and his men marched to the capital of the Aztecs. [time]

ORIGINAL   The baseball game was stopped. Heavy lightning began.

REVISED   The baseball game was stopped **because heavy lightning began.** [cause]

NOTE   When you place an adverb clause at the beginning of a sentence, separate it from the independent clause with a comma.

Reference Note

For more about the **use of commas with adverb clauses,** see page 310.

EXAMPLES   **Although I got up early,** I was still tardy for school.

           When I got home from school, I reorganized my English binder and set my new alarm clock.

Noun Clauses

You can make a sentence into a noun clause by adding a word like *that, how, what, whatever, who,* or *whoever* at the beginning of the sentence; you may also have to delete or move some words. Then, insert the clause into another sentence just as you would an ordinary noun.

ORIGINAL   Manuel has been asked to the *quinceañera*. Selena told me this fact.

REVISED   Selena told me **that Manuel has been asked to the *quinceañera.***

Exercise 5   **Combining by Subordinating Ideas**

Combine each of the following pairs of sentences by turning one sentence into a subordinate clause.

HELP

You may have to add, delete, or change some words in the sentences in Exercise 5. Add commas where necessary.

EXAMPLE   1. For my report topic I chose robots. Robots are automatic mechanical tools.

         1. *For my report topic I chose robots, which are automatic mechanical tools.*

1. The word *robot* originates from the word *robota*. This is a Czech word meaning "drudgery."

2. I thought robots would be an interesting topic to write about. I am fascinated with science fiction.

3. I started my research. I was disappointed to find out that most robots are stationary and consist of only a single arm.

4. I found out that some engineers are building moving robots. These robots are equipped with cameras.

5. These robots also have electronic sensors. The sensors provide feedback.

6. Robotics is an important technology. Robotics deals with the creation of robots for use in industry, science, and other fields.

7. People worry that robots will take over the jobs of humans. There is evidence to contradict the belief.

8. Robots can perform small tasks like assembling watches. Robots are often used for tasks such as drilling and welding.

9. The robot usually follows a set of instructions. These instructions are entered and stored in the robot's computer.

10. Difficult and dangerous jobs need to be done. People can rely on robots.

 Oral Practice **Combining Sentences by Coordinating and Subordinating Ideas**

Read the following sentence pairs aloud. Then, use either coordination or subordination to combine the pairs. There may be more than one way to combine a sentence pair.

EXAMPLE   1. I had heard of Robert Ripley. I didn't know much about him.

   1. *Although I had heard of Robert Ripley, I didn't know much about him.*

1. Robert L. Ripley worked as a cartoonist for the *New York Globe*. He spent his life seeking incredible but true stories.

2. His unusual career started one day. He could not think of an idea for a cartoon.

3. To find an idea, he looked through his files. He hurriedly drew several items about unusual achievements.

4. Ripley's first collection of "Believe It or Not" was published in 1929. The collection was instantly successful.

5. Eventually Ripley's features appeared in more than two hundred newspapers. Even more success lay ahead for him.

6. One of the categories was "Strange Coincidence." This was a category Ripley used as the basis of his features.

7. Two men playing golf together at a famous golf club in California chipped simultaneously at the twelfth hole. Their golf balls collided and dropped into the cup.

8. In one strange incident, an icehouse in Blanca, Colorado, burned to the ground. The ice inside did not melt.

9. In another, a horse named "Lucky Wonder" typed out a psychic prediction. The prediction foresaw the reelection of President Truman.

10. Robert L. Ripley died in 1949. Today his work is carried on by the Ripley organization in Toronto, Canada.

Review A **Revising a Paragraph by Combining Sentences**

Using all the sentence-combining skills you have learned, revise the following paragraph for style. Do not change the meaning of the original paragraph.

EXAMPLE   Babe Didrikson Zaharias is one of my mother's heroes. Babe was an amazing athlete.

Babe Didrikson Zaharias, an amazing athlete, is one of my mother's heroes.

Mildred "Babe" Didrikson Zaharias was born in Port Arthur, Texas, around 1911. She was considered one of the finest track-and-field performers of all time. Babe gained national attention in 1930. She competed in a track-and-field meet in Dallas. She won two events. She broke the world record in a third event. The event was the long jump. Babe competed in the Olympic Games in 1932. She entered the high jump, the javelin throw, and the hurdles. She set records in all of these events. They were world records. Only two of these records were made official. Babe's high-jump performance was disqualified. It was disqualified over a technicality. Babe was a champion in women's track and field for more than a decade. She was a world champion in track and field. Babe later became a world champion golfer.

Chapter Review

A. Revising Sentences by Subordinating Ideas

The clauses in each of the following sentences have been combined by coordinating ideas. Revise each of the sentences by subordinating one of the clauses to the other.

1. The situation at the border was resolved peacefully, and the resolution is a credit to the officials' negotiating skills.

2. I couldn't find that book on the shelf, so I think someone must have checked it out.

3. My uncle's job doesn't leave him much time to exercise, and his job requires him to travel most of the week.

4. Lenny's new baby sister will come home from the hospital tomorrow, and Tara must have told me that.

5. Maria wants to apply to that college, but she'll need to take another year of a foreign language.

6. Those cats belong to my neighbor, and their names are Sandy, Dusty, and Smoky.

7. She was supposed to have been home at three o'clock, but she didn't remember until the phone started ringing.

8. These strawberries just need to be washed and put in a bowl, and they are the sweetest and ripest we've had all summer.

9. Pin the seam in several places, and then the fabric won't slide when you sew it.

10. Please call Mrs. Robinson when the shipment arrives, for she ordered that long, blue dress.

B. Revising Paragraphs by Combining Sentences

Revise the following paragraphs to improve the writing style by combining sentences. To combine sentences, use a variety of techniques: inserting words or phrases; coordinating subjects, verbs, or clauses; or subordinating clauses.

```
        Everyone is familiar with dragons. The
folktales and legends we've heard are full of
dragons. We've heard them since childhood.
Dragons are legendary beasts. Many cultures
```

portray them as scaly, fire-breathing, flying creatures. Usually dragons are an obstacle for the hero of a story to overcome. Sometimes they symbolize evil. Very occasionally, a dragon is portrayed as a friendly, misunderstood animal. That happens especially in children's stories or songs.

Myths and legends about dragons are ancient. Myths and legends from all over the Middle East and the Mediterranean tell of gigantic, snakelike beasts. In some cultures, the beasts were sea serpents. In fact, in ancient Greek, the word *drakōn* meant any large serpent. We get the word *dragon* from *drakōn*.

The dragons of ancient times were often fearsome. They took many forms. The Egyptian god Apepi was a great serpent. It dwelt in a world of darkness. In Babylonian literature, the god Marduk fought the dragon Tiamat. Tiamat looked much like our own idea of dragons. It had a scaly body and wings. The Greeks told of a many-headed serpent. It was called Hydra. A Canaanite poem tells of the struggle between the god Baal and a monster called Leviathan. The Old Testament also contains references to God's ancient battle with a dragonlike creature. That creature was also called Leviathan. In the art of Christian Europe, the dragon came to be used as a symbol. The dragon was a symbol of sin and pagan beliefs.

As magical creatures, dragons were not only terrifying. They had magical protective powers, too. In the *Iliad*, King Agamemnon's shield displayed a three-headed snake. Uther Pendragon used the dragon as a royal symbol. He was the father of King Arthur. Norse warriors carved the prows of their ships into dragons' heads. They used the dragon to frighten their enemies.

In the Far East, dragons were also powerful and magical. They were traditionally viewed as benevolent beasts. The Chinese dragon represents *yang* in the Chinese *yin-yang*. *Yang* is the principle of heaven, maleness, and activity. The dragon was the emblem of the Chinese imperial family. It was on the Chinese flag until 1911. Japanese dragons are like Chinese dragons. Both are usually wingless.

Stories of dragons, sea serpents, and other giant sea creatures have existed for thousands of years. Some of the stories may have developed after sightings of giant squids. Giant squids can grow up to 50 feet long. The most famous modern sea serpent, of course, is the Loch Ness "monster." It supposedly lives in Loch Ness, in Scotland. Many people claim to have seen the Loch Ness monster. Investigations into the existence of the Loch Ness monster have been inconclusive.

CHAPTER

Improving
Sentence Style

Diagnostic Preview

A. Revising Sentences by Varying Sentence Beginnings

Each of the following sentences begins with the subject. Revise each sentence so that it begins with another element of the sentence. The beginning may be a single-word modifier, a phrase modifier, or a clause modifier.

EXAMPLE   1. The weather that day was cool yet pleasant—perfect for a race.

        1. *Cool yet pleasant, the weather that day was perfect for a race.*

1. The hills on the course were long and steep and challenged all but the most experienced runners.
2. Some runners were saving their strength for the final stretch of the race and ran slowly for the first mile or two.
3. Two or three runners were far ahead of the pack within a few minutes of the start of the race.
4. Runners had to train for months if they wanted to be truly competitive in the race.
5. The stragglers crossed the finish line hours later and were proud of their accomplishment.

B. Revising Sentences to Reduce Wordiness

The following sentences are wordy. Revise each sentence to make it more concise, less repetitious, and less pretentious.

EXAMPLE   1. Jim will explain the way in which to display the national flag in a correct manner.

     1. *Jim will explain how to display the national flag correctly.*

6. My friend Alan, who is an accomplished drummer, will be playing with the band tonight due to the fact that one of the regular band members is ill.

7. The woman who was the one who showed us the exhibits at the museum was in all likelihood one of the curators of the museum.

8. We got the raft through the rapids, which were swirling all around the raft, by means of paddling hard and following the instructions that were given to us by our guide.

9. In spite of the fact that Mary had stayed up late because she was studying, the fact was she looked as though she had rested well.

10. Raymond tasted a small piece of the cheese from Ireland and then tried several of the cheeses that had been imported from France.

C. Revising Paragraphs to Vary Sentence Structure.

The following paragraphs are made up of simple sentences. Rewrite the paragraphs, combining sentences and using a variety of sentence structures.

EXAMPLE   1. I would like to visit Egypt. Many fascinating ancient sites are there.

     1. *I would like to visit Egypt, for many fascinating ancient sites are there.*

In ancient Egypt the throne traditionally belonged to men. Many queens were influential. The influence of Nefertiti, for example, is well known. Nefertiti was the wife of Akhenaten. Akhenaten ruled Egypt from 1352–1336 B.C. She helped him to establish the monotheistic worship of Aten. Nefertiti may actually have ruled as pharaoh, according to some scholars. She may have ruled for a short period following her husband's death. Cleopatra VII is another famous queen of Egypt. She is known to us from both history and drama. Cleopatra was the last queen

of Egypt before its total annexation by Rome in
31 B.C. She was not actually Egyptian, however.
Cleopatra was the last of the Macedonian
dynasty founded by Ptolemy in 323 B.C.

One earlier Egyptian queen, Hatshepsut,
became a pharaoh after the death of her husband. The reign of Hatshepsut's husband,
Thutmose II, lasted probably no more than
three or four years. Then Hatshepsut became
regent for Thutmose III. Thutmose III was
about ten years old. Hatshepsut was regent for
the heir. She took control of the government.
She had herself crowned pharaoh. She adopted
a royal name. She wore the complete regalia of
the office, including a false beard.

Revising for Variety

Have you ever looked closely at an intricately woven tapestry or a
beautiful oil painting? What catches your eye? Just as artists can use a
variety of colors and textures to enrich their art, you can use a variety
of sentence patterns to enrich your writing. This technique of varying
sentence patterns applies to almost all writing, whether it is for school,
business, or personal use.

As you read the following passage, notice how the sentences work
together to form a smooth, effective paragraph.

> Grace advanced her hand toward the nearest cobra.
> The snake swayed like a reed in the wind, feinting for the
> strike. Grace raised her hand above the snake's head, the
> reptile twisting around to watch her. As the woman slowly
> lowered her hand, the snake gave that most terrible of all
> animal noises—the unearthly hiss of a deadly snake. I
> have seen children laugh with excitement at the roar of a
> lion, but I have never seen anyone who did not cringe at
> that cold, uncanny sound. Grace deliberately tried to
> touch the rigid, quivering hood. The cobra struck at her
> hand. He missed. Quietly, Grace presented her open palm.
> The cobra hesitated a split second, his reared body quiver-
> ing like a plucked banjo string. Then he struck.
>
> Daniel Mannix,
> *All Creatures Great and Small*

Mannix's carefully crafted sentences add style and interest to his writing. You can improve your own writing style by revising your sentences for variety.

Varying Sentence Beginnings

Have you ever heard or read a story that kept you on the edge of your seat? Chances are the sentence beginnings helped hold your attention. Instead of starting every sentence with a subject and a verb, the storyteller probably began some sentences with attention-grabbing words, phrases, and clauses such as *Suddenly . . ., At the bottom of the cliff . . .,* and *When she opened the door. . . .*

Varied sentence beginnings do more than hold a reader's attention. They also improve the overall style of writing. The examples in the chart below show how you can revise your sentences to open them with introductory words, phrases, and clauses.

NOTE When you vary sentence beginnings, you sometimes must reword the sentences for clarity. As you reword, be sure to place modifiers close to the words they modify; otherwise, you may create a misplaced modifier.

Sentence Connectives	
Subject First	Graphology is the study of how handwriting reveals a person's personality. Scientific handwriting analysis, though, determines the authenticity of a signature.
Coordinating Conjunction First	Graphology is the study of how handwriting reveals a person's personality. **But** scientific handwriting analysis determines the authenticity of a signature.
Subject First	Graphologists use size, direction, and regularity of letters to tell if a person is shy, quick-thinking, or independent. Graphology has not been recognized as a true science.
Conjunctive Adverb First	Graphologists use size, direction, and regularity of letters to tell if a person is shy, quick-thinking, or independent. **However,** graphology has not been recognized as a true science.

STYLE **TIP**

In your reading, you will frequently see coordinating conjunctions used to begin sentences. Because such usage is often considered informal, it is best not to use coordinating conjunctions to begin your sentences in formal, or academic, situations.

(continued)

(continued)

Single-Word Modifiers

Subject First	The letters of Erica's signature are upright and elaborate and might suggest independence.
Single-Word Modifiers First	**Upright and elaborate,** the letters of Erica's signature might suggest independence.
Subject First	Angling letters to the left supposedly indicates shyness.
Single-Word Modifier First	**Supposedly,** angling letters to the left indicates shyness.
Subject First	Two people's signatures may show the couple's compatibility if the signatures are analyzed.
Single-Word Modifier First	**Analyzed,** two people's signatures may show the couple's compatibility.

Phrase Modifiers

Subject First	Birds can close their eyes for sleep by raising the lower lid.
Prepositional Phrase First	**By raising the lower lid,** birds can close their eyes for sleep.
Subject First	The eyes of many birds are located on the sides of the head and provide peripheral vision.
Participial Phrase First	**Located on the sides of the head,** the eyes of many birds provide peripheral vision.
Subject First	Birds have a third eyelid beneath the upper and lower lids to blink and moisten the eyes.
Infinitive Phrase First	**To blink and moisten the eyes,** birds have a third eyelid beneath the upper and lower lids.

Clause Modifiers

Subject First	Birds turn their heads instead of moving their eyes if they want to look at an object.
Adverb Clause First	**If they want to look at an object,** birds turn their heads instead of moving their eyes.
Subject First	Most nocturnal birds have very large eyes, but the New Zealand Kiwi's eyes are tiny.
Adverb Clause First	**Even though most nocturnal birds have very large eyes,** the New Zealand Kiwi's eyes are tiny.

Exercise 1 Varying Sentence Beginnings

Revise each of the following sentences by varying their beginnings. The hint in parentheses will tell you which type of beginning to use.

EXAMPLE
1. Speaking and writing, though we use them often, are not the only methods of communication. (clause)

1. *Though we use them often, speaking and writing are not the only methods of communication.*

1. Sign language is an ancient form of communication, speaking through moving the body. (participial phrase)
2. People have used signs and gestures to communicate their thoughts since prehistoric times. (infinitive phrase)
3. Sign language can flexibly range from pointing and shrugging to subtle movements of the hands and changes of facial expression. (single-word modifier)
4. Chinese and Japanese people are able to communicate with each other by spelling out mutually comprehensible characters on their palms. (prepositional phrase)
5. A system of commonly understood gestures often helped American Indian nations communicate with each other. (single-word modifier)
6. Nations in the Plains area spoke many different languages, so a well-developed sign language was essential for trading. (adverb clause)
7. The scope of the sign language grew as more groups settled on the Plains. (adverb clause)
8. One gesture was used to mean "peace" and was known by many nations. (participial phrase)
9. A circle traced against the sky was used to refer to the moon. (participial phrase)
10. French Sign Language was combined with numerous other systems to create a new sign language called American Sign Language. (infinitive phrase)

Varying Sentence Structure

You can also improve your style by varying the structure of your sentences. That means using a mix of simple, compound, and complex (and often even compound-complex) sentences in your writing.

Read the following short paragraph, which is made up of only simple sentences.

Reference Note

For information about the **four types of sentence structure,** see page 87.

The Bermuda Triangle is located between the
island of Bermuda, the coast of Florida, and
Puerto Rico. It is known for unexplained disappearances. Ships have been disappearing in
the area since the mid-nineteenth century. It
got this reputation. A training squadron of
five U.S. Navy bombers disappeared in 1945.
This incident seemed to set the triangle's
reputation. Another ship is the nuclear-
powered submarine *Scorpion*. It disappeared in
this area in 1968. There have been disappearances. These disappearances may have logical
explanations.

Now, read the revised version of the paragraph. Notice how the
writer has used sentence-combining techniques to vary the structure of
the sentences.

The Bermuda Triangle, which is located
between the island of Bermuda, the coast of
Florida, and Puerto Rico, is known for unexplained disappearances. It got this reputation
because ships have been disappearing in the
area since the mid-nineteenth century. A training squadron of five U.S. Navy bombers disappeared in 1945, and this incident seemed to set
the triangle's reputation. In 1968 another
ship, the nuclear-powered submarine *Scorpion*,
disappeared in this area. However, these disappearances may have logical explanations.

Exercise 2   Revising a Paragraph to Vary
                 Sentence Structure

Decide which sentences in the following paragraph would sound better
with compound, complex, or compound-complex structures. Then,
use sentence-combining techniques to vary the sentence structure.
(You may need to change some wording to create smooth sentences.)

EXAMPLE   1. *Kendo* is a Japanese word. It means "way of the sword."

           1. *Kendo is a Japanese word that means "way of the
              sword."*

This person may look like a villain from a
science fiction movie. He is actually a student of kendo. Kendo is an ancient Japanese
martial art. It requires skill, concentration,

and agility. The contestants fight with long
bamboo swords called <u>shinai</u>. Kendo can be dangerous. The players must wear protective gear.
The gear includes a mask, a breastplate, and
thick gloves. Each match lasts three to five
minutes. The first contestant to score two
points wins. Kendo is a graceful, dignified
sport. Respect for one's opponent is important. A contestant can even be disqualified
for rudeness.

Revising to Reduce Wordiness

Read the following sentence. Could you remove a single word from it
without changing its meaning or lessening its impact?

> At last I knelt on the island's winter-killed grass,
> lost, dumbstruck, staring at the frog in the creek just
> four feet away.
>
> Annie Dillard,
> *Pilgrim at Tinker Creek*

Skilled writers make every word count; they know that conciseness is
essential for good style. You can make your own writing more concise
by eliminating the clutter of extra words.

To avoid wordiness in your writing, keep these three points in mind.

- Use only as many words as you need to make your point.

- Choose simple, clear words and expressions over pretentious,
  complicated ones.

- Do not repeat words or ideas unless it is absolutely necessary.

The following examples show some ways to revise wordy sentences.

1. Take out a whole group of unnecessary words.

WORDY	Every single individual in our class bought tickets to the concert.
BETTER	**Everyone** in our class bought tickets to the concert.

WORDY	At the edge of the river, we boarded a small boat that was floating there on the surface of the water.
BETTER	At the edge of the river, we boarded a **small boat.**

2. Replace pretentious words and expressions with straightforward ones.

WORDY	All attempts to mollify the male being in the early stage of life development and from an educational establishment were unsuccessful.
BETTER	All attempts to **soothe the young schoolboy failed.**

3. Reduce a clause to a phrase.

WORDY	Atul, who was the winner of the sportsmanship award, was asked to give a speech at the sports banquet.
BETTER	**Winner of the sportsmanship award,** Atul was asked to give a speech at the sports banquet.

WORDY	Tori, who is a computer expert, produced a program that detects computer viruses.
BETTER	Tori, **a computer expert,** produced a program that detects computer viruses.

4. Reduce a phrase or a clause to one word.

WORDY	Lenny contacted a reporter from Albania.
BETTER	Lenny contacted an **Albanian** reporter.

WORDY	The price that was confirmed will be honored by the dealer.
BETTER	The **confirmed** price will be honored by the dealer.

Here is a list of wordy phrases and their simpler replacements. Watch out for these wordy phrases in your writing.

Wordy	Simpler
at this point in time	now
at which time	when
by means of	by
due to the fact that	because, since
in spite of the fact that	although
in the event that	if
the fact is that	actually

NOTE Sometimes no replacement is needed for wordy phrases—they can be cut altogether. "The fact is that," for example, is often unnecessary.

WORDY   **The fact is that** I am turning seventeen in five months.
BETTER   I am turning seventeen in five months.

Oral Practice   Reducing Wordiness

Read aloud each of the following sentences. Aloud, revise each wordy sentence to make it straightforward and concise. If a sentence does not need revision, say *correct*.

EXAMPLE   1. Writing is an important, consequential skill.
   1. *Writing is an important skill.*

1. Good writing is precise and straightforward.
2. Have you ever read sentences that seem to ramble on and keep going forever?
3. Annie Dillard, who is a careful writer, revises heavily.
4. Redundant sentences are boring and repetitive.
5. Sentences that are longer than it is necessary for them to be may confuse your reader.
6. A sentence that has too many clauses that are subordinate becomes a mental maze for the unsuspecting reader.
7. Think of the sounds and rhythms of the writing you like best.
8. Sentences stuffed with extra, unneeded words resemble Saint Bernards squeezed into Chihuahua-sized sweaters.
9. The fact is that carefully crafted sentences are like well-tailored suits.
10. William Strunk, Jr., said, "Vigorous writing is concise."

Review A   Revising Sentences to Improve Style

Revise the sentences below as suggested in the parentheses.

EXAMPLE   1. Charles Kingsley was Mary Kingsley's uncle. He was a member of the clergy and an author. (Use a phrase to combine.)
   1. *Charles Kingsley, a member of the clergy and an author, was Mary Kingsley's uncle.*

1. Mary Kingsley set sail for Africa in 1893. (Begin with a phrase.)

COMPUTER TIP

A word-processing program's search feature can help you look for wordy phrases such as those listed in the chart. The command can also find overused words. To choose synonyms for these words, use the thesaurus tool if the program has one.

2. Her father, George Kingsley, had written an unfinished book about African law and religion. Mary Kingsley decided to finish it. (Create a compound sentence.)
3. Kingsley equipped herself as a trader. She hired African guides. She set off into the bush of Gabon and the Niger Delta. (Use a compound predicate to combine.)
4. She visited in 1893 and 1894 Angola, Nigeria, and Fernando Po, an island that is part of what is now Equatorial Guinea. (Begin with a phrase.)
5. Kingsley brought back a variety of animal specimens. She donated them to the British Museum. (Create a complex sentence.)
6. She returned to Africa in December of the next year, becoming the first European to set foot in parts of Gabon. (Begin with a phrase.)
7. Kingsley was a fearless and intrepid woman and was the first person to travel the route north from the Ogooué to the Rembwe River. (Begin with single-word modifiers.)
8. The fact is that she had many exciting, breath-taking adventures. (Reduce wordiness.)
9. Upon her return, Kingsley penned a prodigious tome, the title of which was *Travels in West Africa,* with the aim and purpose of convincing inhabitants of England that the traditions and customary ways of the peoples of the African continent were worthy of their respect and regard. (Reduce wordiness.)
10. After her return from Africa, she journeyed across England giving lectures. The lectures were about her travels and discoveries. (Use a phrase to combine.)

Chapter Review

A. Revising Paragraphs to Reduce Wordiness

Revise the paragraphs below to vary sentence beginnings and sentence structure and to eliminate wordiness.

Wireless operator

Guglielmo Marconi invented wireless telegraphy in the 1890s. Wireless telegraphy was the forerunner of radio. There were many problems with the first wireless messages. The messages were full of static, noise, and unintelligible sounds. Also, they were not very private as well due to the fact that anyone could tune in and listen if he or she had the proper receiving device.

Several ships carried wireless technology by 1912. The famous ship *Titanic* was among them. The *Titanic* struck an iceberg late at night while on its first voyage, and its crew sent out SOS messages on the ship's wireless. The wireless operators on many other ships in the area were no longer on duty, so the *Titanic*'s messages were not received by very many operators. The fact is that after the ship sank, the U.S. government required wireless ship communications to be monitored at all times.

B. Revising Paragraphs to Improve Sentence Style

Revise the following paragraphs, varying sentence beginnings and structures and eliminating wordiness.

Many people dismiss modern sightings of legendary beasts as hoaxes. Other people think they are the result of overactive imaginations. Most supposedly real photographs of the Loch Ness monster have proved without any doubt to be fraudulent. Little solid evidence exists. Tales about Bigfoot, the Loch Ness monster, and others that are like Bigfoot or the Loch Ness monster persist. Many of the people who study or believe the stories have no formal scientific credentials. A small group of scientists who do have professional credentials, however, researches the creatures seriously. These scientists call their field of study cryptozoology. Cryptozoology is the study of hidden animals.

The International Society of Cryptozoology (ISC) has more than eight hundred members. It was founded by a French zoologist, Bernard Heuvelmans. Heuvelmans began to study scientifically unverified animals in the 1950s. ISC members include zoologists, paleontologists, ecologists, anthropologists, and scientists from other fields. The society publishes a newsletter that is published quarterly, and it publishes a journal that appears once a year. Cryptozoologists accept that their field of study is often considered by many to be controversial. They insist that their purpose is to investigate the existence of cryptids in a manner that is objective and uses the scientific method. Hoaxes, frauds, and crackpot theories about extraterrestrial beings or time-travelers only impede the search for genuine evidence.

Cryptozoologists point to discoveries and documentation that have been made relatively recently of new or unknown species. The fact is that reports of African and Australian animals were once ridiculed in Europe, for example. Some large species have only recently become extinct in the last thousand years. The moa was an ostrichlike bird in New Zealand. It became extinct about three hundred years ago. A species of the dodo bird lived until around 1800. The Tasmanian wolf survived in Australia until the early twentieth century.

Discoveries of new species are not uncommon. Many of the earth's species have not been classified even today. Most of the newly discovered species are small. Some recently documented species are large. The okapi looks like a cross between a zebra and a giraffe. It was not classified by zoologists until 1900. The muntjac is also called the barking deer. A new species of muntjac was found in Vietnam in

1993. It was called the giant muntjac due to the fact that it was larger than the other known species. The most famous discovery of an unknown animal happened in 1938. A strange, five-foot-long fish was caught off the coast of Madagascar. At that point in time, a museum curator happened to see the fish. The fish was identified as a coelacanth. Coelacanths were thought to have become extinct with the dinosaurs. More than a dozen of the fish have been caught since. Some species of fish that are similar to the coelacanth that was caught off Madagascar have been discovered off the coast of Indonesia. That is a distance of more than six thousand miles from Madagascar.

CHAPTER

20 Sentence Diagramming

The Sentence Diagram

A *sentence diagram* is a picture of how the parts of a sentence fit together and how the words in a sentence are related.

Reference Note

For more information about **subjects** and **verbs,** see page 33.

Subjects and Verbs

Every sentence diagram begins with a horizontal line intersected by a short vertical line, which divides the subject from the verb.

EXAMPLE   **Judy Garland sang** "Over the Rainbow."

| Judy Garland | sang |

Reference Note

For more information about **understood subjects,** see page 46.

Understood Subjects

EXAMPLE   Close the door.

| (you) | Close |

Reference Note

For more information about **nouns of direct address,** see page 36.

Nouns of Direct Address

EXAMPLE   Hand me the dictionary, **George.**

George

| (you) | Hand |

490   Chapter 20   Sentence Diagramming

Compound Subjects

EXAMPLE   **Ryan** and **Maria** are running a marathon.

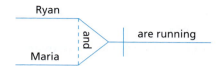

Reference Note

For more information about **compound subjects,** see page 35.

Compound Verbs

EXAMPLE   Eileen **sings** and **dances.**

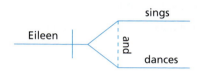

Reference Note

For more information about **compound verbs,** see page 35.

Compound Subjects and Compound Verbs

EXAMPLE   **Art** and **literature can entertain** and **inspire**.

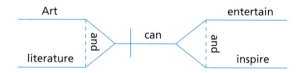

When the parts of a compound subject or a compound predicate are joined by a correlative conjunction, diagram the sentence this way:

EXAMPLE   **Both** Amy **and** Megan have **not only** called **but also** visited.

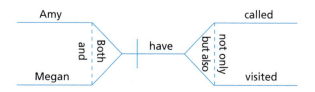

Reference Note

For more information about **correlative conjunctions,** see page 23.

Modifiers

Reference Note

For more information about **adjectives,** see page 9. For more about **adverbs,** see page 17.

Adjectives and Adverbs

Adjectives and adverbs are written on slanting lines beneath the words they modify.

EXAMPLE   **The large** fish **slowly** turned **upstream.**

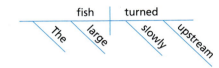

An adverb that modifies an adjective or an adverb is placed on a line connected to the word it modifies.

EXAMPLE   The time passed **incredibly** quickly.

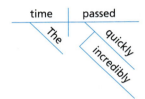

Here, There, and *Where* as Modifiers

Reference Note

For more about questions and sentences beginning with **here** and **there,** see page 37.

EXAMPLES   **Here** comes the rain!

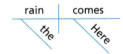

There goes the American cycling team.

Where has the boat docked?

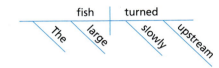

SENTENCES

NOTE Sometimes *there* begins a sentence but does not modify the verb. When used in this way, *there* is called an *expletive*. It is diagrammed on a line by itself.

EXAMPLE **There** are three boys in my family.

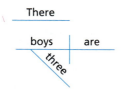

Subject Complements

A subject complement is placed after the verb on the same horizontal line as the simple subject and the verb. A line *slanting toward the subject* separates the subject complement from the verb.

Reference Note

For more information about **subject complements,** see page 42.

Predicate Nominatives

EXAMPLE My cousins are excellent **skiers.**

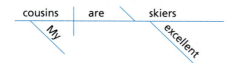

Predicate Adjectives

EXAMPLE This pasta is **delicious.**

Compound Subject Complements

EXAMPLE Sam Shepard is both a **playwright** and an **actor.**

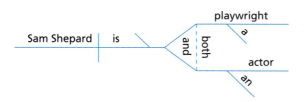

Objects

Direct Objects

Reference Note

For more information about **direct objects,** see page 39.

A direct object is placed after the verb on the same horizontal line as the simple subject and the verb. A *vertical* line separates the direct object from the verb.

EXAMPLE   James opened the **window.**

Compound Direct Objects

EXAMPLE   They recycle **cans** and **bottles.**

Indirect Objects

Reference Note

For more information about **indirect objects,** see page 40.

The indirect object is diagrammed on a horizontal line beneath the verb.

EXAMPLE   I handed **him** a pencil.

Compound Indirect Objects

EXAMPLE   Graham brought **Emily** and **Scott** souvenirs.

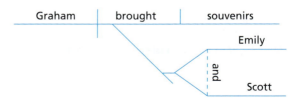

SENTENCES

Phrases

Prepositional Phrases

The preposition is placed on a slanting line leading down from the word that the phrase modifies. The object of the preposition is placed on a horizontal line connected to the slanting line.

Reference Note

For more information about **prepositional phrases,** see page 54.

EXAMPLES   The shallow pool **in the cave** was filled **with microorganisms.** [adjective phrase modifying the subject; adverb phrase modifying the verb]

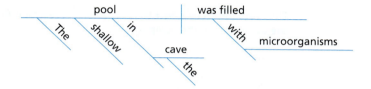

We awoke early **in the morning.** [adverb phrase modifying an adverb]

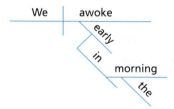

Grandpa told an old joke to **Brian** and **Sam.** [compound object of preposition]

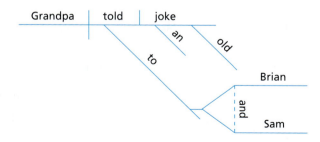

The Sentence Diagram   **495**

SENTENCES

Around the sun and **beyond the planets** orbit many comets. [two phrases modifying the same word]

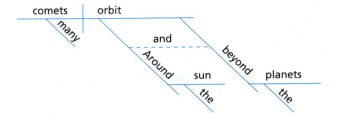

The hermit lived **in a hut by the lake.** [phrase modifying the object of another preposition]

Reference Note

For more information about **participles** and **participial phrases,** see page 58.

Participles and Participial Phrases

Participles and participial phrases are diagrammed as follows.

EXAMPLES   He saw her **waving.**

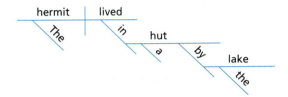

Raising his arm, Bill hailed the taxi **coming around the corner.**

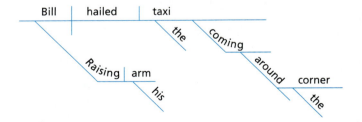

Notice above that the participle *Raising* has a direct object (*arm*), which is diagrammed in the same way that a direct object of a main verb is.

Gerunds and Gerund Phrases

Gerunds and gerund phrases are diagrammed as follows.

EXAMPLES **Diving** is not risk-free. [gerund used as subject]

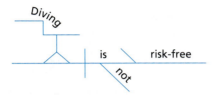

Exercising regularly with friends is definitely a good plan for **developing healthy habits.** [gerund phrases used as subject and as object of a preposition]

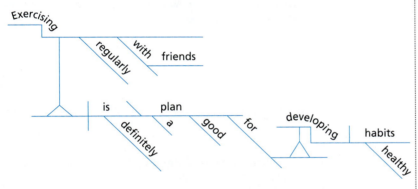

Notice above that the gerund *developing* has a direct object (*habits*).

Reference Note

For more information about **gerunds** and **gerund phrases,** see page 61.

Infinitives and Infinitive Phrases

Infinitives and infinitive phrases used as modifiers are diagrammed in the same way as prepositional phrases.

EXAMPLE   They fought **to survive.** [infinitive used as adverb]

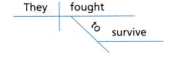

Reference Note

For more information about **infinitives** and **infinitive phrases,** see page 64.

SENTENCES

Infinitives and infinitive phrases used as nouns are diagrammed as follows.

EXAMPLES **To reach the highest peak** requires great determination. [infinitive phrase used as subject]

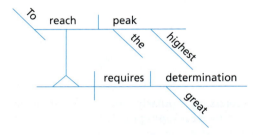

We are planning **to leave New York tomorrow.** [infinitive phrase used as direct object]

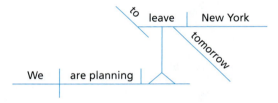

My friend helped **me find my dog.** [infinitive clause with subject, *me,* and with *to* omitted]

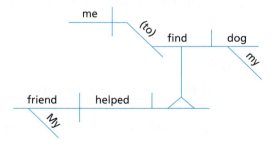

Reference Note

For more information about **appositives** and **appositive phrases,** see page 68.

Appositives and Appositive Phrases

Place the appositive in parentheses after the word it identifies or describes.

EXAMPLES   My sister **Joan** is a surgeon.

Seamus traveled to Kilkenny, **a town in Ireland.**

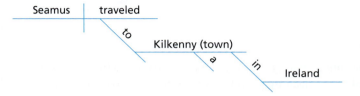

Subordinate Clauses

Adjective Clauses

An adjective clause is joined to the word it modifies by a broken line leading from the modified word to the relative pronoun.

EXAMPLES   The bird **that he spotted** was very beautiful.

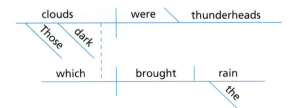

Reference Note

For more information about **adjective clauses,** see page 78.

Those dark clouds, **which brought the rain,** were thunderheads.

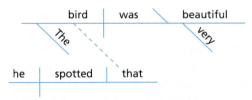

He is the man **from whom I heard the strange tale.**

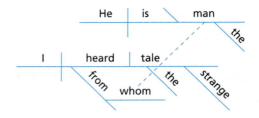

Adverb Clauses

Reference Note

For more information about **adverb clauses,** see page 83.

Place the subordinating conjunction that introduces the adverb clause on a broken line leading from the verb in the adverb clause to the word the clause modifies.

EXAMPLE   **If a drought occurs,** many plants may die.

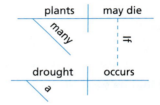

Noun Clauses

Reference Note

For more information about **noun clauses,** see page 80.

Noun clauses often begin with the word *that, what, who,* or *which.* These words may have a function within the subordinate clause or may simply connect the clause to the rest of the sentence. How a noun clause is diagrammed depends on how it is used in the sentence and whether or not the introductory word has a grammatical function in the noun clause.

EXAMPLES   **What he did** surprised us. [The noun clause is used as the subject of the independent clause. *What* functions as the direct object in the noun clause.]

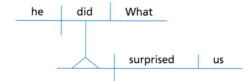

Sam forgot **that Mike needed a ride.** [The noun clause is the direct object of the independent clause. *That* has no grammatical function in the noun clause.]

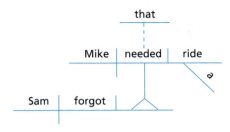

If the introductory word were omitted from the preceding sentence, the diagram would look like this.

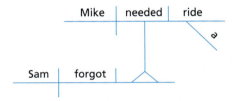

Sentences Classified According to Structure

Simple Sentences

EXAMPLES   The Grand Canyon is a national treasure. [one independent clause]

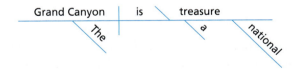

Meredith took a photograph. [one independent clause]

Reference Note

For more information about **simple sentences,** see page 87.

Reference Note

For more information about **compound sentences,** see page 88.

Compound Sentences

EXAMPLE   The enormous icebergs frightened us, but our ship sailed around the danger. [two independent clauses]

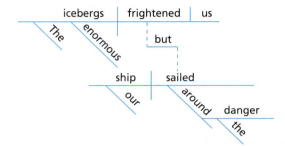

If the compound sentence has a semicolon and no conjunction, a straight broken line joins the two verbs.

EXAMPLE   Svetlana Savitskaya made history in the 1980s; she was the first Russian female spacewalker.

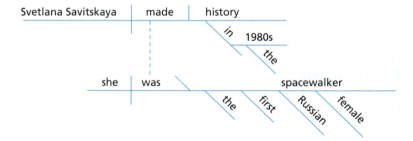

Reference Note

For more information about **conjunctive adverbs,** see page 88.

If the clauses of a compound sentence are joined by a semicolon and a conjunctive adverb (such as *consequently, therefore, nevertheless, however, moreover,* or *otherwise*), place the conjunctive adverb on a slanting line below the verb it modifies.

EXAMPLE   Juan runs daily before sunrise; **therefore,** he can hope to
           win the big race.

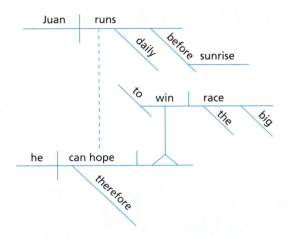

Complex Sentences

EXAMPLE   Before he arrived, the party was dull. [one independent
           clause and one subordinate clause]

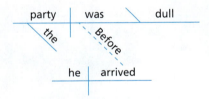

Reference Note

For more information
about **complex
sentences,** see page 89.

Compound-Complex Sentences

EXAMPLE   The museum that Felicia visited was small, but she enjoyed
           the collection. [two independent clauses and one
           subordinate clause]

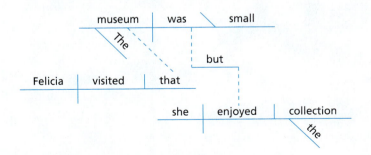

Reference Note

For more information
about **compound-
complex sentences,**
see page 89.

Resources

GO TO: go.hrw.com

Manuscript Form

Why Is Manuscript Form Important?

What is manuscript form, and why should you care about it? **Manuscript form** refers to the overall appearance of a document. A legible, professional-looking manuscript gives the impression that the writer cares not only about what he or she has to say but also about what the reader thinks. A manuscript that is an illegible jumble, on the other hand, gives the impression that the writer is careless, is not thinking clearly, or does not respect the reader.

Such impressions affect our lives every day. For example, a busy employer faced with the task of evaluating multiple job résumés may simply discard the sloppy ones without ever reading them. If we value what we write and want others to understand and value it too, then we should present our ideas in the best form possible. To help you present your ideas as effectively as possible, this section of the book covers basic guidelines for preparing and presenting manuscripts and provides a sample research paper as a model.

General Guidelines for Preparing Manuscripts

The following guidelines are general style rules to use in formal, nonfiction writing. Such writing includes papers and reports for school, letters of application for jobs or colleges, letters to the editor, and press releases for clubs and other organizations.

Content and Organization

1. Begin the paper with an introductory paragraph that contains a thesis sentence.

2. Develop and support your thesis in body paragraphs.

3. Follow the principles of unity and coherence. That is, develop one and only one big idea (your thesis), and make sure that your paragraphs and sentences flow smoothly without any gaps in the sequence of ideas.

4. Place charts, graphs, tables, and illustrations close to the text they illustrate. Label and number each one.

5. Follow the conventions of standard grammar, usage, capitalization, punctuation, and spelling.

6. Include a conclusion.

Appearance

1. Submit manuscript that is legible. Type or print out your paper using black ink; or when your teacher permits handwriting, write neatly using blue or black ink. (Other colors are harder to read.) If the printer or typewriter you are using is printing words that are faint and hard to read, change the ink cartridge or the ribbon.

2. Keep all pages neat and clean. If you discover errors and if you are working on a word processor, you can easily correct the errors and print out a fresh copy. If you write your paper by hand or on a typewriter, you generally may make a few corrections with correction tape and insert the revisions neatly. To replace a letter, word, or phrase, neatly cross out what you want to replace. Then, insert a caret mark (∧) below the line, and write the inserted item above the line.

EXAMPLE

The ~~daily~~ ∧weekly broadcasts continued all that summer.

Paper and Font

1. Use quality 8½ × 11 inch paper.
2. Use only one side of the paper.
3. When using a word processor, use an easy-to-read font size. Size twelve is standard.
4. Use a standard font, such as Times New Roman, that does not call attention to itself. Flowery, highly stylized fonts are hard to read. They look unprofessional, and they dis-tract the reader from the ideas you are trying to convey.

Plagiarism

Do not plagiarize. Plagiarism is the unacknowledged borrowing of someone else's words or ideas and the submission of those words or ideas as one's own. Honest writers document all borrowings, whether those borrowings are quoted or merely paraphrased.

Back-up files

When you are ready to submit your work, be sure to save a copy—a printout, a photocopy, or an electronic file—for yourself.

Academic Manuscript Style

In school you will write some very formal papers—research reports or term papers, for example. For such assignments, you will need to follow not only general manuscript guidelines but also some very specific guidelines especially for academic manuscripts.

The academic manuscript style summarized on the following pages follows the style recommended by the Modern Language Association in the *MLA Handbook for Writers of Research Papers.* Two other popular manuscript styles are the format recommended by the American Psychological Association, known as APA style, and the one published in *The Chicago Manual of Style.* Style manuals are updated from time to time, so be sure you are using the most current version. When formatting papers for school, be sure to follow your teachers' instructions on which manuscript style to use.

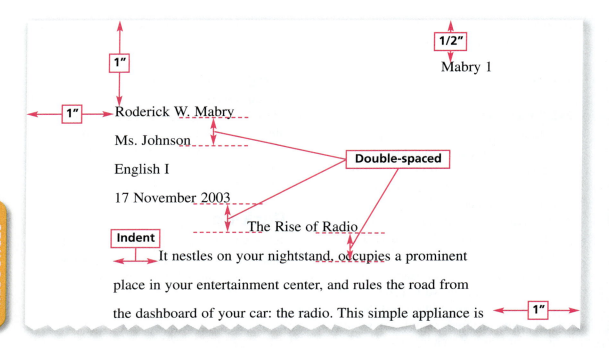

Labels on the diagram:

1"

1/2"

Mabry 1

1"

Roderick W. Mabry

Ms. Johnson

English I

17 November 2003

Double-spaced

The Rise of Radio

Indent

It nestles on your nightstand, occupies a prominent

place in your entertainment center, and rules the road from

the dashboard of your car: the radio. This simple appliance is

1"

Title Page, Margins, and Spacing

1. Leave one-inch margins on the top, sides, and bottom of each page.
2. Starting with the first page, number all your pages in the upper right-hand corner. Precede each page number with your last name. Computer software can help you create this "header."
3. Place your heading—your name, your teacher's name, your class, and the date—in the upper left-hand corner of the first page. (If your teacher requires a separate cover sheet, follow his or her instructions.)
4. Double-space between the header and the heading. Double-space the lines in the heading. Double-space between the heading and your title. (This rule does not apply if your teacher requires a cover sheet.)
5. Center the title, and capitalize the appropriate letters in it.
6. Double-space between the title and the body of the paper.
7. Do not underline or use quotation marks to enclose your own title at the head of your own paper. If you use someone else's title within your title, use quotation marks or underlining, as appropriate, with the other person's title only.

EXAMPLE

An Analysis of Symbolism in Yeats' "The Second Coming"

8. When typing or word-processing, always double-space the lines. (In a handwritten paper, skip every other ruled line unless your teacher instructs you otherwise.)
9. Do not use more than a double-space, even between paragraphs.
10. Indent the beginning of each paragraph one-half inch (five spaces).

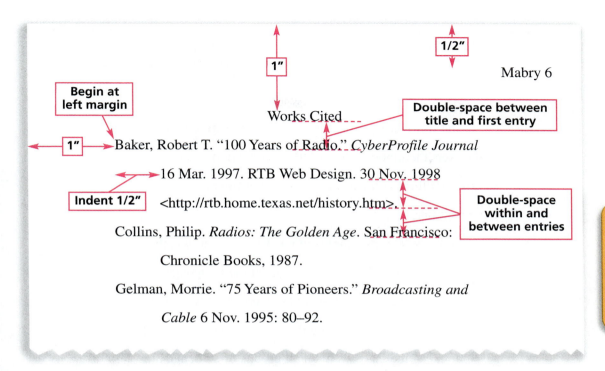

1"

1/2"

Begin at left margin

Double-space between title and first entry

Works Cited

1"

Baker, Robert T. "100 Years of Radio." *CyberProfile Journal*

16 Mar. 1997. RTB Web Design. 30 Nov. 1998

Indent 1/2" <http://rtb.home.texas.net/history.htm>.

Double-space within and between entries

Collins, Philip. *Radios: The Golden Age*. San Francisco:

Chronicle Books, 1987.

Gelman, Morrie. "75 Years of Pioneers." *Broadcasting and*

Cable 6 Nov. 1995: 80–92.

Documenting Sources

Works Cited Page

1. In a research paper or any other paper that incorporates information from other sources, add a works cited page at the end.
2. Continue numbering the pages of your paper through the works cited page.
3. The entries on the works cited page should be in alphabetical order, according to the last name of the author. For works with no author, the entry should be alphabetized according to the first main word in the title.
4. Do not number the sources on your works cited page.

Documentation in the Body of the Essay

1. Use parenthetical citations within the body of your paper to acknowledge any paraphrased idea or quotation that you have borrowed from someone else. The parenthetical citation refers to specific source documentation on the works cited page. Place the parenthetical citations at the **end** of the material that you borrowed from some other source.

EXAMPLE

Newspapers worried that radio would drive them out of business (Henderson 90).

2. If the citation appears at the end of a sentence, the citation comes before the closing period, as shown above. If the citation appears at the end of a dependent clause or after the first half of a compound sentence, the citation comes before the sentence comma.

EXAMPLE

Newspapers worried that radio would drive them out of business (Henderson 90), but it did not.

RESOURCES

3. For quotations of five or more lines, indent all of the lines one inch (about ten spaces) from the left margin. Do not use quotation marks to enclose indented quotations. Also, place end punctuation at the end of the quoted material, not after the closing parenthesis.

In the following passage, we see how effectively the author sets the mood. With a little imagination, we can almost feel the moist air and hear the murmured conversations.

← 1″ → The streetlights along Toole Street, which meandered downhill from the Language Academy to the town, were already lit and twinkled mistily through the trees. Standing at the gates were small groups of students, clustered together according to nationality. As Myles passed by, he could not help overhearing intense conversations in Spanish, German, and Japanese; all of his students had momentarily abandoned English in the urgency of deciding where to go for the weekend and how to get there. (Boylan 58)

Model Research Paper

The following final draft of a research paper closely follows the guidelines for MLA style given on the preceding pages. (Note: The pages of the model paper are smaller than 8½ × 11, and the margins of the paper are less than one inch wide to allow room for annotations.)

Mabry 1

Roderick W. Mabry

Ms. Johnson

English I

17 November 2003

The Rise of Radio

   It nestles on your nightstand, occupies a prominent place in your entertainment center, and rules the road from the dashboard of your car: the radio. This simple appliance is so common that most people take it for granted, yet radio is a relatively new invention. In fact, the first commercial radio station, KDKA in Pittsburgh, did not go on the air until 1920 (Stark 120). Before long, however, the new medium dramatically affected the nation's entertainment, information delivery, and economy.

   The invention of radio was made possible by a number of earlier developments. German physicist Heinrich Hertz, drawing on established mathematical principles, discovered the existence of radio waves in 1887. Eight years later, in Italy,

HEADING
your name
your teacher's name
your class
date

THESIS SENTENCE: tells focus of the paper

TOPIC SENTENCE: tells focus of the paragraph and is a subtopic of the thesis

RESOURCES

(continued)

Mabry 2

Guglielmo Marconi successfully completed the first wireless transmission of Morse code signals. An American invention helped move radio closer to reality: Lee De Forest's 1907 Audion, which made it possible to transmit sounds, not just signals. A full decade before KDKA debuted, De Forest broadcast a live performance by famed Italian tenor Enrico Caruso from New York City's Metropolitan Opera House (Yenne 77).

Few people were equipped to hear that landmark broadcast, however, because radio was still very much a do-it-yourself project; most people built their own receivers. In 1921, one such "tinkerer," twenty-eight-year-old Franklin Malcolm Doolittle of New Haven, Connecticut, even used his homemade transmitter to broadcast the Yale-Princeton football game from his home (Gelman 80). The first commercially produced receivers became available in 1920, when a Pittsburgh department store began offering sets for ten dollars. The response was so enthusiastic that Westinghouse began mass producing the appliances (Baker).

When radio found its way into the majority of American households, it brought the nation together in an unprecedented

FIRST REFERENCE: Full name of inventor is used.

SECOND REFERENCE: last name only

This parenthetical citation indicates that paraphrased information in the paragraph comes from Yenne, page 77. *Yenne* refers to *Yenne, Bill* on the works cited page.

In the Baker citation, no page number is listed because this information comes from an unpaginated online source.

RESOURCES

way. Radio reached into "once dreary homes, reducing the isolation of the hinterlands and leveling class distinctions" (Henderson 44). At first radio programming simply duplicated existing forms of entertainment: singers, musicians, comedians, lecturers. Coping with technical difficulties left little time for creating new types of shows. Later, as the technical problems were resolved, programmers began adapting existing formats and experimenting with new types of shows, including variety shows, serials, game shows, and amateur hours ("Radio as a Medium of Communication"). As programming expanded, radio truly became, in researcher Amy Henderson's words, "a theater of the mind" (144).

The introduction of radio also radically altered the way people learned about events in the outside world. For the first time in history, everyone could receive the same information simultaneously. As sociologists Robert and Helen Lynd, writing in the 1920s, noted, "With but little equipment one can call the life of the rest of the world from the air . . ." (qtd. in Monk 173). Live coverage gave news events an immediacy far greater than newspapers or newsreels could provide. In fact, most people

When parenthetical documentation follows closing quotation marks at the end of a sentence, the period should be placed after the parentheses.

These parentheses contain only the page number because the author is named in the text.

This citation tells us that the quotation from Robert and Helen Lynd was found in a book edited by Linda R. Monk.

(continued)

RESOURCES

(continued)

Mabry 4

first learned of such historic events as the 1941 Japanese attack on Pearl Harbor from the radio (Stark 120).

Equally important was radio's impact on the economy. The first, and most noticeable, effect was to add a new consumer product to people's wish lists. Most early sets were strictly functional—"a box, some wire, and headphones" (Baker). Once the initial demand was satisfied, however, manufacturers began stimulating repeat sales by offering new models each year, with the goal of placing a "radio in every room" (Collins 10).

The demand for sets was a boon to manufacturers, but it struck fear into some other segments of the economy. Newspapers worried that radio would drive them out of business (Henderson 90). Similarly, members of the traditional entertainment industry feared that the new technology would cut into the sales of tickets and recordings (Stark 120).

Surprisingly, advertisers were slow to realize the opportunities radio offered. At first, most business people assumed that profits would come solely from the sale of sets and replacement parts. In addition, paid advertising was considered improper for what was initially viewed as a "new, pure instrument of democracy" (Weiner). Instead, early programs were underwritten by "sponsors," with companies receiving only a brief, discreet acknowledgment in return for their support. Eventually, however, this approach gave way to the direct advertising that is familiar today (Weiner).

Reviewing the rise of radio makes clear how instrumental the medium was in shaping the nation's entertainment, information delivery, and economy. Today, with the advent of television and the Internet, radio is no longer the primary source of news and entertainment for most people, nor is its impact on the economy as far-reaching. Still, each day millions of listeners wake, work, and play to the rhythms of radio, and many would be lost without it. The radio may have been muted, but it has not been unplugged.

Mabry ends his paper with a concluding paragraph that is entirely his own statement. First, he restates the thesis in the form of a conclusion. Then, he places the history of the radio in its modern context.

(continued)

RESOURCES

(continued)

Center and capitalize *Works Cited,* but do not put it in quotation marks or underline it.

Entries are alphabetized according to the last name of the author.

Carefully punctuate all entries.

Indent second and subsequent lines of entries five spaces.

If no author is listed, alphabetize according to the first main word in the title.

The online address (URL) is enclosed by these signs: < >.

Mabry 6

Works Cited

Baker, Robert T. "100 Years of Radio." *CyberProfile Journal* 16 Mar. 1997. RTB Web Design. 30 Nov. 1998 <http://rtb.home.texas.net/history.htm>.

Collins, Philip. *Radios: The Golden Age*. San Francisco: Chronicle Books, 1987.

Gelman, Morrie. "75 Years of Pioneers." *Broadcasting and Cable* 6 Nov. 1995: 80–92.

Henderson, Amy. *On the Air*. Washington, DC: Smithsonian Institution Press, 1988.

Monk, Linda R., ed. *Ordinary Americans*. Alexandria, VA: Close Up, 1994.

"Radio as a Medium of Communication." *The Encyclopedia Americana*. International ed. 1998.

Stark, Phyllis. "On the Air." *Billboard* 1 Nov. 1994: 120–124.

Weiner, Neil. "Stories from Early Radio." *Background Briefing*. 14 April 1996. 28 Mar. 1999. <http://www.backgroundbriefing.com/radio.html>.

Yenne, Bill. *100 Events That Shaped World History*. San Francisco: Bluewood, 1993.

RESOURCES

The History of English

Origins and Uses

A Historical Overview

The English language was first written about 1,300 years ago but was spoken long before that. Since its beginnings, the language has changed so much that English speakers today find it difficult to recognize its earlier forms. Still, there is continuity across the ages. The history of the English language may be divided into four major periods: *Pre-English, Old English, Middle English,* and *Modern English.* The time line below shows approximately when English moved from one period to the next and when other languages influenced the development of English. It also indicates how the number of English speakers has grown over the centuries.

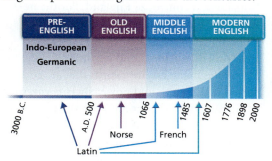

Pre-English   About five thousand years ago, *Proto-Indo-European,* an ancestor of English and other languages, was spoken by peoples in Asia Minor and southeast Europe. Most of the languages of Europe, as well as many of those spoken in northern India and Iran, come from Proto-Indo-European. (*Proto–* means "first or earliest.")

As people who spoke Proto-Indo-European migrated and settled, they developed their own *dialects,* or different ways of speaking the language. One of the groups settled in what is now northern Germany, along the coast of the North Sea. This group organized into several tribes—the Jutes, the Angles, and the Saxons. Their version of Proto-Indo-European, called *Germanic,* is the language from which Modern English is descended.

The Germanic-speaking tribes in northern Europe, known generally as the *Anglo-Saxons,* eventually mingled with Latin-speaking Romans of southern Europe. From the Romans, the Anglo-Saxons took words, called *loanwords,* into their language. Words such as *street, dish,* mile, and *wall* are loanwords borrowed from Latin. Although early English speakers probably took words from other languages, the Latin words borrowed on the continent of Europe more than two thousand years ago are the first loanwords we can be sure about.

Old English   Around A.D. 450, the Anglo-Saxons invaded Britain, taking over land that had been settled earlier by the Celts and colonized for centuries by the Romans. The Anglo-Saxons called the island after themselves, *Englaland*—the land of the Angles—or, as it is known today, England. They called their language *Englisc,* which is now referred to as **Old English.** The invading Anglo-Saxons incorporated very few Celtic words into their language, though several words that referred to features of the British landscape—*crag* and *tor* (a high rock), and *combe* (a deep valley)—became part of Old English. The language was further enriched over the years when the English were converted to Christianity by Latin-speaking missionaries. Latin provided words associated with religious matters, such as *church* and *bishop,* as well as other things, such as *school* and *butter.* Then, from the ninth to eleventh centuries Norse invaders from Scandinavia settled in Britain. The Norse provided English with the pronouns *they, their,* and *them,* as well as many English words that begin with *sc* or *sk,* such as *scared, skirt,* and *sky.*

In many ways, the English spoken by the Anglo-Saxons was very different from Modern English. They used sounds that have been lost over time, as in their word *hnutu,* which became *nut.* When they wrote at all, the alphabet they used was an angular-looking system of characters called runes. Also, Old English words had endings or alternative forms to show how they fit together in a sentence. The order of most

words in the sentence could stay the same, while the forms of the words changed to express different meanings. Below is an example of how word endings affected the meanings of sentences. (The Old English word *guma* means "man" and *boda* means "messenger.")

Modern English	The man gave the messenger an answer.
	The messenger gave the man an answer.
Old English	**Se** guma geaf **thæm** bodan andsware.
	Thæm guman geaf **se** boda andsware.

Although the English language has changed over the centuries, a number of Old English words have survived with little alteration in spelling or meaning. The following lists show the Old English and Modern English forms of several everyday words.

Old English	Modern English
cnif	knife
hus	house
modor	mother
æppel (meaning "fruit")	apple
wyrm (meaning "serpent")	worm

Middle English   In 1066, another group of Norse seized control of England. For the next 150 years, the French-speaking Normans ("north men") made French the language of government, business, and law in England. Therefore, many English words that are connected with wealth and power such as *governor, attorney,* and *fashion,* come from the French. The common people of England, however, still spoke English—a changing form of the language now called ***Middle English.***

The English language did not die out under French rule for three reasons. First, the English-speaking commoners outnumbered the French-speaking rulers. Second, the French-speaking rulers in England gradually lost contact with the French culture and language. Third, a shift was triggered when, in 1204, King John of England lost Normandy, the largest of the English possessions in France. Although England still owned large possessions in France, the loss of Normandy forced the King and his nobles to make England their first priority. Noble families possessing lands in England and France found that they had to choose between the two countries. Later, acts by the kings of England and France made it necessary for the nobility to declare their loyalty to one kingdom or the other. As a result, those nobles who chose England became English-speaking Englishmen.

Three hundred years after the French invasion, English was re-established as the national language of England. By this time, however, it had developed a grammar and structure similar to the English spoken today. In addition, many English words had been replaced with French and Latin vocabulary. For example, the native English word *leorningcild* ("learning child") was replaced by the Latin *studiante* ("student"). Here are some other French and Latin loanwords that entered English in the Middle English period.

French	armée	lettre	palais	prière
Modern English	army	letter	palace	prayer
Latin	alphabetum	ecclesiasticus		
Modern English	alphabet	ecclesiastical		

Modern English (1500–Present)
Despite the Scandinavian and Norman French invasions of England, the English were relatively isolated from the continent of Europe for nearly 1,200 years. Living in small villages, the English were also isolated from one another; consequently, speakers and writers in different parts of the country used different versions of the language. However, as London became the center of commerce and government, the kind of English pronunciation, grammar, and spelling spoken and used there became the standard. Equally important to the development of modern English was William Caxton's printing press, introduced in 1496. Books, previously handwritten and affordable only to the rich, became more available to the masses. Early printers standardized spelling and grammar to the kind of English spoken and written in London. The availability of cheap books meant that more people learned to read and to speak using the new standardized language. The first dictionary showing English usage, spelling, and pronunciation was prepared in 1604 by Robert Cawdrey.

Once standardized, however, the English language did not stop changing. In fact, it expanded into an international language. From the sixteenth century to the nineteenth century, English merchants, explorers, and settlers spread English to other parts of the globe. For example, the first English settlement in North America was established in Jamestown, Virginia, in 1607 and was followed thirteen years later by the more successful settlement in Plymouth, Massachusetts. Later, English settlers and traders ventured to Canada, the Caribbean, India, Australia, New Zealand, South Africa, and other places. The introduction of the English language and culture would permanently influence the native languages and cultures of all these places. At the same time, English people's interaction with other cultures brought many new loanwords into English.

American English

A Brief History

Immigration to the North American colonies by the English in the seventeenth and eighteenth centuries brought about a new version of the language—American English. Separated by an ocean, the two strains of English—British and American—developed into recognizably different varieties. The history of American English is divided into three periods: *Colonial, National,* and *International.*

The Colonial Period (1607–1776) One of the many problems faced by English settlers in North America was to find words to describe things and experiences that had never been seen or described by an English speaker. Often they had to borrow words from the Native Americans or to adapt old words for their new situations. For example, to describe the unfamiliar mammal with the single white stripe down its back, settlers used its Algonquian name, *skunk.* In another example, settlers had no word for the slope that leads down to a running river, characteristic of the deep-cut rivers in America, because in England rivers are mostly level with the land through which they run. Therefore, the settlers adapted the word *bank,* which in England described a hill or mound of earth, and created the expression "river bank." In short, the early English colonists had language changes forced on them almost immediately because of the new conditions under which they lived.

The National Period (1776–1898)
As settlers began to spread westward, more and more words entered the language, and American English became increasingly different from British. When the thirteen original British colonies declared their independence from England in 1776, American English emerged as a separate national standard. A number of the new nation's founders, including Thomas Jefferson, John Adams, and Benjamin Franklin, recognized that the United States had to be independent not only in government, but also in literature, language, and thought. However, the man who did the most toward standardizing American English was Noah Webster, who took the initiative in choosing single American spellings from multiple British ones. (In the eighteenth century, many British words were spelled more than one way.) As a result, British words ending in *–re, –our,* and *–ise,* such as *centre, humour,* and *realise,* became the Americanized *center, humor,* and *realize.* Generations of American schoolchildren learned Webster's spellings in his "Blue-Backed Spellers" and in the many dictionaries he prepared. By the end of the nineteenth century, American English was distinctly American, not British—the differences were documented in dictionaries and grammar books and recorded in its own literature.

The International Period (1898 to the Present) During the twentieth century, American English spread all over the world through the influence of U.S. business, wars and political affairs, popular culture, and technology. The location of the United Nations headquarters in New York City, the presence of U.S. military bases in various international places, and professional and amateur athletes from the United States playing sports around the world have helped spread American English to other lands. Now the French may *golfer* on *le weekend* (play golf on the weekend), the Danes may *zappe* from one television channel to the next, and the Japanese may eat a *hotto doggu* (hot dog) while watching *futtobooru* (football) on the *terebi* (television).

At the same time, of course, American English has also changed. Immigrants to the United States have contributed their vocabulary to the language, and the media have brought various products and ideas from other cultures into U.S. homes. Look at some of the following words that English has borrowed from other cultures in the twentieth century.

Afrikaans: apartheid
Arabic: falafel
Chinese: chow mein
Czech: robot
French: discothèque
German: moped
Greek (classical): cybernetics
Greek (modern): pita
Italian: pepperoni
Japanese: honcho

Latin: spelunking
Mexican
Spanish: bronco
Norwegian: slalom
Portuguese: bossa nova
Russian: perestroika
Spanish: rumba
Swedish: smorgasbord
Swiss German: muesli
Tagalog: boondocks
Yiddish: schmaltz

American and British English

In some respects, American English has changed less than British English. Those who traveled to the U.S. were more conservative in the way they talked than those who stayed in England. For example, most Americans pronounce *r* where it is spelled, as in *roar* and *card*. However, many English people do not pronounce *r* unless it is immediately followed by a vowel, so their pronunciation of *roar* sounds like *raw* and *card* sound like *cod*. The American pronunciation is older, as the spelling suggests.

Similarly, Americans say both "She's got an idea" and "She's gotten an idea" but mean different things by them. "She's got an idea" is equiva-lent to "She has an idea," whereas "She's gotten an idea" means "An idea has occurred to her." *Got* and *gotten* are both past participles of the verb *get,* but *gotten* is the older form. In England today, people do not generally use *gotten* anymore. They have lost one of the forms of the verb, while Americans have kept it.

On the other hand, Americans have added many words to the English language, perhaps more than the British have. Here is a sample of words—both older and newer ones—that Americans have contributed to English.

American Words Added to English

avocado	kerosene	T-shirt
belittle	lipstick	upside-down cake
cedar chest	mileage	
disc jockey	nifty	volleyball
eggbeater	ouch!	waffle
glitzy	parking lot	xerography
hamburger	quarterback	yo-yo
inchworm	road hog	zipper
jampacked	shack	

NOTE American English has also contributed the popular word *OK*. It came into the language first in 1838–39 as an abbreviation for "oll korrect," a comic misspelling used in Boston newspapers. Then, in 1840, a political organization called the "O.K. Club" was formed to support Martin Van Buren's reelection as President of the United States. Van Buren was nicknamed "Old Kinderhook" after his hometown of Kinderhook, New York, and the club adopted the initials *O.K.*, which punned on the newspaper term and Van Buren's nickname. During the election campaign of 1840, the expression *OK* changed from a regional to a national expression. Now, of course, the term *OK* is used internationally to mean "all correct."

English in the Twenty-first Century

English—both the American and British forms—has become the most widely used language in the world. In fact, it is the official language in more than eighty-seven nations and territories. Several countries, such as India, which have more than one native language, use English as a second language for government and education. English is also the world language of diplomacy, science, technology, aviation, and international trade.

As people around the world use and contribute to the language, it continues to grow and diversify. In fact, some people fear that as English is used in different regions around the world, it will break up into many local languages, just as Latin developed into Italian, French, Spanish, Portuguese, and Romanian at the end of the Roman Empire. Local varieties of English are developing, but so is an international standard of English usage. Airplane travel, television, movies, computers, and other forms of mass communication promote uniformity in the language and keep it from changing too quickly.

NOTE The English language is accompanied by hundreds of **gestures,** or "body language," that reinforce, or contradict, what we are saying. Many gestures are universal. For example, when people—no matter what language they speak—are puzzled, they tend to lift their eyebrows and open their eyes wide. Other gestures are particular to a specific language. For example, English speakers say goodbye with an upraised hand, palm extended outward, fingers moving together up and down. In another culture, people wave goodbye similarly, but they turn their palms toward themselves. They say "Goodbye" with a gesture that to English speakers usually means "Come here."

Varieties of American English

Dialects of American English

Like all languages, American English has many distinct versions of speech, called *dialects.* Everyone uses a dialect, and no dialect is better or worse than another. Dialects can communicate much about us—our home locality, education, gender, and age. Each has unique features of grammar, vocabulary, and pronunciation.

Ethnic Dialects   *Ethnic dialects* are the speech patterns of special communities that have preserved some of their heritage from the past. Every group of people that has come to the United States has brought something characteristic of its original homeland and culture. For example, English, Scottish, Irish, Dutch, Welsh, French, Spanish, Scandinavian, German, Yiddish, Polish, Czech, Italian, Greek, Armenian, Indic, Chinese, Japanese, Korean, and Vietnamese have all influenced American English.

One of the most prominent ethnic dialects in the United States is African American Vernacular English. This dialect unites some of the features of West African languages with some features of early Southern speech and yet other usages developed in African American communities. Some features are *aunt* pronounced "ahnt," *He be sick* meaning a continuing rather than temporary illness, and *tote* meaning "carry" (*tote* is of African origin but now is common in all Southern use).

Another prominent ethnic dialect is Hispanic Vernacular English, which has three main subvarieties: Mexican-influenced English in the Southwest, Cuban-influenced English in

Florida, and Puerto Rican–influenced English in New York City and, of course, in Puerto Rico. Early Hispanic influence in the West introduced such words as *vamoose* (from Spanish *vamos,* "let's go") and *mesa* ("table"). Today, Spanish-influenced English uses English words with meanings similar to Spanish words. For example, the English word *direction* is used to mean "address," the meaning of the Spanish word *direccion.* The number of speakers of Hispanic English has grown in recent years, and so has the importance of their dialect.

Of course, not all African Americans or Hispanic Americans use the dialect associated with their groups, and some features of these dialects turn up in other speech communities, too. The boundaries of ethnic and regional dialects are fluid and ever-changing.

Regional Dialects   The United States has four major ***regional dialects:*** the *Northern,* the *Midland,* the *Southern,* and the *Western.* Remember, however, that not everyone in a region speaks the dialect of that region, just as all members of a particular ethnic group do not speak the same way.

The pronunciations of words often vary from one dialect to another. For example, some

Southerners pronounce the words *ten* and *tin* the same way—"tin." Some Northerners tend to drop the *r* sound from words and lengthen the /a/ sound, so that *farm* sounds like "fahm."

Similarly, regional dialects differ in grammar and vocabulary. For example, someone from the South might say "sick at my stomach," while someone from the North might say "sick to my stomach." You might drink *soda, tonic,* or *pop* depending on the part of the country in which you reside. Furthermore, dialects often vary within each of the four major regions. The following table shows some of the distinctive features of pronunciation, vocabulary, and grammar that distinguish regional dialects. (According to linguists, the Western dialect is still developing and is not yet as well defined as other regional dialects.)

Features of Regional Dialects				
	Northern	**North Midland**	**South Midland**	**Southern**
Pronunciation	"greassy"	"greassy"	"greazy"	"greazy"
	"hahg"	"hahg" or hog	hog	"hawg"
	"pahked cah"	parked car	parked car	"pawked caw"
Word Choice	burlap bag or gunny sack	burlap bag	burlap bag	burlap bag or croker sack
	pail	bucket	bucket	bucket
Grammar	quarter of/to you, youse	quarter to you	quarter til you, you'uns	quarter til/to you, y'all

Standard English

Standard English   Standard English is a variety of language that is not limited to a particular place or ethnic group. It is the one variety of English that is more widely used and accepted than any other in the United States. Because it is commonly understood, people from many different regions and cultures can communicate with one another clearly. In the U.S., standard English is usually more a matter of writing than of speech. It is used for treating important matters seriously, and it is especially appropriate for talking with or writing to people we don't know well. It is the language of public affairs and education, of publications and television, of science and technology, and of business and government. People are expected to use standard English in most school and business situations. It is also the variety of English recorded in dictionaries and grammar books.

This textbook presents and illustrates many of the rules and guidelines for using standard English. To identify the differences between standard English and other varieties of English, this book uses the labels *standard* and *nonstandard*. Nonstandard does not mean wrong language. It means language that is inappropriate in situations where standard English is expected. Nobody needs to use standard English all the time, but everybody should be able to use it when it is the right variety to use.

Standard English—Formal to Informal

Depending on your audience and purpose, the language you use can be formal, informal, or somewhere in between.

Formal English, like formal dress and formal manners, is for special occasions, such as writing serious papers and reports or speaking at formal, dignified occasions. The sentence structure of formal English is long and complex; word choice is precise, often technical or scientific; and the tone is serious and dignified.

Informal English is everyday English. Used for writing personal letters, journal entries, and many newspaper and magazine articles, informal English has a short and easy sentence structure and simple, ordinary word choices. Informal English often includes contractions, colloquialisms, slang, and a conversational tone.

■ *Colloquialisms* are the informal words and phrases of conversational language. (The word *colloquial* derives from a Latin word meaning "conversation.") They bring flavor and color to everyday speech and a friendly, conversational tone to writing. Many are figures of speech or **idioms** that are not meant to be taken literally.

EXAMPLE   When my computer crashed the night before my paper was due, I thought I would **lose my mind**.

■ *Slang* is newly coined language or old words used in unconventional ways. Often special language used by specific groups of people, such as students, musicians, and military personnel, slang is sometimes an indication that the speaker is in tune with a particular group.

EXAMPLES
yo!—hello
hot—pleasing, excellent
cool—pleasing, excellent
code red—an emergency situation
punt—to give up on further action

Don't be surprised if many of these slang words seem outdated. Most slang is popular for a short time and then dies out quickly. A few slang words, however, have been around for centuries. The word *duds,* meaning "clothing," dates back to the sixteenth century.

Test Smarts

Taking Standardized Tests in Grammar, Usage, and Mechanics

Becoming "Test-Smart"

Standardized achievement tests, like other tests, measure your skills in specific areas. Standardized achievement tests also compare your performance to the performance of other students at your age or grade level. Some language arts standardized tests measure your skill in using correct capitalization, punctuation, sentence structure, and spelling. Such tests sometimes also measure your ability to evaluate sentence style.

The most important part of preparing for any test, including standardized tests, is learning the content on which you will be tested. To do this, you must

- listen in class
- complete homework assignments
- study to master the concepts and skills presented by your teacher

In addition, you also need to use effective strategies for taking a standardized test. The following pages will teach you how to become test-smart.

General Strategies for Taking Tests

1. **Understand how the test is scored.** If no points will be taken off for wrong answers, plan to answer every question. If wrong answers count against you, plan to answer only questions you know the answer to or questions you can answer with an educated guess.

2. **Stay focused.** Expect to be a little nervous, but focus your attention on doing the best job possible. Try not to be distracted with thoughts that aren't about the test questions.

3. Get an overview. Quickly skim the entire test to get an idea of how long the test is and what is on it.

4. Pace yourself. Based on your overview, figure out how much time to allow for each section of the test. If time limits are stated for each section, decide how much time to allow for each item. Pace yourself, and check every five to ten minutes to see if you need to work faster. Try to leave a few minutes at the end of the testing period to check your work.

5. Read all instructions. Read the instructions for each part of the test carefully. Also, answer the sample questions to be sure you understand how to answer the test questions.

6. Read all answer choices. Carefully read *all* of the possible answers before you choose an answer. Note how each possible answer differs from the others. You may want to make an *x* next to each answer choice that you rule out.

7. Make educated guesses. If you do not know the answer to a question, see if you can rule out one or more answers and make an educated guess. Don't spend too much time on any one item, though. If you want to think longer about a difficult item, make a light pencil mark next to the item number. You can go back to that question later.

8. Mark your answers. Mark the answer sheet carefully and completely. If you plan to go back to an item later, be sure to skip that number on the answer sheet.

9. Check your work. If you have time at the end of the test, go back to check your answers. This is also the time to try to answer any questions you skipped. Make sure your marks are complete, and erase any stray marks on the answer sheet.

Strategies for Answering Grammar, Usage, and Mechanics Questions

The questions in standardized tests can take different forms, but the most common form is the multiple-choice question. Here are some strategies for answering that kind of test question.

Correcting parts of sentences

One kind of question contains a sentence with an underlined part. The answer choices show several revised versions of that part. Your job is to decide which revised version makes the sentence correct or whether the underlined part is already correct. First, look at each answer carefully. Immediately rule out any answer in which you notice a grammatical error. If you are still unsure of the correct answer, try approaching the question in one of these two ways.

■ **Think how you would rewrite the underlined part.** Look at the answer choices for one that matches your revision. Carefully read each possible answer before you make your final choice. Often, only tiny differences exist between the answers, and you want to choose the *best* answer.

■ **Look carefully at the underlined part and at each answer choice, looking for one particular type of error, such as an error in capitalization or spelling.** The best way to look for a particular error is to compare the answer choices to see how they differ both from each other and from the underlined part of the question. For example, if there are differences in capitalization, look at each choice for capitalization errors.

After ruling out incorrect answers, choose the answer with no errors. If there are errors in each of the choices but no errors in the underlined part, your answer will be the "no error" or "correct as is" choice.

EXAMPLE

Directions: Choose the answer that is the **best** revision of the underlined words.

1. My neighbor is painting his <u>house and my brother helped him.</u>

   A. house; and my brother is helping him.

   B. house, and my brother had helped him.

   C. house, and my brother is helping him.

   D. Correct as is

Explanation: In the example above, the possible answers contain differences in punctuation and in verb tense. Therefore, you should check each possible answer for errors in punctuation and verb tense.

   A. You can rule out this choice because it has incorrect punctuation.

   B. This choice creates inconsistent verb tenses, so you can rule out this answer.

   C. This choice has correct punctuation and creates consistent verb tenses.

   D. You can rule out this choice because the original sentence lacks correct punctuation between the clauses and has inconsistent verb tenses.

Answer: Choice C is the only one that contains no errors, so the oval for that answer choice is darkened.

Correcting whole sentences
This type of question is similar to the kind of question previously described. However, here you are looking for mistakes in the entire sentence instead of just an underlined part. The strategies for approaching this type of question are the same as for the other kind of sentence-correction questions. If you don't see the correct answer right away, compare the answer choices to see how they differ. When you find differences, check

each choice for errors relating to that difference. Rule out choices with errors. Repeat the process until you find the correct answer.

EXAMPLE

Directions: Choose the answer that is the **best** revision of the following sentences.

1. After Brad mowed the lawn, he swept the sidewalk and driveway, then he took a shower. And washed his hair.

   A. After Brad mowed the lawn, he swept the sidewalk and driveway. Then he took a shower and washed his hair.

   B. After Brad mowed the lawn, he swept the sidewalk and driveway. Then he took a shower, and washed his hair.

   C. After Brad mowed the lawn. He swept the sidewalk and driveway; then he took a shower and washed his hair.

   D. Correct as is

Explanation: The original word groups and answer choices have differences in sentence structure and punctuation, so you should check each answer choice for errors in sentence structure and punctuation.

   A. This choice contains two complete sentences and correct punctuation.

   B. This choice contains two complete sentences and incorrect punctuation.

   C. This choice begins with a sentence fragment, so you can rule it out.

   D. You can rule out this choice because the original version contains a sentence fragment.

Answer: Choice A is the only one that contains no errors, so the oval for that answer choice is darkened.

Identifying kinds of errors
This type of question has at least one underlined part. Your job is to determine which part, if any,

contains an error. Sometimes, you also may have to decide what type of error (capitalization, punctuation, or spelling) exists. The strategy is the same whether the question has one or several underlined parts. Try to identify an error, and check the answer choices for that type of error. If the original version is correct as written, choose "no error" or "correct as is."

EXAMPLE

Directions: Read the following sentences and decide which type of error, if any, is in the underlined part.

1. Marcia, Jim, and Leroy are participating in <u>Saturday's charity marathon. they</u> are hoping to raise one hundred dollars for the new children's museum.

   A. Spelling error

   B. Capitalization error

   C. Punctuation error

   D. Correct as is

Explanation: If you cannot tell right away what kind of error (if any) is in the original version, go through each answer choice in turn.

   A. All the words are spelled correctly.

   B. The sentences contain a capitalization error. The second sentence incorrectly begins with a lowercase letter.

   C. The sentences are punctuated correctly.

   D. The sentences contain a capitalization error, so you can rule out this choice.

Answer: Because the passage contains a capitalization error, the oval for answer choice B is darkened.

Revising sentence structure
Errors covered by this kind of question include sentence fragments, run-on sentences, repetitive wording,

misplaced modifiers, and awkward construction. If you don't immediately spot the error, examine the question and each answer choice for specific types of errors, one type at a time. If you cannot find an error in the original version and if all of the other answer choices have errors, then choose "no error" or "correct as is."

EXAMPLE

Directions: Read the following word groups. If there is an error in sentence structure, choose the answer that best revises the word groups.

1. Mary Lou arranged the mozzarella cheese and fresh tomatoes. On a platter covered with lettuce leaves.

   A. Mary Lou arranged the mozzarella cheese and fresh tomatoes on a platter covered with lettuce leaves.

   B. Mary Lou arranged the mozzarella cheese and fresh tomatoes, on a platter covered with lettuce leaves.

   C. Mary Lou arranged the mozzarella cheese and fresh tomatoes; on a platter covered with lettuce leaves.

   D. Correct as is

Explanation: The original word groups and answer choices have differences in sentence structure and punctuation.

   A. This choice is correctly punctuated and contains a correct, complete sentence.

   B. This choice contains an incorrect comma, so you can rule it out.

   C. This choice contains an incorrect semicolon, so you can rule it out.

   D. The original word groups contain a sentence fragment, so D cannot be correct.

Answer: Choice A is the only one that contains no errors, so the oval for that answer choice is darkened.

Questions about sentence style

These questions are often not about grammar, usage, or mechanics but about content and organization. They may ask about tone, purpose, topic sentences, supporting sentences, audience, sentence combining, appropriateness of content, or transitions. The questions may ask you which is the *best* way to revise the passage, or they may ask you to identify the *main* purpose of the passage. When you see words such as *best*, *main*, and *most likely* or *least likely*, you are not being asked to correct errors; you are being asked to make a judgment about style or meaning.

If the question asks for a particular kind of revision (for example, "What *transition* is needed between sentence 4 and sentence 5?"), analyze each answer choice to see how well it makes that particular revision. Many questions ask for a general revision (for example, "Which is the *best* way to revise the last sentence?"). In such situations, check each answer choice and rule out any choices that have mistakes in grammar, usage, or mechanics. Then, read each choice and use what you have learned in class to judge whether the revision improves the original sentence. If you are combining sentences, be sure to choose the answer that includes all important information, that demonstrates good style, *and* that is grammatically correct.

EXAMPLE

Directions: Choose the answer that shows the **best** way to combine the following sentences.

1. Jacques Cousteau was a filmmaker and author. Jacques Cousteau explored the ocean as a diver and marine scientist.

   A. Jacques Cousteau was a filmmaker and author; Jacques Cousteau explored the ocean as a marine scientist.

   B. Jacques Cousteau was a filmmaker and author, he explored the ocean as a diver and marine scientist.

   C. Jacques Cousteau was a filmmaker and author who explored the ocean as a diver and marine scientist.

   D. Jacques Cousteau was a filmmaker, author, diver, and scientist.

Explanation:

   A. Answer choice A is grammatically correct but unnecessarily repeats the subject *Jacques Cousteau* and leaves out some information.

   B. Choice B is a run-on sentence, so it cannot be the correct answer.

   C. Choice C is grammatically correct, and it demonstrates effective sentence combining.

   D. Choice D is grammatically correct but leaves out some information.

Answer: Because answer choice C shows the best way to combine the sentences, the oval for choice C is darkened.

Fill-in-the-blanks

Fill-in-the-blanks This type of question tests your ability to fill in blanks in sentences, giving answers that are logical and grammatically correct. A question of this kind might ask you to choose a verb in the appropriate tense. A different question might require a combination of adverbs (*first, next*) to show how parts of the sentence relate. Another question might require a vocabulary word to complete the sentence.

To approach a sentence-completion question, first look for clue words in the sentence. *But*, *however*, and *though* indicate a contrast; *therefore* and *as a result* indicate cause and effect. Using sentence clues, rule out obviously incorrect answer choices. Then, try filling in the blanks with the remaining choices to determine which answer choice makes the most sense. Finally, check to be sure your choice is grammatically correct.

Directions: Choose the words that **best** complete the sentence.

1. When Jack _____ the dog, the dog _____ water everywhere.

   A. washes, splashed

   B. washed, will be splashing

   C. will have washed, has splashed

   D. washed, splashed

Explanation:

   A. The verb tenses (present and past) are inconsistent.

   B. The verb tenses (past and future) are inconsistent.

   C. The verb tenses (future perfect and present perfect) are inconsistent.

   D. The verb tenses (past and past) are consistent.

Answer: The oval for choice D is darkened.

Using Your Test Smarts

Remember: Success on standardized tests comes partly from knowing strategies for taking such tests—from being test-smart. Knowing these strategies can help you approach standardized achievement tests more confidently. Do your best to learn your classroom subjects, take practice tests if they are available, and use the strategies outlined in this section. Good luck!

Grammar at a Glance

abbreviation An abbreviation is a shortened form of a word or a phrase.

- **capitalization of** (See page 284.)

TITLES USED WITH NAMES	**M**s.	**L**t. **C**ol.	**S**r.	**RN**
KINDS OF ORGANIZATIONS	**L**td.	**I**nc.	**D**ept.	**C**orp.
PARTS OF ADDRESSES	**A**ve.	**S**t.	**D**r.	**P.O. B**ox
NAMES OF STATES	[without ZIP Codes]	**L**a.	**F**la.	
		Mich.	**S. D**ak.	
	[with ZIP Codes]	**LA**	**FL**	
		MI	**SD**	
TIMES	**A.M.**	**P.M.**	**B.C.**	**A.D.**

- **punctuation of** (See page 297.)

WITH PERIODS	(See preceding examples.)
WITHOUT PERIODS	SAT DNA NCAA IRS
	DC (D.C. without ZIP Code)
	ml mi gal °F mm
	[Exception: inch = in.]

action verb An action verb expresses physical or mental activity. (See page 13.)

EXAMPLE The herd of zebra **galloped** across the plains.

active voice Active voice is the voice a verb is in when it expresses an action done by its subject. (See page 194. See also **voice**.)

EXAMPLE Mr. Intrator, the museum director, gingerly **handled** the Limoges vase.

┌H E L P┐

Grammar at a Glance is an alphabetical list of special terms and expressions with examples and references to further information. When you encounter a grammar or usage problem in the revising or proofreading stage of your writing, look for help in this section first. You may find all you need to know right here. If you need more information, **Grammar at a Glance** will show you where in the book to turn for a more complete explanation. If you do not find what you are looking for in **Grammar at a Glance,** turn to the index.

RESOURCES

adjective An adjective modifies a noun or a pronoun. (See page 9.)

EXAMPLE   **The** Schmidts live in **a magnificent, spacious** apartment.

adjective clause An adjective clause is a subordinate clause that modifies a noun or a pronoun. (See page 78.)

EXAMPLE   The years **that Mom likes to remember** are the late 1970s.

adjective phrase A prepositional phrase that modifies a noun or a pronoun is called an adjective phrase. (See page 54.)

EXAMPLE   Cars **in Europe and Asia** are generally smaller than cars **in North America.**

adverb An adverb modifies a verb, an adjective, or another adverb. (See page 17.)

EXAMPLE   "I **really** like that desk," said Emily. "It's **almost** perfect."

adverb clause An adverb clause is a subordinate clause that modifies a verb, an adjective, or an adverb. (See page 83.)

EXAMPLE   **While he was driving,** Jerry listened to news reports on the radio.

adverb phrase A prepositional phrase that modifies a verb, an adjective, or an adverb is called an adverb phrase. (See page 55.)

EXAMPLE   **Before dinner,** Dr. Laplace was called away.

agreement Agreement is the correspondence, or match, between grammatical forms. Grammatical forms agree when they have the same number, gender, and person.

■ **of pronouns and antecedents** (See page 111.)

SINGULAR   **Nathan** cannot find **his** driver's license.
PLURAL   The **dancers** train hard every day, striving to perfect **their** performances.

SINGULAR   Does **everyone** in the cast know **his or her** lines?
PLURAL   Do **all** of the actors know **their** lines?

SINGULAR	Neither **Mariah** nor **Claire** has decided whether **she** will play basketball this season.
PLURAL	**Mariah** and **Claire** have not decided whether **they** will play basketball this season.

■ **of subjects and verbs** (See page 96.)

SINGULAR	The **chief executive officer is** confident that the corporation will remain competitive.
	The **chief executive officer,** along with the stockholders, **is** confident that the corporation will remain competitive.
PLURAL	The **stockholders are** confident that the corporation will remain competitive.
	The **stockholders,** along with the chief executive officer, **are** confident that the corporation will remain competitive.
SINGULAR	**Each** of the planets **revolves** around the sun.
PLURAL	**All** of the planets **revolve** around the sun.
SINGULAR	Normally, **Matthew or Julia writes** the club's monthly newsletter.
PLURAL	Normally, **Matthew and Julia write** the club's monthly newsletter.
SINGULAR	Here **is** my **report** on the history of the Japanese theater.
PLURAL	Here **are** my **notes** on the history of the Japanese theater.
SINGULAR	**One hundred dollars is** what we paid for this painting.
PLURAL	**One hundred dollars** with consecutive serial numbers **were found** in an old shoe box.
SINGULAR	***Clubhouse Detectives* is** a good movie.
PLURAL	The young **detectives are investigating** the disappearance of a neighbor.
SINGULAR	**Is physics offered** at your school?
PLURAL	**Are** my **sunglasses** in your car?
SINGULAR	Soledad is one applicant **who qualifies** for the job.
PLURAL	Soledad is one of the applicants **who qualify** for the job.
SINGULAR	Soledad is the only one of the applicants **who qualifies** for the job.

ambiguous reference Ambiguous reference occurs when a pronoun incorrectly refers to either of two antecedents. (See page 148.)

AMBIGUOUS One difference between coniferous trees and broadleaf trees is that they produce cones instead of flowers.

CLEAR One difference between coniferous trees and broadleaf trees is that coniferous trees produce cones instead of flowers.

antecedent An antecedent is the word or words that a pronoun stands for. (See page 148.)

EXAMPLE At **Patti** and **Paul**'s anniversary dinner, **Adrianna** sang a

song that **she** had written especially for **them.** [*Patti* and *Paul* are the antecedents of *them. Adrianna* is the antecedent of *she.*]

apostrophe

- **to form contractions** (See page 349. See also **contraction.**)
  EXAMPLES shouldn'␣t you'␣ll let'␣s '␣99

- **to form plurals of letters, numerals, symbols, and words used as words** (See page 350.)
  EXAMPLES *x*'␣s and *o*'␣s too many *and*'␣s and *so*'␣s

  1990'␣s [*or* 1990s] CD'␣s [*or* CDs]

- **to show possession** (See page 345.)
  EXAMPLES the farmer'␣s wheat crop

  the farmers'␣ wheat crops

  men'␣s fashions

  someone'␣s keys

  during the President and the First Lady'␣s trip to South Africa

  one week'␣s [*or* five days'␣] wages

appositive An appositive is a noun or a pronoun placed beside another noun or pronoun to identify or explain it. (See page 68.)

EXAMPLE I like the novels of the writer **James Jones.**

appositive phrase An appositive phrase consists of an appositive and its modifiers. (See page 69.)

EXAMPLE   James Jones, **the author of *From Here to Eternity*,** lived for many years in Paris.

article The articles, *a, an,* and *the,* are the most frequently used adjectives. (See page 10.)

EXAMPLE   **The** watch, **an** old possession of my mother's, was **a** fine example of Swiss workmanship.

bad, badly (See page 214.)

NONSTANDARD   Do you think this sushi smells badly?
STANDARD   Do you think this sushi smells **bad**?

base form The base form, or infinitive, is one of the four principal parts of a verb. (See page 162.)

EXAMPLE   We thought we heard something **move** downstairs.

brackets (See page 329.)

EXAMPLES   In his introduction to Victorian poetry, the teacher explained, "Many people mistakenly attribute **[**Elizabeth Barrett**]** Browning's 'Sonnet 43,' which begins with the famous line 'How do I love thee? Let me count the ways,' to William Shakespeare."

Of all of the Navajo gods, the most revered is Changing Woman (often called Earth Woman **[**the belief is that her spirit inhabits the earth**]**).

capitalization

- of abbreviations and acronyms (See page 284. See also abbreviation.)
- of first words (See page 269.)
    EXAMPLES   **M**y sister writes in her journal every night.

    Omar asked, "**W**ould you like to play on my team?"

    Dear Ms. Reuben:

    Sincerely yours,

■ **of proper nouns and proper adjectives** (See page 271.)

Proper Noun	Common Noun
Richard the Lion-Hearted	leader
Australia	continent
Costa Rica	country
Santa Clara County	county
Quebec Province	province
Liberty Island	island
Narragansett Bay	body of water
Mount Makalu	mountain
Mesa Verde National Park	park
Petrified Forest	forest
Timpanogos Cave	cave
the Northwest	region
Twenty-fourth Street	street
Parent-Teacher Association (PTA)	organization
Democratic Party (*or* party)	political party
Industrial Revolution	historical event
Middle Ages	historical period
World Series	special event
Labor Day	holiday
January, Saturday	calendar items
Oglala Sioux	people
Shinto	religion
God (*but* the god Thor)	deity
Rosh Hashana	holy days
Veda	sacred writing
First Interstate World Center	building
Presidential Medal of Freedom	award
Uranus	planet
Beta Centauri	star
Corona Borealis	constellation
Dona Paz	ship
Discovery	spacecraft
Chemistry I (*but* chemistry)	school subject
Hindi	language

■ **of titles** (See page 280.)

EXAMPLES **M**ayor Biondi [preceding a name]

Bill Biondi, the **m**ayor of our town [following a name]

Thank you, **M**ayor. [direct address]

Aunt Katarina [*but* my aunt Katarina]

Glow-in-the-Dark Constellations: A Field Guide for Young Stargazers [book]

A River Runs Through It [movie or book]

Planet Safari [TV program]

Landscape with the Flight into Egypt [work of art]

Hymns from the Rig Veda [musical composition]

"**W**onderful **W**orld" [song]

"**T**he **J**ilting of **G**ranny **W**eatherall" [short story]

"**S**topping by **W**oods on a **S**nowy **E**vening" [poem]

National Geographic World [magazine]

the *Denver Rocky Mountain News* [newspaper]

Hi and Lois [comic strip]

case of pronouns Case is the form a pronoun takes to show how the pronoun is used in a sentence. (See page 124.)

NOMINATIVE   Last summer, **she** and **I** traveled to Boston and walked the Freedom Trail.

The only juniors on the prom committee are Chiaki and **he.**

Either one, Margo or **she,** will be glad to accompany you.

We senior citizens are organizing a community walkathon.

Is Gioacchino Rossini the composer **who** wrote the opera *The Barber of Seville*?

Do you know **who** the guest speaker will be?

I helped Simon more than **she.** [meaning *more than she helped Simon*]

OBJECTIVE   Quincy accompanied **her** to Freedom Hall to see the African Heritage exhibit.

Miguel taught **them** some traditional Mexican folk songs.

The first tennis match was between Lupe and **me.**

The Nobel Peace Prize was awarded to both leaders, John Hume and **him.**

Our math teacher explained to **us** students what a magic square is.

Then the math teacher asked **us** to create some magic squares.

My neighbor Mr. Mukai often quotes Shakespeare, **whom** he considers the greatest writer of all time.

One ruler about **whom** I would like to learn more is Hatshepsut, the first woman pharaoh.

I helped Simon more than **her.** [meaning *more than I helped her*]

POSSESSIVE   **Your** computer can process data faster than **mine** can.

Her sliding safely into home plate in the bottom of the ninth inning tied the game.

clause A clause is a group of words that contains a verb and its subject and that is used as a sentence or as part of a sentence. (See page 76.)

INDEPENDENT CLAUSE   Robert Graves was an English poet and writer

SUBORDINATE CLAUSE   who was famous for the novel *I, Claudius*

colon (See page 324.)

■ **before lists**

EXAMPLES   Central America comprises the following nations**:** Belize, Costa Rica, El Salvador, Guatemala, Honduras, Nicaragua, and Panama.

Today, the discussion in our world history class focused on the beliefs and teachings of three philosophers of ancient Greece**:** Socrates, Plato, and Aristotle.

■ **in conventional situations**

EXAMPLES   8**:**45 P.M.

Genesis 7**:**1–17

*Bulfinch's Mythology***:** *The Age of Fable, The Age of Chivalry, Legends of Charlemagne*

Dear Dr. Sabatini**:**

comma (See page 301.)

■ **in a series**

EXAMPLES   Ms. Camara explained the differences between a meteor, a meteoroid, and a meteorite.

On his vacation in Alaska, Jason went kayaking, bob-sledding, and rock climbing.

■ **in compound sentences**

EXAMPLES   Alberto has written three drafts of his essay on transcendentalism, and he is not satisfied with any of them.

I nominated my best friend, Elena, for junior class president, but she surprised me by declining the nomination.

■ **with nonessential phrases and clauses**

EXAMPLES   Pa-out-She, an ancient Chinese scholar, is credited with compiling the first dictionary.

Carlos Chavez, who composed symphonies and ballets, founded the Symphony Orchestra of Mexico.

■ **with introductory elements**

EXAMPLES   On the surface of the moon, a person would weigh about one sixth of what he or she weighs on the earth's surface.

After they had read several of the fables attributed to Aesop, the students discussed the moral lessons that the fables teach.

■ **with interrupters**

EXAMPLES   The most fascinating exhibit in the museum, in my opinion, is the huge Egyptian tomb that visitors are allowed to explore.

Nocturnal animals, such as armadillos, hunt and feed at night and rest during the day.

■ **in conventional situations**

EXAMPLES   On Friday, July 9, 1999, the Wilsons set out on a road trip from Bangor, Maine, to Seattle, Washington.

I mailed the letter to 645 Pinecrest Ave., Atlanta, GA 30328-0645, on 16 October 2000.

comma splice A comma splice is a run-on sentence in which sentences have been joined with only a comma between them. (See page 451. See also **fused sentence** and **run-on sentence**.)

COMMA SPLICE	I asked the librarian to suggest a contemporary novel about family values, she highly recommended *Mama Flora's Family* by Alex Haley and David Stevens.
REVISED	I asked the librarian to suggest a contemporary novel about family values**, and** she highly recommended *Mama Flora's Family* by Alex Haley and David Stevens.
REVISED	I asked the librarian to suggest a contemporary novel about family values**;** she highly recommended *Mama Flora's Family* by Alex Haley and David Stevens.
REVISED	I asked the librarian to suggest a contemporary novel about family values**. S**he highly recommended *Mama Flora's Family* by Alex Haley and David Stevens.

comparison of modifiers (See page 216.)

■ **comparison of adjectives and adverbs**

Positive	Comparative	Superlative
soft	soft**er**	soft**est**
early	earl**ier**	earl**iest**
effective	**more (less)** effective	**most (least)** effective
rapidly	**more (less)** rapidly	**most (least)** rapidly
far	**farther/further**	**farthest/furthest**

■ **comparing two**

EXAMPLES   Our science teacher asked us, "Which is **heavier,** a pound of feathers or a pound of lead?"

Which of these two automobiles do you think operates **more efficiently**?

■ **comparing more than two**

EXAMPLES   Founded in 1636, Harvard is the **oldest** university in the United States.

Of the four debaters on the team, Yosuke argued **most persuasively.**

complement A complement is a word or word group that completes the meaning of a verb. (See page 38.)

EXAMPLES   Papa sent **me letters** and **postcards.**

This room is **quiet;** it will be my **study.**

complex sentence A complex sentence has one independent clause and at least one subordinate clause. (See page 89.)

EXAMPLES   Angel Falls, which is the world's highest waterfall, was named for the aviator James Angel, who crash-landed near the falls in 1937.

As we read the historical play by Shakespeare, the teacher pointed out several anachronisms, which are things that are out of their proper time in history.

compound-complex sentence A compound-complex sentence has two or more independent clauses and at least one subordinate clause. (See page 89.)

EXAMPLES   Animals that live in the desert, such as the camel, the mule deer, and the kangaroo rat, require very little water to survive; in fact, most desert animals can go several days without drinking any water.

Maya Angelou, who is one of our country's most gifted authors, has written short stories, novels, plays, and poems; but she is perhaps best known for her autobiographical work *I Know Why the Caged Bird Sings.*

compound sentence A compound sentence has two or more independent clauses but no subordinate clauses. (See page 88.)

EXAMPLES   The African elephant is the largest land animal, and the Savi's pygmy shrew, also indigenous to Africa, is the smallest.

The first Women's Rights Convention was held in 1848 in Seneca Falls, New York; today, the city is the home of the National Women's Hall of Fame.

conjunction A conjunction joins words or groups of words. (See page 23.)

EXAMPLES   The long line of moviegoers **and** their families **or** friends stretched around the block, **for** it was **not only** a beautiful night **but also** a national holiday.

Turn off the lights **before** you leave.

contraction A contraction is a shortened form of a word, a numeral, or a group of words. Apostrophes in contractions indicate where letters or numerals have been omitted. (See page 349. See also **apostrophe.**)

EXAMPLES you're [you are]	here's [here is]
who's [who is *or* who has]	they're [they are]
wasn't [was not]	it's [it is *or* it has]
can't [cannot]	don't [do not]
'14–'18 war [1914–1918 war]	o'clock [of the clock]

dangling modifier A dangling modifier is a modifying word, phrase, or clause that does not clearly and sensibly modify a word or a word group in a sentence. (See page 232.)

DANGLING   Proofreading his report on mummification and other ancient Egyptian practices, a few errors, including a dangling modifier, were discovered. [Who is proofreading his report?]

REVISED   Proofreading his report on mummification and other ancient Egyptian practices, **Richard** discovered a few errors, including a dangling modifier.

dash (See page 328.)

EXAMPLE   My grandparents—my mother's parents, that is—moved to California before my mother was born.

declarative sentence A declarative sentence makes a statement and is followed by a period. (See page 45.)

EXAMPLE   Euripides was a famous Greek playwright.

direct object A direct object is a word or word group that receives the action of the verb or shows the result of the action, answering the question *Whom?* or *What?* after a transitive verb. (See page 39.)

EXAMPLE   Every Friday night, we eat **fish.**

double comparison A double comparison is the use of two comparative forms (usually *more* and *–er*) or two superlative forms (usually *most* and *–est*) to express comparison. In standard usage, the single comparative form is correct. (See page 220.)

NONSTANDARD   This salsa is more spicier than the salsa that you normally make.

STANDARD   This salsa is **spicier** [*or* **more spicy**] than the salsa that you normally make.

double negative A double negative is the nonstandard use of two or more negative words to express a single negative idea. (See page 261.)

NONSTANDARD	When I met the President, I was so nervous that I couldn't hardly speak.
STANDARD	When I met the President, I was so nervous that I **could hardly** speak.

NONSTANDARD	The field trip to the petting zoo won't cost the children nothing.
STANDARD	The field trip to the petting zoo **won't cost** the children **anything.**
STANDARD	The field trip to the petting zoo **will cost** the children **nothing.**

double subject A double subject occurs when an unnecessary pronoun is used after the subject of a sentence. (See page 252.)

NONSTANDARD	Kiyoshi and his sister, although they are twins, they do not have the same birthday.
STANDARD	**Kiyoshi and his sister,** although they are twins, **do** not have the same birthday.

elliptical construction An elliptical construction is a clause from which words have been omitted. (See pages 84 and 134.)

EXAMPLE   Aunt Zita is much more outgoing **than Mother [is].**

end marks (See page 294.)

- **with sentences**

EXAMPLES   Spanakopita, a delicious Greek dish, is a thin shell of pastry dough filled with spicy spinach and feta cheese. [declarative sentence]

Do you have a recipe for spanakopita? [interrogative sentence]

Yum! [interjection] What a tasty dish this is! [exclamatory sentence]

Please give me your recipe. [imperative sentence]

- **with abbreviations** (See **abbreviation.**)

EXAMPLES   The first American in space was Alan B. Shepard, Jr.

Was the first American in space Alan B. Shepard, Jr.?

essential clause/essential phrase An essential, or restrictive, clause or phrase is necessary to the meaning of a sentence; it is not set off by commas. (See page 306.)

EXAMPLES   Any pilots **who have already logged more than two hundred hours** will be excused from training. [essential clause]

Students **competing for the first time** must report to Mr. Landis. [essential phrase]

exclamation point (See **end marks.**)

exclamatory sentence An exclamatory sentence expresses strong feeling and is followed by an exclamation point. (See page 46.)

EXAMPLE   That's absolutely fantastic**!**

 F

faulty coordination Faulty coordination occurs when unequal ideas are presented as though they were coordinated. (See page 442.)

FAULTY   At the age of sixty-five, my grandmother retired from teaching school, but within a year she grew restless and bored, for she missed the camaraderie of her colleagues and the exuberance of the students, so she decided to become a substitute teacher, and now she is back in the classroom nearly every day, and she is enjoying life again.

REVISED   At the age of sixty-five, my grandmother retired from teaching school. Within a year, however, she grew restless and bored, for she missed the camaraderie of her colleagues and the exuberance of the students. As a result, she decided to become a substitute teacher. Now she is back in the classroom nearly every day and is enjoying life again.

fragment (See **sentence fragment.**)

fused sentence A fused sentence is a run-on sentence in which sentences have been joined together with no punctuation between them. (See page 451. See also **comma splice** and **run-on sentence.**)

FUSED   Last night, a heavy snowfall blanketed our community consequently, all schools and many businesses in the area were closed today.

REVISED   Last night, a heavy snowfall blanketed our community**;** consequently, all schools and many businesses in the area were closed today.

REVISED   Last night, a heavy snowfall blanketed our community. Consequently, all schools and many businesses in the area were closed today.

general reference A general reference is the incorrect use of a pronoun to refer to a general idea rather than to a specific noun. (See page 149.)

GENERAL   To make food called glucose, a green plant uses water from its roots, a chemical called chlorophyll, and the energy from the sun. This is called photosynthesis.

REVISED   To make food called glucose, a green plant uses water from its roots, a chemical called chlorophyll, and the energy from the sun. **This process** is called photosynthesis.

gerund A gerund is a verb form ending in *–ing* that is used as a noun. (See page 61.)

EXAMPLE   **Procrastinating** leads nowhere, as my mom always says.

gerund phrase A gerund phrase consists of a gerund and its modifiers and complements. (See page 62.)

EXAMPLE   **Collecting Beatles memorabilia** is my uncle's hobby.

good, well (See page 214.)

EXAMPLES   Paul is a **good** employee.

Paul works **well** [not *good*] with others and performs his duties effectively.

hyphen (See page 352.)

- **to divide words**

   EXAMPLE   Both Ming and I wish that our school offered computer courses earlier in the day.

- **in compound numbers**

   EXAMPLE   Ms. Hughes served as president of the company for twenty-one years.

- **with prefixes and suffixes**

   EXAMPLES   The football season begins in mid-August.

   I think this salsa is fat-free.

RESOURCES

imperative mood The imperative mood is used to express a direct command or request. (See page 198.)

EXAMPLES **Name** and **describe** the Seven Wonders of the ancient world.

Ladies and gentlemen, please **stand** for the singing of our national anthem.

imperative sentence An imperative sentence gives a command or makes a request and is followed by either a period or an exclamation point. (See page 45.)

EXAMPLES Please return this map to Mr. Miller**.**

Get out of that tree now**!**

indefinite reference An indefinite reference is the incorrect use of the pronoun *you*, *it*, or *they* to refer to no particular person or thing. (See page 153.)

INDEFINITE In this week's edition of our community newspaper, it shows the official ballot that will be used for the upcoming local election.

REVISED This week's edition of our community newspaper shows the official ballot that will be used for the upcoming local election.

REVISED In this week's edition of our community newspaper is a reproduction of the official ballot that will be used for the upcoming local election.

independent clause An independent clause (also called a *main clause*) expresses a complete thought and can stand by itself as a sentence. (See page 76.)

EXAMPLES **The game was afoot,** as Holmes would say, and **no dawdling would be tolerated.**

indicative mood The indicative mood is used to express a fact, an opinion, or a question. (See page 198.)

EXAMPLES Denzel Washington **has received** considerable praise for his performance in the movie.

Denzel Washington, in my opinion, **deserves** an Academy Award.

Didn't Denzel Washington **win** an Oscar for his performance?

indirect object An indirect object is a noun, pronoun, or word group that often appears in sentences containing direct objects. An indirect object tells *to whom* or *to what* (or *for whom* or *for what*) the action of a transitive verb is done. Indirect objects generally precede direct objects. (See page 40.)

EXAMPLE   In Roman mythology, Mercury gave **gods** messages from humans.

infinitive An infinitive is a verb form, usually preceded by *to*, used as a noun, an adjective, or an adverb. (See page 64.)

EXAMPLE   **To understand,** read the book.

infinitive phrase An infinitive phrase consists of an infinitive and its modifiers and complements. (See page 65.)

EXAMPLE   **To play the piano well** has long been an ambition of mine.

interjection An interjection expresses emotion and has no grammatical relation to the rest of the sentence. (See page 25.)

EXAMPLE   **Oh no!** The whole freeway's backed up for miles!

interrogative sentence An interrogative sentence asks a question and is followed by a question mark. (See page 45.)

EXAMPLE   Ma'am, are you sure you spoke to Dr. Ryan in person?

intransitive verb An intransitive verb is a verb that does not take an object. (See page 16.)

EXAMPLE   The dogs **barked** as the camels **passed.**

irregular verb An irregular verb is a verb that forms its past and past participle in some way other than by adding *d* or *ed* to the base form. (See page 164. See also **regular verb.**)

Base Form	Present Participle	Past	Past Participle
be	[is] being	was, were	[have] been
become	[is] becoming	became	[have] become
begin	[is] beginning	began	[have] begun

Base Form	Present Participle	Past	Past Participle
catch	[is] catching	caught	[have] caught
put	[is] putting	put	[have] put
take	[is] taking	took	[have] taken
throw	[is] throwing	threw	[have] thrown

italics (See page 330.)

- ### for titles

  EXAMPLES *A History of the Supreme Court* [book]

  Scientific American [periodical]

  Perseus with the Head of Medusa [work of art]

  A Little Night Music [long musical composition]

- ### for words, letters, and symbols used as such and for foreign words

  EXAMPLES You misspelled ***exhilaration*** by leaving out the ***h.***

  A ***cause célèbre*** is a scandal or a controversial incident.

its, it's (See page 378.)

EXAMPLES **Its** [Canada's] capital is Ottawa.

Brrr! **It's** [It is] cold outside.

It's [It has] been snowing here since early this morning.

lie, lay (See page 177.)

EXAMPLES For several weeks, straw **lay** over all of our backyard.

We **laid** straw on the ground to cover the grass seed.

linking verb A linking verb connects its subject with a word that identifies or describes the subject. (See page 13.)

EXAMPLE As she **grew** older, her ambitions changed.

misplaced modifier A misplaced modifier is a word, phrase, or clause that seems to modify the wrong word or words in a sentence. (See page 230.)

| MISPLACED | Chicle is the main ingredient in chewing gum made from the sap of the sapodilla tree. [Chicle, not chewing gum, is made from the sap of the sapodilla tree.] |
| REVISED | Chicle, **made from the sap of the sapodilla tree,** is the main ingredient in chewing gum. |

modifier A modifier is a word or word group that makes the meaning of another word or word group more specific. (See page 210.)

EXAMPLE   Ronald is **a prominent** attorney **in a small Kansas town.**

mood Mood is the form a verb takes to indicate the attitude of the person using the verb. (See page 198. See also **imperative mood, indicative mood,** and **subjunctive mood.**)

nonessential clause/nonessential phrase A nonessential, or nonrestrictive, clause or phrase adds information not necessary to the main idea in the sentence and is set off by commas. (See page 306.)

EXAMPLES   The tourists on the pier, **who had all agreed to wear the same color combinations,** were becoming restless. [nonessential clause]

Our cats Boots and Bandit, **those two scamps,** are hiding behind the curtains. [nonessential phrase]

noun A noun names a person, place, thing, or idea. (See page 3.)

EXAMPLE   **Tyrell** is a **musician** of great **skill.**

noun clause A noun clause is a subordinate clause used as a noun. (See page 80.)

EXAMPLE   The prize goes to **whoever comes in first.**

number Number is the form a word takes to indicate whether the word is singular or plural. (See page 96.)

| SINGULAR | door | I | loaf | mouse |
| PLURAL | doors | we | loaves | mice |

objective complement An objective complement is a word or word group that helps complete the meaning of a transitive verb by identifying or modifying the direct object. (See page 41.)

EXAMPLE   The Hartleys painted their bookcases **black.**

object of a preposition An object of a preposition is the noun or pronoun that completes a prepositional phrase. (See page 20.)

EXAMPLE   In the **general store** she found a battery for her **watch.** [*In the general store* and *for her watch* are prepositional phrases.]

parallel structure Parallel structure is the use of the same grammatical forms or structures to balance related ideas in a sentence. (See page 443.)

NONPARALLEL   The job requires someone with a college degree in computer programming and who has excellent communication skills.

PARALLEL   The job requires someone **with a college degree in computer programming** and **with excellent communication skills.** [two prepositional phrases]

PARALLEL   The job requires someone **who has a college degree in computer programming** and **who has excellent communication skills.** [two adjective clauses]

parentheses (See page 327.)

EXAMPLES   The seven colors of the spectrum **(**think of a rainbow**)** are as follows: red, orange, yellow, green, blue, indigo, and violet. **(**See diagram C.**)**

participial phrase A participial phrase consists of a participle and any complements and modifiers it has. (See page 59.)

EXAMPLE   The kangaroo, **leaping ever farther and higher,** was soon out of sight.

participle A participle is a verb form that can be used as an adjective. (See page 58.)

EXAMPLE   **Astounded,** Mother could only nod her head in assent.

RESOURCES

passive voice The passive voice is the voice a verb is in when it expresses an action done to its subject. (See page 194. See also **voice.**)

EXAMPLE   Emile **has been given** a great responsibility.

period (See **end marks.**)

phrase A phrase is a group of related words that does not contain a verb and its subject and that is used as a single part of speech. (See page 53.)

EXAMPLES   Goethe, **probably Germany's greatest writer,** represents the best **of the classical and romantic traditions.**
[*Probably Germany's greatest writer* is an appositive phrase. *Of the classical and romantic traditions* is a prepositional phrase.]

Always to tell the truth requires courage. [*Always to tell the truth* is an infinitive phrase.]

Sitting in the bleachers, we cheered our team. [*Sitting in the bleachers* is a participial phrase.]

predicate The predicate is the part of a sentence that says something about the subject. (See page 33.)

EXAMPLE   Ed **throws an unforgettable fastball.**

predicate adjective A predicate adjective is an adjective that completes the meaning of a linking verb and modifies the subject of the verb. (See page 43.)

EXAMPLE   The White House aides seemed **worried** and **uncertain** about the latest developments.

predicate nominative A predicate nominative is a word or word group that completes the meaning of a linking verb and that identifies the subject or refers to it. (See page 42.)

EXAMPLE   My younger brother John is becoming a very influential **reporter.**

prefix A prefix is a word part that is added before a base word or root. (See page 364.)

EXAMPLES	un + usual = **un**usual	il + logical = **il**logical
	re + write = **re**write	pre + mature = **pre**mature
	self + discipline = **self**-discipline	ex + senator = **ex**-senator
	mid + October = **mid**-October	pre + Columbian = **pre**-Columbian

preposition A preposition shows the relationship of a noun or a pronoun to some other word in a sentence. (See page 20.)

EXAMPLE   The house **in** the valley, built **by** my grandfather Ernesto, has a view **of** the forest.

prepositional phrase A prepositional phrase includes a preposition, its object (a noun or a pronoun), and any modifiers of that object. (See page 54. See also **object of a preposition.**)

EXAMPLE   Finally, someone went **for additional refreshments.**

pronoun A pronoun is used in place of one or more nouns or pronouns. (See page 5.)

EXAMPLES   **My** cousin Rich, **who** worked in the Peace Corps when **he** was younger, wants to devote **his** life to helping people.

Everyone should introduce **himself** or **herself** to the group.

question mark (See **end marks.**)

quotation marks (See page 333.)

▪ **for direct quotations**

EXAMPLE   **"**Before I make my ruling,**"** said the judge, **"**I want to meet with both counsels in my chambers.**"**

▪ **with other marks of punctuation** (See also preceding example.)

EXAMPLES   **"**In what year was the Great Wall of China completed**?"** asked Neka.

Is Robert Frost the poet who said that a poem should **"**begin in delight and end in wisdom**"?**

The teacher asked, **"**Who are the speakers in Gwendolyn Brooks's poem **"**We Real Cool**"?"**

■ **for titles**

EXAMPLES   "The Bells of Santa Cruz" [short story]

          "Mother to Son" [short poem]

          "Backwater Blues" [song]

regular verb A regular verb is a verb that forms its past and past participle by adding *d* or *ed* to the base form. (See page 163. See also **irregular verb.**)

Base Form	Present Participle	Past	Past Participle
ask	[is] asking	asked	[have] asked
drown	[is] drowning	drowned	[have] drowned
receive	[is] receiving	received	[have] received
risk	[is] risking	risked	[have] risked
suppose	[is] supposing	supposed	[have] supposed
use	[is] using	used	[have] used

rise, raise (See page 180.)

EXAMPLES   A dense cloud of dust **rose** behind the wild horses as they galloped into the canyon.

          As soon as she **raised** the hood of the car, she saw what was causing the noise.

run-on sentence A run-on sentence is two or more complete sentences run together as one. (See page 451. See also **comma splice** and **fused sentence.**)

RUN-ON   Barney Oldfield (1877–1946) was the first race-car driver to go at a speed of a mile per minute, he won his first race at Detroit in 1902.

REVISED   Barney Oldfield (1877–1946) was the first race-car driver to go at a speed of a mile per minute. **H**e won his first race at Detroit in 1902.

REVISED   Barney Oldfield (1877–1946) was the first race-car driver to go at a speed of a mile per minute; he won his first race at Detroit in 1902.

RESOURCES

semicolon (See page 322.)

- **in compound sentences with no conjunctions**

  EXAMPLE More than six hundred paintings were created by the Dutch artist Rembrandt; nearly one hundred of them were self-portraits.

- **in compound sentences with conjunctive adverbs**

  EXAMPLE Usually, the planet farthest from the sun is Pluto; **however,** because of its orbit, Pluto is at times closer to the sun than Neptune is.

- **between a series of items when the items contain commas**

  EXAMPLE For her research paper Marva wrote about three women who were awarded the Nobel Peace Prize: Jane Addams, a cofounder of the American Civil Liberties Union; Mother Teresa, the founder of Missionaries of Charity in Calcutta, India; and Rigoberta Menchú, a human rights activist from Guatemala.

sentence A sentence is a group of words that contains a subject and a verb and expresses a complete thought. (See page 31.)

EXAMPLE At sunrise the bats returned to the cave.

sentence fragment A sentence fragment is a group of words that is punctuated as if it were a complete sentence but that does not contain both a subject and a verb or that does not express a complete thought. (See pages 446 and 31.)

FRAGMENT A beautiful cantata composed by George Frideric Handel.
SENTENCE The chorus sang a beautiful cantata composed by George Frideric Handel.

FRAGMENT The scene in which an ocean current sweeps the swimmers into an underwater cave.
SENTENCE The scene in which an ocean current sweeps the swimmers into an underwater cave is the most exciting part of the movie.

simple sentence A simple sentence has one independent clause and no subordinate clauses. (See page 87.)

EXAMPLES The relatively long word *sesquipedalian* means "a long word."

Are Justin and Suzanne going with you to Autumn Applefest this weekend?

sit, set (See page 179.)

EXAMPLES   The children **sat** spellbound as the storyteller narrated the Russian folk tale "Baba Yaga."

Dad requested, "Please **set** these crates of aluminum cans in the back of the truck, and take them to the recycling center."

slow, slowly (See page 214.)

EXAMPLE   Led by the school's marching band, the homecoming parade proceeded **slowly** [not *slow*] through town.

subject The subject tells whom or what a sentence is about. (See page 33.)

EXAMPLE   The **aquarium** contains a fascinating array of tropical fish.

subject complement A subject complement is a word or word group that completes the meaning of a linking verb and identifies or describes the subject. (See page 42.)

EXAMPLES   Biarritz is a very popular **resort.**

Biarritz is very **popular.**

subjunctive mood The subjunctive mood is used to express a suggestion, a necessity, a condition contrary to fact, or a wish. (See page 199.)

EXAMPLES   Brad recommended that Katie **be appointed** chairperson. [suggestion]

If I **were** you, Sinan, I would call Yori and apologize. [condition contrary to fact]

Kelly wishes she **were** taller. [wish]

subordinate clause A subordinate clause (also called a *dependent clause*) does not express a complete thought and cannot stand alone as a sentence. (See page 77. See also **noun clause, adjective clause, adverb clause.**)

EXAMPLES   **What you need** is a nap. [noun clause]

The kitten **that Sally wants** is over there. [adjective clause]

The firefighters had to wait **until the wind died down.** [adverb clause]

suffix A suffix is a word part that is added after a base word or root. (See page 364.)

EXAMPLES

love + ly = love**ly**

plain + ness = plain**ness**

remove + able = remov**able**

win + er = win**ner**

ready + ly = readi**ly**

delay + ing = delay**ing**

notice + able = notice**able**

perform + er = perform**er**

tense of verbs The tense of verbs indicates the time of the action or of the state of being expressed by the verb. (See page 182.)

Present Tense

I drive	we drive
you drive	you drive
he, she, it drives	they drive

Past Tense

I gave	we gave
you gave	you gave
he, she, it gave	they gave

Future Tense

I will (shall) drive	we will (shall) drive
you will (shall) drive	you will (shall) drive
he, she, it will (shall) drive	they will (shall) drive

Present Perfect Tense

I have driven	we have driven
you have driven	you have driven
he, she, it has driven	they have driven

Past Perfect Tense

I had driven	we had driven
you had driven	you had driven
he, she, it had driven	they had driven

Future Perfect Tense

I will (shall) have driven	we will (shall) have driven
you will (shall) have driven	you will (shall) have driven
he, she, it will (shall) have driven	they will (shall) have driven

transitive verb A transitive verb is an action verb that takes an object. (See page 16.)

EXAMPLE   Pete **drove** the bus.

underlining (See **italics.**)

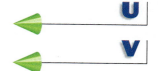

verb A verb expresses an action or a state of being. (See page 13.)

EXAMPLES   An interpreter **translates** languages orally.

Bern **is** the capital of Switzerland.

verbal A verbal is a form of a verb used as a noun, an adjective, or an adverb. (See page 58. See also **gerund, infinitive,** and **participle.**)

EXAMPLES   **Thrilling** as the balloon ride may have been for you, it was certainly **tiring** for me. [participles]

I intend **to win.** [infinitive]

verb phrase A verb phrase consists of a main verb and at least one helping verb. (See page 15.)

EXAMPLE   He **has** rarely **been** so cheerful in the morning.

verbal phrase A verbal phrase consists of a verbal and its modifiers and complements. (See page 58. See also **gerund phrase, infinitive phrase,** and **participial phrase.**)

EXAMPLES   **Uprooted by the storm,** the oak lay across the path. [participial phrase]

Our dog Scooter loves **meeting new people.** [gerund phrase]

voice Voice is the form a transitive verb takes to indicate whether the subject of the verb performs or receives the action. (See page 194.)

ACTIVE VOICE   Wolfgang Amadeus Mozart **composed** the opera *The Magic Flute.*

PASSIVE VOICE   The opera *The Magic Flute* **was composed** by Wolfgang Amadeus Mozart.

weak reference A weak reference is the incorrect use of a pronoun to refer to an antecedent that has not been expressed. (See page 152.)

WEAK   The art teacher explained surrealism, but not until he showed me one did I fully understand his explanation.

REVISED   The art teacher explained surrealism, but not until he showed me **a surrealist painting** did I fully understand his explanation.

well (See *good, well.*)

who, whom (See page 137.)

EXAMPLES   Among the American artists **whom** we have studied is Frederic Remington, **who** is famous for works that depict life on the American plains.

wordiness Wordiness is the use of more words than necessary or the use of fancy words where simple ones will do. (See page 483.)

WORDY   One of the articles in this magazine provides a number of suggestions that are practical for helping a person to make better his or her ability to concentrate.

REVISED   This magazine article provides several practical suggestions for improving concentration.

L

quotation marks, 333–39
semicolons, 322–23
of titles used with names, 315
Put, **principal parts of,** 172

Question marks

abbreviations and, 297, 543
as end marks, 294–96, 543
quotation marks and, 294, 335

Questions. *See also* Test-taking.
indirect questions, 294
punctuation of, 294
test-taking skills and, 526–30

Quiet, quite, 381

Quotation marks

dialogue and, 336
direct quotations and, 333–37, 552
end marks and, 335
indirect quotations and, 333
manuscript form and, 510, 513
with other marks of punctuation, 294–96, 335, 552
single quotation marks, 337
for slang words, invented words, technical terms,
dictionary definitions, 339
with titles, 338–39, 553

Quotations. *See also* Direct quotations.
divided quotations, 334
ellipses in, 342–43
indirect quotations, 333
manuscript form and, 509–10
of long passages, 335–36
punctuation of, 325, 329, 333–337
quotation within a quotation, 337

Raise, **principal parts of,** 180
Raise, rise, 180, 553
Read, **principal parts of,** 172
Real, really, 215
Reason . . . because, 246
Receive, **principal parts of,** 162
Reflexive pronouns, definition of, 6, 135–36
Regional dialects, of American English, 523
Regular verbs, 163, 553
Relative adverbs, 79
Relative pronouns
list of, 78
subject-verb agreement and, 108
understood meaning of, 79

uses of, 7
who, whom, 137–38
Research paper. *See* Manuscript form.
Retained objects, 196–97
Revise, **principal parts of,** 163
Ride, **principal parts of,** 169
Ring, **principal parts of,** 169
Rise, **principal parts of,** 169, 180
Rise, raise, 180, 553
Rout, route, 381
Run, **principal parts of,** 169
Run-on sentences
comma splices, 539–40
definition of, 553
fused sentences, 544–45
as obstacles to clarity, 451–52

Salutations. punctuation of, 315, 326
Say, **principal parts of,** 166
Scarcely, 261
–sede, –cede, –ceed, 364
See
conjugation of, in passive voice, 194–95
principal parts of, 169
Seek, **principal parts of,** 166
Self– **as prefix,** 353
Sell, **principal parts of,** 166
Semicolons
compound sentences formed with, 451, 554
with conjunctive adverbs, 554
between independent clauses, 322–23
between items in series using commas, 323, 554
quotation marks and, 335
Send, **principal parts of,** 166
Sentence(s)
adjective clauses in, 440–41
adverb clauses, 438–39
capitalization and, 269–70
choppy sentences, 78, 460
classified by purpose, 45–46
classified by structure, 87–89
combining sentences, 460–70
complex sentences, 89, 541
compound sentences, 88, 436–37, 468, 481–82, 541
compound-complex sentences, 89, 541
coordinate ideas in, 436–37
declarative sentences, 45, 294, 542
definition of, 31, 554
end marks and, 543
exclamatory sentences, 46, 295, 544
faulty coordination, 442
fused sentences, 451, 544–45
imperative sentences, 45, 295, 546

Index

interrogative sentences, 45, 294, 547

phrase fragments and, 448–49

run-on sentences, 451–52

sentence structure, 87–88, 481–82

simple sentences, 87, 554

subordinate clause fragments and, 449–50

subordinate clauses as, 77

subordinating ideas in, 438–41

test-taking skills and, 526–30

using parallel structure, 443–44

varying sentence beginnings, 479–80

writing clear sentences, 436–52

Sentence clarity, 436–44

Sentence connectives, 479

Sentence diagrams, 490–503

Sentence fragments

definition of, 32, 446, 554

as obstacles to clarity, 446–52

Sentence structure

diagramming sentences and, 501–503

test-taking strategies and, 528

Sentence style. *See also* Style.

clause modifiers and, 480

complex sentences, 541

compound sentences, 541

compound-complex sentences, 541

connectives and, 479

phrase modifiers and, 480

simple sentences, 482

single-word modifiers and, 462, 480

test-taking skills and, 529

varying sentence beginnings, 479–80

varying sentence structure, 481–82

wordy sentences, 483–85

Series of items. *See* Items in series.

Set, **principal parts of,** 172, 179

Set, sit, 179, 555

Shake, **principal parts of,** 169

She, **as double subject,** 252

Should of, 255

Show, **principal parts of,** 169

Shrink, **principal parts of,** 169

Simple predicates, 34

Simple sentences

compound sentences distinguished from, 35, 88, 303

definition of, 87, 554

diagramming sentences and, 501

Simple subjects, 33–34

Sing, **principal parts of,** 162, 170

Single quotation marks, 337

Single-word modifiers

combining sentences and, 462

sentence style and, 480

Sink, **principal parts of,** 170

Sit, **principal parts of,** 166, 179

Sit, set, 179, 555

Slang

definition of, 524

examples of, 524

quotation marks and, 339

Slay, **principal parts of,** 170

Slow, slowly, 214, 555

Some, somewhat, 256

Somewheres, 244

Sort of a, kind of a, 253

Sort of, kind of, 253

Sort(s), kind(s), type(s), 253

Spacing, manuscript form and, 508–509

Speak, **principal parts of,** 170

Spelling

–*cede,* –*ceed,* –*sede,* 364

ie and *ei,* 363

–*ness,* –*ly,* 364

of numbers (numerals), 372–73

plurals of abbreviations, 370

plurals of nouns, 368–70

prefixes, 364

pronunciation as aid, 361

suffixes, 364–66

syllables and, 362

words commonly misspelled, list of, 390–91

words often confused, 375–84

Spelling notebook, 362

Spend, **principal parts of,** 166

Spin, **principal parts of,** 166

Split infinitives, 66

Spread, **principal parts of,** 172

Spring, **principal parts of,** 170

Squinting modifiers, 231

Stand, **principal parts of,** 166

Standard English, 241–42, 524

Stationary, stationery, 382

Steal, **principal parts of,** 170

Sting, **principal parts of,** 166

Straight, strait, 382

Stream of consciousness writing, definition of, 452

Strike, **principal parts of,** 170

Strive, **principal parts of,** 170

Style. *See also* English language; Sentence style.

combining sentences, 460–70

revising sentences for variety, 478–85

sentence connectives, 479

Subject(s)

agreement with verb, 96–108

complete subjects, 33–34

compound subjects, 35, 100–101, 126

definition of, 33, 555

diagramming sentences and, 490–91

double subjects, 252

finding of, 36–37

following verb, 36–37

ACKNOWLEDGMENTS

For permission to reprint copyrighted material, grateful acknowledgment is made to the following sources:

Chronicle Books, LLC, San Francisco: From "Oranges" from *New and Selected Poems* by Gary Soto. Copyright © 1995 by Gary Soto.

Harcourt, Inc.: From "The Jilting of Granny Weatherall" from *The Flowering Judas and Other Stories* by Katherine Anne Porter. Copyright 1930 and renewed © 1958 by Katherine Anne Porter. Electronic format by permission of The Estate of Katherine Anne Porter.

Houghton Mifflin Company: From *Tough Trip Through Paradise* by Andrew Garcia. Copyright © 1967 by the Rock Foundation. All rights reserved.

Harold Matson Company, Inc.: From *All Creatures Great and Small* by Daniel Mannix. Copyright © 1963 by Daniel P. Mannix.

Leslie Norris: From "A Flight of Geese" from *Collected Stories* by Leslie Norris. Copyright © 1996 by Leslie Norris.

Sabine Ulibarri: From "My Wonder Horse" from *Rierra Amarilla: Stories of New Mexico* by Saline Ulibarri. Copyright © 1971 by The University of New Mexico Press.

Viking Penguin, a division of Penguin Putnam Inc.: "One Perfect Rose" from *The Portable Dorothy Parker.* Copyright 1926, and renewed © 1954 by Dorothy Parker.

Bruce Watson: Adapting from "A Wizard's Scribe" from *Smithsonian,* August 1998, vol. 29, no.5. Copyright © 1998 by Bruce Watson.